Managing in the Media

Dedication:

To Kalpana, Elinor and Ruth

Managing in the Media

Peter Block (Editor)
William Houseley, Tom Nicholls and
Ron Southwell

Focal Press

OXFORD AUCKLAND BOSTON JOHANNESBURG MELBOURNE NEW DELHI

Focal Press
An imprint of Butterworth-Heinemann
Linacre House, Jordan Hill, Oxford OX2 8DP
225 Wildwood Avenue, Woburn, MA 01801-2041
A division of Reed Educational and Professional Publishing Ltd

 A member of the Reed Elsevier plc group

First published 2001

© Media Operations Management Ltd 2001

British Library Cataloguing in Publication Data
Managing in the media
    1. Mass media – Management
    I. Block, Peter
    302.2'3'068

Library of Congress Cataloguing in Publication Data
A catalogue record for this book is available from the Library of Congress

ISBN 0 240 51599 4

Composition by Genesis Typesetting, Laser Quay, Rochester, Kent
Printed and bound in Great Britain by Biddles Ltd, www.biddles.co.uk

Contents

Contents

Contents

Preface

I have a particular preoccupation with the production industry, both in television and film. I am anxious to ensure that we continue to produce first-class entertainment for domestic audiences. We have a pool of expertise that I want to see maintained.

Is it really the case that another Brideshead will never be made? Do regulations in ownership restrictions make that rather gloomy prophecy more or less likely to be fulfilled? How is a strong production base best achieved? Is the independent producer quota system working? How independent is independent?

National Heritage Secretary Peter Brooke, addressing the Media Society on Cross-Media Ownership, 17th January 1994

Two key themes are pursued in this book. The first is to look at the reality of the audiovisual industrial environment. The second is to offer some practical tools and techniques to the audiovisual manager who is trying to produce a quality product set against the need to survive in the highly competitive media market.

Peter Block

Acknowledgements

No text of this nature can be anything other than a collaborative effort. My thanks to Ron, Tom and William for their agreement to make their valuable contribution to this work, without which this eclectic set of writings would not have had the sense of the whole I was trying to achieve.

The broad range of material encapsulated here is an amalgam of work and experience drawn from shared experiences from all our colleagues over many years. Much is owed to their knowledge. The chapters on production management would not have been as clearly expressed without Laure Vermeersch and Mark Iliff, with whom I have worked at PricewaterhouseCoopers for the past two years. Their knowledge and questioning of my own position has turned an intuitive set of actions into a method of producing high quality new media programmes.

Special thanks go to Tony Coe, who offered comments and insights on the media management chapters, and to Dr Lesley Perman-Kerr, who reviewed Chapter 8, Organisational behaviour.

Our joint thanks to Caroline Boon, who took on the role of production co-ordinator.

Finally I thank my wife Kalpana, who encouraged me to write this book, has read every chapter, offered constructive comments and tolerated weekends lost to this work.

Peter Block

Statement on reference sources

The bibliography at the back of this book lists all source material texts. They are arranged in alphabetical order. References within each chapter are noted as superscripts and detailed at the end of the chapter in which they have been used.

Recent statistical data has been gleaned from a range of sources, most notably from the World Wide Web (www). The European Union cultural pages have proved a valuable source. These Internet sources have been referenced in the Bibliography as a separate list from the print-based material. In most cases the main 'home' page is referenced. Where a specific reference is used, this appears as a full address to the referring page at the end of the chapter concerned. Due to the changing nature of the World Wide Web, no guarantee can be offered on the reliability on these unique page references. Statements and issues from national or international media organisations have also been used. A key source of collated and commentated data has been taken from Screen Digest, which gives a widely respected assessment of global media issues. Other sources have included the ITC, texts drawn directly from media companies and national newspapers.

General media market intelligences have been drawn from weekly and monthly journals such as *Broadcast* and *Inside Multimedia*.

Wherever required, permission has been sought to use referenced work.

Introduction

Realising that the constant advance of information and communication technology and the large-scale emergence of new transmission and distribution channels will result in increased demand for programmes and increased competition in the programme market; Wishing, therefore, to foster the co-production and distribution of creative cinematographic and audiovisual works in order to take full advantage of the new communications techniques and to meet the cultural and economic challenges arising from their development; ...

Extract from Resolution (88) 15 of the European Community that set up the support fund for the co-production and distribution of creative cinematographic and audiovisual works: *Eurimages*.

This introduction sets out to give you an insight into the style and approach of *Managing in the Media*; to provide you (as you flick through so many texts in the media or management sections of a bookshop) with a reason to buy this text.

Without doubt, the audiovisual industry is a chaotic and complex working environment. The task for the media manager is to understand the media production process and associated technologies whilst dealing with the *'cultural and economic challenges'* (as above) that will have an impact on the programme makers and the products they produce.

This book has been devised for a broad audience. It is based upon the perceived need for a text that amalgamates cultural theories, film and television analysis, management theories and media production practice into one volume.

There are many books on film and cultural studies. Similarly, there are copious numbers of texts written on management. To date, little has been written that analyses the management of the audiovisual industry set against the backdrop of the cultural and economic environment within which the media manager operates.

Introduction

For the practising media manager working in the audiovisual industry, it is intended to provide an introductory body of knowledge.

The growth in media-related courses at undergraduate and postgraduate standard has been in response to the great interest in film and cultural studies. There was, and is (despite the rapid convergence of technologies), a requirement to operate and maintain the technical pieces of equipment that the media practitioner may use. The media industry and the education service over the years have tried to address that need. It has been accepted as implicit that an understanding, or at least an awareness, of the underlying technologies is essential for all working in the media industry. To date, only limited attempts have been made to understand the management processes the media manager has to go through in providing and completing a successful media production. This text is a primer to media management studies.

The convergence of the various media into some form of computer-based system, often termed 'multimedia' or 'new media', requires a new set of management skills that can be applied across all media. This text, especially Part 3, addresses many of the issues that arise due to the needs of 'cross-media' management. It is therefore anticipated that print-based media managers will also find this a useful guide.

The time-scale available for new entrants to the media industry to practise and develop their skills has been compressed from years to months. Whilst not trying to put old heads and experience on young shoulders, this book does address some of the pitfalls and concerns that experienced practitioners have come across. It has been recognised since the break up of the 'cosy duopoly' (the term applied to the period in the UK broadcast industry from 1955–1982 that was the exclusive province of the BBC and the 15 ITV franchise companies) that training strategies have, like the industry itself, become fragmented and dispersed throughout the industry. Skillset, the Government approved lead body, has many initiatives for training within the craft skill areas. At one time, the BBC and several of the older, larger ITV companies provided in-house training for potential media managers. These programmes prepared individuals as they moved from craft skills-based work to areas of responsibility for staff, budgets and management. The new management regimes of 'least cost producer' and 'quick returns for cost-effective programmes', coupled with the even greater casualisation of the labour market, have created a skills gap. Many commentators have noted that the market has failed to deliver appropriate training for potential media managers within the film and television industry. The authors anticipate that this book will provide the support text for company management programmes.

Structure of the content

Managing in the Media is divided into three sections that take the reader from the global to the specific, from the strategic to the tactical. Each chapter discusses specific topics that can be read in isolation, yet contribute to the theme within each part. Taken as a whole, the book provides potential professional media managers and current practising media managers with a framework of issues that will give them an awareness of the range of knowledge needed by the successful media manager.

This book does not try to be a manual to success. The media industry is awash with successful individuals, none of whom needed textbooks to set them on their chosen career paths. Yet these exceptional people prove the rule; that in the main, most media practitioners would benefit from some additional support and guidance, to present to them some of the management issues that have, or will have, an impact upon their working careers.

Part 1: The media environment

Chapters 1–6 examine the history, culture and context within which the media manager operates. Here we set out the background to the UK media market, and consider the European audiovisual industry from industrial and economic standpoints.

There is a cyclical and iterative relationship between the media industry, its customers, and the national governments. This and other factors influencing a media firm are illustrated in Figure I. The chapters in Part 1 introduce these influences and relationships.

Part 2: Management theories and applications to the media industry

Chapters 7–12 look at the behaviour and constraints on the individual firm within the media industry environment. Chapter 7 looks at the behaviour and growth of any firm within an industry, and points out some of the particular issues relating to the growth of business within the media industry. The chapter considers the business issues based upon some models of management and company assessment, in the light of what was learned about the media environment in Part 1.

Chapter 8 considers the behaviour of individuals within the media industry, and their relationship with the firm for which they are working. It is useful

Introduction

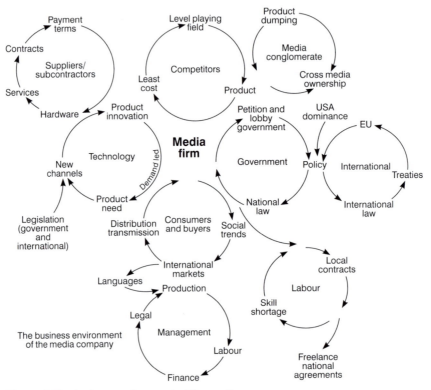

Figure I The business environment of the media company.

to know how individuals function, work in teams, and build working relationships. The chapter also looks at the nature of employment within the industry. The media industry is essentially project (production)-based, with a large percentage of media professionals working in the freelance sector.

Chapter 9 examines strategic management models, and explains why an understanding of strategic management tools and techniques is valuable to the media manager. These processes, such as SWOT, PEST, Value Chain, Environmental Audits and 'Boston Box', may enable media managers to evaluate and analyse the role and position of their own company within the media environment.

Chapters 10, 11 and 12 present the moral and legal boundaries that control and 'constrain' the work of the media manager. Chapters 10 and 11 examine media law. Chapter 12 considers some of the ethical issues and constraints by which a media manager may make a decision or be judged.

Part 3: Media management in action

The final two chapters provide the framework for the individual media project. Part 3 could be used as a guide and template for production management.

Chapter 13 looks at the production process in theoretical terms by presenting some models, ideas and methodologies that the individual project manager has to deal with in a media project. Less tangible and informal matters that relate to the day-to-day issues for a media manager are also discussed.

Chapter 14 presents the production management process in action. It provides a series of project management templates for a cross-media or multimedia production. The multimedia production environment was chosen as the project of choice because it illustrates the broadest range of production issues; film, television, audio, print and new media. There are many excellent texts (several included as recommended reading) that specialise in the production techniques in one of the media sectors in more detail. Part 3 sets the framework for further study or professional development.

The *Managing in the Media* website

The website for *Managing in the Media* (www.mediaops.net) provides a range of support materials.

Organised in chapter headings you will find the following:

- An interview with the author of the chapter giving additional explanation as to his thoughts behind the text
- Reader activity – a series of questions and tasks for the reader to undertake. This could be used to support an academic course. Model responses will be made available to academics and study scheme tutors
- An updated list of further reading. This will change as new references become available.

The website will also carry some of the support material referenced in the main text, such as the nation states' media profiles and the production templates for the Production Project Cycle (PPC).

About the authors

Peter Block is the Head of Production for global self-paced learning programmes within the Management Consultancy Service of PricewaterhouseCoopers. This work requires managing all elements of media that come together to provide a web or CD-ROM-based product. His initial training was at Thames TV, and he has worked in the Media industry for over 20 years. Peter started his career in sound recording, then moved onto video production and computer graphics before specialising in multimedia. He has run three production companies that provided facility services for broadcast programme makers. Peter devised the MA in Media Management, on which *Managing in the Media* is based, whilst lecturing at West Herts College. He is currently the Visiting Fellow in Media Management at the University of Hertfordshire. Peter wrote Chapters 1, 7, 8, 9, 12, 13, 14, and edited the overall structure of the text.

William Houseley LLM has lectured on media law at West Herts College since 1992. As of March 2000, he is working for the Wellcome Trust's IP Management Subsidiary, Catalyst Biomedica Ltd. He was called to the Bar in 1999, and is a member of Lincoln's Inn. William wrote Chapters 11 and 12.

Tom Nicholls is a Senior Lecturer in Media Theory at the University of Lincolnshire and Humberside. Previously, he worked at West Herts College teaching Media Policy on the MA in Media Management: Film and TV course. His contribution to this book reflects that teaching experience – public service broadcasting, film policy and EU media policy. He was involved with the development of the GNVQ (Advanced) Media: Communication and Production course as a member of the NCVQ Advisory committee, and contributed to a number of British Film Institute conferences on media education for 16–19 year olds. Tom wrote Chapters 2, 3 and 4.

Ron Southwell began his career in the world of the media on leaving school and joining the distribution and exhibition branch of Rank Film industries, where he learned to love the products of the film industry. He moved into film production when he worked for a small film production company, where he experienced all the aspects of film making from shooting to editing, including production planning and sound recording. At this time he began to study film and photography on a part-time basis at The Polytechnic, Regent Street. He moved to the University College London, where he worked in a wide area of media production. He has been involved in media education for over 25 years, during which time he has taught vocational and theoretical students at all levels. He has gained a BA degree in Photographic

Media Studies at Harrow College of Higher Education and a MA in Film and Television Studies at Westminster University. Currently, he is Course Director for BA Hon Media Production Management and Area manager for Media Production at West Herts College, Watford. He is also a visiting lecturer in Cultural Studies at the University of Hertfordshire. Ron wrote Chapters 5 and 6.

Part 1

The media environment

Chapter 1

The media industry – into the millennium

1.1 Summary

This chapter describes the historical and economic background to the film, broadcast television and non-broadcast media markets within the wider audiovisual industry. In essence, it is an introduction to the British audiovisual industry. Where appropriate, references to global models are made. We recognise that any attempt to categorise a media product is bound to raise questions of definition, so the terms used in this text are only used to provide boundary conditions for discussion. For example, for the purposes of this book, non-broadcast media include:

- industrial and corporate video production
- secondary sales of feature films and television programmes
- training and education programmes
- other non-broadcast or non-broadcastable programmes (such as pornography).

On the associated web site there are thumbnail assessments of several nation states and economic blocks' audiovisual industries. These notes are provided to give you support notes for comparative studies.

Media products, especially film and television programmes, are not just another commodity sold to the consumer or viewer; they come laden with cultural baggage from the society that created the product. During the 1993–1994 Uruguay round of GATT (General Agreement on Tariff and Trade), France led an EU driven complaint about the USA/Hollywood influence on, and dominance of, the audiovisual industry. The French delegates accused the USA of employing unfair price competition by dumping film and television programmes into the European market. Surprisingly, it was the most contentious aspect of GATT. This was not just about the economic concerns of the Europeans, feeling that the media industries within their own countries were under threat; it was also about a perception of a cultural imperialism that they felt was undermining their own cultural mores – a fear of the 'Hollywoodisation' of the entire audiovisual industry.

Many other governments are also concerned about their audiovisual industry and culture having to compete with that of the USA. An exported media product is more than just a commodity for resale, a means of generating a favourable balance of trade. Whether intended or not, it carries at least some of the prevailing social, cultural and political assumptions of the country that produced it. For this reason, the economic model can only be one part of any analysis or assessment of the global audiovisual industry. Therefore, this chapter begins by looking at the changing audiovisual industrial environment set within the context of the social, economic, technical and cultural values that underpin the industry. At the back of the book a media timeline is provided, to illustrate the links between political, economic, technical and media environments in the UK, which will allow you to place the British audiovisual industry within an historical framework.

At this point, an analysis of the British media industry alone may seem surprisingly parochial. However, there are several good reasons why the British audiovisual industry provides a benchmark for audiovisual industries elsewhere in the world. First, the BBC was the first public television transmission system. Second, the UK is the first national environment and industry in which the three possibilities of delivering digital television signals to the domestic user – satellite, cable and terrestrial – are already in place. Third, the British audiovisual industry, especially television, has often been the laboratory for innovative media productions. However, that is not to say that the impact of Hollywood should be dismissed – indeed, Hollywood undermined the British film industry almost from the start, a situation explored in more detail in later chapters.

This chapter introduces the debate between public or state control of the media and the notion of the independent or free market. Many media observers around the world are amazed, and sometimes appalled, that within the British media environment we accept the idea of the licence fee as a means of 'paying for our television'. Yet, by definition, their notion of the 'free market' cannot exist for the following reasons:

- Regulation at national level determines airwave allocation.
- Treaties at the international level (or the attempt to do so through GATT, for example) moderate and control sales across international boundaries.
- Sales of products from one economic entity to another are, in theory at least, protected by copyright.
- Technology agreements have to be reached about standards. Image conversion and the methods of distribution provide marketing opportunities, but without these agreements no single format programme can be shown or sold in all global markets. The delay in launching DVD occurred more through concerns of product protection than through any technical constraints.
- Internal markets are monitored by monopoly commissions.
- Government audiovisual agencies/departments regulate output.

In countries where regulatory bodies do not exist, anarchy rises to such a level that being able to watch a programme at all can become a hit or miss affair. The very function of being able to provide the air space or bandwidth to enable terrestrial transmission to take place restricts the number of channels available to the analogue broadcasters. Within the UK, this limit was reached with the licensing of Channel 5. Even so, a massive campaign of re-tuning domestic VCRs throughout the country was required to enable Channel 5 to transmit without interfering with the pre-set channel of the majority of domestic videotape recorders. The UK had reached its limits in terms of analogue terrestrial transmission.

A primary driver for change is new technology opening up new possibilities for production and distribution. Yet the audiovisual industry has many forces acting upon it that constrain the opportunities for media practitioners, company owners and business managers to exploit these opportunities. Governments and international bodies seek to regulate and control these opportunities, either to sweep away competition and opposition, or to act as a barrier to the entry of predatory products from other nation states that may possibly overwhelm the indigenous cultural offerings.

New technology, in the form of digital transmission and digital storage, means that images may be transmitted and replicated with no loss of quality. Global distribution networks are possible. Hence the panic and concern in Hollywood about the Digital Versatile Disk (DVD); once a feature film is committed to a digital form, the distribution and replication of the product is harder to control. Price control through segmented markets collapses, and in poorly regulated countries and markets a thriving black market will copy and distribute the product.

There is a continuing fragmentation of the production process. The pessimistic assessment of this is that it reduces still further the influence that the craft skill operators have on those managing and owning the means of production. Alternatively it can be viewed as the embodiment of the post-Fordist production line artisan returning to his or her studio in the Cotswolds, yet using the digital superhighway to form virtual production networks to produce the next Hollywood blockbuster – the ultimate post-modernist vision of movie making.

This fragmentation is underpinned by the economic and social debate over public versus private broadcasting. The potential for more unsatisfactory results from any current round of GATT talks will continue to create a dynamic ebb and flow in the fortunes of the national and international media who trade with the USA. Only when the concept of the nation state and the definitions of what is an American, British or French product become indistinct and insignificant, might the barriers to free trade finally be removed. We are already part way there. If an American company based in Hollywood and owned by a Japanese conglomerate produces a film directed by an Italian and whose leading stars are from England, France and Germany, what determines where this product actually comes from? Or in the UK, will a future Culture and Heritage Secretary make the expedient decision to change yet again the definition of a British film so that it might remain British? Does this matter? Perhaps the answer is to work out who has made the most profit out of such an enterprise – although when we then discover that it is the Icelandic leading actor or actress, where does that leave us? Is the mass viewing audience really concerned about film that reflects the cultural identity of a people or nation state, or do they just want to be entertained? While this debate rages, the reality of a global product designed and produced in a global virtual workshop still has some way to go.

This chapter therefore presents the reader with an overview of the past, present and the possible future of the audiovisual industry as summarised in the media timeline.

1.2 Objectives and key issues

This chapter is not designed to give a blow-by-blow account of the British audiovisual industry. There are many texts that give full and complete histories of the film, television and even (despite its short life span) the multimedia industry. The purpose of this chapter is to highlight some of the activities, behaviours, actions and reactions of players in the audiovisual industry. At the back of the book is a media timeline reference chart, which will enable you to position any discussion mentioned here in its historical context. There is little advantage in giving a detailed chronological account of the media and communication industry because there have been many texts dedicated to that purpose; instead this chapter examines some of the business behaviours manifested in the audiovisual industry in the period since the Second World War.

It is usual to think of audiovisual products as having a three-stage life cycle; production, distribution and exhibition (although to some extent exhibition has become wrapped up in distribution, as the film model becomes a smaller percentage of the total audiovisual offering to the audience). Internet sales of audio material are already challenging the traditional distribution model for music. It is surely no coincidence that Virgin began moving into the communications business, with mobile phones and links to Microsoft, in early 2000. These expanding opportunities to reach a new audience have become known as 'channels to market'.

Throughout the life of the media industry there has been a continual change in the players at each stage of this production process. For example, the model of film production that the media industry would currently accept as standard is not the process by which films were made in its earliest days. Chapter 6 explores some of the issues about the development of the Hollywood system of film-making. Since the 1980s, the relatively low barriers to entry and the continual churn of internal competition have encouraged many to join the film and television production market. The intentions of any government to create a 'free and open market' will be undermined by their very intervention as they perturb the system. In any case, the resourceful entrepreneur will always seek (and often find) ways to undermine government strategies if they are not in their interest. The future of the audiovisual industry will be determined by the current debate about ownership, technology and globalisation.

1.3 The audiovisual industry – past and present

1.3.1 The British film industry

In the early days of film-making, there was genuine naiveté about the role and demarcation of tasks in the production process. George Pearson, one of the earliest directors and producers, thought of his film crew as a team of interchangeable sportsmen. This seems rather a good analogy since, in the early days, production and craft roles were not clearly defined. As explained in Chapter 6, it was only with the establishment of film as a commodity with a formal production process that clear craft and management roles emerged, creating what Orson Wells described RKO studios as being – 'the biggest electric train set any boy ever had!'.

As production became more complex in its scope and use of technology, so the division of labour, production management and senior management became more formal. Once the division of labour had been established, the three stages in the production lifecycle emerged – production, distribution and exhibition. Throughout this book, reference is made to these stages.

Most students of media will be aware that production embodies the 'manufacturing' stage, comprising pre-production, production and post-production. As any product and its associated manufacturing process becomes more mature and has an impact on the economy of the nation, governments inevitably intervene (see Chapters 2 and 3 for British government policy on TV and film).

In Chapter 9, we consider Michael Porter's model of competitive strategies in some detail and illustrate some of the issues pertinent to the audiovisual industry. In this chapter we set the scene for the analysis that will be further explored in Chapters 2, 3 and 4.

If you look at the media timeline, you will see that various British governments have taken all of the following approaches to media production:

- *Laissez faire* – do nothing and let the market decide
- Regulate – through government agencies that control the infrastructure
- Legislate – to determine industry structure (i.e. use of independent companies by the broadcasters)
- Provide funds – grants, tax breaks
- Change the terms of reference for the industry – i.e. the definition of a British film.

In turn, organisations in the media industry have responded by:

- Competing – nationally and globally
- Specialising – developing products for niche markets (arts, science, religion, news etc.)
- Seeking protection from government – to control imports, definitions of national product to obtain central funding etc.

- Seeking support from the government – by legislation and/or regulation
- Creating barriers to entry – trade associations, unions, standards.

Depending on the government in power, there has been a match or mismatch between government and industry objectives. These behaviours operate across all aspects of the media industry between and within nation states. Suppliers to broadcasters want formal 'preferred supplier' status. Established agency and facility companies create trade associations to protect standards, and in doing so also create barriers to entry. Governments have sought to control the channels to the audience as a means of controlling the power of others (independent broadcasters) and maintaining their own (see Chapter 7, reference to Competition Commission). And so it goes on. In the remainder of this section we will consider some of the features of the audiovisual industry that have changed as the industry has matured.

1.3.2 Labour relations

It was only a few years after the birth of the industry in the UK that the first organised labour group was formed. The National Association of Cinematography Operators (1907) took on issues of wages, Sunday opening and training. The government also acted early on in the life of the industry. In 1909, the first act to regulate performances and Sunday trading was passed. This Act was also marginally concerned with wages and qualifications. So from the earliest days governments legislated to control the industry. Over the next 60 years, Labour unions formed and then reformed:

1910   National Association of Theatre and Kine Employees (NATTKE)
1921   Musicians Union
1932   Film Artistes Association (for extras)
1932   Association of Cine Technicians (ACT), became Association of Cinema and Television Technicians (ACTT), representing all technical staff in the independent sector. Renamed as Broadcasting, Entertainment, Cinema and Theatre Union (BECTU) when ACTT and BETA (the BBC staff union) amalgamated.

According to Betts[1]:

> These union bodies, of course, were outside the structure of the industry, but they could bend it and disrupt it, and sometimes they did so.

This quotation illustrates the attitude of many commentators of the film and television industry – that the unions were outside the structure of the industry, and hence the artisans who made the programmes and formed unions were central to the industry's activities but not central to its structure.

Until the 1980s, the broadcast industry operated a closed shop. All employees had to be a member of an approved union (ACTT, NUJ, NATTKE, EQUITY etc.). In so-called 'Middle England', there was a growing hostility to the trade union movement and towards media unions in particular, especially when it impacted on what people did (or rather didn't) see on their TV screens. It became the view of media industry leaders, and certainly that of the first Thatcher Conservative government of 1979, that the unions were actually counterproductive to the industry's success. This view is important in understanding the rationale for the break up of the terrestrial broadcast system into the publisher–broadcaster model, and the growth of independent programme makers during the 1980s.

1.3.3 A short history of the British television industry

The history and structure of the British television industry can be divided into four eras:

1 The BBC monopoly (1926–1956)
2 The ITV and BBC duopoly (1957–1981)
3 Deregulation and uncertainty (1982 to about 2000)
4 The digital age (2000 onwards).

The BBC monopoly (1926–1956)

Broadcasting began in the 1920s with radio transmission, and this developed into the concept of public service broadcasting (PSB; see Chapter 2). The broadcast television industry grew from the new technologies that enabled the development of cameras and transmission systems. The BBC was established as a public body in 1927 by a Royal Charter, and the publicly funded licence fee kept the government at arm's length. The major expansion of the BBC came after the Second World War. As television began in earnest, there was a need for skilled staff. At the time the British film industry was in another of the many slumps that endlessly beset it, and the opportunity was at hand for film technicians to transfer to the television industry, which many successfully did, taking their institutions and practices, as well as their skills, with them.

Hence by the early 1950s the PEP report (of 1952) could state that the ACT was in an exceptional position; 'the only union in the country not to have known serious unemployment since the war'. At the same time, the report criticised the ACT for 'restrictive practices ... which so inflate costs – overtime bans, demands which force production units to carry superfluous personnel, and over-rigid demarcation of jobs'. It was precisely these kinds of accusations that were revived by the Thatcher government.

Creatively, the early days of the BBC established a long tradition of protecting its creative workers from the need to consider administration and finance. As one senior administrator put it in the book by Tom Burns[2]:

> One is always frightened, in administration, of stopping something. You know, we preach the gospel, that we're only here to help – blah blah blah – but this is true. Therefore people tread rather warily.

And[3]:

> We did have in the BBC a deep suspicion of so-called pure administration. It's a dirty word.

At least, so it seemed. Much of the philosophical argument that runs through the media industry concerns the tension between creativity and management, and then between management and government. In the early 1990s, the term 'Birtism' became synonymous with the perception of low quality programming driven by the requirement of least cost production. Although many observers believe that the changes in the BBC to a more financial focus began with the first Thatcher government, this is not so. The reorganisation began as early as 1968, as a result of trying to balance the conflict of interests between departments. Already by the late 1960s Burns identified that those lower down the organisational hierarchy believed that management were in charge and not the programme makers. As Horrie and Clarke pointed out in *Fuzzy Monsters: Fear and Loathing in the BBC*[4]:

> The inconvenient fact that the BBC had started to change well before Birt's arrival … was therefore overlooked as Birt made his bid for a place in the history books.

The language of the early 1990s presented the professionals as the creative people with a concern for the programme *output*, and the new management as those concerned with *control* – with what the programme makers called bureaucracy.

Duopoly of the ITV and BBC (1957–1981)

In 1957, the first independent television (ITV) broadcasters began transmission. The UK was segmented into 15 regions, and the ITV companies awarded the regional franchise were granted their licences on the basis of creating programme capital from advertising revenues. The 1960s and 1970s were a period of stable, policed compromises of legislation and commercial control. The licence fee rose in keeping with inflation through submissions by the BBC to the government of the day. Everyone who made broadcast programmes either worked for the BBC or for one of the 15 regional ITV companies. The in-house full-time employees had secure and predictable career paths. Production staff were represented by relatively strong unions – BETA for the BBC, and ACTT for ITV. These unions took their stance from film and newspaper unions; they operated a card-based closed shop with clear task and skill demarcation lines, although in the BBC BETA was more akin to a trade association. The growth of ITV actually gave BBC staff greater leverage than they would have had otherwise, because of new job opportunities and the higher salaries offered by ITV companies.

Once an ITV company had been awarded a franchise, it then had a regional monopoly for broadcast advertising. Many compromises of competition were operated between the commercial and public broadcasting services. For example, the balance between new productions and imports was set at about 18 per cent of programme output This was as a consequence of a gentlemen's (*sic*) agreement between the BBC and ITV. There were few head-to-head battles other than the usual, some thought phoney, ratings war.

While they recognised that there were restrictive practices within the industry, the franchise owners and management of the ITV companies did not want to challenge this system. They were making huge profits from commercial television for their shareholders and, in some cases, parent companies. Prior to 1979, both Conservative and Labour governments were receiving substantial revenues from the industry. The unions also had a vested interest in maintaining the *status quo*; working conditions were good, and staff earned up to double the comparable salary in other industries. As newspaper proprietor Lord Thompson put it[5]:

> (commercial television) is like having your own licence to print money...

The period of deregulation and uncertainty (1982–2000)

To the Conservative Thatcher government of 1979, the television industry represented twin thorns; a subversive left-wing BBC, and managerially weak ITV companies. The media industry structure also substantiated the right-wing theory that the unions controlled too many areas of industry. It became a central element of the Conservative economic strategy to embark on a programme that would radically change the structure of the television industry. The decade from the start up of Channel 4 to the 1990 Broadcast Act became one of rapid change, with the 'free market' of programme making being the goal of the Thatcher government. Small companies were considered the best means to stimulate competition and enterprise as part of the regeneration of industry in general, and of the television industry in particular.

In February 1990, *The Economist* published an article called 'Thatcherites of the Small Screen'; it illustrated how on a budget of £150 000 for two 1-hour C4 programmes, the producer/director would make £50 000 for 6 months' work – 'nice work, if you can get it'. If you believe this myth, then we hope this book will go some way to reveal just how much talent and hard work is required for most productions.

Political events of the 1980s radically shook up the broadcast TV structures of the 1960s and 1970s. The introduction of new and reliable digital technologies within the television industry took away the need for traditional engineering skills within the production chain, and made technicians no more than skilled operators. (The same was true within the print industry; the computer was eliminating several intermediate steps from the journalist's VDU screen to the printed page.) Laws restricting trade union power had a major impact on the unions' control of the new working practices that the new technologies offered. Until this time, communication workers, including those in the television industry, were party to 'Spanish practices' (see Glossary), which the Thatcher administration sought to curb.

There were many legal and real battles during this time as the Thatcher government took on the unions in the media industry. Eddy Shah started the confrontation with the print unions, which ended with the street fights in Wapping. Marmaduke Hussey, as chair of the Board of Governors of the BBC, initiated an era of business commercialism as the driving force behind the BBC. John Birt, the new Director General (1992–2000), gave this philosophical shift managerial substance in a style of management that became known as 'Birtism', loosely interpreted as an obsessive concern with the 'bottom line' and 'value for money'.

The final showdown and subsequent demise of the ACTT was actually accomplished as early as November 1987. At TV-am, Bruce Gyngell locked out the technicians and replaced them with managers and administrative staff who were actually able to run the station and broadcast for a short while. The revival, and many say the saving, of TV-am was driven by an ambitious executive, Greg Dyke (aided by the puppet Roland Rat), now the Director General of the BBC.

1.4 The implications of the restructuring of British broadcasting

In the 1970s, there was a relatively small independent production sector (IPS). By 1994, there were 1200 members of the Producers' Alliance In Cinema and Television (PACT). The creation in 1982 of Channel 4, as the first 'publisher–broadcaster', initiated and developed the model of buying programmes from independents as the main method of filling scheduled slots (see www.channel4.com, where the week's schedule shows slot, programme cost and production company).

For the BBC and the ITV companies, the 1990 Broadcasting Act set a target of 25 per cent contracting out of original programme making to the independent sector. The IPS was seen as the means to combat the excessive vertical integration that the government considered counterproductive to efficiency (Broadcast White Paper 1989, p. 6). The 1990 Act also auctioned off the franchises, which earned the government an extra £100 million.

Until 1990, the regional franchise ITV companies sold the advertising slots transmitted by Channel 4. Under the new Act, Channel 4 became an independent corporation and began selling its own airtime. This established, for the first time, competition for advertising revenue on terrestrial television.

As far as the BBC was concerned, the (still) Conservative government was no longer willing to increase the licence fee (in line with a funding formula) as a matter of course. In the era of John Birt, processes needed to be restructured for efficiency and financial control. Part of this restructuring was the creation of producer choice, which enabled programme makers to establish competitive tendering for production facilities from both inside and outside the corporation.

Producer choice created an internal market. It separated technical production from programme production by turning each programme-making department into a business unit with its own budget. Producers were given budgets that, in principle, fully costed the production. This would lead to greater financial prudence and give better value to the licence payers – or so it was believed. They were then charged internally for all services, such as studios, post-production, library music etc., under a tariff charging system. For the first time, producers had to know the 'below the line' costs in addition to the 'above the line' costs that they were used to budgeting. This created inefficient and expensive anomalies – like BBC studios standing empty while Soho facility houses were crowded with BBC programme-making staff due to lower production costs.

Anomalies that apparently still persist:

It struck Greg Dyke as 'odd' to find not much going on in BBC studios, but then to find two BBC sit-coms being made at Teddington Studios. 'Something has to be wrong there.'

Greg Dyke, BBC Director General, in an extract from the BBC in-house magazine *Ariel*, February 1, 2000.

Along with the changes in infrastructure and technology, the demise of the closed shop was completed, with freelance workers no longer required to be members of ACTT. Productions for broadcast no longer needed to use union crews. Additionally, retained salaried staff in all broadcast companies were being shed rapidly. On average, employment in 1992/3 was 60 per cent of the 1987/8 levels. The television industry is now largely a casual labour market, with 'fewer people employed in television in 1996 than in 1987'[6], despite the proliferation of channels and broadcasters.

Broadcasters are now busy *not* making programmes. In the 1980s, the average costs of network television programme making were over £80 000/hour, whilst premier drama programmes would have budgets exceeding £500 000/hour. In 1990, Sky boasted that their average costs were about £6000/hour. The media industry of the 1990s was under pressure to reduce costs, but faced criticism on quality from the regulatory bodies. In answer to the ITCA's concern at the start of 2000, Channel 5 announced an increase in budget to produce 'a greater number of cheaper 30-minute dramas backed by budgets of £120 000 an hour' (*Broadcast*, 7 January 2000).

1.5 The global industry

The Conservative government believed that deregulation and a flexible work force in the British television industry would by extension help the British film industry become the Hollywood of Europe. It was felt that there were many natural advantages, including:

- skilled technicians
- the English language
- mature supplier relations

- a diverse production base
- good studio and location facilities.

The European Union (EU) also sought to encourage the small- and medium-sized enterprise (SME). Within the audiovisual industry, there was a policy of promotion of the programme production industry as part of the philosophy of 'television without frontiers'. The government predicted the demand for independent programmes to expand from 19 000 hours in 1989 to 35 000 hours in 1999.

The EU measures were intended to:

- help co-productions and cross-frontier co-operation
- give priority to the SME
- recognise and help cultural diversity.

If proof were needed that the restructuring of the television industry has not yet been successful, an examination of the balance of trade is a useful benchmark. In the early 1990s, the British balance of trade in television programmes fell into a deficit for the first time in many years.

The stated objective for breaking up the duopoly was to establish a vibrant and efficient industrial audiovisual sector and, by so doing, develop a capability to compete on the world market. In fact, the strategy was primarily designed to break the power of the unions and shake up the complacent attitudes of the broadcasters. The IPS was used as the agent of change to reduce union power and reduce wages, and therefore efficiently produce cheaper programmes. Their main function was to shift the programme-making base 'away from making new kinds of programmes towards the same kind of programmes more cheaply'[7].

1.6 The independents and the broadcasters – a new model of contractual relationships

The vital element to the survival and growth of the independent sector was the contractual relationship it had with the broadcasters. In the early 1990s, the number of programmes commissioned by the BBC increased by 18 per cent on the 1980s to 744 hours. This represented about 11 per cent of the qualifying 7448 hours of new production material. The target set by the government was 25 per cent. The strongest representation occurred in the areas of music and arts (over 50 per cent produced by independent programme makers) and light entertainment (LE) (20 per cent produced by independent programme makers). Conversely, the ITV companies reduced the number of commissions from 1323 hours in 1991 to 1104 in 1992, although the average price paid per hour had also steadily fallen.

Channel 4, the first publisher–broadcaster, has a close relationship with the independent sector. The total number of hours allocated by Channel 4 to the independent sector had increased to about 25 per cent during the late 1980s. The push to lower cost had also been in evidence, with the fall of average cost per hour to £69 000 in 1991 and £78 000 in 1992, from £120 000 in 1988.

Another issue that affects the independent programme maker is the distribution of contracts from the broadcasters. Again using Channel 4 as the primary example, the distribution of programme payments across the IPS has consistently reduced since 1982. The companies that are receiving the large contracts of over £1 million slowly grew during the 1980s to become relatively stable at about 27/28 contracts per annum during the early part of the 1990s. More interestingly, the number of small contracts, which had shown a steady growth during the 1980s, actually fell during the early 1990s – the inference being that fewer companies were winning contracts, and that they tended to be the same companies. For example, *Brookside*, a major Channel 4 soap, is shown as just one yearly contract.

1.7 The independent production sector (IPS)

The changing role of the IPS in the provision of broadcast programmes has been an essential element in the restructuring of the British television industry during the 1980s and 1990s. This restructuring was not in fact driven by market forces, but by a government that considered it essential to break up what Prime Minister Thatcher called the 'cosy duopoly' of the BBC and the ITV companies, and also the power of the trade unions in the television industry, which Thatcher, when addressing a meeting of senior television managers, referred to as 'the last bastion of restrictive practices'[8]. They represented the last of the 'enemy within', and needed to be broken. The new legal framework provided a two-pronged attack on the industry structure.

First, the government changed the industrial landscape with the Broadcast Acts. Second, through labour laws, the government virtually eliminated union power within the industry. This legislation separated the function of production and transmission. The broadcaster no longer had to make programmes – the product – and the programmes no longer had to be produced at the time of consumption. With a few exceptions, such as the news, weather and sport, most programmes can be pre-recorded months before the transmission date. However, many are still recorded quite close to transmission: *Top of the Pops*, which links live bands with those pre-recorded as live, chat shows like *Parkinson* and *TFI Friday*, topical reference programmes such as *Have I got News for You*, audience participation programmes such as *Live and Kicking*, and so on.

Prior to the shake-up by the early Thatcher administration there was a view, as explored by Cornford and Robins[9], that the 1970s were a highly stable period which represented the zenith of the 'cosy duoply' between the BBC and the ITV companies, and to some a golden age of broadcasting. However, borrowing a phrase from an earlier period in British political history, the 'winds of change' were already blowing through the corridors of the BBC. Tom Burns, in his extensive study of the BBC (*The BBC – Public Institution and Private World*), suggested that as early as 1968 the days of the programme maker being the driving force behind the BBC were numbered. The more commercially driven regimes that typify modern broadcast structures were already being established.

The independent production sector as a force in broadcast television was effectively created with the establishment of Channel 4. Richard Paterson[10] suggests that:

> The increasing role of independent production in the changing environment of British television was the result of one of the most successful lobbying campaigns of the '80s.

The campaign leaders (PACT) were in fact pushing against an open door, making representations to a government who wanted to fundamentally change the structure of the British television industry. The nature and boundaries of the audiovisual firm were not being shifted by an organic response to the changing market, but by legislation imposed to create and then regulate the free market.

John Ellis[11] comments that: 'the (audiovisual) sector has as a whole becomes an example of the "post-Fordist" industrial strategy'. It is interesting to consider whether the actual market forces created by the then current and subsequent radical changes in technology, and the consequent changes in production techniques, would have been by themselves sufficient to have caused some or all of the fundamental changes that the legislators imposed on the industry. As Paterson[12] suggests:

Any account of 'independent' production must define the factors of dependency and mutuality in any relationship between contracting parties, including any regulatory dimensions.

This mutual dependency is also relevant to the film industry in the UK – an industry that, as suggested at the start of this chapter, continues to struggle to find any model of stability.

The new form of television industry, with its increasing reliance on the small independent enterprise, was in keeping with the Thatcher idea of regenerating industry. The small and medium-sized enterprise (SME) was seen overall as the best means of stimulating and revitalising British industry.

According to Ellis[13], 'since even the largest of independent production companies tend to specialise in a few areas of production', the independent production sector (IPS) would therefore fall into the definition of 'the craft based SMEs: the niche and flexible specialisation options' as expressed by Hilbert et al. (1994)[14]. The debate on flexible specialisation within the film industry was first discussed by Michael Storper[15], who examined the structures of the Hollywood film industry. By being flexible, companies can respond to a changing demand by buyers. By being specialised, they concentrate their skills in particular niche markets. Their strength is in flexibility to change; the weakness is the focus on market segment.

The main interest in this chapter is the economic model of the audiovisual industry. It is the internal structures of the typical very small IPS (VSIPS), its business viability and the relationship between the VSIPS (the suppliers) and the broadcasters (the buyers) that, as the VSIPS grows, provides a useful analogy to the growth of the industry itself. The growth of the entrepreneurial enterprise is examined further in Chapter 7.

1.8 The origins of the independent production sector (IPS)

Since the start of film-making in the United Kingdom, there has been a cluster of small independent production companies located around the Soho district of London. These had established themselves alongside the distribution companies, cinema chain owners and the British representatives of the Hollywood production companies. They had been set up to provide the programme shorts, trailers, news and cinema advertisements that supported the feature films. In some cases these embryonic forms grew and established themselves as companies in Pinewood, Elstree and Ealing, aiming to produce feature products to rival the American imports. The 1930s, 1950s and 1980s stand out as three periods when the UK most clearly tried to compete with the US model of production. The last period was led by Goldcrest (see *My Indecision is Final: The Rise and Fall of Goldcrest Films*[16]), the production company that produced *The Killing Fields*, *Gandhi* and *Local Hero*, as well as *Chariots of Fire* – a film that indirectly produced the oft-quoted promise (or threat?) delivered by Oscar-winning screenwriter Colin Welland at the Academy Awards of 1982, 'The British are coming'. More recently, following *'Four Weddings and a Funeral'*, Polygram also saw themselves as 'a contender'. Alongside these film-makers were the support services provide by set builders, sound studios, dubbing suites, rostrum camera facilities, etc.

From the 1950s to the late 1970s, these production companies produced industrial and corporate films, cinema shorts, government information films, advertisements and general film production services. From them came film-makers like Ridley Scott and Alan Parker, who learnt their film craft through directing advertisements. It is worth noting that British advertisements, especially those for television, have always been seen as the industry standard. Others specialised in the cinema short, now a lost art since multiscreen cinemas replaced the town centre cinema and the single evening presentation of the feature film. For economic reasons driven by the distribution companies, more showings equate to more money. After the *Star Wars* blockbuster phenomenon, audience habits started to change; the film had become part of the evening entertainment, not the whole.

Typically, these film-based companies would be established by one or two film-makers. This would often be, say, a director and camera operator or editor. With these skills within the business, they could pitch, write, shoot and edit a complete programme. All that was required was a small cutting room in Soho. All the other production services, such as dubbing suites, graphics, equipment hire, film labs and crews, were within easy reach. This style of partnership was the pattern for the establishment of a start-up production company, where a number of people with what they believed to be complementary skills set up in business after becoming disenchanted with the larger company or corporation for which they worked. This traditional model of a start-up media business, although challenged now by the multimedia business environment, is explored further in Chapter 8.

During this period (the 1950s–1970s), the process of obtaining a commission to make a programme was relatively simple because:

1 There were relatively few independent production companies.
2 The idea of having a corporate or industrial film made was novel – often companies had films produced as an offshoot of personnel, public relations or the training department. It was not a media event, nor a specialised internal management area for many companies. The commissioning company relied heavily on non-specialist contract managers to supervise the project.

Many of these film companies specialised in niche markets and obtained commissions by identifying who might need a programme in their particular market. The potential client was identified by scanning the newspapers, journals and corporate or charity reports for major projects etc, and the company then made the approach. For example, one company[17] researched that the Hong Kong Government was opening up a new trade centre, and suggested a cinema short-style programme and organised distribution. They got the commission. British Airways saw the film, liked it, and also commissioned a cinema short to support their new service to Hong Kong. There was relatively little competition, and company budgets were flexible. It was also shot on film. This was a key factor in limiting the number of potential entrants to the industry. Film was the province of skilled artisans who had received their craft training in the big studio. The independent sector was a stable cottage-style industry up until 1981/82.

1.9 Technology and legislation

Two events in the early 1980s changed this structure.

The first was technological, in the introduction of the lightweight video camera and the videocassette format recording medium. Until this time, colour video cameras were huge, heavy, studio-based units. The camera body alone needed a four-strong team to lift it on and off a dolly (the camera mount). Up to five technicians were required in the image chain; the camera operator, the cable basher (who kept the heavy cable out of the way of the camera as it traversed the studio floor), the vision control engineer (who controlled the aperture and colour quality), the rack engineer (who lined up the camera at the beginning and end of the day) and the maintenance engineer (who had intimate knowledge of the camera and its particular idiosyncrasies). This was before the picture was mixed with other cameras and then recorded by a videotape (VT) engineer. Both Philips and Sony introduced a camera that could be shoulder-carried by a camera operator and mounted on a lightweight tripod. It was portable, and the industry now had immediate access to video pictures from locations. The skill of the camera operator was no longer paramount. The director could look at the monitor and review the recorded 'takes' instantly, or even view them as they were shot. This was much to the anger and frustration of the film cameramen who had taken up the new technology. Until this time the director had relied heavily on the judgement of the camera operator, and there was a high degree of trust, as the pictures would not be seen until they came back from the labs. The implications now were that anyone could record images and use a camera.

The independent sector and its support facility houses have always been at the forefront of the adoption of technical innovations. They have helped to change working practices, develop multi-skilling in order to keep production costs down, shorten the production timetable and so maximise their turnover and profit. Sadly, it is the obsession with new technologies that have since caused many production companies and facility houses to go into liquidation. The potential client calls, discovers that the supplier does not hold the latest piece of technology, and thus moves on to the next company. Supply companies become trapped on the technological treadmill, trying to keep up. Offering 'new' services therefore has more to do with commercial fear than with good business practice.

The second event to change the structure of the audiovisual industry was political, and was embodied in the 1981 Broadcasting Act. Through it the government established Channel 4, the first designated publisher-broadcaster, whose first transmission was on 2 November 1982. By 1985, emboldened by their Channel 4 experience, the independent producers formed a lobbying group to submit to the Peacock Committee the proposal that they should have the opportunity to make programmes for the BBC and ITV as well as for Channel 4. The Peacock Report (1986), in line with Government thinking, wanted the British television industry to function within the demands and disciplines of market forces, to break up the 'cosy duopoly' of the BBC and the ITV companies:

> One way of introducing competition even when the duopoly remains, is by enlarging the scope of independent programme makers to sell to existing authorities, as already occurs in the case of Channel 4.

The government agreed, and in 1987 announced that, by 1992, 25 per cent of newly originated programming transmitted on BBC and ITV should be supplied by independents. The existing broadcasters' rhetoric of 'new voices' and 'innovation' and the sense of 'team spirit' were no longer felt to provide sufficient drivers for change. It wasn't enough that programmes should be made by the independent sector; programme making throughout the industry must be made more accountable. Cost-effectiveness was the core issue, and the term 'Birtism' (derived from (Sir) John Birt, Director General of the BBC 1989–2000) was coined to describe an obsession with the financial efficiency, usually to the detriment of programme quality.

At the start of the 1990s, it was anticipated that this would improve competitiveness and open up the television sector to market forces. However, at the time there were only a limited number of transmission outlets for an independent producer. Although that situation has apparently changed with the onset of satellite, cable and digital channels, the amount of airtime to fill has driven budgets down even further, and the means of distribution – the broadcasting – is still in the hands of a small number of big players. This means that it was, and still is, a buyer's market – the broadcaster or the publisher–broadcaster imposes the financial terms on the supplier, who must either like it or leave the business.

The range of programmes that is transmitted by the franchised independent broadcasters is determined by the 1990 and 1996 Broadcast Acts. They are regulated by the Independent Television Commission (ITC), who also license the channels. As the *2000 Media Guide* puts it: 'the ITC's job is to limit the independence of the independent broadcasters'. So, independence for the producer is most definitely not the same as independence for the broadcaster.

It is therefore hard to believe that independent production companies have produced such a wealth of programme diversity; the Government determines what is transmitted and transmittable, and the commissioning company determines the cash flow and the profit. In addition, the programmes are in many cases being made by ex-BBC or ITV employees. In the 1980s, and then again in the mid- to late 1990s, the independent sector was flooded with freelance workers made redundant by the broadcast companies who originally employed them.

A major change in the industry brought about by independent production is the method by which programmes are produced. The independent production sector relies on bought-in facilities and crews to make the programmes. Budgets are tight and closely monitored. According to several suppliers to the BBC, BBC programme makers of the 1950s to the 1980s did not have a true indication of how much a programme really cost to make. BBC staff spoke glibly of 'above the line' and 'below the line costs', without really knowing or even caring what the true financial implications were for the Corporation. It was not considered relevant or useful to know. If a studio was available, then it could be used. Meanwhile, the independent production sector had to work to accurate cost accounting for production, project planning and cash flowing the budgets imposed on them by the constraints of a tender process, an implicit requirement of project management. This was virtually absent for the producer and director in the BBC[17].

1.10 The growth of the independent production sector (IPS)

In the early 1980s, there was a huge growth in the IPS. The listings in *Kemps*, the key journal at the time, grew from 300+ to over 1000 in a matter of a few years.

These production companies were established to capitalise on the potential projects from Channel 4. The independent production sector was booming. This relatively homogeneous sector provided a range of programme material of a few hours each, under conditions which the *Producers' Guide to Channel 4* quaintly described as '– the proverbial man, dog and answerphone'.

Some of these companies grew and became commercially stable on a steady diet of Channel 4 commissions – most typically (and successfully) Mersey TV, who produced the Channel 4 soap *Brookside*, and Hat Trick, with comedy programmes such as *Who's Line is it Anyway?* A number of the start-up companies have since become well-established production houses – Wall to Wall, Illuminations, Tiger Aspect and so on. The sector has become fragmented and diverse. There are still the small companies, formed to produce one commission, but increasingly there are larger companies, such as SelectTV, who now have an annual turnover of £50 million or more. The reshaping of the production landscape meant that the largest of the independents were getting listings on the stock exchange. There were also formal and informal mergers and cartels with aspirations to bid to become a broadcaster in the franchise round at the beginning of the 1990s. Increasingly, the smaller independents have to present ideas to the major independents first, as a way of gaining access to the broadcasters.

In the space of 15 years, the free market that was supposed to open up television to 'new voices at every level' (John Ranleigh, Channel 4 commissioning editor), has been reduced to a very few broadcast companies supported by a few dozen major independent companies.

In the beginning, when the independent production sector as providers of broadcast programmes was legislated into existence in 1981, the programme makers felt that they were part of a concerted effort to change the face of broadcast television. According to John Ellis, producer and author of *Visible Fictions*[18]: 'We were part of a team approach, on the same side ...'. There were other views, too. Stanley Marks (film-maker and producer) stated that[19]: 'Anyone with a camera and an office in Soho and some second-rate proposal could get a commission as long as you were not an established programme maker'.

The question now, with the model of publisher–broadcaster, is, who is taking the risk? Where are the new voices? Will the 'dumbing down' of British television entertainment programmes and the lack of aggressive television journalism, as argued by many disaffected TV staff and more objective observers, continue in the even more accelerated environment of change of the twenty-first century?

1.11 The future – into the digital age

Most commentators would agree that profound changes have taken place in the communications industry, of which the media and, more specifically, the audiovisual industry is a part. In the first few weeks of the twenty-first century, Time Warner (a content owner) merged with AOL (a provider and carrier) along with EMI (more content, especially popular music). By doing so, they have ensured that they will be able to reach the audience/customer by whichever electronic channel is being used. The three factors that have been pivotal to this change have been ownership, globalisation and technology. As shown in Figure 1.1, these three seem set to continue to drive the audiovisual industry for the immediate future.

Bandwidth and broadband services are the current mantra of the communications industry. Digital technology has delivered the possibility of the uniform data stream decoded by the user's device appropriate to the product's interface. The personal computer (PC) presents the web page with television inserts, the linear TV programme will be enhanced by text and graphics, and the WAP phone will present just the text highlights. The revolution in computing systems and local networks of the past 20 years has yet to be matched by the telecommunications systems. Whilst fibre optics and satellite systems offer narrow cast and broadcast bandwidth, a fully integrated infrastructure has yet to emerge. The amount of traffic carried over the Internet is said to be doubling every 100 days. In the near future,

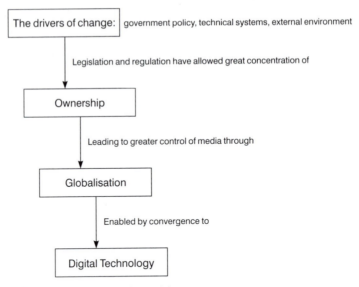

Figure 1.1 The condensing media model

the data stream volume will exceed that of voice on a system that, for the domestic subscriber, was designed to carry low bandwidth continuous analogue signals. Ideally, digital data can be sent in short bursts of broadband signal.

The media industry is driven by new technology. Three themes emerge in digital media:

1 Convergence
2 Compression
3 Interactivity.

The convergence to a transferable digital format offers many opportunities and many concerns. In the audiovisual industry, digital technology is almost universally accepted as the means for the reproduction, storage and transmission of information in all media. All content, sound, vision, text and data have become independent of the medium. This has contributed to the erosion between telecommunications and broadcasting companies. This data stream will become complete as digital television makes an impact on the domestic market. This, coupled with the Internet, is now blurring the boundaries between the models of distribution. For example, while working on-line and connected via the web to a radio station, its current programme output or even archive material can be listened to whilst using the computer. The single portal to communication channels has arrived.

This proliferation of digital channels gives rise to the concern by content owners regarding how their intellectual property rights (IPR) might be protected. The risk of piracy and misuse will increase. The music industry has already witnessed the use of sampled material from existing works. On-line digital still image libraries are now commonplace. CD-ROM production music will be replaced by searchable on-line database systems with keyword searches for the style, era, format etc. Key frame library footage and degraded inspection copies will allow content owners to re-sell their material to a global market. Each one of these, and other ideas yet to come, will help reduce production costs and research time. It is now accepted practice that research starts on the Internet. For each of these potential benefits, there are enormous problems in the management and reuse of assets. Control of brand and product identity has become more complex and, in a market place in which time to market is measured in months, legal wrangling over the minutiae of the contract could fatally delay speedy exploitation of rights.

The impact of compression of this data stream is twofold. First, the distinction between on-line (connected and live) and download (stored and time-shifted) has to date been about quality – on-line is degraded and download is full bandwidth. As access to digital systems inproves through fibre optics and digital modems the distinction will be eroded; the only reason to store data will be to listen or view when off-line. Digital home juke boxes that can digitally store the equivalent of hundreds of audio CDs and many tens of full feature films are being market tested. Will this be the final demise of the album cover?

Secondly, new business models will emerge. Will the consumer buy the individual programme direct from the production company, or still subscribe to the channel? What rights will content providers have to share in the new revenue streams? The supply chain will become more complex and fragmented. Any government's regulatory system also faces new challenges as delivery systems converge. The same piece of content could be subject to excessive and/or inconsistent regulation from different regulatory bodies. The risk for the audiovisual industry, as for content providers, is that opportunities may be 'jeopardised by (government) regulatory overlaps and anomalies'[20].

Within the first few months of taking up his post as Director General of the BBC, Greg Dyke spoke on the importance of education. The Internet started as a common platform for data delivery, became a communication tool, expanded to a business medium, and is now becoming an education medium. Each of these stages has required a higher degree of interactivity. It has been predicted that the revenue generated by educational materials on the web will eclipse all other markets. Education on the web will require the most sophisticated user interface to provide a challenging learning environment. Yet content remains king – as with old computers and new systems, 'garbage in, garbage out'. The content must be good; programmes have to be engaging. It has got to be appropriate and useful, and remain informative, educational and entertaining.

This chapter has sought to introduce some of the complexities of the audiovisual industrial environment. The debate will continue between policies that ring-fence audiovisual products, or leaving the free global market to find its own stability. This clearly will not happen with so many commercial and national interests at stake. We have also tried to indicate how 'players' in the industry seek to control their external environment and limit the impact of new entrants. We now see some of these behaviours manifesting themselves in the rush to be part of the Internet by merger and acquisition.

1.12 References

1. Betts, C. (1973). *The Film Business: A History of British Cinema 1896–1972*. Allen and Unwin.
2. Burns, T. (1979). *The BBC – Public Institution and Private World*, p. 247. Macmillan Press Ltd.
3. Burns, T. (1979). *The BBC – Public Institution and Private World*, p. 252. Macmillan Press Ltd.
4. Horrie, C. and Clarke, S. (1994). *Fuzzy Monsters: Fear and Loathing at the BBC*. Mandarin.
5. Referenced in *The Oxford Dictionary of 20th Century Quotations*. Oxford University Press, 1999.
6. Ursell, G. (1995). *Organising Employment for Higher Performance in the UK Television Industry*. Paper presented at The 1995 Annual Conference of the Employment Research Unit, Cardiff Business School.
7. Davis, J. (1991). *TV, UK – A Special Report*, p. 76. Knowledge Research.
8. Davidson, A. (1992). *Under the Hammer: Greed and Glory Inside the Television Business*, p. 10. Mandarin.
9. Cornford, J. and Robins, J. (1990). *Beyond the Last Bastion: Industrial Restructuring and the Labour Force in the British Television Industry*. Centre for Urban and Regional Development Studies, University of Newcastle upon Tyne.

10. Paterson, R. (1992). *New Questions of British Cinema*. British Film Institute.
11. Ellis, J. (1992). *Visible Fictions*. Routledge.
12. Paterson, R. (1992). *New Questions of British Cinema*, p. 127. British Film Institute.
13. Ellis, J. (1992). *Visible Fictions*. Routledge.
14. Hilbert, J., Sperling, H.J. and Rainnie, A. (1994). SMEs at the crossroads – scenarios on the future of SMEs in Europe. *Future of Industry Paper Series*, Vol. 9. Commission of European Communities.
15. Storper, M. (1985). *The Changing Organisation and Location of the Motion Picture Industry – A Research Report*. UCLA Publishing.
16. Eberts, J. and Ilott, T. (1992). *My Indecision is Final: The Rise and Fall of Goldcrest Films*. Faber and Faber.
17. Block, P. L. (1996). *Strategies for Survival – The Small Television Production Company*. Stanley Marks Interview, University of Hertfordshire.
18. Block, P. L. (1996). *Strategies for Survival – The Small Television Production Company*. John Ellis Interview.
19. Block, P.L. (1996). *Strategies for Survival – The Small Television Production Company*. Stanley Marks Interview, University of Hertfordshire.
20. *Regulating Communications* (1998). Green Paper, HMSO.

Chapter 2

British public service broadcasting

2.1 Summary

This chapter will consider a variety of definitions of public service broadcasting (PSB), tracing the history of the concept from the establishment of the British Broadcasting Company in 1922 to the multichannel broadcasting system we have today. The Broadcasting Research Unit's definition will be considered, together with the findings of commissions on broadcasting. Public service broadcasting has, from its inception, been seen to be vital to the formation of a national identity. This chapter will therefore consider theories of identity, and debate what identity is created by the British broadcasters.

This introduction to PSB will mainly focus on the British broadcasting environment, but a comparison with other national systems (e.g. Canada and Germany) will be included to demonstrate the diversity of methods of regulation that exist. In the UK context, PSB will normally encompass the five terrestrial television channels and most radio stations, but the chapter will seek to demonstrate that Reith's aim to 'educate, inform and entertain' has a wider influence. Finally, the future of PSB will be considered – can it survive the expansion of digital broadcasting?

2.2 Objectives and key issues

Public service broadcasting, PSB, might easily be dismissed as a twentieth century concept that has little relevance to the production or consumption of audiovisual texts in the new century. As we shall see, the concept dates from the 1920s, but not only are public service broadcasters still reaching the majority audience within the UK; they also set much of the agenda for the production and consumption of broadcast programmes. Cable, satellite and new digital television programmes are frequently judged in comparison to the output of the terrestrial, PSB channels. It is sometimes suggested that the advent of digital broadcasting and the possibilities for broadcasting through the Internet will inevitably lead to the end of PSB. However, it is worth considering that many terrestrial broadcasters are involved in both of these developments (e.g. BBC, Granada and Carlton).

2.3 Introduction to policy as a critical concept and managerial tool

In contrast to textual methods of studying films and television programmes, e.g. *mise en scene* or semiotics, which draw out an analysis from what is seen on the screen, policy can be loosely grouped with contextual methods of study. The approach of these three chapters is to look at the relationship between media policy, film and television texts. This is illustrated in Figure 2.1.

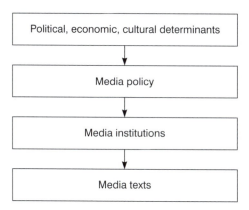

Figure 2.1 The relationship between media policy, film and television texts.

Thus, analysis of the media text should reveal both the influence of media policy and the political, economic and cultural factors which shape it, rather than, for example, the director's intentions or its links with other films within a genre. The policy line can be traced back from the film or television programme to the institution that produced it (e.g. film company, broadcaster or independent). From there, we can consider the influence of media policy upon the institution (e.g. PSB charter, film funding policy), and finally relate this policy to the political system and economic, political and cultural factors which shaped that policy.

As a simple example, we could consider the popular television drama series, *Minder.* A detailed background is given to the production company, Euston Films, in Manuel Alvarado and John Stewart's book, *Made for Television: Euston Films Limited* – regrettably, there have been few studies which are so detailed since. In the first chapter, Alvarado and Stewart explain how Euston Films came into existence[1]. Thames set up a film production company mainly in order to increase overseas sales and improve earnings because of the tax structure for ITV's profits in the 1970s. This limited earnings within the UK, because if advertising revenue grew too great it was largely paid over to the government in tax. Thus, the taxation policy and the intention of limiting the growth of ITV audiences led to a very particular group of programmes being made in the late 1970s and early 1980s, i.e. produced on film so that they could earn money from overseas sales and so that contractual conditions of service from the film industry rather than television could be utilised.

We can trace a policy 'line' from broadcasting policy through to Euston Films and, finally, *Minder.* This would lead to very different conclusions about the production techniques, largely based on low-budget feature film practice, than we might deduce from an analysis of the programme alone. For example, the use of dialogue recorded on location, with little improvement in post-production, might be perceived as an attempt to make the series as naturalistic as possible – appearing to be really taking place on the streets of London. However, as Michael Winterbottom explains[2] in the same study, the lack of post-synchronisation of dialogue is also a product of the production cycle for the series; determined very much by the budget and hence restricted schedule.

2.4 Introduction to key terms and definitions

We need to start this investigation with a clear definition of the state.

2.4.1 State

The origins of the state go back to the division of labour; this produced a class of administrators who were freed from primary labour. The state can be seen as the apex of a class structure, having the right to limit citizens' freedom, and ultimately having the right to imprison them through the judicial system. This chapter will be concerned with the policy making and cultural activities of the state, rather than its repressive role (although some might see these activities as repressive in another way).

2.4.2 Distinction between state and government

There is an important distinction between government (an executive body) and the state (which administers affairs). The state is seen as providing continuity, but government will change (although to some extent this view altered during the 1980s, when senior civil servants changed more frequently). Apart from the policy-making areas of government, the state is more traditionally seen to be composed of the judiciary, the clergy and the military, and sometimes the mass media are included in the definition. Government is advised by the civil service (state), and is therefore heavily dependent on it (see Yes Minister or Yes, Prime Minister! for an exaggerated television representation of this).

The state can be seen as self-sustaining and, although dependent on primary producers (in Marxist terms), separate from society and therefore not directly accountable to it. Broadcasting in the UK has been defined from this perspective – i.e. in a neopluralist model of the media, media producers are considered as a professional elite with a degree of autonomy and independence from the state but working within guidelines, the law and, in the case of terrestrial broadcasters, a charter from the state.

2.4.3 Distinction between nation and state

One definition of nationalism is that each nation should have its own state – i.e. each cultural group, each race etc. This would mean, for example, a Scottish state or a Native American state. We can see, therefore, that nation and state do not necessarily go together (even though we may be moving slightly closer to this in the UK, with a Scottish and Welsh assembly). In his book Nations and Nationalism[3], Gellner claims that nationalism is the dominant ideology of the twentieth century; this he attributes to the collapse of imperialism. He suggests language is the key to nationality and identity; a shared language will produce a shared identity.

In Key Concepts in Communication and Cultural Studies[4], John Hartley adopts a different approach to the concept of 'nation'. He suggests that not only is nation not defined by the state (territory in this case), but it is also not defined by race or ethnicity, language or an organic or indigenous culture. It is culture and a manufactured identity that define nation and nationality. Popular culture, particularly film and television, is the key transmitter of this concept of nation.

Terrestrial television, for example, offers a wide range of contrasting representations of the nation, from live coverage of those events concerned with the government and the monarchy (the state opening of Parliament, trooping the colour, the Budget etc.) to international sporting events, where the emphasis of coverage is frequently on England and the United Kingdom described as 'us' against a foreign adversary (less commonly, coverage centres on Wales, Scotland or Northern Ireland). It is not just factual or news programming that transmits the concept of nation and national identity. There are many examples within television drama, soap opera and situation comedy, such as the contrasting but intrinsically English content of *Last of the Summer Wine* and *Goodness Gracious Me*, which immediately highlights differences between a single culture nation and a multicultural society. More properly, we would need to consider the whole breadth of broadcasting content to assess fully the range of representations and therefore, by extrapolation, concepts of national identity which are in circulation.

2.4.4 The nation state

The nation state is a modern, twentieth century form of the state conceived in terms of political sovereignty, not economic sovereignty, because of international capitalism. Multinationals will operate across borders and, to some degree, outside national control. The concept is now in question and hotly debated, particularly in the UK, because membership of the European Union potentially cedes political sovereignty to the EU. This contradiction emerged during the Thatcher government, and led to the 'twin track'[a] approach to the EU (very much a British perspective). Globally, nation states are now merging into larger blocks. For example, in Europe, membership of the EU is set to expand, America has established a free trade zone with Mexico and Canada, and there could be an Islamic trading block in the future.

The concept of the nation state informs the relation of television to the state; public service broadcasting is a national system regulated by a single nation state. However, satellite developments (from the 1980s onwards)

---

[a] The 'twin track' approach to the EU emerged during the Thatcher years, and has not entirely disappeared. It suggests that the UK will cede legal power to the EU when it is deemed to be in the UK's interest, but insists on the second, national track when it does not.

make the concept of 'national television', the cornerstone of PSB definitions, less credible.

2.4.5 National identity

The mass media are the principal agencies that create and maintain the concepts of nation, nation state and national identity. Indeed, this is an integral part of the charter that regulates the programming policy of terrestrial broadcasters. One way of conceptualising the transmission of nation and national identity was suggested by Benedict Anderson in his 1983 book, *Imagined Communities: Reflections on the Origin and Spread of Nationalism*[5]. The term 'imagined communities' was used to explain the process by which we can 'experience' the nation through symbolic representation (signification), since we cannot literally experience it. Even if we travel extensively, we cannot know all the inhabitants of the nation in the way that we could have known all the inhabitants of a pre-industrial village. Television, as the most widely consumed medium, is identified as the primary agency for building 'imagined communities'.

There are dangers inherent within the concepts of nation and national identity. Gellner, in *Nations and Nationalism*[6], also alludes to the inclusivity and exclusivity of the concepts. Clearly, they are frequently used divisively in order to support prejudice, both within a nation and between nations.

2.4.6 Four models for the state

Let us now consider four models for the state.

Functionalist or authoritarian

This states that all parts of a society are integrated; they have a part to play in the whole (closely associated with the work of the philosopher, Hegel). This is an organic conception of society evolving through history to a unified entity. The state prevents society from breaking up, and holds sectional interests and individualism in check.

Hegelian concepts were connected with fascist ideology after the First World War, and thus fell into disrepute[b]. However, Hegelianism was strongly

[b]It is important to distinguish between a political philosophy and how it has been applied to a political system. It is possible to conceive of a unified society which would not be oppressive, for example a religious order, although the events of the twentieth century give us many examples of the appalling consequences of authoritarian regimes.

entrenched in Oxford University until 1922, and was a major influence on both John Grierson and John Reith (first Director General of the BBC), who saw broadcasting as the method for holding the nation together – 'the social cement'.

Pluralistic conception of the state

This states that society is composed of a number of forces; the state is not dominant. The constitutions of France and USA were based on this model, which is based on a concept of three estates – the military, the judiciary and the clergy. In this model, the mass media is seen as the 'fourth estate', and is therefore able to regulate the power of the state. This is in contrast to the authoritarian model, where it has the right, indeed the duty, to comment on and criticise the workings of the state.

This concept of the state arose from the sixteenth century onwards, and the context to these changes was the rise of capitalism, replacing feudal states, after the agrarian and industrial revolutions. A new class emerged that was capable of challenging the power of the state – e.g. in the repeal of the Corn Laws, a growing industrial bourgeoisie was able to change the law.

In a pluralist state, groups within society cede power to the state, but there are limitations to the power of the state. The concept of individualism emerges, and rights of the individual are stated but checked by the state to ensure that no one group becomes dominant. The state has a regulatory function, but is itself regulated, to ensure that no one estate dominates the others. Therefore, there is a strong role for the state.

O'Leary and Dunleavy's 'New Right Theory' of the state

O'Leary and Dunleavy's theory is based on the idea of a minimal state within a free market economy, where the state will not limit the activities of successful market capitalists. It derived from the work of economist Adam Smith, although Smith suggested that the state would have to regulate capital in order to maintain the free market.

However, the New Right Theory rejects the concept of regulation except in limiting monopolies to ensure an open market. It takes a more radical position than Adam Smith, suggesting that if market forces are unregulated, this will produce a natural balance or harmony – the 'hidden hand' or 'self-righting process'. The state must not intervene to sustain pluralism, since this will artificially interfere with the balance of the markets. This philosophy was one of a number that informed Thatcherism and Reaganism in the 1980s and, more importantly for broadcasting, was a key part of the philosophy of the Broadcasting Act 1990.

Neopluralist conception of the state

An attempt to adapt classic libertarian ideas to corporatism, neopluralism relates to British broadcasting.

This approach is derived from the notion of society as autocratic and technocratic. The business sector dominates, and pluralism refereed by the state is therefore impossible. This is an admission of the inadequacy of pluralist theory, and therefore an inherent acceptance of dominance by capitalism.

Neopluralism is based on a concept of industrial society being so complex that it needs an equally complex administration to govern it. New structures will emerge – e.g. the EU and social democratic structures. These will be run by professional bureaucrats, who will become an elite, and governments will then have to cede power to these professional elites, who can run a complex society. This overturns the notion of real democracy; popular democracy does not work in this theory.

Broadcasters are one of these groups of professional elites who are granted autonomy from the state in their own professional sphere. This produces a separate professional society and culture. (For a detailed description of the BBC in these terms, see Tom Burn's *The BBC – Public Institution and Private World*[7].) In this model the state will construct the regulatory framework and have some notional input, but the professionals are able to maintain their autonomy.

For the BBC, the regulatory framework is set by the Charter, and BBC governors are nominated by the government[c]. Nevertheless, broadcasters are able to run a complex industry with a degree of autonomy; therefore, broadcasting fits neatly into the neopluralist model. (Other elites, such as lawyers, have their own 'public service' regulations, which prevent government interference.)

[c]There is no provision for a democratic approach to the operation of PSB except by the indirect route of an elected government. Many would argue that broadcasting is too complex and powerful a medium for viewers to elect the BBC governors, the ITC or the Director General of the BBC.

2.4.7 Theories of the media

How does the mass media operate within these models of the state?

Authoritarian model

The state controls the media in the interests of society, and the state is seen as the most important society within society. This model refers back to Plato and the theory of a common culture. Underlying this is a notion that individualism is irrational and damaging to society. The mass media is used to unify society, and control can be exerted through patronage, censorship, legal prosecutions or state subsidy. Whilst this model could be seen as outdated, such a system still exists, for example in China.

It can be argued that there is no absolute distinction between an authoritarian and a liberal broadcasting system, since there are always controls extant in any society. Television is rarely unregulated in western societies; it is not allowed to range over a complete spectrum of views within a society. However, in the French and United States constitutions the freedom of the media from state intervention is stated.

Libertarian model or pluralism

This model is based on the notion of social unity being achieved through maximum range of expression. Individuals are able to express their own opinions. State and media are totally separate, and the state will not regulate content. This model emerged from seventeenth and eighteenth century libertarian theory – the individual is rational, an objective view exists. There are a variety of opinions, but only the true opinions will be perceived and survive, whilst others will fall away. Individual citizens are able to make this choice without intervention by the state.

The mass media are not only independent, but can also now become an adversary of the state – the 'fourth estate'. This was embodied in the American constitution, but in Britain there is no written constitution and therefore no set role for the media. Thus the value of the pluralist model lies in media's ability to voice dissent against the state or society. However, it does not address the way that power is distributed within society, and therefore the consequent inequality in access to the media. The mass media may be independent of the state, but could be controlled by market forces, reflecting media owners' opinions rather than the breadth of views within society. From this position, opinions succeed not because they are objectively true but because they are supported by powerful groups.

Libertarianism was part of the background to the Broadcasting Act 1990 – the 'competition of ideas' lies behind the argument to increase cable and satellite channels.

The model does not address ideas of irrationalism (can humans rationally judge?), because the theory pre-dates psychoanalysis and notions of the unconscious.

Social responsibility theory

The basis for this theory is that the state should intervene in the mass media to some extent, to ensure that it serves the breadth of society, and that market forces alone do not produce this. This approach developed alongside the growth of mixed economies, e.g. The New Deal in the USA in the 1930s. After the Wall Street Crash of 1926, unregulated capitalism was seen to be flawed. (**NB**: Soviet economy was then growing, unaffected by the crash.)

In a social responsibility model, the mass media have obligations to society, and governments have to intervene to ensure that they act responsibly. Hence Stanley Baldwin's comment on the press that they had 'power without responsibility'. The media are held to be responsible to:

1 Keep the electorate informed on a wide range of issues
2 Act as a critic of society and government
3 Provide a variety and quality of output.

That is, 'to educate, inform and entertain', in Reith's words; this responsibility is still embodied in the BBC and ITV companies charter.

Thus the media have autonomy, but have to comply with regulation. Two basic rights are involved; first, the media's right of free expression, and this is qualified by the second, the public's right to be informed. Free expression is therefore subservient to the public's right to information.

Broadcasting companies operate within criminal and civil law, bias, impartiality, acceptance of censorship and so on, all of which limit their autonomy. Therefore, the closest comparison for the British public service broadcasting system is to a neopluralist model of the state; professional groups who are autonomous within regulation.

2.5 The concept of public service broadcasting in the UK and elsewhere

Public service broadcasting (PSB) is not a concept unique to the UK – other European countries have their own systems (e.g. RAI in Italy, ZDF in Germany) – but the method of regulation and range of stations is specific to the UK.

Public service broadcasting is a difficult concept to define precisely; it is partly rooted in the 'public service' traditions of public utilities and services (e.g. health, education, the civil service). As Paddy Scannel points out in *Public Service Broadcasting – The History of a Concept*[8], the debate about setting up the broadcasting system in the UK was concurrent with the establishment of many of the public utilities – e.g. gas and water. The term also refers to nature of programming and assumptions about the audience.

In the UK, all the terrestrial television stations (BBC1, BBC2, the ITV companies, Channel 4 and Channel 5) can be considered to be PSB broadcasters. Cable and satellite stations are not, although they may choose to offer community and access channels.

There are several distinctions between the two systems:

1 Method of payment – PSB is funded by a licence, cable and satellite by subscription.
2 Programming – PSB has mixed programming, cable and satellite has generic programming. The PSB stations' charter demands that they offer a range of services, while cable and satellite can choose to offer only generic (e.g. movie channel, sports channel, home shopping!).
3 Regulation – the PSB stations work to charter, and are controlled through the BBC board of governors and the ITC (see Negrine, *Politics and the Mass Media* for details[9]). Cable and satellite stations are regulated through the ITC, but this exercises far less influence over programme content.
4 Availability – PSB should be available to the whole population, while cable and satellite need only be available to some.

At first sight, some of these distinctions between a PSB system and cable and satellite might seem to be trivial, but it is argued that they have a significant effect on both production and consumption.

The licence fee distinguishes PSB – certainly the BBC – from cable and satellite stations, because it breaks the link between audience size and income. This can be represented as part of the paternalistic nature of PSB – that the broadcasters know what is best for the audience, rather than the audience exercising consumer choice between a range of channels and programmes. The latter approach approach to broadcasting considers programmes as marketable goods rather than cultural artefacts – a direct comparison is sometimes made with print media; there is a huge range of publications to choose from, and their success or failure will be decided by the consumers. The ITV companies, Channel 4 and Channel 5 are funded by advertising, and so one could argue that, although not directly funded by the viewer, they are heavily reliant upon the audiences that they can supply to advertisers. (Audience size is not of course always the key factor here, as advertisers are also interested in a range of other factors such as gender, income or region.)

The wide range of programmes offered by PSB stations is intended not only to serve the diverse tastes and interests of the audience, but also to broaden their experience. It is sometimes argued that generic programming will prevent viewers finding programmes by chance, and that their experience of television will be diminished. Again, this approach to PSB can be represented as paternalistic (broadcasters rather than viewers control-ling the schedules) or it can be defended as maintaining pluralism within the schedules, since minority audience interests can be served. The remote control and more recent pre-selecting controllers for digital television reduce the argument that viewers will find new programmes simply because they cannot be bothered to change channels. Indeed, programmable remote controls for digital broadcasting will allow viewers to create a generic selection, e.g. feature films or sport, from a group of mixed programming channels.

The differences in regulation reinforce the different characteristics of the two systems; cable and satellite stations have minimal regulation, whereas the balance of the programme schedule and even individual programmes are considered by the BBC governors and the ITC. Since 1992, when the ITC took over from the IBA (Independent Broadcasting Authority), there has been less regulation of the commercial PSB stations, ITV, Channel 4 and Channel 5. For example, in the autumn of 1999 the ITC announced that it was not part of its remit to dictate the time of the ITV news programme, *News at Ten*. The proposal to move *News at Ten* was debated in the House of Commons, and was widely condemned because it was felt that this was prioritising other programme types over the news within the schedule. For the ITV network the motivation was partly financial; they had only been able to run films and drama from nine o'clock in the evening if they had a

40-minute break to allow for national and regional news programmes, and a reduced number of viewers returned after the break. The ITC's decision not to intervene despite concerns raised in Parliament demonstrates a shift away from a regulation of ITV's public service function (providing news to the widest possible audience) to a recognition of the economic constraints under which broadcasters operate.

Availability is central to PSB; the signal should as far as possible be available to the whole population regardless of cost. (Channel 5 is the exception here in that the 1990 Broadcasting Act only required it to be available to 80 per cent of the population). National availability invites comparisons with the postal service, also costing a flat fee regardless of the cost of delivery, and other services such as water and electricity. It also allows PSB stations to claim that they are part of a national culture and national identity.

2.5.1 Definitions

A variety of definitions of Public Service Broadcasting have been suggested. We need to consider the source of these – are they formed from a particular political and/or social perspective?

John Reith's purpose for the BBC, first outlined in 1922, is still an everyday guideline for the function of not just the BBC but the whole PSB system – 'to inform, educate and entertain'. However, a cursory glance at contemporary schedules demonstrates that the emphasis has shifted towards entertainment and away from education.

The Broadcasting Research Unit drew up a definition of public service broadcasting, which they then submitted to the Peacock Committee on Broadcasting (1986). This government committee considered the future of the BBC, and particularly whether the licence fee should be retained as a method of funding, or whether advertising should be introduced.

The research unit found it difficult to obtain a definition of PSB from broadcasters, who held a variety of views as to what PSB was and how it should function, but they drew up eight main principles for PSB[10]:

1 Geographic universality – broadcast programmes should be available to the whole population
2 Universality of appeal – broadcast programmes should cater for all interests and tastes
3 Minorities – all minorities, and especially disadvantaged minorities, should receive particular provision

4 National identity – broadcasters should recognise their special relationship to the sense of national identity and community
5 Vested interests – broadcasting should be distanced from all vested
interests, and in particular from those of the government of the day
6 Universality of payment – one main instrument of broadcasting should be
directly funded by the corpus of users (currently the licence fee)
7 Competition – broadcasting should be structured so as to encourage
competition in good programming rather than competition in numbers
8 Guidelines – the public guidelines for broadcasting should be designed to
liberate rather than restrict programme makers.

Given the perception that the Peacock Committee might be about to break
up the PSB system, and there was speculation that the BBC might be
partially privatised, this list can be read as a defence of the existing
system.

Let us now consider the principles in more detail. Those that deal with
reception and funding have already been considered. Principles (2) and (3)
seem to be in direct contradiction to each other – universality of appeal, and
serving minorities, However, the principles apply to the whole PSB system
rather than one programme or strand of programmes. Thus essentially the
two principles call for pluralism within the system – for a range of 'voices'
rather than simply the most popular programme formats. Both BBC2 and
Channel 4 were required by their charters to serve minority audiences, and
these were initially defined by demographic categories, primarily gender and
race, and more recently sexual orientation – in other words, by the
audience served. Channel 4 extended this approach to define minority
programming by content, for example minority sports (e.g. Kabbadi) or
minority interests (e.g. programmes on fishing).

Principle (4), concerning broadcasters' relationship to the community and
national identity, is as problematic. As discussed above, british television is
perceived as an important transmitter of what it is to be British (or English,
Welsh, Scottish or, much less often, Irish). How far can we define a national
identity in a complex society? It is not credible for a single identity to be
created for all viewers. However, this function is considered essential for
PSB's survival; if identity was not important then the source of programmes
would be irrelevant, and commercial broadcasters could easily supply
American programmes more cheaply than the PSB broadcasters' product.

Principle (5), freedom from vested interests, has always been important for
PSB, whether the interests are political, independence from the government
of the day, or financial independence from corporations. For the BBC,

political independence was tested as early as 1926, during the General Strike. John Reith, the first Director General of the newly formed British Broadcasting Corporation, was asked to broadcast government speakers' and the government's view of the strike, and not to allow the strikers' view to be put. Publicly Reith resisted the government's intervention, but privately, writing in his own diary, he was appalled that they had felt the need to ask for his support and had not simply assumed that he would uphold the government view. This incident is often referred to in histories of broadcasting because it demonstrates the consensus between the BBC in particular (and broadcasters in general) and the government. This was to break down dramatically during the time of the Thatcher government in the 1980s. The notion of an 'arm's length' relationship between broadcasters and government has a number of paradoxes attached to it. The BBC's licence fee is set by Parliament, and so the government is intrinsically involved in the funding process. The government is also involved in regulating the PSB system; it recommends appointments to the BBC board of governors, and regulates the ITC.

Governments, most notably the Thatcher government, have intervened directly to ask broadcasters not to transmit individual programmes. The most famous of these cases was Thames Television's documentary *Death on the Rock*, which was transmitted in 1986 in the *This Week* programme. The programme considered the shooting of three IRA members on active service in Gibraltar, and claimed that they may have been shot without warning. Thames was asked not to transmit the programme by the Thatcher government, on the basis that it might prejudice the coroner's court, which had not then been held. Geoffrey Howe, then Minister at the Foreign Office, approached the IBA to hold back transmission, but they approved the programme. *Death on the Rock* could therefore be seen to prove the independence of PSB broadcasters from government. However, given that Richard Dunn (the Chief Executive of Thames) was dining privately with Douglas Hurd, then Home Secretary, on the eve of transmission, there must be some question as to how much distance there was between Thames and the government[11]. This is less a question of government intervention, and more a product of a 'common culture' between broadcasters and external bodies. Many other programmes were not transmitted, or transmission was postponed, following a government request to delay transmission. Jean Seaton, in *Power without Responsibility*, gives a full account of the changing relationship between government and broadcasters in the 1980s[12].

The last two principles reinforce the traditional PSB model of programmes as cultural production rather than economic goods. It is significant that the distinction is made between 'good programming' and 'good numbers'. This restates a standard assumption of broadcasting, indeed of popular culture in general, that popular programmes cannot be 'good' (though what good means in this context is not easy to define). Certainly, a number of challenging drama serials have had good ratings – for example, *Boys from the Blackstuff* in the 1980s, and *Our Friends in the North* in the 1990s. The BBC has recently promoted its most popular programmes – in particular *Eastenders* and *Casualty* – as popular, quality drama.

Let us now consider a critique of the principles. Ralph Negrine, in his book *Politics and the Mass Media in Britain*, points out that it is not clear whether the principles relate to a real model (e.g. the BBC or Granada) or the underlying philosophy which we would relate to such an organisation. Negrine sums up this difference between the ideal model and the reality[13]:

> If it relates to the BBC *per se* then it conveniently overlooks its seedier and more questionable aspects, whilst if it relates to some imaginary institution it ignores the real pressures on institutions which make them somehow less ideal than one would desire.

Negrine also quotes Krishnan Kumar, from *Public Service Broadcasting and the Public Interest*[14], which gives another range of definitions. PSB should provide a[15]:

> ... daily service that is that is continuously and thoroughly infused with a sense of its public function. That is serving the public as a living audience with potential for growth and development.

A breadth of programming should be provided, from Shakespeare to *Minder*, for:

> without such breadth public service broadcasting can become elitist and authoritarian.

However, Negrine suggests that Kumar is in danger of being elitist by distinguishing between *Minder* as a useful programme, and *Dallas* and *Dynasty* as showing a contempt for the audience. Kumar was writing in the mid 1980s; there are certainly those who feel that the range of programming has narrowed considerably since then in terms of the demands it makes on the audience. One should also consider the diverse ways television is consumed, from the careful attention that may be afforded to a current affairs programme or soap to the ambient sound and pictures which late-night television may provide – an audience may not always want to be faced with challenging television throughout the schedule.

2.5.2 Public service broadcasting in Canada and Germany

In order to consider other approaches to PSB, this section will very briefly look at the Canadian Broadcasting Corporation (CBC) and the structure of the German PSB system as it was constituted in the 1980s.

Canadian broadcasting – a warning for Europe?

In the 1980s, Canadian public service broadcasting and its battle for survival against American competition was seen as a model for the future of European PSB[15]. With the benefit of hindsight, we can see that for much of Europe, and particularly the UK, the model did not apply. However, with the arrival of digital television distribution, many of the same issues are being debated again – for example, what is the role of a public service broadcaster in a multichannel environment. The similarities in language and culture between the USA and Canada are probably the most important factors here; it could be argued that many Canadian viewers were not primarily concerned with the source of programming. This could explain why many European PSB systems, who were distinguishable by culture and language, did not encounter all of the problems of Canadian PSB.

Let us consider the history of Canadian broadcasting up until the 1980s. The public service broadcaster is the Canadian Broadcasting Corporation (CBC), similar to the BBC, and the focus of national goals for PSB. The CBC was established in 1936, somewhat later than the BBC (1926).

The history of PSB in Canada

Canada was formed in 1867. From the foundation of the Canadian nation, national identity was a priority; the government identified the need for a coast-to-coast communication network to achieve this. (Canada is world's second largest nation state, in area terms, with a population of about 23 million, mainly located in the east.) The physical geography of the country was a key factor in the way that communications were established. As Richard Collins points out in *Canada: Nation Building Threatened by the US Dominated Media?*[16]:

> The geography of Canada is such that although east–west water communications stretching from the Atlantic to the Rocky Mountains facilitated early exploration and exploitation of a large land area, in much of the country north–south connections are as convenient as

east–west. Physical communications with the United States are, in Western and Atlantic Canada, as easy, or easier than they are with central Canada.

A series of government acts defined the role of broadcasting – to strengthen the social, cultural, political and economic fabric of Canada.

Key dates

In 1919, the first licence to broadcast was granted to the Marconi company (**NB:** this was granted to Marconi in the UK in 1922).

By 1923, there were 34 private radio stations in Canada and 556 operating in the USA. This created problems for Canadian broadcasters because American stations were easy to receive in Canada – the majority of Canadians live within 200 miles of the border with the USA. American performers, primarily music, were popular in Canada, and therefore many Canadians could and did tune in to American stations.

In 1932, the First Canadian Broadcasting Act was passed as a result of the report of the Canadian Broadcasting Commission. The Act defined the role for Canadian PSB as a publicly owned service to protect against American cultural product, which would be nationally available (as in the British system) and allowed for government control.

In 1936, the Second Broadcasting Act was passed; this established the CBC.

In 1939, the national network was established. Unlike the BBC, the CBC only operated transmitters in centres of population, because of a lack of financial support from government for a public, national network. They worked with affiliates – private companies who would broadcast CBC product. So from the beginning the CBC was short of money and had to rely on affiliate stations; hence programming had to be popular. (The CBC could not, and cannot, produce minority programming in English.) Lack of funding meant that cheap but popular American product was bought in, thus undermining one of the key principles of the 1932 Broadcasting Act.

During the war, the national radio network was important in giving a Canadian voice rather than an American voice; this was seen as a confirmation of the need for a Canadian Broadcasting Service. News became vital programming in creating the CBC identity. (Again, one could draw parallels with the function of the BBC during the Second World War.)

In 1952, CBC TV was established. Television had similar problems to radio in competing with American stations. By the time it arrived, Canadians already had 150 000 sets picking up American stations. Cable TV was already established for picking up American programmes, so it was easy to receive, whereas off-air reception was a problem.

In 1959, the Board of Broadcasting Governors imposed a quota for Canadian product on both private and public channels. In 1962, the quota was set at 55 per cent minimum of Canadian programming.

In the early 1980s, satellite became available and thus there was more American competition (e.g. in 1992 in Toronto, 59 channels were available on satellite). This fragmented the audience, reducing further the advertising revenue available for CBC.

In the early 1990s, Canadian PSB consisted of two CBC radio stations (one in English and one in French), and two television stations (again one in English and one in French). CBC was under threat from a wide variety of other channels, a high percentage of Canadian homes are cabled or own satellite receivers, and therefore receive a variety of American stations.

National goals for broadcasting – the 1968 Broadcasting Act

This was an important statement of broadcasting policy for Canada, but it was more of an ideal than a reality. The Act had the following goals:

1 To strengthen unity and common destiny. This is difficult to achieve; it is claimed there isn't unity in Canadian society, so why should it be the case in broadcasting? Canada is often seen as two nations, English and French speaking, particularly in Quebec. This is reinforced by Quebec's frequent (and narrowly lost) referenda to secede from Canada. Post-war Canada has encouraged immigration, creating a multicultural state and encouraging multiculturalism.
2 To exalt the independence of Canada, politically, socially and economically. This is problematic because, as we have seen, Canadians have always consumed American product; 50 per cent of CBC programming is from American producers. Also, post-Second World War, Canada became much more economically dependent on the USA (75 per cent of its export trade is with the USA). In 1987 the Free Trade Agreement removed barriers to US, Canadian and Mexican trade, in a similar way to EU agreements. Thus, even if Canada could achieve cultural independence, which seems unlikely, it is fundamentally tied to the USA in economic terms.

3 To reinforce a single broadcasting system in Canada. Canada's system is pluralistic; a mix of Canadian and American programming mirrors trade in other areas. Therefore, the current broadcasting system is in direct contradiction to this aim. The Canadian Government is dedicated to protecting industry and the consumer; this is not served by a single broadcasting system.

Canadian programming

There are high ratings for Canadian news and sports, particularly ice hockey. It is often argued that this represents Canadian culture on television, and that the source of TV drama is irrelevant to most Canadian viewers. For example, a very successful Canadian drama serial (both in Canada and the USA), *Conspiracy of Silence* (CBC, 1991), conforms to American television drama conventions of narrative, genre, camera and editing styles. More recently, *Due South* (Alliance) was based on taking its Canadian hero south of the border to Chicago in order both to emphasise the stereotypes of Canadian identity and to produce a distinctly American-style detective series.

The Canadian model has been used for analysis of the future of European broadcasting. However, European nation states have stronger national identities than Canada. One view is that Canadian broadcasting problems are largely self-inflicted; there is not a strong desire from the audience for a Canadian public service broadcasting system. This is exacerbated by insufficient government funding. However, the advent of digital broadcasting has led to a revisiting of some of these predictions for the future of PSB in Europe. Again, there are fears of American dominance in schedules and the gradual decline of terrestrial, PSB stations.

2.5.3 German public service broadcasting

The German public service broadcasting system is now based on the former West German model, and we will consider this in some detail in order to compare to PSB in the United Kingdom. The system would appear to offer greater democratic control of broadcasters and to break down the dominance of a paternalistic system – a frequent criticism of PSB in the United Kingdom, particularly the BBC.

Germany had the earliest mixed economy in Europe – a corporate society from the late nineteenth century. The individual was part of that corporation, and related to the state (following the philosophy of Hegel).

This affected broadcasting; during the Nazi period (1933–1945) broadcasting and film were controlled by the state, and used by the party.

In the post-war years, the Allies were determined to prevent the re-emergence of a unified state. Germany was not only partitioned, but in West Germany a Federal Republic was established. Eleven *Länder* were established, and power was devolved to each of these regions under a new constitution, Basic Law. Cultural policy and power were also deliberately devolved to the Länder in order to prevent the reforming of a nationalist culture.

Article 5 of Basic Law provides for the freedom of expression, but also limits it. Expression has to comply with both the criminal law and the constitution; it must not threaten the constitution, for example by arguing for the abolition of federalism.

Article 15 places emphasis on the public ownership of broadcasting, seen as the only feasible option post-war. It provided a continuity of public ownership and public control.

The West German broadcasting system was split into nine stations, one station per *Länder*, apart from the two smallest ones. This is clearly a different approach from the UK, although there are some parallels with the regional division of the ITV network (ITV stations are required to represent their region as well as forming part of a national network). Each station has a similar organisational structure, and is responsible to its local region.

In the late 1950s, there was pressure for a commercial broadcasting system to be established. The conservative Federal government (the Bund) was interested in a national network to compete with regional broadcasting, because of concerns over regional bias and local interpretation (the stations were thought to be broadly left of centre). The Bund tried to set up a national service, but the *Länder* were able to take them to constitutional court and win because of Articles 5 and 15 of the constitution. This event highlights the role of a written constitution and the function of broadcasting stated within it. The court also ruled that all types of opinion should be broadcast; balance and impartiality would be achieved over a year's schedule and not within a single programme. Thus, the court recognised that broadcasting would be important in shaping public opinion and could take up an adversarial role in politics. Programmes could have a certain tendency or bias, which was unacceptable in the UK until the Broadcasting Act (1990).

However, the *Länder* recognised the need to accommodate the Bund's demands and they established a second channel, ZDF, which was controlled regionally but broadcast nationally. This was more conservative.

Funding for broadcasting is through the licence fee and advertising. By the late 1970s/early 1980s, advertising made up 30 per cent of PSB income. The broadcasting system is not so threatened by American programming because of the language difference and quotas. The licence fee is on a sliding scale, not a fixed fee as in UK; income is distributed between *Länder*. Advertising was initially tightly controlled, with a maximum of 20 minutes per day and no advertising on Sundays. As with other European countries, the public service system was threatened by the emergence of cable and satellite in the late 1970s/early 1980s.

Structure of policy management

The German broadcasting system is often said to have pluralism all the way though it, placed there by the Allies. How is this achieved?

The regulatory framework for each station required it to have representatives from the local community, and to provide access for the local community. There was freedom from commercial and central state pressures, and ideally this would provide the autonomy and freedom to experiment. For example, the WDR's *Arbeiterfilm* (workers' films) in the 1970s were naturalistic dramas from a broad left perspective. They had some common ground with Garnett and Loach's early work for the BBC but were more overtly political. However, despite achieving relatively high ratings, the *Arbeiterfilm* were cancelled. It is claimed that powerful forces were mobilised to oppose them, principally the business sector and the right, and that the broadcaster, WDR, caved in. This illustrates an important gap between theory, policy indeed, and practice, which is an important consideration for debates about reforming or enforcing PSB policy.

Within each station, the regulation was carried out by:

1 The Broadcasting Council, which was elected by members of the state assembly, for a 5-year term. The political spectrum of the *Länder* would be represented, because Germany has proportional representation in its electoral system (for WDR, the Council had 21 members).
2 The Director General (Intendant), who was appointed for a fixed term to carry out policy decisions.
3 The Programme Advisory Council, which was elected from local interest groups (e.g. church, industry and women's groups). Not every station had a Council; in the WDR's case this consisted of 20 members, 19 of which were elected by the Broadcasting Council. Again, this provided a link between the political spectrum represented by electors and the management of the television station.

4 The Administrative Council, which was elected by the Broadcasting Council to achieve a balance between the Social and Christian Democrats and other parties. This group met once a month, and was the real power base of the system in Porter and Collins view[17]. The Broadcasting Council appointed the Intendant, who then needed the Administrative Council's approval for the appointment of programme director, directors of administration, studio directors, legal advisors, director of transmissions and technical directors[18]. Their approval, however, was not needed for posts 'with exclusively artistic duties'. Hence, there was separation made between the management of broadcasting resources and the breadth of content, and decisions about individual programme content. (A comparison could be made with the BBC governors and their remit.)

If programming became too partial over the year, the Administrative Council would step in to ask for balance. Although Broadcasting Councils allowed for a range of political views, this tended to lead to parties 'siding' for political ends with either the Social or Christian democrats, and this in turn led to minority views (such as the Greens) being squeezed out.

The system can be seen as democratic, but allowing for direct political intervention in programming in a way that would be unacceptable in the UK. This type of structure answers some of the criticisms of the lack of accountability of PSB, but it also raises the prospect of broadcasting becoming closely allied to party politics.

Cable and satellite have now made inroads into the PSB system. In 1987, a court accepted that private broadcasting could go ahead as long as balance and representation were maintained. (PSB was identified as functioning to maintain democracy, but private systems only had to maintain 'a minimum standard of pluralism' – they were left freer in programming terms.)

In the 1990s, the German television industry was seen to be in crisis, hampered by a high degree of regulation to maintain balance and pluralism (pluralism here including non-federal views, which are unconstitutional). There was a potential problem with the EC/EU post-1992, since Germany's regulation of PSB could be deemed to contravene a European free market and therefore be challenged in the European court as a restrictive practice. The fragmentation of revenue, by both an increase in the number of public stations and the arrival of satellite and cable, has limited programme making, whereas in the 1970s German PSB funded 'New German Cinema' (e.g. the films of Wim Wenders, Werner Herzog,

Fassbinder and Margerethe von Trotta). It is now almost squeezed out of film co-production.

West German PSB was considered a model for the 'social responsibility' system of PSB. Media reformers in the UK pointed to it because of its role being defined by the constitution and protected by it. It appeared to allow for a real democratic input to PSB, but to some extent a real breadth of programming could not be delivered. In the light of the technological, economic and political changes of the 1980s/1990s, this may need to be re-evaluated.

2.6 The history of British public service broadcasting

The history of public service broadcasting in the UK is often recounted as a history of regulation. Broadcasting in the UK was established as a public monopoly after a short trial period as private monopoly. This is clearly not the only model; in the USA broadcasting was largely left to the market, although there was still regulation on technical grounds because of the scarcity of wavelengths.

This brief history details the main developments in public service broadcasting in the United Kingdom, particularly those related to television. For a fuller account see the reading list at the end of the chapter, which details a number of histories of broadcasting.

2.6.1 Context

Radio communication was developed by the military during the First World War; post-war they were reluctant to see it developed for civilian purposes. Parliament was lobbied because of concerns about interference from civilian signals affecting the efficiency of military use of the airwaves. A second factor that delayed the start of public broadcasting in the UK was the Russian revolution (1917). There was concern about the power of broadcasting to subvert the state because the new medium could be used to call people to revolt, and indeed the initial broadcasts were carefully controlled by the Postmaster General to prevent any subversive use. The consequence of these concerns was that, whilst the USA and many other countries established radio stations during 1919 and 1920, broadcasts were delayed in the UK until 1922.

2.6.2 Regulation of broadcasting

Paddy Scannel's writing in *Understanding Television* suggests that, when considering the history of regulation[19]:

A useful starting point is to distinguish between public service as a responsibility delegated to broadcasting authorities by the state, and the manner in which the broadcasting authorities have interpreted that responsibility and tried to discharge it.

Key dates, Acts and government committees

In 1922, the British Broadcasting Company was founded as a private monopoly.

In 1923, the Sykes Committee considered the future of broadcasting ('The control of such a potential power over public opinion and the life of the nation ought to remain with the state'[20]).

In 1925, Reith was asked to submit a proposal for future of broadcasting to the Crawford Committee. He recommended a public utility. The Crawford Committee maps out the guidelines for British public service broadcasting.

In 1926, the British Broadcasting Corporation became a public utility, and John Reith became its first Director General. The BBC's independence from the government was tested by the General Strike in the same year. All the newspapers except for the government's *British Gazette* were closed down, and the Home Secretary, Winston Churchill, wanted to use the BBC to broadcast the government line. Reith wrote in his diary afterwards:

They want to be able to say that they did not commandeer us, but they know they can trust us not to be really impartial.

In 1932, the BBC World Service was established. This is the only part of the BBC directly funded by government (the Foreign Office) and not by licence fee. Ironically, it is sometimes suggested that it is the most independent service, particularly in terms of its news coverage.

In 1933, Radio Luxembourg was founded and competition arose because the BBC was unwilling to broadcast popular music, especially on Sundays.

In 1936, BBC television started, although it was only available in the South East of England and programmes and transmissions were limited (typically 20.30–22.00 hrs). The BBC management was seen as being indifferent to it, and funding continued, in the main, to be for radio.

In 1939, the television service closed down for the war (it was seen as a luxury), although radio continued. Television broadcasting eventually resumed in 1946.

In 1950, the Beveridge Report recommended that the BBC should remain as monopoly broadcaster.

In 1954, the Television Act legislated for the creation of independent television. Only one-fifth of households had a television; this was a low percentage compared to the USA, but was much higher than in the rest of Europe.

In 1955 to 1956, the monopoly was broken and ITA was established. The first stations, including Granada, started broadcasting.

By 1957, the audience had been largely drawn to independent television – 75 per cent watched ITA and 25 per cent BBC. Reith was unable to deliver popular culture, whereas the ITA companies were broadcasting gameshows and American programmes.

In 1960, the Pilkington Report criticised the low standards on ITV, and forced companies back from mainly popular programming ('a licence to print money') to their public service remit. As a result of the Pilkington Report, the third TV channel was awarded to the BBC in 1964. BBC2's charter required it to function as a minority channel.

Between 1964 and 1982, the three channels operated in equilibrium and competition. This period is now often described as the 'Golden Age of Television'. BBC1 had a 40 per cent audience share, BBC2 10 per cent and ITV 50 per cent. It was in the government's interests to maintain a stable audience for each, and if ITV exceeded a 50 per cent share, a government levy on advertising income would reduce profits. Instead of competition for audience, there was competition for quality – broadcasters wanted to win awards as well as ratings.

This created openings for oppositional programme makers such as Tony Garnett and Ken Loach (*Cathy Come Home*), Sidney Newman (*Armchair Theatre*, *The Wednesday Play*) and Peter Watkins (*The War Game*). There was less pressure on broadcasters to deliver ratings, and a desire to experiment with new 'voices'. Senior management and production staff in ITV and BBC had similar social backgrounds; they shared a common culture and would not have to compete with each other, and there was a growing similarity in the ideology of both broadcasters. This all created a unique system of PSB in the UK, despairingly labelled as 'the liberal broadcasting tradition' by Margaret Thatcher.

In 1967, pirate radio stations were closed. BBC started Radio 1 and renamed the other services ('the Light' became Radio 2, the 'Third Service' became Radio 3 and the 'Home Service' became Radio 4).

In 1972, ILR started (LBC and Capital Radio were early stations) and broke the BBC radio monopoly after 46 years. (Note that this was 17 years after the television monopoly was broken.)

In 1977, the Annan Report criticised the 'cosy duopoly' of broadcasters, with BBC and ITV split roughly 50/50 with little competitive scheduling. BBC2 was unable to cater for minorities, as society was now more politically and culturally fragmented, and PSB needed a new station to serve the whole breadth of population. This fourth channel was to be independent. (Initially it was funded by the ITV companies, although it is now reliant on advertising revenue.)

In 1982, Channel 4 started. This was the first national, independent television station, and it had a remit to serve minorities. Jeremy Isaacs, the first Chief Executive, claimed that if the channel reached more than 10 per cent of the audience, then it had failed. In the same year, the Hunt Report on cable was published; this aimed for a complete British network to allow for free market competition, as in the USA. Private companies were to be used to develop the network, unlike West Germany, where public funds were used to create the national system.

In 1986, the Peacock Report was published regarding the funding of the BBC and whether the licence fee should be abolished. This report was directly responsible for the 1990 Broadcasting Act, which was the key legislation for the 1990s; its fallout is still working through the broadcasting industry. This was a move away from PSB principles towards the market. The act articulated Thatcherite policy in a similar way to Health Service and Education reforms of the 1980s (although it was moderated by more than 200 amendments as it passed through Parliament). The Act led to a number of significant changes in broadcasting, including:

1 Franchise auctions for Channel 3; IBA became ITC, and Channel 3 was deregulated
2 Freeing up of radio regulations and the creation of incremental stations (e.g. Kiss FM, Jazz FM), community stations and independent national radio (e.g. Classic FM, Virgin 1215)
3 The 25 per cent rule for independent production for both BBC and ITC companies, which had implications both for employment in television (creating a tendency towards casualisation) and for programming (easier

access to the network meant that programming could be more innovative)

4 The proposal of Channel 5 as an independent national broadcaster, although it was not required to broadcast to the whole country.

In 1995, the government published a White Paper on digital broadcasting.

In 1996, the BBC charter was renewed after much debate about the corporation's future role (see Green Paper, *The Future of the BBC*, and the BBC's reply, *Extending Choice*).

In 1997, Channel 5 eventually started broadcasting.

In 1998, digital distribution started (Sky Digital, Ondigital). Ondigital included BBC1, BBC2, Channel 3 and Channel 4, as well as the new BBC channels (BBC Choice and BBC News 24), Channel 4's FilmFour, and new Carlton and Granada channels. This could be the beginning of commercial PSB or, alternatively, the beginning of the end of PSB.

2.6.3 The future of public service broadcasting

This chapter has considered the history of PSB in the UK, Canada and Germany. One conclusion that can be drawn from this is that there appears to have been a general trend during the 1980s and 1990s towards market-led broadcasting. The accusations of a producer-led, rather paternalistic, system have now given way to criticisms of 'dumbing down' current affairs, news and drama in order to attract more ratings. Despite the fact that the BBC might be perceived as free from chasing ratings, since its income is not directly related to them, they are still essential to the Corporation in order to prove its relevance. If audiences are fragmented by the availability of channel choice and BBC television ratings drop, then the justification for the licence fee (rather than a subscription fee) will be lost. A variety of figures have been debated, but it is often assumed that 25 per cent of the audience, on a weekly basis, is required to maintain the BBC's position. For any government, raising the licence fee is always an unpopular measure; abolishing it, however, would be met with delight by some. Not least of these would be subscription channels, whether cable, satellite or digital, since the licence fee is a significant brake on their expansion. Some viewers are reluctant to pay further for access to television channels, but if there was no licence fee to enter the system (as in the USA) they might well choose, and be able to afford, to subscribe to additional stations.

The end of PSB has been forecast for some 20 years, since the advent of satellite broadcasting. Falling audience share is a major concern for broadcasters – it erodes the notion of a national broadcaster 'speaking' to the whole nation, and threatens programme budgets which might provide distinctiveness (as in Canadian broadcasting). However, public service broadcasters are involved in the new technologies of distribution, with new digital stations (BBC Choice, News 24) and websites (the BBC website is a highly popular and fast expanding example). Finally, as in Canada, the public's desire (or otherwise) for a distinctive public service broadcasting system will probably determine its survival.

2.7 References

1. Alvarado, M. and Stewart, J. (1985). *Made for Television: Euston Films Limited*, Ch. 1. British Film Institute.
2. Winterbottom, W. (1985). In production: *Minder.* In: *Made for Television: Euston Films Limited* (M. Alvarado and J. Stewart, eds). British Film Institute.
3. Gellner, E. (1983). *Nations and Nationalism.* Blackwell.
4. O'Sullivan, T. *et al.* (1994). *Key Concepts in Communication and Cultural Studies.* Routledge.
5. Anderson, B. (1991). *Imagined Communites: Reflections on the Origin and Spread of Nationalism.* Verso.
6. Gellner, E. (1983). *Nations and Nationalism*, p. 7. Blackwell.
7. Burns, T. (1977). *The BBC: Public Institution and Private World.* Macmillan.
8. Scannell, P. (1990). Public service broadcasting: the history of a concept. In: *Understanding Television* (A. Godwin and G. Whannel, eds), pp. 11– 29. Routledge.
9. Negrine, R. (1992). *Politics and the Mass Media in Britain.* Routledge.
10. The Broadcasting Research Unit (1985). *The Public Service Idea.* BRU.
11. Dunn, R. (1994). The 1990 Broadcasting Act: Benefit or Disaster? Lecture given at the RSA London, 16 November 1994.
12. Seaton, J. (1998). To be or not to be the BBC: broadcasting in the 1980s and 1990s. In: *Power without Responsibility* (J. Curran and J. Seaton, eds), pp. 209–36.
13. Negrine, R. (1992). *Politics and the Mass Media in Britain*, p. 106. Routledge.
14. Kumar, K. (1986). Public service broadcasting and the public interest. In: *The BBC and Public Service Broadcasting* (C. MacCabe and O. Stewart, eds) (quoted in Negrine, 1992). University of Manchester Press.

15. Juneau, P. (1984). Audience fragmentation and cultural erosion: a Canadian perspective on the challenge for the public broadcaster. *EBU Rev.*, **35(2)**.

16. Collins, R. (1985). Canada: nation building threatened by the US dominated media. In: *The Politics of Broadcasting* (R. Kuhn, ed.), p. 197. Croom Helm.

17. Collins and Porter, V. (1981). *WDR and the Arbeiterfilm: Fassinder, Ziewer and Others*. British Film Institute.

18. Collins and Porter, V. (1981). *WDR and the Arbeiterfilm: Fassinder, Ziewer and Others*, p. 18. British Film Institute.

19. Scannell, P. (1990). Public service broadcasting: the history of a concept. In: *Understanding Television* (A. Godwin and G. Whannel, eds), p. 11. Routledge.

20. Scannell, P. (1990). Public service broadcasting: the history of a concept. In: *Understanding Television* (A. Godwin and G. Whannel, eds), pp. 12–13. Routledge.

2.8 Further reading

Nation, nationality and identity

Anderson, B. (1983, 1991). *Imagined Communities: Reflections on the Origin and Spread of Nationalism*, especially Chapters 2 and 3. Verso.

Gellner, E. (1997). *Nations and Nationalism*, especially Chapters 1 and 4. Blackwell.

Hutchinson, J. and Smith, A. (eds) (1994). *Nationalism*. Oxford University Press.

Kedourie, E. (1985). *Nationalism*, pp. 68–91. Hutchinson.

O'Sullivan *et al.* (1994, 1995). *Key Doncepts in Communication and Cultural Studies*. Routledge.

Smith, A. D. (1991). *National Identity*, especially Chapters 1, 4 and 7. Penguin.

Public service broadcasting

Briggs, A. (1961, 1965, 1970, 1979). *The History of Broadcasting in the United Kingdom*: Vol. 1 *The Birth of Broadcasting*; Vol. 2 *The Golden Age of Wireless*; Vol. 3 *The War of Words*; Vol. 4 *Sound and Vision*. Oxford University Press.

Budd, A. (1989). *The Peacock Report: Some Unanswered Questions*, pp. 63–75. Institute of Economic Affairs.

Collins, R. (1990). National culture: a contradiction in terms. In: *Television: Policy and Culture*, Chapter 11. Unwin Hyman.

Curran, J. and Seaton, J. (1998). *Power Without Responsibility*. Routledge.

Godwin, A. and Whannel, G. (eds) (1990). *Understanding Television*, especially Chapter 1. Routledge.

Hood, S. (ed.) (1994). *Behind The Screens, The Structure of British Television in the Nineties*. Lawrence & Wishart. (A useful source for articles on deregulation and the charter renewal in the nineties.)

Negrine, R. (1989, 1990). *Politics and the Mass Media in Britain*, especially Chapters 2, 5, 10 and 11. Routledge.

Peacock, A. (1989). *The Future of Public Service Broadcasting*, pp. 51–62. Institute of Economic Affairs.

The Broadcasting Research Unit (1985). *The Public Service Idea*. BRU.

Tracey, M. (1998). *The Decline and Fall of Public Service Broadcasting*, especially Chapters 1, 2, 3, 11 and 14. Oxford University Press.

Veljanovski, C. (1989). *Freedom in Broadcasting*. Institute of Economic Affairs.

Programme case studies

Bolton, R. (1990). *Death on the Rock and Other Stories*. W. H. Allen.

Hinds, H. (1996). Fruitful investigations: the case of the successful lesbian text. In: *Turning It On, A Reader in Women and Media* (H. Baehr and A. Grey, eds). Arnold.

Reports

Extending Choice (1992). BBC.

Green Paper: The Future of the BBC (1992). HMSO.

Programmes and People (1995). BBC.

Report of the Committee on Financing the BBC (1986) (The Peacock Report). HMSO.

The Broadcasting Act (1990). HMSO.

Canadian and German PSB

Collins, R. (1985). Canada: Nation building threatened by the US dominated media? In: *The Politics of Broadcasting* (R. Kuhn, ed.), pp. 197–232. Croom Helm.

Collins, R. and Porter, V. (1981). *WDR and the Arbeiterfilm: Fassbinder, Ziewer and Others*. British Film Institute.

Desaulniers, J.-P. (1987). What does Canada want? (or l'histoire sans lecon). *Media Culture Soc.*, **9(2)**.

Dorland, M. (1996). Policy rhetorics of an imaginary cinema: the discursive economy of the emergence of the Australian and Canadian feature film. In: *Film Policy* (A. Moran, ed.), pp. 114–27. Routledge.

Juneau, P. (1984). Audience fragmentation and cultural erosion: a Canadian perspective on the challenge for the public broadcaster. *EBU Rev.*, **35(2)**.

Williams, A. (1988). The impact of the new technologies on the West German media. *Contemporary German Studies*, Occasional Papers No. 5. Strathclyde University.

Chapter 3

British film policy

3.1 Summary

This introduction to British film policy will compare and contrast the cultural and economic dimensions of film policy. A brief comparison with broadcasting policy will demonstrate the very different relationship the state has had with the film industry. The history of policy will be reviewed considering the Eady Levy, quotas for British film exhibition, the National Film Finance Corporation and its successors, and the variety of public funding bodies (e.g. the Arts Council, BFI and Regional Arts Authorities). These will be considered in the light of cultural policy (the need to create a national film culture to prevent American films swamping the UK) and economic policy (the desire to create a thriving British production base which will encourage inward investment to the UK).

The Thatcher government's decision to leave the film industry's future entirely to the market will be contrasted with the measures taken during the Major years (tax incentives and National Lottery funding). The Blair government's policy and in particular the report from the policy working party on the British film industry, *A Bigger Picture*, will be discussed. The new initiatives for film education and proposals for expansion of the distribution networks indicate a clear shift to a broader approach to film policy, moving away from a focus on production funding. The chapter will conclude with a discussion of where this policy may lead the British film industry in the near future.

3.2 Objectives and key issues

This chapter sets out to offer a brief historical overview of British film policy as a backdrop to the dilemmas facing British film-makers.

The key issues for policy decisions on British film are:

- film as a cultural artefact
- film as an industrial product
- protectionism of national industries
- protectionism or levies – too much effort for too little return.

3.3 British film policy

Until recently there was little film policy to consider in the UK; the few writers who dealt with the subject either constructed a historical survey or lamented the lack of state intervention and support for the industry. With the sharp increase in cinema ticket sales in the late 1980s and 1990s (54 million in 1984, 94.5 million in 1989 and 137 million in 1997[1]) and new markets in video, cable and satellite television, there seems a real possibility of re-establishing the British film industry. Ever since Oscar-winning screenwriter Colin Welland's boast 'The British are coming' at the 1982 Academy Awards Ceremony, when Hugh Hudson's *Chariots of Fire* won Best Picture, there have been a series of one-off successes at breaking into the American market. However, despite films such as *Four Weddings and a Funeral, Trainspotting* and, more recently, *Notting Hill* (which is part American-financed), the British industry has yet to stabilise and thus to break out of its cycle of 'boom and bust'.

3.4 History of past measures

Fears for the future of the British film industry have a long history and stretch back at least to the 1920s, when British film production came close to extinction (Hartog, 1983). However, during the 1990s such fears have been aired with increasing frequency.[2]

Direct and specific intervention by the state in the British film business began with the Cinematograph Films Act (1927). Since then each new decade has had its own new Films Act, and the state's involvement with films has been crucial to the development of the business, and particularly of British film production.[3]

The state's involvement with the film industry is clearly different in both its extent and its nature to the establishment and regulation of public service broadcasting. British film policy, such as it is, is concerned with, in Simon

Hartog's words, the 'state protection of a beleaguered industry', and rarely with content or reception/consumption issues (prime concerns for broadcasting in the UK). Production policy is usually determined by the market, and it is self-evident that cinemas are not required to programme a balance of genres in that way that PSB broadcasters have to carry mixed programming[a]. However, there are similar concerns about the source of material, primarily that American product will swamp local production.

As both Hartog and Hill point out, the British film industry has been in a state of crisis since the 1920s. Indeed, the boom years for the British industry were before World War One; many histories of film take 1915 or 1916 as the date that Hollywood gained dominance over the European industry. In the years 1900–1920, British films were exported in quantity to the USA and in a number of cases influenced American production. For example, *Daring Daylight Burglary*, produced by the Sheffield Photographic Company, was a source for *The Great Train Robbery* (Edwin S. Porter, 1903).

Leaving aside the licensing of cinemas and certification of films through the BBFC, both essentially methods of state censorship, British film policy has been concerned with financing and protecting an industry. However, with the establishment of the publicly funded British Film Institute in 1934, policy was extended to film education and film culture. Thus, post-war, we can see two distinct but often overlapping approaches to policy – first an economic approach, and secondly a cultural one. Let us first explore the economic approach to policy.

John Hill describes three approaches that were taken to protect and develop the British film industry; quota, the Eady levy and the National Film Finance Corporation.

Quota

This was established by the Cinematograph Films Act (1927). It required 'distributors and exhibitors to handle a minimum percentage of specifically British films' (John Hill, *British Film Policy*). This was set at 30 per cent, and was then reduced to 15 per cent in January 1982, before being abandoned by the government on 1 January 1983.

[a]The difference in approach to the two media can partly be explained by the time difference in their development. Film exhibition developed very rapidly between 1895 and 1900, in contrast to broadcasting, which in the UK was developed during the public service era of the 1920s.

The Eady levy

This was devised by a Treasury official, Sir Wilfred Eady, introduced voluntarily in 1950, and made compulsory by the Cinematograph Films act of 1957. The levy was raised from exhibitors' earnings; essentially a levy on cinema ticket sales, and this was used to fund production. It was administered by the British Film Fund Agency, and was abolished by the 1985 Films Act on the grounds that it was a burden on the exhibition industry (cinema attendance hit an all-time low in 1984 in the UK). Moreover, more specifically it was not 'an efficient way of encouraging an economic activity that should be essentially oriented towards the market' (Department of Trade, *Film Policy*).

The National Film Finance Corporation

The NFFC was established in October 1948 as a specialised bank to make loans to support production and distribution, in what was thought to be a temporary crisis in the industry post-war. By the end of the 1970s, the NFFC had invested in some 150 feature films. Financial problems in the 1970s limited it to supporting only 29 features between 1972 and 1979. Support was cut, by the first Thatcher government, to a proportion of the money raised through the Eady levy; when this was abolished in 1985 the Corporation was effectively 'privatised' and became the British Screen Finance Consortium (subsequently British Screen Finance Limited).

John Hill comments on the effectiveness of these three measures in his article in *Film Policy*[2]. His main argument is that their withdrawal was not a problem – they were not wholly effective anyway – but the lack of a coherent policy to replace them was problematic.

3.4.1 Film on Four

Film on Four is often represented as providing the springboard for the renaissance of the British film industry. In policy terms, it represents an important development in funding. Part public finance and part private, it was based on the German PSB model of film finance in the late 1970s/early 1980s, through which WDR and ZDF, in particular, created the financial environment for New German Cinema. Although financially limited, 20 feature films were made in the first year for approximately £5.5 million; Channel 4 partially funded 170 films between 1981 and 1990[4]. This was a far higher number than the National Film Finance Corporation had been able to support in the 1970s.

David Puttnam, talking about the first batch of films, represented a widely held view[5]:

> ... the like of which many of us had lost hope of seeing in our own language, arriving like a gift of the gods in a parched land.

Mike Leigh may exaggerate slightly when he claims that, 'During the 1970s and 1980s all serious film-making was done for television'[6], but for a while in the early 1980s it seemed that any serious work was carried out for *Film on Four*. Where protectionist policies had failed, and were in any case repealed in the 1980s, Channel 4 succeeded. Admittedly there were limits to film budgets but, as Mike Leigh's quote suggests, 'serious' filmmaking was possible. Importantly, Channel 4 films enabled television drama directors such as Stephen Frears to broaden out into features, and experimental directors such as Peter Greenaway and Derek Jarman to work on feature films.

The films represented a wide diversity of form, content and to some extent intended audience. Many were given a cinema release first (particularly successful during the early 1980s were *The Ploughman's Lunch*, *The Draughtsman's Contract*, *Another Time, Another Place* and, later, *My Beautiful Laundrette*). However, as James Park points out in his book, *Learning to Dream, The New British Cinema*[5], even these successes rarely made a profit on theatrical release, although they did boost audiences for the television screening and built up PR for sales abroad – both to television and for theatrical release.

Paul Giles also made criticisms of content[4]; Derek Jarman described them as 'Films to complement the ads'. Director and critic Chris Petit saw them as 'television hardback'[6]. Lindsay Anderson's comments on the financial and the subject restrictions are more illuminating[6]:

> I think the real difference is the kind of subject liable to be financed by Channel 4, which leads to some of the new British films being a bit lacking with the ambition one associates with a cinema film. There is a certain restriction of imagination or idea, rather than the feeling that if you make a film financed by television you have to restrict it in terms of technique or style.

Whether restricted or not, the films clearly carried out Channel 4's remit to serve minority audiences and to allow new voices to be heard. As part of a PSB system, though co-funded by a variety of commercial and public institutions (principally the BFI), *Film on Four* could be seen as 'public service cinema'. Thus, it fulfilled the cultural component of film policy – the need for a national cinema to produce and circulate images of the nation. Clearly the films were also produced in an economic context, but they have less value as earners of foreign currency or as a method of providing employment and subsidising regional economies. Paradoxically, some of the UK's most successful exports to the USA were Channel 4 films (e.g. *Trainspotting* and *Four Weddings and a Funeral*), thus suggesting a degree of overlap between the economic and cultural approaches to film policy and indeed film-making. However, one would have to consider how far these two films would contribute to a British film culture and a sense of identity.

3.5 Recent developments

3.5.1 The Thatcher and Major governments' policies

During the Thatcher years a group of key figures from the film industry, including David Puttnam and Richard Attenborough, met at Downing Street to discuss the future of the industry and possible government intervention. The seminar, held in June 1990 and chaired by Margaret Thatcher herself, was called to deal with the crisis in British production; according to John Hill, the number of British films in production in 1989 fell to 30. John Hill's article[7] gives a complete account of the outcomes, but in the medium term these were restricted to greater involvement in the EU's media programme and support for marketing films abroad. John Hill describes film policy during the Thatcher years as 'aggressive non-intervention'[7].

The Major government introduced five measures to assist the industry, moving slowly towards more government intervention, but without a clear statement of policy:

1 The British Film Commission was established to market British films abroad and attract inward investment. This was followed by the London Film Commission, mainly concerned with promoting London as a base for production, and, more recently, Herts Film Link, promoting the Hertfordshire studios (Elstree, Leavesden etc.). Regional film offices have been established throughout the UK, often working with or as part of the Regional Arts bodies.
2 A European co-production fund was set up.
3 The subscription to Eurimages was paid (withdrawn in 1995, due to be repaid by the Blair government in 1998). Eurimages is the Council of Europe's production and distribution support fund.
4 Tax relief was introduced by Norman Lamont in 1992.
5 Lottery funding was made available through the Arts Council for feature films and shorts. To date, 160 film starts have been funded, although there

has been widespread criticism of the number of these films which failed at the box-office or were never released.

In contrast to the Thatcher government's non-intervention, during John Major's premiership we saw a gradual move to support the film industry. Whilst there would seem to be little evidence of a coherent cultural policy on film; there was clearly the development of an economic film policy. The establishment of the British Film Commission and a number of regional equivalents in its wake demonstrated the determination to expand the UK as a film production base. This was seen to benefit not just the existing infrastructure and workforce of the film industry, but also a variety of businesses and industries within the geographical region of production of an individual film. From this perspective, the cultural element of film production would always be secondary to the economic advantages – it would be just as valuable to attract a Hollywood film as a 'runaway' production, as it would be to produce indigenous films.

3.5.2 'New Labour' film policy

Labour has yet to make any radical changes to film policy in terms of legislation. However, it has commissioned a study by the Film Policy Review Group to look at supporting and expanding the industry. They published their report, A *Bigger Picture*, in March 1998. This concentrated on production, distribution, marketing and training, and a number of initiatives will be developed from it. For example, there could be an investment in film literacy for schoolchildren in an attempt to build a British film culture (the Film Education Working Party considered this in January 1999, running seminars throughout the UK).

The Film Policy Review Group set out their principal aim in *A Bigger Picture* – not just to expand British film production, but to set up British distribution and exhibition networks. (It is worth remembering that the renaissance in British cinema attendance is largely attributed to multiplexes, which are mainly American-owned, e.g. Warner Brothers and UCI.) Because of budgetary restrictions and the need for New Labour to operate within Conservative spending limits during their first term, there is no public funding at present to assist in this process. The intention is to create an industry with an infrastructure similar to Hollywood, although clearly on a smaller scale.

Amongst a whole range of suggestions concerning marketing and training for the industry[8], there is also a proposal for various changes to the qualifying criteria for tax relief on films produced in the UK. Briefly, the suggestion is that the definition of a film that will attract tax relief should be changed to any film where at least 75 per cent of its budget is spent in the UK. If the film has a specifically British content but needs overseas shooting, this would be reduced to 60 per cent subject to certain requirements – for example, post-production work must take place in the UK.

A cultural definition of a British film is also proposed for purposes of marketing, PR and monitoring industry performance. This is based upon the nationality of the leading production personnel (scriptwriter, producer, director and director of photography), the subject matter of the script, the labour cost and production spend (a minimum of 75 per cent for each). Points are allotted for each category, and if a certain total is reached the film will be judged to be British[9]. Whilst the system is easy to criticise, it does allow for a more flexible definition than others that are more generally applied – source of funding, where production takes place, or the subject matter. The definition also implies a balance between economic factors and cultural ones, although it is debatable whether a director of photography or an editor's input, for example, is determined by nationality. As with public service broadcasting (see Chapter 2), the concept of a national identity, the British subject matter of the script amongst many other elements, of a film is problematic in a diverse society. If we take *Notting Hill* (1999) as an example, the most successful British film ever in box-office terms, but partly funded from the US (Polygram Filmed Entertainment), there has been considerable debate about the representation it offers of the Notting Hill district of London. It would, however, qualify as a British film according to the proposed cultural definition – if we accept its subject matter as British – because of the nationality of cast and crew.

The Film Council

From April 2000, a single body has been created. The Film Council is to be responsible for all Department of Culture, Media and Sport funding for film, except for the funding of the National Film and Television School. It will carry out two prime aims of the Blair government's film policy[10]:

1 To develop film culture by improving access to and education about the moving image
2 To help develop a sustainable domestic film industry and encourage inward investment.

The Film Council is also involved in funding training and script development, and aims to promote European co-production. Overall, it has a responsibility to carry not only the economic policy associated with the film industry but also the cultural policy of promoting a British film culture.

It is too early to assess the outcome of this development, but it suggests that more importance will be granted to film policy than by previous administrations, and it also demonstrates a continuing policy rather than a series of one-off measures. The Film Council was proposed by the Film Policy Working Party in *A Bigger Picture*.

Whilst the British film industry can never compete directly with the American film industry, the future would seem to lie both in promoting the UK as an alternative production base for Hollywood films[b] and in establishing a marketing and distribution system that will sustain indigenous production.

Alan Parker, chair of the new Film Council sums this up[11]:

> No-one is ever going to take the place of Hollywood, no-one in the world can do that. What we can do is actually offer alternatives to it, a different kind of talent base, and different technical base, and I think that's very healthy.

3.6 References

1. Film Policy Review Group (1998). *A Bigger Picture, The Report of the Film Policy Review Group*, p. 36. Department of Media, Culture and Sport.
2. Hill, J. (1996). British film policy. In: *Film Policy* (A. Moran, ed.), pp. 101– 13. Routledge.
3. Hartog, S. (1983). State protection of a beleaguered industry. In *British Cinema History* (J. Curran and V. Porter, eds). Wiedenfeld & Nicolson.
4. Giles, P. (1996) History with holes: Channel 4 films of the 1980s. In: *Television Times, A Reader* (J. Corner and S. Harvey, eds), p. 118. Arnold.
5. Park, J. (1984). *Learning to Dream, the New British Cinema*, p. 107. Faber and Faber.
6. Giles, P. (1996). History with holes: Channel 4 films of the 1980s. In: *Television Times, A Reader* (J. Corner and S. Harvey, eds), p. 120. Arnold.
7. Hill, J. (1996). British film policy. In: *Film Policy* (A. Moran, ed.), pp. 110– 11. Routledge.

[b]A recent publication of the Foreign and Commonwealth Office, The Department of Trade and Industry and the Department of Culture, Media and Sport, *Britain, The Big Picture* is a DVD primarily designed to attract productions to the UK, particularly American production.

8. Film Policy Review Group (1998). *A Bigger Picture, The Report of the Film Policy Review Group*, pp. 48–50. Department of Media, Culture and Sport.
9. Film Policy Review Group (1998). *A Bigger Picture, The Report of the Film Policy Review Group*, pp. 53–4. Department of Media, Culture and Sport.
10. Taken from DCMS website – www.culture.gov.uk
11. Parker, A. (2000), speaking in *Britain, The Big Picture* (DVD, 2000). Foreign and Commonwealth Office, Department of Trade and Industry and the Department for Culture, Media and Sport.

3.7 Further reading

Curran, J. and Porter, V. (eds) (1985). *British Cinema History*. British Film Institute.

Department of Trade (1984). Film Policy. Cmnd 9319. HMSO.

Film Policy Review Group (1998). *A Bigger Picture, The Report of the Film Policy Review Group*. Department of Media, Culture and Sport.

Giles, P. (1996). History with holes: Channel 4 films of the 1980s. In: *Television Times, A Reader* (J. Corner and S. Harvey, eds), p. 120. Arnold.

Hill, J. (1996). British film policy. In *Film Policy* (A. Moran, ed.). Routledge.

McIntyre, S. (1996). Art and industry: regional film and video policy in the UK. In: *Film Policy* (A. Moran, ed.). Routledge.

Park, J. (1984). *Learning to Dream, The New British Cinema*. Faber and Faber.

Websites

The Arts Council of England – www.artscouncil.org.uk

British Film Commission – www.britfilm.co.uk

British Film Institute – www.bfi.org.uk

The Department for Media, Culture and Sport (DCMS) – www.culture.gov.uk

The Film Council – www.filmcouncil.org.uk

NB: most of these provide extensive links to other sites. The BFI site has a links page to all the others listed here.

Chapter 4

European Union media policy

4.1 Summary

Since the 1980s, EC film and TV policy has been based on mass media's role in the formation of identity. There has been a distinct shift away from policy concerned with the free trade of film and television programmes to a culturally led approach. This chapter will briefly consider the history of the European Union and explain its structure. The history of media policy will be reviewed, beginning with the three medium-term plans of the 1970s and 1980s, and then considering in more depth the statement on broadcasting policy, *Television Without Frontiers*. The more recent MEDIA and MEDIA II funding programmes will be described. The implications of co-production, which is an essential element in EU policy, will be discussed.

4.2 Objectives and key issues

The European Union has developed a number of funding initiatives, which aim to promote a European film and television industry and a European film and television culture. There are a number of similarities between the objectives of the MEDIA I and MEDIA II projects and those proposed for the British film industry by the Film Policy Working Group (see Chapter 3) – for example, the dual approach to policy, which is concerned with both economic and cultural policy.

The cultural approach to media policy can be seen as part of the much broader project of the political and economic integration of Europe. This chapter deals with the history of the EU and the way in which media policy evolved from issues of copyright and distribution in the 1970s and early 1980s to production and distribution in the late 1980s and particularly in the 1990s. The range of agencies and funding initiatives is now very broad, but behind much of the EU's support for the audiovisual industry lies a desire to create an industry that can compete with the USA.

4.3 History of the European Union

If we were beginning the European Community all over again, we should begin with culture.

Jean Monnet (in Morley and Robins, 1990)[1]

European – someone who watches American soaps on a Japanese television set.

Anon.[1]

The EC was created in the aftermath of the Second World War; locking Germany into Europe was considered of prime importance to prevent the resurgence of nationalism and, by implication, fascism. The method adopted was economic; the integration of Europe would be achieved through the creation of a free market – if European countries' economies were interdependent, they would be less likely to go to war.

Key dates

In 1950, the Schumann Plan was devised. French and German Coal and Steel industries became interdependent, and this was important in symbolic as well as economic terms. Coal and Steel were perceived as the essential materials for warfare.

In 1951, the European Coal and Steel Community (ECSC) was founded – the precursor to the EEC. Italy, Holland, Belgium, Luxembourg joined France and Germany.

In 1957, the two Treaties of Rome were made. The first founded the EEC (European Economic Community) and created the written constitution for it. This was the basis for community law, and therefore European media policy. The second founded the EAEC (European Atomic Energy Commission), which was clearly of vital importance to post-war stability in Europe;

however, since it does not relate to media policy it will not be considered further in this chapter.

The first Treaty enlarged the community and established a common market for goods and services. The EEC was created to regulate European trade, but the founders also wanted to establish a future European political union. It is important to note that this was laid down from the foundation of the EEC and is embodied in the Treaty, even though political discussion about whether union should take place is still extant within the UK. (Currently this centres on monetary union within Europe and whether the UK should adopt the Euro. Other controversial issues include a unified defence force and the possibility of an EU foreign policy.)

The objective for the community, as stated in the Treaty of Rome, was[2]:

> To lay the foundations for an ever closer union between the peoples of Europe, and remove the barriers between them.

The move towards full political integration comes principally from France, and was particularly advanced during the Presidency of Jacques Delors. It is often assumed that the French experience of invasion, in both World Wars, is one of the key reasons for this.

4.3.1 The UK joins the EEC

The UK was invited to talks on the foundation of the EEC and subsequently to sign the Treaty of Rome, but did not because the Macmillan Conservative government was unsure that it would work. Empire and Commonwealth interests also conflicted with the ideals of integrated trade in Europe, and the British government was concerned about loss of trade with the USA (although the business community wished to join for political and economic reasons). A further perceived restriction on membership was that the UK would require greater adjustments to legal and economic structures than other countries in order to comply with EEC regulations. There were also those in government who recognised the political implications of the treaty – that it would lead to political and economic integration.

In 1961, the UK applied to join the Community but France (under the Presidency of General DeGaulle) vetoed this. Although this is sometimes represented as simply a long-held antagonism between the two nations, the more likely explanation was that the UK was seen as a potential threat to the integration of Europe. This was because it was too tied, by language and trade, to the USA, and this could create a 'back door' route for American imports into Europe.

In 1973, the UK joined the EEC with Ireland and Denmark; the Heath Conservative government had partial support from the Labour opposition, but many Labour MPs were against membership. In 1975, the Callaghan Labour government held a referendum on membership, which confirmed the electorate's wish to remain as members. Greece joined in 1981, Spain and Portugal in 1986, the former GDR in 1990 (automatically brought into membership by the unification of Germany), Austria, Finland and Sweden in 1995, bringing membership to 15 states and a population of 370 million.

An increasing number of former Eastern Block countries now wish to join, including Poland, Hungary and Czechoslovakia. The EU will expand considerably in the next few years. During the Thatcher and Major years it was sometimes claimed that Britain was in favour of broadening membership, because it slowed, or possibly would even prevent, social and political union. Now the perception is probably of a larger market, and new opportunities for economic expansion by Western Europe. This is potentially relevant to film and television production, since there were substantial film studios, and film schools in Eastern European countries, particularly in Hungary. (To some extent this change has already taken place, with a number of television dramas being produced in Eastern European countries – e.g. *Maigret* in the early 1990s in Hungary, and more recently Alan Bleasedale's adaptation of *Oliver Twist*, shot in Czechoslovakia for ITV and transmitted in December 1999.)

Why are so many countries interested in joining the EU? There are a number of advantages to membership, some political – membership offers the opportunity to influence policy within Europe on a wide range of issues such as agriculture and the environment – and others economic. The economic advantages are probably the prime motivation for joining. The prolonged economic booms in France, Italy and Spain during the 1980s are attributable to EU membership, and the EU is the largest trading block, now constituting 40 per cent of world trade. This makes the EU the largest export market for the USA, which is important for the American film and television industry, as it is for a wide range of other American industries.

4.4 The structure of the EU

There are four institutions of the European Union that devise, debate, enact and enforce legislation[3].

1 The European Commission – membership is composed of one member from each state, and this is sometimes described as the 'think tank' for Europe. Commissioners are appointed by member states' governments, but should act with European interests in mind and place these above national interests. Commissioners are appointed for a fixed term, and therefore should remain in post regardless of changes in member states' governments – most commonly as the result of an election. Thus, the commission can be seen to be more constant and less political party orientated than a national government. A parallel can be drawn with the UK Civil Service; it is not directly accountable to the electorate, and does not, in principle, operate as part of the political party system. The Commission enforces legislation through conventions and directives. Conventions are general instructions to member states, who then decide how to implement them; i.e. they are advisory (e.g. *Television without Frontiers* (1989), the EU Convention on transnational television). Directives are binding on member states, and supersede national law.

2 The European Council – this is the Union's most powerful institution. Twice a year it becomes a council of prime ministers, and for the rest of the year the relevant ministers attend, depending on the issue. Proceedings are secret.

3 The European Parliament – this is composed of elected representatives (MEPs) organised in political blocks. The Parliament is seated in political divisions and not in member states. In contrast to the British House of Commons, the Parliament has no executive power and currently performs a similar role to the House of Lords (they consider legislation, not formulate it).

4 The European Court of Justice – this upholds the Treaty of Rome and EU law. It includes the European Court of Human Rights, where an individual can act against a member state. It rules on disputes between member states, EU and member states, institutions, and individuals in the community, and on international agreements. The EU Court of Justice will uphold an individual EU resident's right to residence in other member states, and any restriction on free trade between member states. This includes any restraint on the free trade of film and broadcast material, subject to certain minimum legal requirements.

4.4.1 The process of formulating and passing legislation

The Commission formulates policy. The Council debates policy and makes a decision to accept or reject it. If accepted, the European Parliament will debate the detail further, providing a consultation stage. The policy, possibly

Figure 4.1 The EU process for formulating and passing legislation.

amended, then returns to the Council, which finalises the legislation. This passes to the European Court of Justice, where it becomes Law. Member state governments then adopt and enact the legislation (Figure 4.1).

4.5 European Union media policy

Three medium-term plans were created between 1976 and 1991 to carry out media policy. During the last period of the last plan the MEDIA programme was created to provide a wide range of support to the film and television industries, this has been followed by MEDIA II and, more recently, MEDIA 2000. In broad terms, the policy has shifted from issues of copyright to the expansion of production, distribution and exhibition.

The first medium-term plan (1976–1981)

European media policy began with copyright issues. Television programmes were being screened without copyright fees being paid to the producer, and the EU sought to extend national copyright regulations to cover the whole of Europe. This period was primarily concerned with legal and copyright issues. As the plan wore on, non-legal aspects were reported on – for example, the creation of a European market for television. Another important step was that legal issues were not divorced from cultural ones; the plan gradually extended to cover how the mass media should function to speed up European integration and bring about the single market.

The second medium-term plan (1981–1986)

The second plan had a much wider remit; there was an important change of responsibility from the legal sphere to the human rights sector. This led to important changes in rights issues.

The main emphasis of the second medium-term plan was to look at how new technology (cable and satellite transmission) could speed up European integration and the establishment of a common market. Media policy during this plan was dominated by civil rights issues derived from the European Treaty of Human Rights (e.g. freedom of information, freedom of communication, limitation of censorship). Media policy tended towards a libertarian approach; policy was concerned with consumers' rights rather than, for example, public service broadcasting issues.

The third medium-term plan (1987–1991)

The plan was based on the maintenance of pluralism within broadcasting – essentially maintaining a diversity of views in film and television products. There was a new concern, the freedom of reception of programmes within Europe. The 1992 Single European Act was committed to removing tariff barriers in order to create a single European market. This was also to be applied to television – not principally in the trading of programmes between broadcasters, which already took place to a limited extent, but in the freedom of reception of television signals. This would allow broadcasters to reach audiences outside their own national barriers.

The principles of PSB, which were based on national identity, were perceived to be under threat, because governments would not be able to restrict the reception of television signals within their own national borders. This raised questions about smaller countries and regions within the EU – could larger broadcasters overwhelm their language and culture? (For example, Luxembourg by French broadcasting or Holland by German television stations.) It could be assumed that there would be little threat to the UK, because the language difference has always been a barrier to the large-scale importation of European programming.

In 1986, at the end of the second medium-term plan, the first European Ministerial Conference on the mass media was held and Ministers discussed the development of a united media policy for the EU. This was a major development in policy; it clearly signalled that the future of European media was a serious concern within the EU. The key issue for the conference was how to promote the development of an integrated European broadcast system that would compete with American software (films and pro-grammes) and Japanese hardware (both broadcast and domestic). The outcome was a convention, not a directive, on transfrontier television.

4.5.1 Television without Frontiers (1989)

This was a key statement of EU media policy primarily concerned with the relaxation of national regulatory policy on television. However, the EU was still concerned to protect public service traditions. This clearly raised a contradiction between the needs of a European free market and individual member states' need to preserve their own national television systems. If the intention of *Television without Frontiers* was carried out, national PSB would always be subordinate to the need to relax regulations.

The document argued for common minimum standards throughout Europe, based on the European Declaration of Human Rights. The free market in broadcasting, and therefore the right to reception of programmes, would be moderated by the following minimum standards:

1 The protection of children, which could be ensured through encrypted services, rather than the UK tradition of a 9.00 pm watershed for adult viewing.
2 The right to reply, given to institutions, organisations or individuals. This would entail an equal 'space' being allowed for the complainant to reply. (The UK practice has tended to offer minimal space in the press for retractions, or very limited time, outside 'primetime', for adjudication by the Broadcasting Complaints Commission. In both cases, the individual, institution or organisation is not given access to the media.)
3 Protection against incitement to racism. For most member states, this would already be enshrined in national law.
4 Breaking of copyright. This was an existing requirement, but one that new methods of distribution might challenge.

There would be a guarantee of freedom of reception subject to these minimum standards – that is, individual countries can operate their own systems within their borders, but cannot prevent the reception of programmes from outside. This freedom of exchange is enshrined within the Treaty of Rome – the free movement of labour, trade and capital. Thus for many in the European Union, television is seen as cultural commodity and not cultural practice, and is therefore governed by free trade regulations.

National PSB systems will get in the way of EU policy, promoting national identity and not European, and wishing to exclude the reception of overseas competitors. In EU terms, television, as we have seen, is a branch of commerce or trade. In the UK, it has been regarded as part of cultural practice. Therefore, UK policy will need to go through a lengthy process of change[a].

4.5.2 European broadcasting policy

The initial strategy was distribution led rather than production led. The EU funded satellite and cable developments. It was felt that only by creating a pan-European market could the EU cope with Japanese and American competition. Theoretically, production would then expand to fill this increasing broadcast time and market. Little was spent on programming; billions of ECUs were spent on distribution systems. It was widely believed that economic recovery in Europe could only be brought about through development of new technology. However, this was a smokescreen; production did not follow distribution, because this ignored the financial requirements of new production and its ability to fill new markets and outlets. (The majority of the initial satellite and cable stations programmed existing television material, primarily American in origin, or films.)

By the middle of the 1980s, European policy had shifted to the view that European production would bring about a common European identity. The1982 Hann Resolution was concerned with identity. Information was seen as the most decisive factor in creating identification. European identity

[a]During the 1990s policy did change, through a combination of the 1990 Broadcasting Act, technological change and the decision not to regulate heavily the growth of cable and satellite television. With the advent of digital distribution the 'privatisation' of broadcasting is set to expand, and it could be argued that the medium is no longer perceived, in the UK, as primarily concerned with the dissemination of culture.

relies on there being an identity that is recognisable; this depends on that identity being transmitted (see Chapter 2).

To some extent, policy ran behind technology; Transfrontier satellite 'footprints', made new policy essential. Therefore, individual countries were faced with freedom of reception as a reality before the EU formulated the policy (*Television without Frontiers*). Apart from the minimum standards mentioned above, the only reason for restrictions being placed on transmission of signals would be a threat to national security, or evidence that programming damaged culture. This would be difficult to prove, since an individual state would have to prove it was damaging to a free society in general and not just to their national identity. (Bias and impartiality were also not covered by EC minimum standards, and these have always been important issues in UK public service broadcasting.)

The EU has applied quotas against non-European television product, primarily from the USA; all members are to strive for 50 per cent European programming. However, it is apparent that this can never be achieved – it was estimated that by 2000, 20 per cent of primetime television would be European. (Presumably, this would be achievable within UK terrestrial broadcasting.) Is the quota merely a PR exercise? The EU commissioners knew that this proposal contravened the spirit of the GATT, (General Agreement on Tariff and Trade), which aims to reduce barriers to global free trade, and hence the USA was vehemently opposed to it. In the Uruguay round, concluded in 1994, this was the only significant area of disagreement between the USA and the EU (1994). Indeed, news coverage at the time of the agreement included a statement by the American negotiator that you could not conduct a free society on this basis (a statement given with such lack of emotion that it belied the very real anger over the EU's determination not to allow for free trade in film and television with the USA). The statement was later revised to a 50 per cent quota to be achieved where practicable. Such protectionism ignores the very problem of European audiences who want American productions such as *Friends* or *ER*, in a similar way to the demand for American films over European ones[b].

[b] There is, however, a clear difference in the level of demand, at least in the UK; whereas American films dominate in mainstream cinemas, the most successful American series tend to be on the minority channels (e.g. *Friends* and *ER* on Channel 4; *Buffy the Vampire Slayer* and *Star Trek: The Next Generation* on BBC2). *The X-Files* is a clear exception here, although it was initially perceived as a minority programme and transmitted on BBC2.

4.6 Issues of co-production

Co-production assumed greater importance in the 1990s because of the EU's view that European identity can only exist if it can be effectively transmitted. This clearly suggests a number of questions and areas of research – for example, what that identity is, the factors that might form it, and the ideological values that it might transmit. For the EU, and perhaps Europe as a whole, the key problem is to define being European in terms of a cultural identity. (The simplest definition, for film and television, tends to be 'not American'.) Defining and transmitting a European culture is now seen as one of the most important tasks to create a fully integrated community. As Jean Monnet stated, 'If we were beginning the European Community all over again, we would should begin with culture'[1]. In fact, of course, it started with trade in iron, steel and coal.

Co-production existed in the 1920s and 1930s, but increased in the 1960s and 1970s, particularly between France, Germany and Italy. It is often criticised for producing bland films – 'Europuddings' as William Fisher (amongst others) has called them[4]. However, it should be remembered that many of the films of Federico Fellini and Luis Bunuel and the later films of Ingmar Bergman were co-productions (e.g. *La Dolce Vita* (1960), directed by Federico Fellini, France/Italy; *The Discreet Charm of the Bourgeoisie* (1972), directed by Luis Bunuel, France/Spain/Italy; and *Fanny and Alexander* (1982), directed by Ingmar Bergman, Sweden/France/West Germany).

The larger budgets and greater pool of talent might also produce films that could compete with American product within Europe, and even compete within the USA – although this seems somewhat fanciful, given language barriers. Anglo-European co-productions, for example *The Land Girls* (David Mamet, 1998), an Anglo-French co-production, overcome this barrier, but are not likely to be highly successful at the box-office within the USA. (The success of *Notting Hill* in the USA suggests that American/British co-productions are much more acceptable to mass American audiences.)

There are three main forms of co-production, also known as international joint ventures (IJVs):

1 Official co-productions. These are co-production treaties between named countries, and offer the benefits of tax concessions and free or cheaper facilities.
2 Co-ventures. These have private financial arrangements and do not benefit from tax concessions etc. There is therefore no access to government or state subsidies.

3 Twinning packages. This method involves two countries collaborating to make programmes for each other, which results in a greater available market – e.g. France/Italy or France/Germany. It is unlikely that twinning will increase, because there is only a slight increase in profit unless an American company is involved in the co-production.

There are a number of benefits to IJVs, but the reduction of financial risk for producers is clearly the most important. The pooling of financial resources enables larger projects to be taken on, and may enable producers to access locations within the partner(s) country, either free or at a reduced rate. Government subsidies are available, except in the case of a co-venture. The film gains access to the partner's market, and the production company gains experience from the partner.

There are also clear disadvantages to these co-produced films, some of which are sometimes evident in the final film. For example, there is a loss of cultural specificity, which often leads to the adoption of American narrative forms and technical style (particularly camera and editing) in order to transcend national differences. Specific cultural references to places, people and events will tend to be excised from the script, leaving little national identity within the film. More transaction and negotiation is involved in pre-production, which is often concerned with the desire of each producer to ensure the accessibility of the film to their national audience. This leads, in the worse cases, to international casts working in several languages, and an excessive use of locations to represent each producer's country. Larger partners are able to force through decisions (for example on script or casting) based on their larger investment and market share. The process may also create more formidable competitors who, having gained knowledge of their production partner's market and production methods, may be better equipped to compete in the future – although within Europe, language barriers might restrict this.

The European assumption would be that these disadvantages are maximised in co-production with the USA. However, IJVs tend towards American pacing, narrative development and generic models so that they are accessible to American audiences and indeed to pan-European audiences, whose common ground is likely to be American models of narrative and genre (unless the film adopts the conventions of European Art Cinema). Cultural resistance may largely depend on language difference – for example, in Canada the French language service of the CBC (Canadian Broadcasting Corporation) thrives because of its differentiation from American broadcasting (see Chapter 2).

American/German co-production would provide for the largest market group, but the language difference makes it very rare. Thus, co-production cannot just be addressed in financial terms, as it would be in many other industries; cultural considerations are vital to the financial success of a film or television programme.

Twinning packages are the most advantageous method in co-productions between European countries, because they provide an increase in market size without a corresponding loss of control. The producer can maintain autonomy, and, to a degree, cultural specificity is possible (although, clearly, references to regional geography and events are likely to be inaccessible to the partner's audience). Because twinning tends to take place between partners with similar sized markets (for example, the UK and Germany, or, more commonly, France and Italy), a stable relationship can be developed between equal partners.

However, twinning packages produce a relatively low increase in financial returns, and indeed all European co-productions will tend to be limited in their income. Given the desire to promote co-operation between member states' industries and the need to build up pan-European rather than national cinema, the EU established a funding programme specifically to promote co-production.

4.7 MEDIA I and II programmes

The MEDIA programme was established in 1991 to promote co-production, distribution and the financing of projects within the European Union[5]. The programme funded script development, the negotiation process to find backers, cinema distribution and video distribution. A number of critically successful films were produced with part MEDIA funding, although their financial success was very varied (e.g. *Toto the Hero*, 1991, directed by Jaco van Dormael, Belgium/France/Germany; *Orlando*, 1991, directed by Sally Potter, UK/Russia/France/Italy/Netherlands).

MEDIA II continued the work of the initial programme, and was launched in January 1996 with a total budget of 310 million ECU (approximately £280 million). It will run until December 2000, when it is proposed that a further 5-year programme will be launched (MEDIA plus 2001–2005).

A significant development of the second programme was the funding of training programmes for the European audiovisual industry. As with production, these involve more than one European member state, so that training also involves co-operation within the Union. Three areas were identified for training; economic and commercial management, new technologies (multimedia, computer graphics in various applications and the use of new technology for archiving), and screenplay techniques[6]. Production funding was also extended to cover multimedia products, and programme development and distribution continued to be supported. We can see some similarities with recent developments in British film policy, which also, much more recently, broadened its aims to include training and distribution.

The common language between the USA and the UK has benefits for attracting American productions to the UK, but is problematic in terms of European co-production. British audiences are generally reluctant to watch subtitled or even dubbed films, and so co-production will, in the main, involve productions made in English (this may also be seen as an advantage by some co-producers, since, in theory, it allows them access to an American audience). Consequently, British involvement in the MEDIA programme was initially limited. However, during 1999 the UK became one of the main recipients of MEDIA II funding[7] and won the MEDIA prize (awarded for an internationally successful MEDIA-supported first feature) at Cannes with Damien O'Donnell's film *East is East*.

The aim of EU policy is to develop an industry that can compete with the USA, or at the very least maintain a cultural 'fence' against the mass of American product. The aims and objectives are clearly on a larger scale than the UK's film policy. Apart from language and cultural differences, the EU is also hampered by lack of funding in this task. Although producing an impressive array of initiatives, the MEDIA II programme is equivalent to £55 million per annum, and this is a small sum when compared to the development, marketing, distribution and training budgets of Hollywood.

4.8 References

1. Morley, D. and Robins, K. (1990). Non-tariff barriers: identity, diversity and difference. In: *The Single European Market and the Information and Communication Technologies* (N. Locksley, ed.). Belhaven.
2. European Commission (1987). *Treaties Establishing the European Community*. European Commission.

3. Budd, S. (1991). *The European Community, A Guide to the Maze*. Kogan Page.
4. Fisher, W. (1990). Let them eat Europudding. *Sight and Sound*, **59(4),** 224–7.
5. Commission of the European Communities (1986). *The MEDIA Programme*. Commission of the European Communities, X/253/86.
6. MEDIA II, *A Programme of the European Union*, available at www.mediadesk.co.uk
7. Details from www.mediadesk.co.uk

4.9 Further reading

Alvarado, M. (1996). Selling television. In: *Film Policy* (A. Moran, ed.), pp. 62–71. Routledge.

Budd, S. (1991). *The European Community, A Guide to the Maze*, pp. 87–108. Kogan Page.

Cheneviere, G. (1990). Chairman of the ECA Programme Committee. The European co-production association is five years old. *EBU Rev.*, **XLI(6)**.

Collins, R. (1989). Broadcasting – the United Kingdom and Europe in the 1990s. *Rundfunk and Fernsehen*, **37**.

Commission of the European Communities (1986). *The MEDIA Programme*. Commission of the European Communities, X/253/86.

European Commission (1987). The institutions of the community. In: *Treaties Establishing the European Community*. European Commission.

Fisher, W. (1990). Let them eat Europudding. *Sight and Sound*, **59(4)**.

Jackel, A. (1996). European co-production strategies, the case of France and Britain. *Film Policy* (A. Moran, ed.), pp. 85–100. Routledge.

Miller, T. (1996). The crime of Monsieur Lang: GATT, the screen, and the new international division of cultural labour. In: *Film Policy* (A. Moran, ed.), pp. 72–84. Routledge.

Morley, D. and Robbins, K. (1990). Non-tariff barriers: identity, diversity and difference. In: *The Single European Market and the Information and Communication Technologies* (N. Locksley, ed.). Belhaven.

Porter, V. (1985). European co-productions: aesthetic and cultural implications. *J. Area Studies*, **12**.

Schwartz, I. (1985). Broadcasting without frontiers in the European Community. *J. Media Law Practice*, **6(1)**, 26–46.

Stephane, R. (1988). Cinema and television in Europe: present situation and future prospects. *EBU Rev.*, **39(2)**.

Websites

This is the best way to keep up with the range of funding and policy issues that the EU is constantly developing.

European Union Website – www.europa.eu.int

Audiovisual index at EU website – www.europa.eu.int/comm/dg10/index_ en.html

UK Media Desk – www.mediadesk.co.uk (this provides links to many other relevant sites)

Chapter 5

Mass media theory

5.1 Summary

During the nineteenth century, a number of changes took place in Europe that were to influence the development of mass communication and the growth of the mass media during the next century and a half. Major changes were the establishment of mass urban communities, the decomposition of a fundamentally agrarian society that had existed since medieval times, and the establishment of an economy based upon industry rather than the land. Ferdinand Tonnies expressed this change as the contrast between *Gemeinschaft* and *Gesellschaft* – the development of a community based upon tradition and kinship to one based upon contract.

The year 1848 saw the publication of the *Communist Manifesto*, and was a year during which almost every country in Europe experienced a failed political revolution. The intellectual energy released by these two events was to generate the creative underpinning for the period between 1850 and 1914, which came to fruition in the artistic products of high modernity and the social products of the mass media.

As well as creating mass-produced consumable goods, which were improving the lives of the people, technology had facilitated the concept of reproduction. Reproduction enabled the masses to access the cultural products of their society, although the products had lost the implicit significance of originality. As Walter Benjamin explained in *The Work of Art in the Age of Mechanical Reproduction*,[1] the very nature of mass communication changes the implication of the work itself.

By the turn of the nineteenth century, western society had developed into one where the people were largely living in cities and involved in industrial production. Physical and social mobility had encouraged the growth of education, and literacy was becoming an essential factor in individual development and success. The 1870 Education Act marked out the system and content of education for the next four decades.

At the turn of the twentieth century, the influence of the mass media upon society was becoming recognised and had become the focus of argument about how it operated and who controlled it. Its significance became particularly important during the two World Wars, when it was perceived as another arm of the war effort. During this century, film, radio, television and (more lately) the developments in multimedia brought about a sea change in the way people saw their lives and the world in which they lived. These changes have been the results of the technical developments of media products, the creative innovations made by the authors of media products, and the changes in the consumption of media products.

The stratification of society has been measured against divisions in the products of the mass media, the implication being that the products are divided into groups for class consumption – that there is high, popular and low media material, which caters for the stratification in society. This view is undermined by the evidence that the mass media is the agency for changing this theory.

The mass media is now a subject in its own right, with an increasing body of critical theory being written about it since the days of Hoggart and McLuhan. The structure of its form is now discussed in terms of the symbolic representation, ideology and representation that it takes.

Three main questions should concern the student of the mass media:

1 What does the mass media say?
2 Who is saying it?
3 How does it say it?

5.2 Objectives and key issues

The prime objective of Chapters 5 and 6 is to introduce some of the cultural and sociological events and influences that have underpinned many of the current views held about the mass media. It aims to give a foundation for further reading, and to instil an initial understanding of the complex range of factors that have developed the cultural studies of the media.

The issues developed in this chapter explain the roots of the underlying fear that the establishment has of the media and mass society, and why, despite the liberalising development in the perception of the media during the second part of the twentieth century, there still remains an inherent apprehension about its influence and who controls it.

The roles and constraints of the groups of producers and consumers who influence the media are debated, and a number of models proposed that could be related to other areas of the book (especially media ethics; see Chapter 12). The background to the current debate concerning 'dumbing down' in the media is explained, and the reader can analyse the various perspectives that can be taken in the argument surrounding the status of popular and high culture portrayed in the media.

Two major aspects of media critical theory are presented in the chapter (language and meaning, and the auteur theory), with the intention of providing the reader with a resumé of some of the intellectual reasoning that motivated media studies during the twentieth century. It is these concepts, debates and arguments, which began in universities and academic journals, that have had an increasing influence on the young graduates who are now achieving significant roles in the industry. A manager with a reasonable grasp of the basis of media critical theory has the advantage of understanding the creative workforce with whom they are working, and the material they produce.

5.3 The mass media and society

The major questions posed by media and cultural studies are the new and different ways of looking at life. All developments in the media destabilise the existing beliefs about the ability and the right of ordinary people to acquire knowledge beyond their own experience, and raise questions about the perspective from which public knowledge is manufactured. Communication, in the generally humanising sense, is the production, perception and grasp of messages bearing man's notion of his philosophy (defined in terms of what exists), his politics (expressed as what is important) and his morality (defined as what is right).

For a long time the messages and images that composed the matrix of popular culture were produced within the small unit of the tribe, village or family. As people became aware of the exterior influences beyond their own family, tribe or village, social interaction became primarily aural, and increasingly took on a regional point of view rather than a purely localised one. It was the Industrial Revolution that gradually replaced the age-old process of filtering down and person-to-person transmission of information with a system of mass production, bringing an almost simultaneous introduction of information, ideas, images and products at all levels of society. The changes in the early part of the nineteenth century as a result of the transformation of Europe from an agrarian into an urban society gave rise to the concerns about the concomitant changes in the minds and the hearts of the people. Ferdinand Tonnies, writing in 1887, developed the theory of the contrast between the *Gemeinschaft* and the *Gesellschaft*. He describes all that that was intimate, private, exclusive, the living together in understanding; as *Gemeinschaft*. *Gesellschaft*, on the other hand, he signified as public life. *Gemeinschaft* is with one's family; one lives in it from birth to death, and is bound to it. He observed that one goes into *Gesellschaft* as one goes into a strange country. Tonnies introduces his proposal on the difference between city and countryside thus[2]:

> There exists a Gemeinschaft of language, of folk ways of mores and beliefs, but by way of contrast Gesellschaft exists in the realm of business, travel and science. Gemeinschaft is old; Gesellschaft is new as a name as well as an occurrence.

He points out that *Gemeinschaft* extols and gives all praise to rural life[2]:

> The people living in Gemeinschaft are stronger and therefore more alive. It is the lasting and genuine form of living together and this is in contrast to Gesellschaft. Accordingly Gemeinschaft should be understood as a living organism; Gesellschaft as a mechanical aggregate or artefact.

This view of modern urban society was the basis of the fear that society was disintegrating as the individual was becoming an atomised, dehumanised figure, who was seemingly easily manipulated and controlled by political movements and individuals. The concept of mass society arose at this time, and was associated with the growth of the mass media.

During the latter part of the eighteenth century and the first part of the nineteenth century, newspapers had become major vehicles of mass opinion and influence. During this period the conditions for a radical, reforming newspaper industry had largely disappeared. Mass production and the centralisation of capital investment needed for the establishing of the complex technology of newspaper production had centred ownership of the major newspapers within the hands of a small group of press barons.

This led to the central concern about the mass media; that is, the questioning of the position from which the influence propagated by the mass media is generated. In the early part of the nineteenth century the anxiety was that the press was in the hands of radical revolutionaries who had to be restrained by legal persecution. In the latter part of the nineteenth century the concern was that the ownership of newspapers was in the hands of a limited number of people who would have the power to use the newspapers to their own ends. With the advent of film, later wireless, and finally television, the debate about the ownership, influence and system used in the mass media became the main discussion points surrounding mass society and cultural studies.

During the First World War, propaganda was used in a concentrated way for the first time and, at the conclusion of hostilities, it was commonly believed that it had had a profound effect on the outcome of the War. There was little doubt that the mass media were an extremely strong influence on the attitudes and behaviour of mass society in the 1920s. In the USA and Germany, research studies were established in attempts to understand how it worked. The introduction of mass media research accompanied the growth of the wider study of social science, with its concentration on the implications of mass society and popular culture. Throughout the nineteenth century political power had been shifting from the upper to the middle and lower classes, thus bringing about in this century what Gustav Le Bon has called the 'era of crowds'. He states[3]:

> Today it is the traditions which used to obtain in politics and the individual rulers which do not count, while on the contrary the voice of the masses has become preponderant.

The *Gemeinschaft/Gesellschaft* theory of Tonnies, coupled with the work of Emile Durkheim, led to the view that the social nature of human beings was focused with an equally developed theory of their psychological nature. Briefly, human conduct was thought to be largely a product of a genetic endowment; that is, the causes of behaviour were sought within a biological structure. This developed into the early twentieth century model of the social organisation of industrial capitalist societies, which characterised them as made up of a vast workforce of atomised, isolated individuals, without traditional bonds of location or kinship, who were alienated from their labour by its repetitive, unskilled tendencies and their subjugation to the vagaries of the wage relationship and the fluctuation of the market. It was felt that such individuals were entirely at the mercy of totalitarian ideologies and propaganda and, secondly, of the mass media, comprising in this period the emergent radio and cinema. This line of thought was to have important implications for the early interpretation of the mass media.

5.4 Media theory and philosophy

The transfer of meaning and the system of transmitting messages can be considered as the denoting elements of the process. The process by which the messages are sent and received and the assignation of meaning can be considered as the connotative element of the communication system. In all studies of communication, it is these two elements that occupy the prominent position. Defined in general terms, mass communication refers to the relatively simultaneous exposure of a large, scattered and heterogeneous audience to messages transmitted by impersonal means from an organised source for whom the audience members are anonymous. The media theorist's interest penetrates into this phenomenon at several points. The chief concern is directed towards the social effects and functions of mass communications, which means examining consumers' views and responses to mass media material. Sociological analysis can also illuminate prior considerations – for example, the social influences operating in the production and distribution of symbols in a mass system. At one end of a mass communication chain is the source of information, a complex organisation, itself a product as well as a potential moulder of social forces. At the other end are the receivers of information. Taken as a whole they constitute a mass, since these are large numbers of anonymous persons coming from all walks of life who are seen in terms of the ways they sense, interpret and act upon information. The audience members, although anonymous to the communicator, are embedded in a network of primary and secondary groupings highly relevant to the understanding of the mass communicative process. This interest in mass communication does not confine itself simply to asking what people do, or even why they do it; it is also concerned with the problem why people must do what they do. In other words, we are interested in exposing the underlying factors that impose limitations and constraints on mass communication, and their understanding will reveal how systems are constructed to communicate and how they are used by the consumers of communication. In the 1960s, George Gerbner identified six constraints that affect decision-making in mass communication.[4] These he defined as:

- client relationships
- patron relationships
- logistical relationships

- leverage
- legal requirements
- supervisory relationships.

He described client relationships as those with investors, advertisers and sponsors, or other groups and institutions that furnish major capital and operating costs in exchange for products and services rendered. He pointed out that communications industries such as the press, broadcasting and magazines are producing organisations much like other industries. However, unlike other industries they derive little or no revenue from the sale of their products to the consuming public, who therefore have no direct client relationship with these media. They are also service organisations, to sell a group of people. In the case of television, they are selling audience time and attention to a special type of client – the advertiser. The advertisers underwrite the bulk of the operating costs in return for the time and attention of consumers, concentrated in market areas providing a base for profitable operation. The quantity and quality of the audience is determined by the value and price of the media service to these clients.

Patron relationships are with those who directly patronise the media – that is, the audience. It is true to say that often this audience demand is neither explicit nor specific. However, it is frequently the necessity for gratifying and cultivating some of the expectations of this consumer group that is important in decision-making. It is often patron relationships that set the broad limits of acceptability, within which the media select the policies that are most responsive to their clients' needs and pressures.

Logistical requirements are imposed by the availability and cost of resources. In the case of newspapers, these include paper, technology and manpower; in the case of film, they include technology, plastics, actors, manpower and the supply of creative ability. Distribution facilities are another major factor in the film industry. In television, logistical factors include production facilities, transmission facilities, infrastructure, franchise problems and manpower.

Leverage may be exploited by non-client groups and external bodies, through boycotts, blacklists, strikes, legislation, influence over clients and so forth.

As with other business organisations and licence carriers, the legal requirements that pertain to the media industry are normative expectations that include the general and often also legal obligation to serve some socially valued function (or at least avoid posing major threats to the prevailing moral political order).

The last of Gerbner's six identified constraints is supervisory relationships. This is the chain of command or administration internal to the organisation. This includes trade agreements and the organisation's self-regulation codes, and all working calculated to maximise the value and minimise the risk inherent in all other institutional relationships and constraints.

There are three models for the mass media industry working within the western capitalist societies; the market model, the mass manipulative model and the interactionist model.

The market model is the model that conforms to the principles of a liberal democratic society with a market economy. In this system, the audience is seen as being made up of consumers, who thus influence the output of the media by providing profits for the owners. The owners are therefore controllers and producers seeking audiences – they compete to provide what is demanded, and there is no conspiracy between the owners and governmental agencies. A wide range of opinions is offered, and only the illegal and the unsellable are excluded. Events in the news are seen as having an objective reality, and are selected for broadcasting and publication by journalists and editors on a professional basis. Criticism of this model comes from Marxists, who raise the issue of oligarchic control (that is, government of the media by the privileged few), and Liberals, who claim state interference and control.

The second of the models is the mass manipulative model. This is seen as the opposite of the market model in that the audience, instead of being the major influence on the media, is considered as a passive and uncritical receiver of the media messages. It is the Christian Right, epitomised by Mary Whitehouse and the American moral majority, who still support the pre-war 'hypodermic syringe' view, and see a conspiracy to corrupt conventional standards through the portrayal of sex, violence and other challenges to traditional morality. The Marxist version of this model is much more common among sociologists. There is an internal Marxist debate between the instrumentalists, led by Ralph Milliband, who see fairly direct control over media production by the ruling class, and the structuralists, led by Louis Althusser and Herbert Marcuse, who see journalists and editors as being influenced by ruling class ideology and willingly conforming to the interests of capitalists. Criticisms of this model come from both Liberals and interactionists, who suggest that the evidence of concentration of ownership or even bias in input is insufficient to demonstrate particular effects on the audience.

The final model is the interactionist model, which combines some of the elements of the previous two theories. The media are seen as reflecting the existing attitudes of the audience, as well as helping to create and reinforce a consensual view of the world. The prevailing consensus is divided by writers within this perspective as pro-capitalist, sexist and racist, and thus this model has become associated with the Left, at least in Britain. It is the selection and presentation of news being influenced by both technological and ideological factors. In this case, the news is seen as a socially constructive object rather than a neutral description of real events. The process is described as the manufacture of news, and the outcome as agenda setting.

Ethnomethodologists see the interpretation of news by academics as a similar process to the manufacture of news by journalists. Sociologists, like other viewers and readers, interpret media output according to their own common-sense assumptions. Meanings are read into stories and images according to the audience's expectations. The central task of a mass communication organisation is to formulate the content that is transmitted to its patrons, the audience, and an event that is ultimately to reach the audience is shaped by a complex of social forces. The originating or sponsoring source of the content is frequently an organisation such as a government agency, a business association or a political organisation. Directly as clients, indirectly as patrons, as manipulators of leverage or guardians of the normative order, such groups are responsible for the bulk of the content that moves into media channels. The mass media industry has many special interest groups surrounding it, signifying that mass communication is the form of communication typical of a society in which many secondary group associations thrive. In fact, in modern society, members of secondary groups are frequently bound together into a functioning whole through the ties created by various forms of mass communication. Thus, on a national level, the media provide a nation with many of its shared experiences. A key role in the processing of information is that of the trained professional who makes the initial contact, direct or indirect, with the originating source. Journalistic tradition in many western societies gives this role the mandate to exercise independent judgement in defining what is news and how to gather information. The media personality is enmeshed in critical social relations with his or her sources, employers and public. Whatever the balance of these forces, it is highly unlikely that his or her role can ever be simply that of a sponge, soaking up the environment, or of an open gatekeeper, passing unmodified and unselected information into channels of mass communication. As messages move from the originating source through the media personality into the media organisation and out over the channels to the audience, they are influenced by various supervisory relationships and policies. The general effect of this process is to funnel down the content. It is a selective processing of material in a social context. Another interest to the media theorist is the extent to which patron relationships enter into the decision-making process as to what content the media will offer in the first instance. Is communication a one-way flow of information, or is it, like interpersonal communication, a process of interaction? Certain elements of the general definition of mass communication underscore contrasts between mass and interpersonal communicative processes. In the interpersonal case, more sensory channels are usually involved than in each communicative act. Participants can see, hear, and even touch and smell each other. The result is that direct information and auxiliary cues move rapidly back and forth between persons, each of whom is serving both as a sender and as a receiver in the communicative act. In mass communication, the flow of information is on the surface and traditionally largely unidirectional; technology has made it possible for the few to speak directly (and almost incessantly) to the many. There is also a technology to reverse the flow. The Internet and multimedia technology are opening up a world of interaction; in the third millennium this will be the main motivator of mass communication theory. However, the mass communicator at present is not cut off from audience feedback entirely. The few, the communicators, do make decisions according to some image of the many, the audience.

5.5 The stratification of media products

In 1933, when Hitler came to power, a group of German intellectuals known as the Frankfurt School opposed the new regime and attempted to explain the Fascists' success by concentrating on the nature and effects of the mass media. They observed that the press, radio, films, comics and popular music were endorsing the influence of the family, which they felt nurtured the idea of the 'authoritarian' personality from which fascism arose. It was their view that the mass media strengthened the habits and attitudes that made people susceptible to fascist arguments. When some members of the School emigrated to the United States as refugees from the Nazis, their views on the effects of the media were confirmed. To them, American mass culture appeared to be a corrupting influence that was undermining the elite and superior cultural tradition of Europe. 'What was worse', Seaton explains, was that they believed 'mass culture produced precisely the kinds of personality trait that made the population vulnerable to fascist domination'[5]. The Frankfurt School felt that the conditions in the USA were conducive to it turning to fascism. The attitude of European intellectuals towards the products of the popular mass media in the United States was one of contempt and suspicion. This response was expressed by the literary critic, F. R. Leavis, who, in an essay called *Mass Civilisation and Minority Culture*, said[6]:

> The prospects of culture then are very dark. There is less room for hope, in that a standardised civilisation is rapidly enveloping the world.

Leavis' attitude to American culture was formed largely by reading the book *Middletown* by Robert and Helen Lynd, which pointed out many of the effects of American mass culture upon society. They singled out the isolation of the individual and social fragmentation as two of the main effects. Two leaders of the Frankfurt School, Herbert Marcuse and Theodor Adorno, were prime movers in dismissing what was modern, mass and American. It was, they thought, the failure of liberalism that had created an individualism that was corrupt and selfish, and that the mass media had played a major role in this process by the vulgarising of societies' culture. For the Frankfurt School, the function of the media was seen as aiding capitalism by influencing and controlling the public. Theodor Adorno and Max Horkhiemer believed that a 'culture industry' had been created that had lost its capacity to nurture true freedom and individuality, and that it was producing safe, standardised products geared to the requirements of the capitalist economy. The products of this industry (Hollywood movies, radio, mass-produced journalism and advertising) were only different at the most superficial level. The views of Adorno and Hockheimer were reflected by Leavis when he suggested a form of literary studies, later known as Leavisism, which re-disseminated what is now commonly called cultural capital, a term coined by Pierre Bourdieu. What Leavis advocated was an educational system based on the best examples of literature. He argued for the strict canon of work, which excluded modern experimental work and celebrated the great tradition of English literature – for example, Jane Austen, Alexander Pope and George Eliot. Leavis said that literature was not simply a leisure activity, reading works of a great tradition, but was a way of installing a concrete and balanced sense of life. Leavis and Adorno both believed that mass culture was the main threat to this sense of life. Leavisism was in tune with the social democratic power block, the predominant post-war British political stance of government. Intervention in the private sector both socially (health and housing) and culturally (education and the arts), and the expansion of the educational system in the 1950s and 1960s, was largely based on the Leavisite view of forming citizens and their sensibilities. Richard Hoggart and Raymond Williams approached the Leavisite attitude with ambivalence; they were both from working-class backgrounds and educated in the ways of the dominant high culture. They accepted the concept of the canonical text as being superior to that of the so-called mass culture. However, they saw that Leavisism erased, or at the very least did not come into contact with, the communal background from which they had come. Hoggart's book *The Uses of Literacy* demonstrates his schizophrenia towards Leavisism. The first part extols the values of his boyhood culture, and the second is a critical attack on mass culture. Hoggart believed that both high and low culture could exist alongside each other because they both stood apart from temporary commercial culture, and therefore were both under threat. In his article *Culture is Ordinary*, published in 1958, Williams draws our attention to the nature of the concept of culture. He says: 'There are two senses of culture; there are two colours attached to it.' He observes the 'teashop culture', where he says[7]:

> Here is a culture not in any sense I knew but in a special sense the outward emphatically visible sign of a special kind of people, cultivated people. They were not, the great majority of them, particularly learned, they practised few arts, but they had it and showed you they had it. They are still there I suppose, still showing it though even they must be hearing rude noises from outside from a few scholars and writers that they call, how comforting a label it is, angry young men. As a matter of fact there is no need to be rude; it is simply that if that is culture, we don't want it, we have seen other people living.

He is critical of the fussiness of this teashop culture, their trivial differences of behaviour, their trivial variations of speech habit. He is critical of those who, like him, would dislike the teashop culture, but would in turn pacify and categorise culture and bar it from ordinary people and ordinary work. He extols the culture of his boyhood home: 'I know from the most ordinary experience that there is interest there, the capacity is there'[7]. For him, that old social organisation in which these things had their place has been broken. He says: 'Culture is ordinary through every change, let us hold on to that'[7]. The other sense of colour of the word 'culture' he associates with the only words that he says rhyme with it, sepulchre and vulture. A sepulchre is the act of burying the dead in a special place for the dead, and of course a vulture is a carnivorous scavenging bird. Culture is ordinary, and interest in learning or the arts is simple, pleasant and natural; a desire to know what is best and to do what is good is the whole positive nature of man. While at Cambridge, Williams was influenced by two things; Leavisism and Marxism. Marxism informed him that a culture must be finely interpreted in relation to its underlying system of production, that a culture is a whole way of life and the arts are part of a social organisation which economic change clearly affects. It was self-evident that most of the English working class was excluded from the powerful bourgeois English culture, although the doors were slowly opening. However, to say that the English working class is excluded from English culture is nonsense. He said[8]:

> They have their own growing institutions, a great deal of English cultural institutions and common meanings are in no sense the sole product of the commercial middle class.

Williams rejects the Marxist perspective element of culture; the advocacy of a different system of production is in some way a cultural directive. He says[9]:

> There was an old, mainly agricultural England, with a traditional culture of great value. This has been replaced by a modern, organised industrial state whose characteristic institutions deliberately cheapen our natural human responses, making art and literature into desperate survivors and witnesses while a new mechanised vulgarity sweeps into the centres of powers.

He says in true social democratic vein: 'The only defence is education'[9]. Williams questions the elitist view of the failure of progress, which he points out has released the working classes by offering them choice. Contrasted with the Frankfurt School's perception of the mass media, Williams' is a view that states that there is nothing fundamentally in the structure or character of high culture that distinguishes it from popular or low culture, or *vice versa*. If this is held to be true, then it is also important to understand that there are likely to be economic, political and historical motifs that operate to establish a society's sense of that distinction. The belief underpinning this idea is that television tends to blur the boundaries between high, popular and working-class culture through 'flow'. This theory, developed in the 1970s, suggested that the very nature of television makes it difficult for most viewers to select their viewing and restrict themselves to particular programmes. If setting out to explain the grammar or form that television takes, it would be imperative from the beginning to suggest that its prime component is not the single programme, but the much larger sequence of which that programme is part, and which is a much more complex presentation altogether for the viewer to relate to. It was also felt that the problem encountered of not switching off the television set when a programme had finished had produced a drug-like effect in the audience. Raymond Williams argued that it was better to perceive the real unit of television to be the 'flow' of an evening's programmes, rather than the single programme unit. The form of an evenings viewing is therefore not the one imposed on the audience by the programme planners, but one of accidental positioning of items in the sequence produced by the pattern of flow on each channel, and the viewers' selection from that flow. It was also suggested that the audience for programmes made up of essentially working-class material (programmes with their roots in the music halls and working man's club tradition and sporting events) did not draw their audiences exclusively from the working class. One effect of television was to make uncertain the boundaries between high, popular and working-class cultural objects. It was also proposed that if television could change working-class cultural material into popular culture, then the object of popular culture could be elevated by television to the status of high culture. In the post-war period this theory was applied to movies, notably those featuring Bogart, Chaplin, the Marx Brothers et al. These films became worthy of discussion and debate as art objects, and became the material of retrospective examinations of the work of a particular director or actor. However, the blurring of the boundaries between high and popular cultural object does not always have obvious stages. Raymond Williams cites television drama as one of the main elements in this process. Most people have access to high cultural drama through television. It has also been pointed out that, although the mass audience encounters drama through television as though it were an intrinsic aspect of day-to-day life, it is a particular sort of drama that they are presented with. The major part of the material they watch in the form of series, police adventure series, soap operas, situation comedies etc. is significantly naturalistic in style and content. The relationship between these programmes and the realistic novel (often in its most naive and popular form) is felt to have been a major factor in television's failure to develop its own intrinsic televisual form. The process of change was not only upwards; the blurring of the demarcation between the three strata of culture could be directed to the transition of high to working class and vice versa. This process of television changing the status of cultural material must be seen in the context of a larger historical process. In this process, one class and its interests ultimately prove to be the controlling factor in the cultural domination of the mass media. Television in particular has been prone to this process. In its early years it was undoubtedly influenced by middle-class values, which resulted in an overall process of 'bourgeoisification' of its material. It has been said of television during this period that if it was a window on the world, then the windowpane has a particular middle-class tint. Williams elaborates this point when he states that the British early experience of becoming an industrialised society with a complex communication infrastructure covering a small area produced a nationalised culture which was controlled by the establishment.

5.6 Sociology and technology

Mass communication is the extension of institutionalised public enculturation beyond the limits of other personally mediated interaction. This only becomes possible when technological means are available and social organisations emerge from the mass production and distribution messages. The media of mass communication are organised to select, compose and record symbols and images. Through a continuous flow of public messages, the mass media become the central arms of the social order from which they spring. Mass media policies reflect not only stages of industrial development and general normative order but also types of organisational constraints, which give various priorities to artistic, political and economic considerations, govern overall media operations, affect their relationships with other institutions and shape the public functions of mass communications.

The extension of literacy and the development of democratic processes have broadened the need for information and widened the range of public whose opinions are taken into account. The developments in technology have had a profound effect upon society; the inter-relationship of sociology and technology is of two kinds, one involving study of the social situation, which gives rise to invention and discovery, and the other involving the study of the effects upon man and society of the uses of the inventions and discovery.

Marshall McLuhan[10] has described the drastic effects of the mass media upon society. To McLuhan, it is not just that man is spending time with the media that is important, nor the patterns of messages transmitted; what is significant is the media itself. His analysis begins with the simple premise that there have been three ages of man; the pre-literate or tribal, the Guttenberg or individual, and the present electronic or re-tribalised age. McLuhan's thesis is this. In the pre-alphabet age, the ear was dominant and hearing was believing. Man lived in acoustic space, the world of tribes, emotions, mystery and communal participation. Later, with the phonetic alphabet, there was a transition from the ear to the eye, and then with Guttenberg and printing the transition was complete, individualism was born, thought was separated from action and man began to comprehend in a linear, connected fashion that shattered the old tribal unity.

Finally, in the nineteenth century, McLuhan suggests, electronic circuitry began to bind the world up in a web of instant awareness. Today, high-speed communications annihilate the time and space of the world, contracting it into a global village in which everyone is involved with everyone else – the haves with the have-nots, races of different colours with one another, adults with teenagers, and science, art, industry, politics and religion together. For McLuhan, involvement is the key word in the present age of electronic mass communication. Previously in human history each medium highlighted a particular sensory channel, which set the way that man felt, thought and acted about information. Now the electronic media, particularly television, provide a minimum of information but a maximum of involvement of all the senses simultaneously.

It is for these reasons that McLuhan stresses the concept that the medium is the message. His idea becomes especially plausible and takes on sociological significance when consideration is given to the distinguishing characteristics of the most modern communication media. Television now makes it possible for communicators to convey to mass audiences messages and dramatic content that simulate primary interaction.

A more traditional view than McLuhan's holds that the agencies of mass communication are merely transmitters that provide the means whereby people may constantly and instantly become aware of and react to situations far beyond their horizons. These are the organisational and technological developments that, in the words of Edward Sapir[11], lessen the importance of mere geographical congruity so that parts of the world that are geographically remote may in terms of behaviour actually be closer to one another than adjoining regions that, from the historical standpoint, are supposed to share a body of common understanding. This means a tendency to re-map the world, both sociologically and physiologically.

5.7 Language and meaning

The dominant threads in the attempts to describe how films and television work find their locations in the numerous and complex propositions broadly labelled as structuralist. The emphasis here is, crudely speaking, formalist, with the interest residing in the text rather than authors and audiences, and the endeavour is to discern structures common to a large number of individual texts. Structuralist theory was a very useful way of countering the journalistic tendency to consider the prime quality of film in its relationship with the real world – that is, how true to life it was. Structuralism developed from the work of the Swiss linguist Ferdinand de Saussure, who insisted that meaning was created by differences existing inside the structure of language. By analogy, a structuralist reading of a film would deal with the film as a particular aspect of a structure that is found across the whole spectrum of films. One such structure may define how a film follows the classical Hollywood narrative pattern of stability–disruption–return to stability; another may concentrate on the role of the hero; and yet another might reveal how the text is constructed around the set of oppositions, some thematic (community/anarchy) and others formal (repose/violent action). A particular strength of structuralism is that it can be used to express absences as well as presences – i.e. not only what the text says about a particular theme, but also a latent text. The semiological approach also took its inspiration from the insights of de Saussure, and described the cinema (like language and other social phenomena) as a complex system of signs. Its strength lies in its systematic nature, in its capacity to reveal a whole set of codes in films, and how individual films are made understandable mainly by reference to others. Most importantly, semiology distinguishes between codes specific to the cinema (for example, the structured use of camera movement) and codes incorporated into a film but not necessarily specific to it (usually in the form of literary devices in the narratives). The three models that have been most involved in these developments are those of Vladimir Propp, Claude Levi-Strauss and Christian Metz.

Ferdinand de Saussure initiated the modern approach to the study of language; he perceived it as a natural system that could scientifically investigate developing structures, frameworks and analytical concepts. He defined language (*langue*) as a self-contained whole, and a principle of classification that could not be confused with human speech (*langage*), of which it is only a definite part. Language is both a social product and a collection of necessary conventions that have been adopted by the social body to permit individuals to exercise that faculty. These conventions are headed by the use of the *langue* as an abstract synchronic pattern, which defines the rules of language, and the *parole*, which describes the diachronic performance that takes place within the *langue*. Putting it crudely, the *langue* is the set logical sequence of communication, and the *parole* the various choices that can be used within the sequence. Another of Saussure's major contributions was the concept of the sign, the signifier and the signified, in which he analysed the process of linking the name of an object with the object itself. Expressed simply, the sign is an arbitrary unit, the word, which we use to communicate the concept of the signifier (a symbol of physical form), which signifies the object being described. The object is signified in the mind. The sign is the process of signification, which in language is always a sound. The system of linguistics developed by de Saussure became a master plan for other studies of systems where there was felt to be a need for rules and conventions. In the morphology of the folk tale, Vladimir Propp proposes an underlying structure to the plots of some hundred-plus folk tales whose apparent content and subject matter changes from one story to another. He argues that the tales he studied had been classed together by investigators because they possessed a particular construction, which was immediately felt and determined the category. He maintains that the structure of the tale should be made explicit or transferred into formal structural meanings. Previous studies had proposed that plots in the folk tales were composed of motives, such as the dragon kidnaps the king's daughter, but, says Propp, this motive can be varied without changing the plot; the dragon can be replaced by any villainous force, the daughter by anything beloved, the king by any father figure, and the kidnapping by any form of disappearance. He proposes that the functional unit of the plot for the reader is the paradigm with various characters from which any number can be chosen for a particular narrative. There are two units or components for Propp in folk tales; the first are roles filled by various characters, and the second (which constitute the plot) he calls functions. A function is an act of dramatic persona that is defined from the point of view of its significance for a course of action in a tale as a whole. It is this definition that forms the crux of Propp's analysis. He enquires what other actions could take the place of a certain action without changing its role in the story, and the overall class that includes all these actions then serves as the name of the function in question. Propp isolated some 31 such functions that he suggests can be used to form an ordered set, and the presence or absence of which in particular stories can be used as the basis for the classification of plots.

Claude Levi-Strauss's work on the structural study of myth seems to have been more often invoked than applied in accounts of film criticism. The model has been primarily applied to authorship studies, although it is more suited to accounts of the general underpinning of text. A Levi-Straussian analysis posits the revealing of hidden content through a model of binary oppositions and bundles of relations. Levi-Strauss has investigated the structure of myth to illustrate how these binary oppositions and bundles of relations can be listed in columns of what he called mythemes. These mythemes in each list expressed a particular aspect of the narrative; for example, in the Oedipus myth these are an over-rating of blood relation, an under-rating of blood relation, the killing of a monster and the connotation of the surnames of Oedipus' father-line. By comparing and opposing these themes, a complex structure of meaning can be deduced. Of the three models, it is the semiological work of Christian Metz that is most specific and elegant. It is specific because it investigates the visual narrative and concentrates particularly on the nature of film. Metz believes that although film is like a language, the image is not a word and the sequence is not a sentence. Cinema fails as a language because it is a one-way system of communication and it uses no arbitrary signs. His work departs from the structures of linguistics and focuses on the phenomenon of film – what follows what (syntagma) and what goes with what (paradigm) – and the importance in film of the difference between denotation and connotation. The syntagma of a film or sequence shows its linear narrative structure, and the paradigm represents the choices possible at stages in the syntagma (shades of de Saussure's langue and parole). In his work *The Grande Syntagmatic*[12], Metz redefined montage and *mise en scene* as syntagmatic and paradigmatic categories. Thus he placed film theory where it belongs, investigating film narrative taking place in time and space.

The application of the various systems of structuralist analysis has been seen to offer solutions to some problems and at the same time present new ones. Peter Wollen has used both Propp's and Metz's work in a desire to set plot paradigms and thus describe a story-generating system. In the case of Propp he used the Hitchcock film *North by Northwest* and, insofar as the text has been convoluted so as to accommodate the 31 functions, the application can be considered to be successful. However, it is apparent that the application the system derived from such a narrow base does highlight the limited value of the system for use with other films. In the case of Metz's syntagmatic, Wollen used *Citizen Kane*, and since the system has been designed to assess a visual pattern in film the process seems to work reasonably well – although whether the process brings the expected fruition is debatable. Wollen was keen to revitalise the concept of the auteur by defining a structure of repeated motifs within a body of directors' films, and, with Geoffrey Nowell-Smith, Jim Kitses and other English film theorists, developed the auteur structuralist ideology. The attempts to formalise the work of an auteur within a structure brought considerable criticism from other theorists, particularly Robin Wood, Charles Eckert and Brian Henderson, whose main objection was that the process[13]:

> … reduced the play of text to its underlying structure giving the critic no way of accounting for anything other than the structure and tempting him or her to believe that it is only the structure which gives the text value.

Some auteur structuralists (a loosely applied term), including Jim Kitses, indicated that the forceful and complex body of themes against which the auteur defined his or her work provided the underpinning for the concept of genre and criticism. The auteur theory tends to treat popular art as if it were high culture. For this reason, some critics turned to genre criticism to find an alternative method of writing about popular cinema. Laurence Alloway makes the point[13]:

> ... our reflex homage to personal originality too often makes us dismiss as aesthetically negligible a formulaic film that may be an interesting, valid, even original development within the convention.

There are two genres that have been especially important to the development of Hollywood; the western and the gangster thriller. Each genre has developed its own recurrent iconography and its own themes against which the individual artists have reflected their personal vision, often following closely the formulaic nature of the genres, as in the case of John Ford or Howard Hawks. It is one of the non-naturalistic (mythical) qualities of genres that they find ways of making their unique sensibilities seem normal to a wide audience. Both the western and the gangster film have a particular relationship with American society, both dealing with significant stages in the development of American history. It could be seen a case of America talking to itself about its agrarian past in the case of the western, and its urban, technological present in the case of the gangster. In describing the western, Jim Kitses says[14]:

> First it is American history, needless to say this does not mean that the films are historically accurate or that they cannot be made by Italians: more simply the statement means that American frontier life provides the milieu and mores of the westerns.

As in the case of the debate over whether the study of the author could be substantiated by the claim of the theoretical status, the concept of genre has also been discussed in similar terms. However, it soon becomes obvious that its use is as a set of organising principles rather than an applicable theory. To describe a film as a western, a whole range of films that appear to fulfil the role have to be examined to enable a set of themes or motifs to be ascribed to the nature of the genre. In his study *Virgin Land*, Henry Nash Smith has traced how the west as a symbol has functioned in America's history and consciousness. He asks[15]:

> Is the west a garden of natural dignity and innocence offering refuge from the decadence of civilisation, or a treacherous desert, stubbornly resisting the gradual sweep of agrarian progress and community values?

With this ideological perspective pervading the genre, it is possible to include a wide range of antinomies within the basic elements of form. Kitses lists a series of antinomies: the wilderness from which the flow of concepts of freedom, honour, self-knowledge, integrity, self-interest and solecism come; the community embracing restriction, institution, illusion, compromise, social responsibility, democracy; nature/culture and the west/east. These, he suggests, are not only exclusive to early western genre, but have a national world view for the special problem that affects America. In films such as John Ford's *My Darling Clementine*, *The Man Who Shot Liberty Valence*, and *The Searchers*, it is relatively simple for the post-modern audience to identify and deride the mythic presentation of the west and America. However, it is worth considering the assertion made by Will Wright in his work *Six Guns and Society* that[16]:

> ... a myth is a communication from a society to its members. The social concepts and attitudes determined by the history and institutions of a society are communicated to its members through its myths.

Wright builds his case for a structural study of the western upon an eclectic use of the works of Levi-Strauss, Propp and de Saussure, and makes a convincing case for such a analysis. The main objection to the structuralist approach to film criticism is that since those who propose it extol its scientific nature, then like any scientific process it should be applicable in all the situations for which claims are being made. The argument appears to be that unless the system works completely, it does not work at all. This is a difficult position to accept, because it is only the most elementary theories in science that are not open to debate or variation. It is therefore more than appropriate that the systems proposed by the structuralists should be taken seriously and used to develop an understanding of how films work. The difficulties begin to become apparent when a theorist attempts to apply a single system exclusively to a film. There appears to be a large area of overlap between the approaches. If we consider the elements of authorship, structure, myth and genre as being set at the four points of a square that represents film theory and criticism, then by using a whole superstructure of study we can attempt to analyse film.

5.8 The auteur debate

The nature of both film and television demands a corporate activity; however, since the earliest days of film there has been a tendency to define the authorship of a particular text. To some extent this still applies to television productions. The aim of this section is to indicate the range of the various discussions of the auteur theory within film criticism, and in particular to specify the various concepts used in such criticism. Auteur theory undoubtedly exists in the sense that critics, reviewers, film theorists and students of film continually refer to it, and the ordinary cinemagoer uses it as a rough classification system. The question, however, is, what is the critical significance of the term? Is it effective? Does it do more than simply refer to a rough rule of form and consistency within a canon of individual films? Does the theory do more than simply establish a set of arbitrary taxonomies within the general concept of film? Film criticism and theory has a number of systems with which to substantiate the value of a film or group of films. The term 'theory' is in general applied to the more abstract analysis of film, and the term 'criticism' has a more practical application. All systems are either descriptive or prescriptive, the prescriptive critic/theorist being concerned with what film should be and the descriptive critic/theorist with film as it is. A critic/theorist taking an aesthetic perspective would simply imply a prescriptive set of values, as would a theorist taking a semiotic view, whereas a theorist applying psychoanalytical or infrastructural viewpoints would use descriptive values. In 1931, Paul Rotha wrote that editing was 'The intrinsic essence of filmic creation'[17]. Although Rotha praised it in an extreme way, such a view was usual amongst formalist film theorists. Before André Bazin's dissent in the 1950s, the cinematic became featured as the prime criterion of excelling the purity that could align film with music, visual arts and literature. Mainstream film theorists, led by Rudolf Arnheim, distrusted any technical development in film production. This view crystallised into a particular reverence of silent film, with all its shortcomings, as a recorder of reality. With the advent of sound, colour, improved film stock and lenses, orthodox film theory became more and more remote from the cinema as it operated, and from the needs and methods of criticism. Bazin's response to two decades of obscure film theory and criticism was to apply aspects of phenomenology to the theory of realism. For Bazin, realism was more a matter of psychology than of aesthetics. He was more concerned with the significance of film not for what it was, but for what it could do. James Monaco suggests that what Bazin was after in his criticism was 'functionalism'[18] rather than simple realism. In 1951, Bazin, with Doniol-Valcroze and Loduca, founded *Cahiers du Cinema*. This magazine published articles by Francois Truffaut, Jean-Luc Goddard, Claude Chabol, Eric Rohmer and Jacques Rivette, amongst others. These cineastes used the journal to express their views and policies, and developed concepts of film history, which they were to implement in their work as directors. The major theoretical principle proposed in *Cahiers du Cinema* (January 1954) was expressed by Truffaut in the article *Une certain tendence du cinema Francais*, in which he described the '*politique des auteur* theory'. However, he explained that he was not expressing a theory to be proved, but rather a policy to be achieved. Some years later, he defended the concept of the auteur as merely being a polemical weapon for a given time and place. The American theorist Andrew Sarris has stated that there is no definition of the auteur theory in the English language – that is, by any American or British critic. It is apparent that the theory does not make any claim of prophecy, nor the possibility of any extra cinematic perspective – e.g. a bad director will not always make a bad film, but almost always; a bad director is a director who has made many bad films. The major premise of the auteur theory is the perception of the distinguishable personality of the director as a criterion of value[19]:

> He must exhibit certain recurrent characteristics of style over a group of films which serve as his signature; the way a film looks and moves should have some relationship to the way the director thinks or feels.

The ultimate claim of the theory is concerned with the interior meaning, the ultimate glory of the cinema as art. Interior meaning is extrapolated from the tension between a director's personality and his or her material. Many of the choices that the director of a film has to make are matters of craft; the aim is to make the scenes vivid and varied so as to present an interesting combination of the characters and the narrative. The director's basic task is to disguise poor casting, dull writing and poor sets. Even a good script and competent actors are not enough to prevent a film falling flat; often the fault lies in the director's inability to bring the material convincingly to life. Bazin's reaction to the formalists' emphasis on montage as an essential element of cinema was to denote *mise en scene* as the crux of realist film (by the term *mise en scene* he means particularly deep focus and sequence shots). However, subsequent critics and theorists have redefined and elaborated the concept to include a wide range of techniques and effects. These include (from theatre) the staging of action, the plastics (e.g. sets, props, make up, lighting etc.), and the centre of action, the animate objects (e.g. people and animals). The nature of the frame, its static state and its movement dimensions, lens, angle of view and perspective have become the other governing factor of *mise en scene*. The length of time that a shot appears on the screen also has a profound effect on the concept. A director who shows competence in using these factors obtains the status of *metteur en scene*, a director who demonstrates total responsibility for the pace, rhythm, timing structure and assumes the transcendent theme values and ideologies of raw materials of film-making is acclaimed an auteur. The argument for opposing the auteur theory was largely based upon the concept of form. Fereydoun Hoveyda takes an extreme attitude when he states that[20]:

The story in no way constitutes the underlying significance of the film. Indeed, in the hands of a great director, even the most insignificant detective story can be transformed into a work of art.

He believed that it is form, rather than content, that offers cinema its specificity. Hoveyda focuses on what he calls 'the essential importance of the concept of *mise en scene*' to substantiate the policy of the auteur, but claims that it is not a pure artistic form but, on the contrary, a form with a meaning.

Opposing this position were many of the contributors to the British film journal *Sight and Sound*. These articles took the view that it is content (expressions of the human situation) that is significant in film. Penelope Houston criticised the *Cahiers du Cinema* group for 'barely admitting to experiences which do not take place in the cinema'. She stated that the *Cahiers* debate had become no more than 'an insular shop talk', and that cinema is about human relationships[21]:

If cinema is the art we think it is, then it is entitled to the kind of critical analysis that has traditionally been devoted to the theatre and the novel.

This criticism, to be useful, is likely to be liberal. The major criticism of the auteur theory was that it had become exclusive and arbitrary. Once a director had been accepted by the *Cahiers du Cinema* as an auteur, it automatically followed that all the subsequent (and even previous) works were *ipso facto* excellent. It was felt that it took a long time and some very poor films before the *Cahiers* team changed their mind about a director once he or she had been admitted to this pantheon. 'To Hoveyda, as to many French critics, *x* number of beautiful shots = a great film'[22]. Pauline Keal states that[23]:

The director should be in control not because he is the sole creative intelligence but because only if he is in control can he liberate and utilise the talents of his co-workers who languish, as directors do, in studio production.

She believes that the most applicable interpretation of a director's claim to authorship is not that he did it all himself, but that he suffered from a minimum of interference with the choices and ultimate decisions.

Peter Wollen offered the director Howard Hawks as a test case for the auteur theory. He explains that Hawks had worked for many years within the Hollywood system and to the format of the classic Hollywood text. He also made films in almost all genres, which exhibit the same thematic preoccupations, the same motifs and incidents, the same style and tempo. It is not difficult to appreciate the appeal of a Hawks film to two types of people. First, the supporters of the *Cahiers* group would feel gratified that Hawks shared their tastes for the shock effect, the classy pulp thriller and a teenager's perception of human relationships operating in a male-dominated society. His low regards for social and psychological influences, combined with the absence of a big subject in his work, appears attractive to them. Second, the ex-*Cahiers* film-maker would be intrigued by Hawks' mainly anonymous career – one of the problems of an inspired, honest craftsman of the comparatively unimportant. But why should we recognise Hawks' films as being more significant than the ordinary? John Ford is by far a better director of the western, Sturges has directed more passionate comedies, and Huston's *Maltese Falcon* is a more significant thriller than *The Big Sleep*. It is the overt enthusiasm and all round expertise that attracts us (the audience) to Hawks' work. It is his respect for an intelligent non-expert viewing public who will recognise his work for interesting non-art (even anti-art) dextrous narrative content. Hawks is a romantic; men of action facing danger and death fascinate him, and these fill his outdoor films. His indoor films utilise urbane, eccentric women, whose role is to play upon the vulnerability of gullible, eccentric males who, often, are usually of professional status and show the reverse of those qualities much admired and used by Hawks in the adventure films. Within each genre, says Robin Wood, Hawks does not merely improve on its predecessor in technical proficiency and general know how; it is inevitably a 'richer and denser and more personal work'[24]. Two films particularly characterise Hawks' stylistic pattern. In *Only Angels Have Wings* (1939) the action takes place in South America, in a community filled mostly by men and isolated, geographically, from the rest of the world. The major characters operate in this foreign environment, in an environment that is completed ignored for the rest of the film. The male lead, Cary Grant (Geoff Carter), is a cynical professional pilot running a company delivering the mail across the Andes. He is surrounded by a set of competent and loyal men, each of who has a specific role within the narrative. The female lead, Jean Arthur (Bonnie Lee), arrives on the scene from the outside, and immediately presents the possibility of a difficult romantic invasion of the all-male group. However, as the plot deepens and develops she becomes accepted because of her own level of competence – in the case of Bonnie, her abilities as a performer at the piano. These characteristics are repeated in most of Hawks' adventure films. In *To Have and to Have Not* (1944), Bogart plays the competent cynic and Bacall the talented performer. In *Rio Bravo*, Wayne and Angie Dickinson play the parts. The supporting cast is made up of stock types, such as the loyal sidekick with a physical or psychological problem. In *Angels*, Thomas Mitchell plays Kid Dabb, who is losing his sight; in *To Have*, Walter Brennan plays Eddy the Rummie, an alcoholic; and in *Rio Bravo* he plays the disabled Stumpy. All these characters 'used to be good'. Another set of characters have 'let the side down', and their function in the plot is to achieve redemption through the committing of a brave if foolhardy act. Hawks' use of these familiar types doing and saying similar things could prove tedious in the hands of a lesser director. It is Hawks' mastery of *mise en scene* and his apparent rapport with actors and writers that enhances the production to the extent of offering few barriers to the audience suspending their disbelief.

The other picture that typifies Hawks' output is the comedy *Bringing Up Baby* (1938). In this film Cary Grant again stars, but at first sight his character appears to be ineffectual. It is not until the film has progressed that it becomes clear that in the face of the manic character played by Katherine Hepburn, no one would appear to be effective. The zanyness and apparent lack of logic on the part of Hepburn's character, Susan, overpowers Grant's academic character, palaeontologist David Huxley. The outcome is a retardation of man's behaviour that Andrew Sarris describes thus[25]:

> This film passes beyond the customary lunacy of the period into the bestial *walpurgisnasht* during which man, dog and leopard pursue each other over the Connecticut countryside until the behaviour patterns of men and animals become indistinguishable.

Hawks' films not only exhibit a thematic and character consistency; they also demonstrate the advantage of the Hollywood studio system when used by a director/producer of Hawks' quality. His ability to operate within the economic constraints of the system enabled him to benefit from a level of personal freedom that many other directors fail to achieve. The success of most of his films made him a safe and profitable bet, which meant he could cultivate a style, unaffected by the interference of studio bosses. He built up groups of stars, writers, cinematographers and composers who he used in groups of films at different periods of his career. With Hitchcock, Ford and von Sternberg, Hawks and a few others were able to build up a recognisable personal signature from film to film during the great age of Hollywood. However, for the main part Hollywood productions were the joint effort of groups of craftspeople, directors, actors, cinematographers, writers, designers and producers.

The significance of the auteur theory is not only its application as a system of criticism, but also the result of the tensions it has created with the other systems of theory and criticism, i.e. genre, semiotics, formalism, expressionism, realism etc. These tensions have produced a profound dialectic, which has initiated a dialogue that is far more wide-ranging than would be possible using any one of the systems alone. The implication of the auteur theory has contributed a great deal to this debate, because by nature it offers a dichotomy between production and meaning, i.e. the system demands a close scrutiny of both production techniques and implied meaning. Through auteur theory we do not only seek to analyse a director's film by form and style, we are also constantly seeking those clues to the essence of creativity within the human spirit. The theory also has the potential for both descriptive and prescriptive use. It can present a set of predetermined values, which have been empirically justified by studying a group of films by a director and applying these values to subsequent products in expectation of a continuing policy. Briefly, the fruits of the descriptive process become the tools of a prescriptive application. Criticism of the theory has effectively taken the edge off the extreme and often suspect claims made for the system by critics such as Hoveyda, and at the same time established its prime role amongst the other methods of critical analysis. Monaco expresses his view of the current position[26]:

> What seems clear in general about the present course of film theory is that description as an attitude which reached its apex in the early days of film semiotics has in a sense merged with the prescription that characterised the early film theorist.

He makes the point that film theory today should take the far-reaching and inter-related oppositions involved in film, and use them as a never-ending set of codes and sub-codes that raise fundamental questions about the relationships of life, art, reality and language. The desire on the part of film theorists and critics to put film into context with the other visual and narrative arts has led to a confusion of the complex issues involved. Of course there is a need to put film in its correct place, but there has been too much effort to relate to and compare with these other forms. The growth of the influence of cultural studies has clarified some of the confusion about the nature of film as art and an artefact of popular culture, and is enabling film to achieve its true status in the spectrum of cultural experiences. The development of film theory during the last three decades has been greatly influenced by the work carried out by literary theorists, many of whom were reaching towards the policies proposed by F. R. Leavis, in which he posited the concept of a canon of excellence. This canon of work, he insisted, 'was ultimately the product of individual human beings, and there is a measure of spiritual autonomy in human affairs'[27]. This idea was in direct opposition to most views held by Marxist critics, who proposed that the driving forces in literature (as in all things) were materialism and production. George Lukacs and Lucien Goldman felt that, in the last resort, it is the group and not the individual that is the 'true author of the work, i.e. the expression of the work is trans-individual'[28]. It would at first sight appear that Leavis' concept and the auteur theory in film have a good deal in common; however, Leavis viewed the work of the cinema as the model for mass vulgarity, and he tested the popular novelist as a cynical technician working to a formula to produce a saleable work. Leavis saw any popular cultural product as a means of undermining the concept of a good work – that is, a work from the canon of high culture, which sets the standard of excellence. The Marxist dialectic of criticism would naturally dismiss the auteur theory.

There is a third proposition, which is a result of this development of cultural studies in the 1960s. Raymond Williams drew on the philosophy of European Marxists which, combined with the liberal tradition of literary criticism, stressed the value of cultural materialism (which holds that the super-structural activities we call culture have as good a claim to form the basis on which social relations depend as do the forces of production). Williams asserts that production includes social production, one aspect of which is art – including popular art. Thus, while Marxism does not admit the concept of the auteur, when used in conjunction with the liberal tradition of literary criticism it can produce a suitable cultural philosophy for film. The other factor in his case uses Antonio Gramsci's concept of hegemony. This suggests that the ruling class exerts control over other social groups in ways other than crude political economic pressures. This is in effect the hearts and minds method, which is rarely understood as a conscious strategy, even by members of the ruling class. It is perhaps in this area that the investigation of the auteur, particularly as it operates in the Hollywood system, should take place. The contribution of the auteur theory to film criticism and theory during the last 40 years has been significant, if sometimes uneven. Many of the factors originally used to quantify the status of the auteur no longer operate in the way they did in the Hollywood system of production – the power of the studio system has declined, the star system no longer operates, the economics of film production have changed, and so has the audience. Cinema is no longer the prime product of the popular culture. Is it possible for the system to be current, or is it now an historical phenomenon? Is it possible to assess the work of Scorcese, Stone, Scott, Greenaway, Lynch or even Spielberg in the same way we have Hawks, Hitchcock, Ford, Huston et al.? Perhaps the time has come to reassess the system in the light of the present situation, and not only attempt to quantify the work of modern directors but also to apply similar criteria to the other contributors to the creative process in an attempt to widen the debate.

5.9 References

1. Benjamin, W. *The Work of Art in the Age of Mechanical Reproduction.* Reprinted in G. Mast, M. Cohen and L. Braudy (eds) (1992). *Film Theory and Criticism*, Fourth Edition. Oxford University Press.
2. Tonnies, F. (1887). *Community and Association RKP 1955*, p. 37. RKP, Germany.
3. Le Bon, G. (date unknown). *The Crowd*, p. 15. Ernet Benn.
4. Gerbner, G. (1966). An institutional approach to mass communications research. In *Communication, Theory and Research* (C. C, Thomas, ed.).
5. Seaton, J. (1991). *Power Without Responsibility*, p. 250. Routledge.
6. Leavis, F. R. (1930). *Mass Civilisation and Minority Culture*. Minority Press.
7. Williams, R. (1958). *Studying Culture (An Introductory Reader)*. In *Convictions*, (McKenzie, ed.), p. 7. MacGibbon and Kee.
8. Williams, R. (1958). *Studying Culture (An Introductory Reader)*. In *Convictions*, (McKenzie, ed.), p. 9. MacGibbon and Kee.
9. Williams, R. (1958). *Studying Culture (An Introductory Reader)*. In *Convictions*, (McKenzie, ed.), p. 10. MacGibbon and Kee.
10. McLuhan, M. (1964). *Understanding the Media (The Extensions of Man)*. Sphere Books.
11. Sapir, E. (1948). *Communication Encyclopedia of the Social Sciences*, Vol. IV, p. 80. Macmillan.
12. Crofts, S. (1976). Metz' Grand Syntagmatique. Summary and Critique. *Film Form*, No.1, pp. 78–90.
13. Alloway, L. (1971). *Violent America: The Movies 1946–64*, p. 60. Museum of Modern Art, New York.
14. Kitses, J. (1969). *Horizons West*. Thames and Hudson/BFI.
15. Smith, H. N. (1950). *Virgin Land*. Harvard University Press.
16. Wright, W. (1975). *Six Guns and Society*. University of California Press.
17. Rotha, P. and Griffith, R. (1960). *The Film Till Now*. Twayne.
18. Monaco, J. (1981). *How to Read a Film*, p. 329. Oxford University Press.
19. Sarris, A. (1962–3). *Film Culture*. Winter.
20. Hovegda, F. (1960). Sunspots. In *Cahiers du Cinema*, No. 1120, reprinted in *Cahiers du Cinema*, Vol. 2, 1986, BFI/RKP.
21. Houston, P. (1960). The critical question. *Sight and Sound*, **29(4)**.

22. Roud, R. (1960). The French Line. *Sight and Sound*, **29(4)**.
23. Keal, P. (1985). *The Citizen Kane Book – Raising Kane*, p. 72. Methuen.
24. Wood, R. (1981) *Howard Hawks*, p. 12. BFI.
25. Sarris, A. (1972). The World of Howard Hawks. In: *Focus on Howard Hawks* (J. McBride, ed.). Prentice-Hall.
26. Monaco, J. (1990). *How to Read a Film*, p. 346. Oxford University Press.
27. Bull, J. A. (1988). *The Framework of Fiction*, p. 32. Macmillan.
28. Bull, J. A. (1988). *The Framework of Fiction*, p. 42. Macmillan.

5.10 Further reading

Alvorado, M. and Thomson, J. (1990). *The Media Reader*. British Film Institute.

Bordwell, D. and Thomson, K. (1990). *Film Art: An Introduction*, 5th edn. McGraw-Hill.

Monaco, J. (1990). *How to Read a Film*. Oxford University Press.

Negrine, R. (1989). *Politics and the Mass Media in Britain*. Routledge.

Chapter 6

Media and its cultural implications

6.1 Summary

This chapter extends and elaborates on the content of Chapter 5. It opens with an explanation of the various attempts to investigate and analyse the effects of films upon an audience. This takes the form of a review of the major experiments that have been used in the attempts to understand the effect of the mass media upon the audience. The areas covered are the behaviourist, pluralist and gratification theories.

This is followed with a description of the development of the Hollywood system of production in terms of its industrial, social and political influences. The section on realism investigates the suitability or desirability of the use of film to demonstrate a realistic perspective of the world, and the nature of realism in film.

The penultimate part of this chapter examines the portrayal of modernism and modernity in media material during the first half of this century, and uses the rise and decline of *avant-garde* film and the nature of the reproduction as its central themes. The chapter ends with an attempt to uncover the current situation in the media/culture debate. The section uses the elusive term 'post-modern' as an indication of the *Zeitgeist* under discussion.

6.2 Objectives and key issues

This chapter elaborates on the issues raised in Chapter 5, and begins by setting out some of the main methods of measuring the effects of the media upon the audience. This controversial area of study has been the source of the conflicting political calls for restraint and censorship of the media. The aim here is to supply managers with the tools for a discourse that will underpin their understanding of media law and policy.

The section on Hollywood has been included with the aim of giving an historical perspective to the organization of the current media industry. In the development of industrial Hollywood, much of the ideology that has influenced (and still is influencing) the present management structure of the media industry is visible. The reader should be able to relate the economic, industrial and cultural developments of Hollywood to many of the present day structures in the media industry.

The nature of media products and their influence upon their audience has to be understood against an understanding of how they seem to reflect a view of how people operate in the society. Here, this is described in terms of the various attempts to establish an understanding of how the media represents realism. The aim of this aspect of the chapter is to enable the reader to understand that the term 'realism' can be applied to a wide range of styles of media presentations.

The aims of the last two sections are to enable the reader to gain an understanding of the terms 'modernity', 'modernism' and 'post-modernity' by using film as a vehicle. In the section on modernism, the issues of reproducibility and the avant-garde are offered in order to give a perspective of progress in terms of creativity. Finally, the current concept of post-modernity is expressed in order to give the reader an insight into the current debate about society and media products.

Considered together, Chapters 5 and 6 should enable the reader to form an understanding of media and cultural studies. It should be possible for the reader to flesh out the bones of the major issues that have generated or influenced the ideas and attitudes about the media industry.

6.3 The audience

The earliest experiments in measuring the effects of the mass media took place in the USA in the 1930s, and specifically investigated the influence of film and radio. These studies applied a behaviourist approach, and used scientific methods to identify specific events. They investigated the influences of the media on behaviour, emotions, attitudes and knowledge. What is peculiar to behaviourist research is not so much the particular kinds of effects studied, but the methods used. These included experimental research, done in the controlled environment of a laboratory, and survey research, using representative, random or stratified samples of audiences – assessing media in the field. Researchers employing these methods were convinced that they were producing hard evidence about the effects of the mass media. This conviction was based upon the belief that only scientific methods were capable of discovering the facts about the power of the media.

In the USA, the Paine Foundation Studies (1929–1932) were the first significant theories or surveys. These evaluated the influence of film on children. Thirteen studies were published in 10 volumes, focusing on audience composition and content analysis of themes. It was the classical conditioning experiment that fired the imagination of the psychologists involved in these studies. The experiments relied heavily on the distinctive S and R (stimulus and response) theory made popular by the physiologists Ivan Pavlov and Vladimir Bekhterev. This introduced the idea of association and signification, and described the learning process in terms of the Black Box theory. This proposed the view that to measure a change of attitude by the influence of an external source, the relationship between the stimulus input and the response output should be assessed and a hypothesis formulated about what was going on in the box. This hypothesis was assumed to indicate a psychological change in the subject. These studies investigated six paradigms of audience response:

1 Propaganda persuasion – the effects of moulding the attitude, called a soft modification, and changing behaviour, called a hard modification.
2 Imitation – the effects of copying what is received. This is particularly important in research done with children.
3 Desensitisation – the effect of dulling sensitivities.
4 Escapism – the effect of creating a fantasy world; the defunctioning effect of the media.
5 Reality construction – the effect of the media explaining the world.
6 Agenda setting – the effect of the media establishing the importance of the subject.

Patterson and Thurlston carried out one of the major experiments sponsored by the Paine Fund. They employed a range of techniques to isolate the influence of selected films upon a group of children of similar cultural background. Applying the stimulus response theory, and making the assumption that few extraneous influences affected the children between the pre-screening and post-screening tests, they concluded that any differences of attitudes recorded were a direct result of watching the film. Thurlston devised a scale with which to measure the attitude of the subjects. These were given to each member of the audience before they saw the film, and the results of the group were computed to give an indication of their combined attitude to a number of points. The following day, the scale was given again and the new position of the group computed. Any response higher than the original figure represented a negative shift and a lower figure a positive shift in the attitude of the group to the subject. A test was given at various periods after the screening to enable the permanence of the changes to be assessed. The extensive developments used 4000 subjects selected from mostly junior or high school age groups. Between 600 and 800 films were reviewed, and 13 were selected as being most likely to produce a noticeable change in attitude. The popular films dealt with such subjects as the Chinese (*Son of God*), war (*All Quiet on the Western Front*) and black issues (the D. W. Griffith film, *The Birth of a Nation*). The experiments took place in small towns around Chicago so as to enable a selection of films that children were not likely to have seen.

The results of these experiments suggested that films could affect information acquisition, modify cultural attitudes, stimulate emotions and disturb sleep. At the time, it was thought that the outstanding contribution of the study was the setting of the attitude of children towards social values, which could be immeasurably changed by exposure to one film. A second fact discovered during these attitude studies was the cumulative effects, which demonstrated that the influence of two or more films with similar themes was much greater than the effect of a single film. It also appeared to show that the shifts created by exposure to the films had a long-term effect. The Patterson and Thurlston studies did not specifically investigate the effects of film on behaviour, but the assumption made was that because information was a factor in behaviour and film was influential in imparting information, then there was a connection between the two. W. Charters said[1]:

> We may assume that attitudes towards social objects affect conduct. If one is friendly toward an objective of action in a situation, he will be influenced to build one behaviour pattern; if unfriendly to build another.

Other surveys of the time used the more real life approach of field studies. One such study[2] carried out by Herbert Blumer used an autobiographical technique supplemented by interviews, accounts of conversations and questionnaires and a wide spectrum of society. Blumer went to great lengths to achieve error-free results. He explained that the comparison of large numbers of documents coming from different groups of people with no knowledge of each other made it possible to ascertain the general run of experiences. He went on to say that the content of the documents coming from different sources yielded substantially the same general kind of experience. Charters substantiates this point by saying that the mass and consistency of this project proves the validity of the conclusion[3]. One of the significant points made by Blumer was the elaboration of the phenomenon of emotional possession, during which a child watching in the darkness of the cinema sees the actors and actions of a film as being part of the real world. His emotional condition may get such a strong grip on him that even his efforts to rid himself of it by reasoning may prove to little avail. They also demonstrated how films stimulate a wide range of emotions, including fright, sorrow, love and excitement, and give children techniques of actions in situations of interest to them, ranging from the trivial techniques of the playground to disturbing cues for the delinquent. This childhood state is finally altered by what Blumer describes as emotional detachment, when young people at first affected sophisticated detachment from serial thrillers and then showed genuine dislike of them. The outcome of the Paine Fund studies was to reinforce existing public concern and lead to an industry self-censorship system that lasted in the USA until the 1960s. As should be expected, differences in design methodology and manipulation of the data have produced some disagreement among researchers. The major criticisms of the behaviourist studies were:

- an objection to the assumption that the audience was composed of individuals who operated in self-contained isolation rather than in complex relationships
- that the experiments were unrealistic in the sense that subjects responded knowing that their views were part of an experiment, and therefore the results measured what tended to be unnatural and unrepresentative attitudes.

These film studies had begun to acknowledge the variable nature of the media product, the media audience and the environment in which the media are consumed. The behaviourist surveys of the 1930s raised a range of assertions about the power of the mass media, which were questioned by researchers who took a broader sociological view of mass society and mass media. Theirs was a pluralistic perspective. They felt that the previous surveys did not make adequate allowances for the complex set of factors that act upon the process of media influence. They were concerned with the understanding of the effects of those variables in society that acted as filters on the reception of the media messages. These act on the reception of the message, and fall into four categories; informational, physical, psychological and cultural. Filters or conditions are ways in which we learn or are trained to receive or ignore messages. A number of subsequent works – namely the *Invasion from Mars* survey, which studied the effects of the Orson Welles' radio broadcast *The War of the Worlds*; the *Peoples Choice* study, which analysed voting predispositions in the American 1914 presidential elections; and the war time study *Why we Fight* – focused on some of the variables at work in the process of mass media communication.

In his hastily compiled study *Invasion from Mars*, Hadley Cantril regarded as causal any psychological condition in the listener or the listening situation that endangered and sustained the belief that the broadcast was news. He continued[4]:

> We have seen that a variety of influences and conditions are related to the panic resulting from this particular broadcast. We have found no single observable variable consistently related to the reaction although a lack of critical ability seemed particularly conducive to fear in a large proportion of the population.

The study also concluded that the excellent quality of the production and the point at which people joined the audience contributed to the reaction. It was found that individuals with weak personalities, low educational levels and strong religious beliefs were most susceptible to panic, and that, once frightened, people stopped listening altogether or would not believe all was well despite other stations being on the air. The political tension in Europe and the depressed economy was said to have created cultural conditions that contributed to the overall panic. Cantril acknowledges that this field study does not give a strictly behaviourist explanation of the panic engendered, and suggests the absence of conditioning as an explanation. However, he explains, the particular accounting relationships we have given to a greater subsumptive power in conceptualising the rich and varied experiences we have dealt with in this very realistic phenomenon of our social life[4]. *The Peoples Choice* was the first to use the tools of the social scientist on a large-scale field study, and found that political propaganda activated voters to remain loyal to their political beliefs rather than change them. Variables such as religion, socio-economic status, age, occupation and urban versus rural residence were also identified as important. The study suggested that media content moves through a two-step flow, in which opinion leaders influence less active information seekers and these interpersonal social contacts are more important than exposure to the media. It was the concern for the effects that the variables had on the influence of the mass media that initiated the pluralist studies. In the words of Blumer and Gurevitsch[2]:

> Pluralists see mass society as a polarity of potential concentrations of power, albeit not necessarily equal to each other, which are engaged in a contest for ascendancy and dominance.

The mass media within this view can be seen as a stage on which this contest is conducted and the public support for one or another grouping or point of view is mobilised[2]. The identification of the variables has major effects on media influence, and has been the cause of criticism of the approach. Most pluralists would list four primary sets of variables:

1 Content
2 Media
3 Audience
4 Interaction.

Nonetheless, many variables and combinations of variables remain. The problem is expressed by Richard Dembo[5]:

> When the magnifying power of our social microscope is increased one does not find people acting as alienated automatons in an enormous social universe, but as persons with definite set ties of sentiment and shared experience on the premise of mutual trust. Each individual is seen as being his own kind of social scientist, going about and organising a world that is meaningful to him.

He was working in the 1970s on the effects of television on teenage boys, and poses the view that each subject uses and gains gratification from the medium of television in terms of the variables each brings to bear on the material he views. Opposing this pluralist perspective were George Gerbner and Larry Gross, who asserted that television is the central cultural arm of American society. It is an agency of the established order, and as such serves primarily to extend and maintain rather than alter or weaken conventional conceptions, beliefs and behaviours. Its chief cultural function is to spread and stabilise social patterns, and to cultivate not change, but resistance to change. Television is a medium of socialisation of most people into standardised roles and behaviours. Its function is, in a word, 'enculturation'[6]. This critical or dominant approach reflects the view that critical theorists see the audience as dependent, passive and organised on a large scale, and vulnerable to very powerful ideological effects that confirm the established social order. This view has its followers in Britain, who believed that only by taking a theoretical perspective based on ideology could the media be understood. In 1948, Bernard Berelson attempted to summarise the status of the fields of research into the effects of the mass media as it then existed. He noted that the older stimulus response theory of the all-powerful media had largely been abandoned, and he identified five central factors that seemed to be a guide to new directions of research[7].

In the 1940s a body of empirical research began to accumulate which provides some refined knowledge on the effect of communication on public opinion, and promises to provide a good deal more in the next few years. But what has such research contributed to the problem? The proper answer to the general question, the answer that constitutes the most useful formulation for research purposes, is this: some kind of communication on some kind of issues brought to the attention of some kinds of people under some kinds of conditions had some kinds of effects.

In spite of its simplicity, this serves as a guide for new directions of research and still is the kind of general statement of the salient categories, factors and variables which, along with individual differences, must be considered in trying to understand the effect of the media on society. All the methods used during the last 60 years to analyse the effects of the media have shown apparent contradictions when put into the context of the society to which they are applied. The behaviourist method depended on the scientific approach, which ignored the variables influencing the effects of media. The pluralist method reflected the balance of forces within society, but ignored the extent to which the weaker and unorganised groups are excluded from the process altogether – although it is the pluralist method that leads back into the determinist explanation of the real or supposed role of the media as an instrument of class domination. The determinist method, in terms of class manipulation and exploitation, is too mechanistic, and obscures the series of complex relationships, which have not yet been explained.

6.4 The development of the Hollywood system

The foundations of the media industry were laid in the early part of the last century, particularly with the foundation of the film industry in Hollywood. It is to the form and structure of Hollywood that current media organisations can be traced. The classic Hollywood form and style began to invade the world of cinema from 1910 onwards. The restrictions imposed on the development of the American film industry by the actions of the Motion Picture Patents Company, headed by Thomas Edison, were finally removed in 1912, when a court decision ended its monopoly of equipment. The MPPC had tied up the hardware needed to produce films in a web of patents, which had prevented the competition that could have grown from the expansion of the industry due to the relatively low capital outlay needed to start in the film industry at that time. The MPPC's profits came not from production, distribution or exhibition of film, but from the sale or licensing of the equipment required to make and show films. Films were made to fuel the use of equipment.

The nature of film's status as a distinctive commodity was not immediately stated. The act of film-making at this time could be said to be an artisanal craft activity. The early exhibition of films used the kinetoscope, a device for the individual to view moving pictures. However, this system proved to be a false start, as cinema did not obtain comparable status with other forms of theatre entertainment until the public projection of films made it possible for tickets to be sold to an audience for communal viewing. The foundation of a material audience for consuming film initiated a collective mode of appropriation, which generated a film-making practice. This was dependent upon a sequence of scenes being projected, with some form of introduction. The individual segments were usually scenic shots reminiscent of nineteenth century still photography – topicals, news reporting, great events, variety acts from vaudeville, trick film and short narratives – with the emphasis in the early exhibitions on spectacle rather than narrative. The freeing of the industry from the MPPC monopoly encouraged the independent firms to merge and expand to establish a system that was to dominate the Hollywood film industry for many decades and produce the dominant product in film history – the classic Hollywood film.

There were three factors that had been pivotal in establishing the form of the classic Hollywood film; the development of the narrative form of film, the status of film as an industrial commodity subject to the economic constraints of a capitalist society, and the changes in the production method of films. The contribution made by each of these factors will be the main substance of this chapter. Noel Burch points out that in its early days the cinema addressed itself exclusively to the urban lower classes, and that its practitioners were, for the most part, still of humble origin[8]. He suggests that the form of film during the first two decades was largely influenced by the aggregate of folk art kept alive by the urban working classes in Europe and the USA at the turn of the century[8]. The early stories used in films did not follow the traditional closed world of the bourgeois novel, in which the plot, narrative and characteristics are introduced to the reader as being invented and existing only in the text[9]. They were made on the assumption that the audience had a thorough knowledge of the story being shown – a limited series of moving tableaux were shown to audiences, who were left to fill in enormous narrative gaps themselves. Burch explains that the pictures reflected in form and content the infantilism of the working classes. As long as the audience for cinema was primarily from the working class, the motivation to produce films that used elaborate narrative was absent. The development of a more elaborate narrative form came as a result of the desire to find a more linear chain of spatio-temporal sequentiality in the early genre of the chase films. The cuts from chased to chaser and back again in subsequent shots substantiated the possibility of the audience 'reading' a naturally developing story, and being introduced to the form of closure. Burch describes this as the first decisive step towards the linearity of the institutional mode. These films tended to offer heterogeneity of events in tableaux scenes strung together to form a story, but nevertheless the scenes were discreet and each demanded that the spectator understood what was going on. This primitive cinema, as Burch calls it, demanded a different way of viewing[10]. Charles Musser described the early cinema as a transitional phase between the magic lantern show, with its moving slides and mixed still and moving slides, and early narratives in film. He suggested that it was during this period that the unique struggle with temporality took place. Porter's early films are examples of the early cinema's specificity. All the scenes are complete and whole in their own right; overlapping action in successive shots, repetition and a lack of linear progression demonstrate the absence of the seamless continuity for which Hollywood is renowned. The earliest attempts at narrative came through the use of montage; the use of several shots temporally and spatially disjointed and linked principally by knowledge of the story to which they refer – Porter's *Uncle Tom's Cabin* (1903) in the USA and the vast number of films made after 1896 on the theme of the *Passion* being examples of this development. Burch points out that during the first 10 years of the cinema it addressed itself exclusively to the urban lower classes and was produced by people from similar background, although cinema could not escape the influences of bourgeois modes of representation (specifically literature, painting and especially theatre). However, the characteristics of working-class culture, which comprised both modes of representation and narrative or gestural material deriving from melodrama, vaudeville, pantomime (in England), conjuring, music hall and circus, were the influences that most affected the cinema-going public of the period. These influences, for the main part, did not rely on a rigid linearity as much as the bourgeois mode of representation. Burch explains that the melodrama undoubtedly constituted a theatrical form quite distinct from those of the bourgeois theatre. Kristin Thompson and David Bordwell questioned Burch's view that the primitive cinema is marked by contradictions arising from the fact that film-makers had not yet set out to capture a mass audience[11]. Film-makers responded to the conflicting influences from bourgeois art, nineteenth century theatre, painting, the novel, and proletarian art forms. Thompson and Bordwell particularly criticise his selection and use of historical evidence, claiming that his data tend to be either insufficient or inaccurate. Thompson argues that the development of the classic Hollywood film was not so much shaped by the formation of a narrative tradition brought about by the change from a working-class audience to one that was increasingly bourgeois, but was caused by fundamental changes in production, distribution and exhibition practices. She makes the point that no single cause, but rather a combination of conditions (the early exhibition, links to vaudeville, the very short length of individual films), encouraged film makers to model their works upon vaudeville forms, the simple narratives that resulted demanded few spatial or temporal shifts, thus minimising the need for editing guidelines. However, the steady demand for more footage, supplemented by the nickelodeon boom after 1905, encouraged longer narratives made in more systematic production circumstances. The economic practices of Hollywood operated in two main areas; first in the changes that took place in the exhibition of films in custom-built theatres – the development of the nickelodeon and picture palace – and secondly in the economic mode of production. The transition of cinema to nickelodeon in the period between 1905 and 1914 took place concurrently with film becoming a form of mass entertainment, and required an equivalent mass production base[12].

As early as 1911 Thomas Ince had introduced practices from other industries to film, such as Taylor's concept of the production line and the scientific management much favoured by Henry Ford. By 1910, the nickelodeons were attracting 20 per cent of the population of the USA. It is also suggested that the audience was emerging more from the middle classes. Three factors that revisionist writers relate to the economic growth of the cinema are specifically connected with the status of the nickelodeon. The first is the correction of the view that nickelodeons were squalid, crowded and in bad locations. In fact, most were in the traditional entertainment districts between middle-class and working-class areas, and locations were selected to encourage vaudeville patrons into the new cinemas. This encouraged the second factor, the rise of the middle-class element, in that the audience promoted the use of narratives that were familiar to the middle class, extending the dramatology of films. Charles Musser points out that although story films appealed to both working- and middle-class audiences, there was a move towards a more elite form of narrative. Thirdly, the nickelodeon offered a symbiotic relationship between vaudeville and cinema. Films were accompanied by live acts, a reversal of the previous situation when film was seen as one of the acts. This offered the possibility of the inclusion of special attractions to the middle classes. The nickelodeon had developed an entertainment package. The proliferation of nickelodeons introduced the necessity for the frequent change of programmes, and companies calling themselves exchanges were set up. Exchanges purchased films from the production companies, and rented them to the exhibitors. Before the distributors began to send out programmes to the exhibitors, it was the exhibitors or camera operators who controlled the major of the film text, but after distribution it became the director and subsequently the producers who assumed textural control. Distribution also established the reel of film as a basic industrial commodity, separating distribution from exhibition. The distribution aspect of the film industry, generated in the first place by the nickelodeon and then by the picture palace, produced the concept of profit dominated exhibition, which pressured film production until well into the 1940s.

The development of the importance of exhibitions to the economics of the film industry was a continual movement up a class from the nickelodeon to the picture palace, and redefined the cinema-going experience. The picture palace became one of the central economic commodities of the Hollywood film industry and was an important influence upon the type and style of products produced, as well as being the area of greatest investment in the film industry. Cinema followed other members of the retail industry, such as the chain store Woolworths, by locating picture houses in most large towns. The cinema circuits built elaborate air-conditioned picture palaces with a staff of ushers, and they showed feature length films with themed presentations and recognisable performers. By 1915, the standard film being distributed and finding an enthusiastic audience throughout the main cinema circuits was a reeled 75-minute feature film.

The Hollywood feature film is characterised by being a scripted drama, play, novel or short story, which is presented as smoothly flowing and uses self-effacing techniques that aspire to a visual clarity. The feature films produced by Hollywood in the 1920s, 1930s and 1940s had become mass-produced products for consumption by a mass audience. The standard practice in the economics of Hollywood film production in the

1920s was a system of vertical integration; the co-ordination of production, distribution and exhibition.

Within this system of mass production, the American cinema became definitively orientated towards narrative form. Porter's *The Great Train Robbery* (1903), an early prototype for the classical Hollywood film, has the action developing with a clear linearity of time, space and logic. From 1908 until 1913, D. W. Griffith made hundreds of one and two reelers (running about 15 and 30 minutes respectively). These films introduced relatively complex narratives in short spans. Griffith's contract with the Biograph Company included a bonus clause for production speed and quality. These industrial products could be regularly made in the studio, costs carefully controlled, and the predictable release programme required by the cinema circuits achieved. Charles Musser suggests that the increasing number of films being produced meant that the concept of the viewer having previous knowledge of a film could not be relied upon, and therefore the narrative form had to be strongly identified. Self-sufficient narrative films were developed, which depended upon the use of elaborate inter-titles. The economic practices that had developed during the nineteenth century, when applied to the emerging film industry, generated particular forms of representation. Efficiency justified the standardisation of products. Thus the film industry began in a general industrial structure of a well-developed corporate capitalism, positioned between the economic practice of standardisation for efficient mass production and the economic practice of product differentiation. At the most functional level, the style of productions was influenced by such cost factors as the re-use of sets, scenery and costumes. This had the effect of encouraging the production of films with particular genres, themes, serials and series. Companies often called for scenarios that would use established sets. The multiple use of sets and costume meant that it was possible for the Hollywood producer to budget for the most lavish material, knowing that it would be economically put to use in many productions. Advice to freelance writers in 1913 suggested that unity of place was also of economic importance for the production, permitting the use of the same settings for many scenes. In this way the producer felt justified in spending more money upon settings themselves. As he was more or less limited by the owner of the motion picture company as to the outlay for each picture, the result could be more elaborate and artistic stage effects. In the same manual, the writer was advised to use fewer characters in the plot because it allowed the producer to budget for more settings and costumes. All aspects of production were costed. Jeanette Staiger points out that a handbook author wrote that the cost factors related to the techniques of style were significant[14]. Rehearsals were cheaper than retakes, dissolves less expensive than double exposures, and having characters discovered in scene rather than using entrances cut costs. Another effect of the emphasis of budgetary constraints was that innovations could be financed. These were important in promoting the studio's style and identity for brand name advertising. The rise of the narrative film developed the discourse on acting, and admitted the possibility of acting in film rather than posing. This led to the producers supplying performers' names in response to public demand. The picture personality and his or her work became linked, and the production companies began to circulate information about actors[14].

By 1914, the fully-fledged 'star' system that has come to signify much of the classic Hollywood style had emerged. The life of the actor outside the workplace became part of the public domain. The star system introduced a new element into the economics of Hollywood and the cinema institution; the economics of publicity, printed material (including advertisement), hobby cards, trade and fan magazines, items in newspapers, approach to film manufacturing, and the separation of conceptualisation from production. This created minute divisions of labour for those involved in the industry. Ince's company, for instance, used six units shooting at the same time with a pool of six writers and nine directors. At the top of this bureaucratic pyramid, Ince took full responsibility for overall planning. This became known as the central producer system, and developed between 1912 and 1931. The mass production and the central producer system created a studio identity, the maintenance of a regular output in terms of quality, quantity and budget (the budgets were meticulously prepared), and the introduction of a continuity of script (paper planned) prepared by the management for the workers to follow. This took the form of a blueprint for shot breakdown, *mise en scene* and titles. The status of the director changed; he controlled the actors and the crew, bound by the management's paper model. The introduction of the industrial mode of production into the Hollywood system was instrumental not only in putting a particular style and form of presentation into the hands of a select band of managers, but also in bringing about the consolidation of the industry into a limited number of companies, who prospered under the studio system by producing the classic Hollywood film. It would be convenient in summing up to suggest that the classic Hollywood film was shaped equally by narrative concerns, economic constraints and industrial modes of production. However, it would also be true to say that it was equally affected by the unique ideological constraints operating in the USA during the period. The moral and religious codes imposed by the various states resulted, in many cases, in a high degree of self-censorship in the industry, and the over-patriotism of many of the first-generation immigrant movie moguls dictated a preference for narratives demonstrating positive political values such as progress, success, etc. The unique qualities of the classic Hollywood film were largely a result of the studios being geared for efficiency. However, there is an underlying complex ideological significance in the classic Hollywood film. It allows identification, the standard signifying practice; it declines to call attention to its own construction through editing; and it organises spectator attention – for example, through centring the image and thus creating linearisation through pictorial composition. This results in the audience having little or no choice when viewing the film, but at the same time it involves the viewer by promoting spectator identification. The audience becomes the uncritical consumer of entertainment. By denying criticism, the form substantiates the dominant ideology of the USA, that of capitalism. The film's narrative tells stories in the traditional way, by using the disruption of equilibrium and its restoration as the basis for the plots. The films centre on individual protagonists who resolve the problems of the plot by action and romance. The implicit ideology is patriarchal and individualistic.

The results are only troubled in two ways; when the star is a woman, and when problems cannot be given full social significance because of closure. Classic Hollywood films do not question capitalism or individualism; in fact they depict both as being solutions to problems. The history of the form can be seen as a social drift from depicting the working-class poor towards showing the wealth and consumption of the upper class. The classic Hollywood film is a good example of the effect Raymond Williams has called 'cultural materialism'; that is, the creation of an object by the operation of the various agencies working in the economic, cultural and political aspects of society. The three elements of narrative, economics and mode of production have worked in an intricate way in a complex ideological system to produce the manifestation of the American film industry, the classical Hollywood film.

6.5 Realism

Although the pioneers of film considered it primarily suitable for scientific research, the commercial development of the technology began almost immediately after the first exhibitions. The Lumière brothers sold their commercial interests to Charles Pathé in 1900, and this paved the way for large-scale commercial development. The first films were not structured narratives, but brief, one-shot recordings of everyday life. George Melies is usually credited with the development of the narrative feature film. His important contribution was to free screen time from real time by the implementation of editing techniques, which enabled the narrative to be constructed (i.e. speeded up or slowed down); in short, composed. The use of fade-out as a method of transition, closure, and lap dissolve as a more elegant method of transition, were early examples of the development of techniques that have become conventions determining both film- and television-making practice and the audience understanding of the narrative.

Within 20 years of the beginning of film, directors and theorists such as D. W. Griffith and Vachel Lindsay added development arguments, definitions or prescriptions for the aesthetic characteristics of film. Film had become a companion to sculpture, painting or literature; the seventh art. The concept of the film-maker as artist became popular with the American intelligentsia in the 1920s, although they showed a preference for the more expressive products of the state-funded European film industries of Germany and Russia. German expressionism and Soviet montage demonstrated a more vigorous use of an aesthetic approach to film, and came close to challenging Hollywood's leadership in the formal development of silent film. The reshaping of the raw material printed on celluloid in an expressive way so as to use images of the real world had become the paramount convention of film; the debate concerning the suitability or desirability of the use and potential of film to be able to demonstrate a realistic perspective of the world and the nature of realism in film had begun.

A succession of film-makers within the Marxist tradition attempted to express an ideological perspective in their work against the changing political and aesthetic climate of the last 75 years. A resolution of the Thirteen Congress of the all Union Soviet Communist Party in 1928 was the motivation for Soviet directors to use film to express the political, economic and social reality of the Revolution. 'The cinema,' it stated:

> the most important of all the arts, can and must play a large role in the cultural revolution as a medium for broad educational work and communist propaganda, for the organisation and education of the masses around slogans and tasks of the Party, their artistic education, their wholesome relaxation and entertainment.

This statement established the importance of film within the Soviet state, but the method that the film-makers were to use to play their part in the

Cultural Revolution was less clear. Although Marx had been somewhat ambivalent on the subject of literature's relation to society, his collaborator, Frederick Engels, was suggesting that the relationship between economic forces and cultural achievement could be very indirect. 'It is not so much the economic situation,' he says, 'that is cause, active by itself all alone and all the rest only passive, rather', he goes on, 'it is the mutual interaction based upon economic necessity that always realises itself ultimately'[16]. Engels was clearly alerting us to the problem posed by defining the form that a true Socialist novel should take (the difficulty that Soviet film-makers had four decades later when defining a true Socialist film). One candidate for such a criterion was obviously 'truth to reality'; that is, an accurate description of the class basis of society. However, Engels was aware of the difficulties made by this demand for realism (or Socialist realism, as it came to be called when incorporated later into the official cultural programme of the Soviet Union). In a letter to Mrs Kautsky in 1885, Engels advised against an explicitly political approach in favour of allowing the reader to draw his or her own conclusions. He says[16]:

> I think, however, that the solution of the problem must become manifest from the situation and action themselves without being expressly pointed out, and the author is not obliged to serve the reader on a platter the future historic resolution of the social conflicts which he describes.

He suggests that choice has a major part to play in the tendentious nature of literature; a view that Berthold Brecht would later espouse with respect to both film and theatre. However, three years later he expressed a conflicting view to Margaret Harkness when he advocated resource to 'typicality', which later Marxists such as George Lukacs have recommended ever since[17]. Engels states: 'Realism to my mind implies, besides truth of detail, the truthful reproduction of typical characters under typical circumstances.' Thus he gives contradictory views, the first suggesting the role of the audience selecting a meaning from a text and the second suggesting that the text should be 'normative' – that is, representing things as they ought to be. He criticises Margaret Harkness for depicting the working class as a passive mass, whereas the rebellious reaction of the working class against the oppressive medium that surrounds them belongs to history and therefore must lay claim to a place in the domain of realism, he says. Against the background of the Soviet state's desire to use film and the contradictory and Marxist aesthetic to guide the film-maker, there was formed a group of film-makers who saw the potential of film as a means of expressing the Revolution in filmic terms. One of the most important individuals investigating the potential of film as an expressive art was the exponent of montage, Sergei Eisenstein. His interest was not simply the reproduction of the reality he had filmed, but the creation of something new. Eisenstein went beyond the real (and cinema's relation to it). He rejected any view of film that would relegate it to a category of a simple recording agent, believing that the edited film was no more than a mechanical reproduction of reality. At first he viewed the single shot as the basic material of film, then he adopted the complex concept of attraction, which takes into account the activity of the viewer's mind, and not simply the action of the film-maker's will. This he formed into the theory of montage, where the meaning of a film is created by an audience contrasting or comparing two shots – in simple terms, the idea that the juxtaposition of two images on the screen creates a third that is unseen. Eisenstein set out to shock the audience by using montage to tear reality apart and reassemble it in such a way as to guide the ideas of the audience along the lines of propaganda, which gives the viewer the greatest emotional effect. Although his attitude to montage is often seen to be unswerving, Dudley Andrew points out that while Eisenstein seems to have conceived of montage within the psychological model of Pavlov, his later writings on the issue seem much closer to the developmental psychology of Jean Piaget[18]. Once again his simple mechanistic notions were questioned and altered by the more complex and less predictable variant, one that brought a respect for the power of the spectator and for the serious workings of perception and understanding.

While Eisenstein was making world-famous masterpieces using montage to express the truth of the Revolution, other Soviet directors such as Kuleshov and his disciples Theodore Otsep and Boris Barnet were making films by adopting American techniques and conventions to Soviet themes (the Mismen (1926) series being a good example), and it was these films that Soviet audiences wanted to see. Party activists were quick to point out that in the films of the *avant-garde* directors, form often seemed to outweigh content and they were unintelligible to the masses – their point being that if a film was not accessible to the millions, then its claims to realism were suspect. Eisenstein was by no means the only Soviet film-maker thinking that a revolutionary society needed a revolutionary culture that would instil a revolutionary consciousness into the masses. This culture had to find new forms, untainted by a bourgeois past, and Eisenstein felt that the cinema was the ideal vehicle for this. Other artists went further in search of form appropriate to the revolutionary Soviet cinema by denouncing fictional film altogether. Dzidga Vertov wrote[19]:

> From today neither psychological nor detective dramas are needed in the cinema, everything can be included in the new concept of the newsreel film.

He was a leading exponent of the inherent superiority of the documentary and newsreel format, the founder and leading member of the Kino-Eye group. His premise was that film (particularly the film camera) had been captured by the bourgeoisie for their own ideological purposes. The drama film he described as[20]:

> the new opium of the people, like drunkenness, religion or hypnosis. To such stuff and ideas, such and such conceptions, into the subconscious representation of the world and thus engaged in the struggle against the ideology of the visible against the mystification that visual phenomena *per se* reveal the truth of the world.

In his film *Man with a Movie Camera*, Vertov represents a systematic attempt to combat the traditional bourgeois forms of cinematic representation and to expose to the workers the bourgeois structure of the world. The camera, he believed, should not only be the unmediated recorder of reality, but should also transcend and interrogate this way of seeing, so as to reveal the methods by which perception both in the cinema and out of it is socially structured and conditioned. In other words, he wanted to reveal the workings of ideology beneath or behind the immediately visible. Vertov's aims were quite literally revolutionary. Already his anti-realist stance was distinctly at odds with what had become accepted cinematic practice. As he put it, 'Up to today we have coerced the film camera and made it copy the work of our own eyes. From today we are liberating the camera and making it work in the opposite direction, further away from copying.' Kino-Eye was a means of making the invisible visible, the obscure clear, the hidden obvious and the disguised exposed. Vertov wanted it to open the eyes of the people to connections between visual and social phenomena; in other words, Vertov was primarily interested in the cinema as an ideological practice, as a system of representation through which social relations are expressed and understood. So *Man with a Movie Camera* is not so much a film of a day in the life of a city or in the life of a cameraman, but more an examination of the whole process of film production and consumption, from shooting through editing and viewing. It is a film whose subject is cinema itself, and in which cameraman, editor and audience are the main characters. However, the days of the ascendancy of the formalist film-makers in the Soviet Union were coming to an end. The main emphasis of the speakers at the Soviet Writers Congress in 1932 was directed to the establishment of an orthodoxy of realism that was specifically socialist; that is, a realism that rejected all claims of bourgeois societies' literature to represent reality in any legitimate form. 'The literature of dying capitalism has become stunted in ideas. It is unable to portray those mighty forces which are shaking the world. All the styles which were evolved by past bourgeois art, and in which great masterpieces were created, realism, naturalism, romanticism – all this has suffered attrition and disintegration; all this exists only in fragments, and is powerless to produce a single convincing picture.'[21] The term 'Socialist realism' is attributed to the Soviet leader Joseph Stalin, although the theory had been formulated by Maxim Gorky[21]. He contrasted it with the 'critical realism' of nineteeth century literature, which he said only exposed societies' imperfections. Socialist realism he cited as creative; its chief characteristic was the development of people, to help them achieve wealth and love and life and turn the earth, in its entirety, into the magnificent dwelling place of mankind united in one big family (the socialist utopia)[22]:

> Socialist realism means not only knowing reality as it is, but knowing whither it is moving towards the victory of the international proletariat. And a work of art created by a socialist realist is one which shows whither that conflict of contradictions is leading which the artist has seen in life and reflected in his work.

That 'reality' was the supremacy of the masses and the victory of Communism. The formalist realism of the *avant-garde* film-makers did not match the requirements of this regime. Soviet Socialist realism was not narrow and not a style. Tragedy was acceptable, and even the fairytale might fit so long as the general tenor was true to human nature and society; it was not pessimistic, but helped to strengthen confidence and hope for the future.

Eisenstein's experiment-laden *Battleship Potemkin* (1925) suited the definition just as well as the seminal 'realist' film *Chapayev* (1934). However, later the battle between socialist realism and formalism became bitter, with the terms being used as weapons. Soviet Socialist realism was an accolade without argument; formalism became the ultimate sin. Actually, of course, realism is no synonym for 'naturalism', and formalism 'does not mean "experiment in form" – a sense in which it was often far too casually employed – but a distortion of reality for the sake of formal experiment'[23]. Although *Chapayev* fits clearly into the principle of Socialist realism, there was never any conflict between the theoretical school and those who liked the film. The Vasilievs (who directed *Chapayev*) were actually favoured pupils of Einsenstein, who went out of his way to praise the film, greeting it as heralding a third period in Soviet film history, synthesising the mass film of the first period with the individual, naturalist stage of the second (or sound) period. The later somewhat sinister political ideology of Soviet socialist realism was expressed by Stalin when he defined writers as 'engineers of the human soul'. The concept of socialist realism degenerated into a method of standardising Soviet art[24]:

> Novels and cinema followed psychologically realist models, dealing principally with political (Stalinist) education of heroes, and idealist contemporary conditions. In so fictional orientated a cultural ethos, documentary was relegated to a purely utilitarian status.

Much of the subsequent work produced under the standard of socialist realism took the form of revolutionary romanticism. These films relied on the concept of typicality, described by Engels and taken up by the Hungarian critic George Lukacs – the role of the typical character, be it the masses in Eisenstein's *Battleship Potemkin*, which had already made the crowd a central agent in the film's action, or the individual as in *Chapeyev* (the Soviet-socialist realist film of 1934):

> ... is not that of the average person to whom things happen ... but who have a representative function in the narrative which contributes to the reader–spectator's understanding of the development of social and class forces in the historical moment being presented.

The difference between the Soviet view of typicality and Lukacs' is that he argues that 'these typical figures are only effective if presented as individuals in their own right'[25]. Lukacs fell foul of the orthodox Soviet view by proposing that some nineteenth century bourgeois literature writers, such as Scott, Zola, Balzac and even Dickens, demonstrated an ideology of social realism by highlighting the current historical social debate. This concept of 'critical realism' influenced the development of realism in the West in as much as it moved directors such as Jean Renoir to focus on the relationship between the individual characters and the environment in which they operate. Renoir used a mobile camera and the development of long-take, deep-focus photography; a cinematic style that encouraged what André Bazin described as 'the visual apprehension of the world of physical reality'[26]. Lukacs' criticism of the use of typicality was particularly aimed at the works of Willi Bredel and Ernst Ottwalt, who was a close collaborator and associate of Bertolt Brecht. The root of this criticism was Lukacs' setting out of the:

> ... main categories and principles of the doctrine of literary criticism ... the reiterated antithesis between naturalism and realism, the notion of

the typical character as a nexus of the social and individual, the rejection of both external reportage and internal psychologism, the distinction between passive description and active narrative.

Those modern artists who ignored or contravened these regulative norms of literary creation were insistently pilloried for 'formalism' by Lukacs. Brecht responded by accusing Lukacs himself of formalism, stating[25]:

> The formalistic nature of the (Lukacs) theory of realism is demonstrated by the fact that not only is it exclusively based on the form of a few bourgeois novels of the previous century ... but also exclusively on the particular genre of the novel.

True realism for Brecht was a political and philosophical vision, not only an aesthetic one; for him it meant[25]:

> Discovering the casual complexes of society/unmasking the prevailing view of things as the view of those who rule it, writing from the standpoint of the class which offers the broadest solutions for the pressing difficulties in which human society is caught, emphasizing the element of development/making possible the concrete, and making possible abstraction from it.

Brecht's political view demands that the drama should offer more questions than answers and that the audience should be confronted with a situation with which they can and should react. Apart from *Whither Germany* (1932), Brecht felt that the films with which he was associated betrayed his aesthetic; however, his influence on European directors such as Jean-Luc Goddard and Jean-Marie Straub has been profound. Goddard's work in particular demonstrates[27]:

> ... a superbly Brechtian evolution; i.e. a refusal of doctrine, the insistence on questions rather than answers. And this questioning concerns both the nature of the aesthetic artefact (what is film? what is theatre?) and the nature of its relationship to society and social issues.

For Goddard, the realism of the formal conflict and struggle is taken up not by the content of images but between the different codes and between the signifier and signified. It is the apparent impression of necessity in bourgeois communication; the binding of a signifier to signified that in Goddard's view provides a convincing representation of the world. He not only wants to create an alternative world or worldview, 'but to investigate the whole of signification out of which a worldview or an ideology is constructed'.

Goddard's early films were intended to create this new kind of meaning and, in common with the films of the early Russian *avant-garde* directors, did not find mass audiences. His first complete film after the suppression of the struggles of 1968, *Tout Va Bien* (1972), abandoned 'avant-gardism for a stylized didacticism, set within a classical realist frame'; echoing the position of radical authors following the revolutions of 1848. Most of the attempts to express a realist aesthetic that have been described from a Marxist perspective largely ignore the commercial constraints of film-making, making a profit. In André Bazin's seminal work *Qu'est-ce que le Cinema?* he takes Hollywood films (commercial capitalist texts), specifically the work of William Wyler, and demonstrates[26]:

> To produce the truth, to show reality, all the reality, nothing but reality is perhaps an honourable intention, but stated in that way, it is no more than a moral precept. In the cinema there can only be a representation of reality.

In the early stages of this piece of work it was stated that Marx himself does not have anything specific to say about the nature of realism in literature (or any art form). It appears correct to propose that all the approaches described here have value, in so much as they have experimented with the concept of realism in conjunction with a world ideology. Films are produced and consumed in particular social conditions, and the methods by which realism is portrayed at any time, in varying conditions, will change, and the changes will be relative. Bazin puts it thus[26]:

> The realist tendency has existed in the cinema since Louis Lumber and since Marey and Muybridge. It has been through many mutations, but the forms in which it has appeared have survived only in proportion to the amount of aesthetic invention (or discovery) — conscious or not, calculated or innocent — involved. There is not one, but several realisms. Each era looks for its own, that is to say the technique and the aesthetic which can best capture it.

6.6 Modernism and the *avant-garde* in film

In 1935, Walter Benjamin, in his article 'The work of art in the age of mechanical reproduction', pointed to a new meaning in art. He proposed a Marxist view of production, and suggested that his thesis brush aside a number of outmoded concepts, such as creativity and genius, external value, eternal value and mystery concepts, whose uncontrolled application would lead to a processing of data in the fascist sense. He explains that reproducibility of art has always existed, but mechanical reproduction is relatively new. Printing, he states, is a special case. Engraving and etching led to lithography in the nineteenth century, and lithography enabled the illustration of daily life. This in turn foreshadowed photography, which in its time preceded the movie film. He pointed out that by 1900 technical reproduction had reached a standard that allowed all transmitted works of art to be reproduced and to find a place among the artistic processes. It is the elements of the authentic that he describes in these terms. It is unique to a time and place. It is determined by its history; for example, the changes it has suffered and its various owners. Changes can be revealed by physical or chemical analysis, and this of course is not possible on a reproduction. Finally, ownership is subject to a tradition that must be traced from the situation of the original. For Benjamin, authenticity is outside the sphere of technical reproduction. Value reproduction is usually called forgery. Confronted by forgery, the original retained all its authority; this was not so vis-à-vis technical reproduction. Technical reproduction is more independent of the original than the manual reproduction (the forgery), and is therefore more open to manipulation that will express or expose more of the original. Photography is a good example of this. Reproduction enables the original to meet the beholder half way. Benjamin says: 'The cathedral leaves its locale to be received in the studio of the art lover'[28].

The act of reproduction deprecates the quality of the presence of a work of art. The authenticity of a thing is the essence of all that is transmittable from its beginning, ranging from its substantive duration to its testimony to a history that it has experienced. He says the eliminated element in a reproduction is the work's aura. Reproduction separates the copy from the domain of tradition, and this shattering of tradition is the result of permitting the reproduction to meet the beholder or listener in his or her own situation. This process is intimately connected with contemporary mass movements. Film is the most potent non-oral art, and its social significance is inconceivable without its destructive, cathartic (purging) aspect; that is, the liquidation of the traditional value of the cultural heritage.

It is in the concept of reproduction that current debates are being carried on by cultural critics and philosophers with special reference to electronic image-making, Simulacra and the development of hyper-reality, which tends towards production of pastiche nostalgia, often criticised as being phoney or ersatz.

The practice of cinema began in the 1890s, and there were a number of converging reasons why intellectuals took note. It was a time when decadent poets were fascinated by music hall and low life, painters loved to find subjects in cabarets and circuses, and left-wing thinkers were beginning to take a serious interest in the entertainment of the people. Cinema at the outset evidently belonged very much to that world. In the years following the First World War, there was a period of rejection of both the critical and cultural values of the pre-war world. In Europe, those artists working at the forefront for a radical change in art, literature and film were the *avant-gardes*. The relationship between these artists and the society in which they operated, the work they produced and the ideological and aesthetic attitudes they held, is the basis for this section, which more specifically investigates the claims made that *avant-garde* film reflects and embodies the modernist impulse. The three forces of the modern movement – modernism, the condition of modernity and cultural modernism – are reflected in the definitions used here to explain the concept of modernism and the relationship it has with art, film and society. These definitions are change and progress, experimentation, closing the gap between high and mass culture, and commodification–massification. There are views of modernism that focus on the changes in mass society, urbanisation and technology that took place in the nineteenth century and were to be the major factors during the first three-quarters of the twentieth century.

From the beginning of popular cinema, intellectuals were intrigued by the significance and content of the films of Chaplin, tracing and spelling out his connections with the theatrical traditions of the Commedia del Arte and taking pleasure in his anarchic spirit. 'The first Chaplin films demonstrated the mechanical style. With this mechanical style he has invented a mode of expression appropriate to the technological form of the cinema'[29]. The anarchy of Chaplin's films has much in common with the disruption from which emerged the *avant-garde* art of Dada, which used shock effects; early Surrealism, with its emphasis on the irrational and unconscious; and the futurists, whose belief in being modern for its own sake involved an obvious interest in and sympathy for the most modern form of artistic communication that existed at the time – film. Film also had the added attraction for the futurists (who wished to worship 'the machine') of being machine-made. The characteristics of *avant-garde* film are best seen in its relationship to the qualities of the mainstream (or what we might call dominant) cinema. The style of mainstream film is dependent upon realism and narrative. The relationship between realism and narrative in mainstream cinema signifies its social and political implications. Narrative is relative to realism; the realism of the image proposing an unmediated continuity between the real image and the spectator is what fixes the spectator in a position of specula control through recognition of the film image[30]:

> Narrative similarly is a further tendency in which the text which by assimilating and subordinating other tendencies and discourses for instance through the typical narrativisation of spatial and temporal co-ordinates, offers itself as a vantage point from which the text may be recognised, controlled and understood. Narrativity and realism then play an ideological role in placing films and their spectators, spectators and their films, in relativity to each other.

Mainstream cinema induces a hegemonic acceptance of the ideology of the dominant culture, whereas *avant-garde* film was produced outside the dominant system of production and exploitation, and therefore did not fill the same film/spectator function. It established its own economic and social determinates; economically outside the commercial context, it offered a radical, social alternative to the monolithic integration of production–exhibition–distribution systems. This freedom offered an opposition to the classic realist text by its application of a wider and more disparate set of styles. The relative autonomy of the artist did not only extend to subject matter, but also to methods used to produce images themselves. This led to the classic modernist debate of form over the content and the social nature of film practice.

The *avant-garde* film-makers in post-war France were led by the film's first aesthetic theorist, Louis Delluc. Delluc rejected all previous French cinema tradition except perhaps Lumière and Linder (Melies was almost completely forgotten at the time). In particular, he abhorred the practice of adaptation, which had been predominant in French cinema since the heyday of Film de Arte. Delluc worked entirely within the commercial cinema, making very straightforward story films, such as *La Femme de Nulle Part* (1922) which were notable for their lack of elaboration and their concentration on purely visual storytelling. The group of enthusiastic film-makers who Delluc gathered around him acquired the title 'impressionists', because many of the films they produced sought pictorial effects similar to those of the impressionist painters of the preceding century. Delluc died in 1924, and to some extent his ideas were carried on in the narrative-based films of Abel Gance, Jean Epstein and Marcel L. Herbier, although Gance and Herbier were already mainstream directors. Gance's epic film *Napoleon* (1925–1927), although of dubious historical value, was revolutionary in its use of techniques. He gave the camera a mobility and freedom it had not known before. He used dozens of cameras, put many of them on automatic stands, mounted others on special elevators, and used numerous new camera techniques. Above all, Gance used images to shatter the senses of the audience. The editing was rapid, many shots lasting only a frame or two. He used superimposition, multiple images and a system in which three images were projected side by side on a giant panoramic screen. Sometimes these images would be different and complimentary in their imagery, and sometimes they would be linked together into one vast panorama. He introduced hand-held cameras at a time when cameras were almost too heavy to lift. It was over a quarter of a century before such freedom was used in film-making. There were, however, film-makers and artists who had become interested in film and wanted to free themselves from the traditional narrative modes altogether. One way of doing this was through abstraction, and in 1924 the French *avant-garde* produced an important example, *Ballet Mechanique*, a collaboration between the French cubist painter Barnard Leger, Fernand and American modernist artist Dudley Murphy, which consists of a series of photographic images that are distorted, double-exposed and intercut to create an abstract effect. Like Leger's paintings, the film celebrates geometric form and mechanical motion. As Richter puts it[29]:

> The *avant-garde* emerged gradually by the extension of problems posed in the fine arts. How to present rhythmic processes, not just in space and on a flat surface but also in time. These problems led to film. Their proponents had in common the attempt to create a pure language of cinema, to free the cinema from the chains it had been in since Melies' production, by the rhythm of sequences of images, to create a film poetry with all the meaning provided by the transportation of objective reality by the camera.

The impressionist movement is often called the 'first *avant-garde*' to distinguish it from the 'second *avant-garde*', which grew out of cinema's contact with the literary and artistic *avant-gardes* of the 1920s. Deriving from the cubist and futurist movements, and taking in Dada and surrealism, futurism took issue with the form and function of film, and in the 1916 manifesto *The Futurist Cinema* we find an expression of the futurist vision of film[31,32]:

> At first look the film born only a few years ago may seem to be futurist already, lacking a past and free from tradition. Actually by appearing in the guise of theatre without words it has inherited all the most traditional sweepings of literary theatre.

Consequently, everything we had said and done about the stage applies to the cinema. The cinema is an autonomous art, the cinema must above all fulfil the evolution of painting, detach itself from reality, from photography, from the graceful and solemn; it must become anti-graceful, deforming, impressionistic, synthetic, dynamic, free-working. *One must free cinema as an expressive medium in order to make it the ideal instrument of new art, immensely vaster and lighter than all the existing arts. We are convinced that only in this way can one reach that poly-expressiveness towards which all the most modern artistic researchers are moving.*

The earliest attempts of the *avant-garde* to involve themselves in film production were limited by financial constraints. The futurist films, made around 1910, showed an interest in cinematic and quasi-cinematic processes, such as stop motion, which owed much to the analytical, photographic work of Eadweard Muybridge and Etienne Marey in the nineteenth century. Other modern artists saw the possibilities of a mobile painting produced on a cinema screen. About the same time the Russian-born painter Leopold Survage made a series of colour slides in sequence for a proposed abstract film, although the problems of colour cinematography at the time put an end to his experiments. 'Futurist cinema would emerge as an expressive medium most adapted to the complex sensibility of a futurist artist'[32]. Most of the futurist films have been lost, leaving only contemporary documents and photographic stills from which to draw any conclusions. What is clear is that the Russian and Italian futurists were not following the abstract direction, but making films of eccentric *ballesque* similar to the then popular *grand guignol* cinema. The accumulative process of futurism, gathering all that was new and dynamic to itself, had to be seen to be at work.

The definition of futurist cinema is the sum total of all the events to date, painting plus sculpture plus plastic dynamism plus words, freedom plus composed noises, plus architecture, plus synthetic theatre, plus futurist cinema.

In Russia, just as the political authorities had recognised the propaganda potential of the silent film, so a new generation of artists proclaimed the cinema as a medium of artistic expression. As the new art form for a new time, initially the political view merged with the artistic. However, the political requirement of a medium of mass communication began to conflict with the need for artistic experiment, so the *avant-garde* soon lost the support of the powers that be. Vladimir Mayakovsky, in the midst of the Revolution, found time to write and act in three films alongside other members of the futurist group, but the political tide was turning against *avant-garde* film. In subsequent years most artists turned to the theatre rather than the cinema, yet from the modernist, constructivist Soviet theatre in the early 1920s emerged Sergi Eisenstein. He made his first film, *Stachka*, in 1924, bringing together the two streams of early Soviet cinema (the newsreels of Dziga Vertov and the story film of Lev Kuleshov) into a dynamic personal creation. Vertov, in his documentary films, was one of the first to undertake to structure the accidental rhythms of the shots and to form them artistically, and as a result he bequeathed to the cinema a musically based unity. In the fictional montage film, this style led to the musical arrangement of pictorial expression that we admire in the furiously working machines of *Battleship Potemkin*.

As a specific modern artistic movement, German expressionism roughly spanned the years 1914–1924, firstly in poetry and painting and later in film and cinema. In fact, the film generally considered to be the first example of German expressionism, *The Cabinet of Dr Caligari*, did not appear until 1919, towards the tail end of the movement, and an audience today may find this film flat and two-dimensional. However, its decor does reveal a good deal about the role of set designs in German expressionist cinema; they became means of expression, reflecting and evoking the characters' states of mind and helping to create the film's evocative feelings. Seigfried Kracauer points out that in *The Cabinet of Dr Caligari*, the settings amounted to a perfect transformation of material objects into emotional ornaments – oblique chimneys of pell-mell roofs, its windows in the form of arrows or kites, and its tree-like arabesques that were threats rather than trees[33]. Hans Janowitz and Karl Mayer intended their story to be a modern pacifist parable, with Cesare as a symbol of the people and *Caligari* as the state, seemingly benign and respected but in fact ordering the people to kill (in wars). The meaning of the ending (in which *Caligari* is unmasked and overthrown) is clearly anti-authoritarian, but when the film was finally completed the director, Robert Weine, had added a framing device to the script (a prologue and an epilogue), making the story told by a madman. The result was to completely reverse the original meaning of the story by robbing it of its subversive intent. Kracauer also suggests that the theory of the German cinema directly reflected the mentality of the German people in foreshadowing the rise of the Nazis; in particular, he saw *Caligari* as the first of a series of power-crazed tyrants in German film to whom the other characters in the situation submitted without question. He said[34]:

> Caligari is a very specific premonition in the sense that he uses hypnotic power to force his will upon his tool (Cesare), a technique

foreshadowing in content and purpose that manipulation of the soul which Hitler was the first to practice on a gigantic scale.

This view is considered too precise and mechanistic. The fact is that *The Cabinet of Dr Caligari* is an expressionist film, and to what extent it fits the remit of expressionism is debatable. The work of expressionist painters before the First World War was characterised by subjectivism, emotionalism and anti-naturalism. In literature, the main expressionist themes were alienation, anti-authoritarianism, pacifism, salvation through love, and hostility to bourgeois society. Some of these factors were present in the original script, but the framing device negated them. The visual style of the settings designed by the expressionist artists Herman Warm, Walter Reimann and Walter Rohrig, enhanced by the style of acting of Werner Krauss (who played the maligned Caligari) and Conrad Velts' somnambulist, a slender, hollow-eyed, ashen-faced living corpse, are the major factors in making *The Cabinet of Dr Caligari* one of the few totally expressionist films. Whatever else it was, it was a horror film drawing on the themes of death, tyranny, fate, disorder and ghosts, mummies, vampires and somnambulists associated with German romanticism stretching back to the folklorists, the Brothers Grimm and the dramatist poet Schiller.

The influence of expressionism film on mainstream film has been significant, although to call all films which use a marked visual or theatrical style expressionist is to lessen the meaning of the term. In France, the impressionists were coming under increasing attack because their aesthetic was tending towards purism and away from the debate with narrative cinema, which was the genus of the *avant-garde* cinema. The American photographer, Mann Ray, a central figure of Dada, presented his first film to the Coeur A Barbe (the last major Dada event in 1923). The film, *La Retour à la Raison*, was reputed to be the product of one night's work, and consisted of a series of Rayograms (cameraless photographic images) mixed with unrelated camera footage. Between Ray's first and second films, André Breton and many other Dadaists (including Ray) adopted the concept of surrealism. It was at this point that the first Dada cinema gave way to the second, in which the traditional elements of representation and narrative became the subject of Dada subversion and, as Mann Ray put it, the aim was deliberately to try the patience of the audience. Dada had already made some impact on the cinema in Germany through the work of Viking Eggeling, continued by Hans Richter, Walter Ruttman and Oskar Fishinger. Of the four, only Fishinger had not been a painter before turning to film-making; the other three were already deeply committed to abstract art. As early as 1918, Viking, Eggeling and Hans Richter had started painting abstract images which assumed quasi-cinematic form and led to their trying to work in film, initially in an animation studio provided by the UFA Company in 1920. The collaboration between Eggeling and Richter broke up, but each continued to work on his own abstract cinema, Eggeling completing one film before his death in 1925 (the rigorously abstract *Diagonal Symphonie*, which concerned the play of ever-changing forms in front of the camera). Richter made several short films of this kind, such as *Rhythmus 21* (1921), *Rhythmus 23* (1923) and *Rhythmus 25* (1925), before becoming involved with the French surrealists. The surrealist movement was opposed to the *avant-gardes*, who they thought supported bourgeois art with its purist aesthetics. In the case of cinema they instinctively attacked the impressionist *avant-garde*, and in opposition devised an alternative pantheon, including maverick Hollywoods (Stroheim), popular French cinema (Fuillades), crazy comedy (Keaton) and, in 1928, the start of specifically surrealist cinema with Un Chien Andalou. The first effect of the surrealist counter-*avant-garde* was anti-modernist, in favour of a neo-romanticism movement. There was a political and psychoanalytical perspective to surrealism, a desire to redefine the spectrum of activities that it should address. It constructed its own *avant-garde* cinema, reflecting subversion, rupture and the dysfunction of dominant narrative cinema. Walter Benjamin states[35]:

> Since Bakin, Europe has lacked a radical concept of freedom. The surrealists have won; they are the first to liquidate the sclerotic liberal–moral–humanistic idea of freedom. Because they are convinced that freedom that on this earth can only be bought with a thousand of the hardest sacrifices must be enjoyed unrestrictedly in its fullness without any kind of pragmatic calculation as long as it lasts.

For a surrealist, the only cause worth fighting for is liberation in its simplest revolutionary form. The 1920s were obviously great days of the cinema's flirtation with modernism. It is arguable that current ideas of the experimental in all the arts are rooted in that period. A current experimental novel is likely to resemble one of the twenties. Experimental art of today is likely to go further than the wider aspects of Dadaism, and contemporary experimental film seems to persist in restating the past. The significance of the *avant-garde* art movements of the 1920s and 1930s was to shake the perfection of bourgeois art. Cinema had developed under different conditions to that of the other arts. Historically speaking, the cinema is an instrument for the spiritual and artistic development of the people: 'it is above all the history of masses in their artistic development'. The accessibility of film makes everyone an expert. As Walter Benjamin puts it[28]:

Mechanical reproduction of art changes the reaction of the masses towards art. The reactionary attitude towards a Picasso painting changes into a progressive reaction to a Chaplin movie.

In the case of the early abstract films, such as Richter's *Rhythmus 21* and Deslav's *La Marche des Machines*, they use shots which picture reality of another dimension in such a manner that the real objects they represent change into abstract patterns. The question is whether such works should be considered cinema at all. As Kracauer puts it[36]:

Many animated cartoons are outside the concept of the photographic film and in the case of most the intention of their creators was not the use of film as a photographic medium but as a means of setting imaginative designs, preferably non-objective ones, in motion. On the whole these films are not intended as films; rather they are intended as an extension of contemporary art into the dimension of movement and time.

He suggests that films like *Ballet Mechanique*, with its cubist references, comes straight out of Lagalle's canvasses, and should be looked upon as a new branch of the established arts. The abstract or fantasy film survived more or less at the periphery of the mainstream narrative cinema, in an attempt to set cinematographic technology against the naturalistic theatricality of the fiction film. The objectives of the *avant-garde* included revolution in the stagnant form of cinema, freeing it from tradition and furthering its development. The extent to which the *avant-garde's* using abstraction had fulfilled these objectives is debatable; however, their contribution to the spirit of modernity is considerable. The central issue with the first *avant-garde* film-makers was the contradiction between cinema as industry and as an art form. With the growing sophistication of Hollywood and the birth of Swedish naturalism and German expressionism, the choice was between trying to work to promote the aesthetic qualities of the commercial cinema or establishing an *avant-garde* enclave. The artists who took the second option soon found themselves marginalised rather than independent, and the marginalisation either meant incorporation or reduction of operation. The outcome was the economic and aesthetic decline of the first *avant-garde*. In terms of modernity, the first *avant-garde* film-makers offered a somewhat ambiguous perspective; on the one hand the impulse for change and progress was profound, but change and progress in what? One has to look hard to see the results of the *avant-garde* abstract film upon mainstream film production, either at the time or later. However, the experiment had considerable influence on other artists, such as those involved in the Bauhaus, although the modern impulses of closing the gap between high and mass culture and commodification and massification seemed to be the antithesis of the intentions or results of the work of the early *avant-gardists*. In his influential essay *The Two Avant-gardes*, Peter Wollen poses the concept of there being two broad tendencies in the evolution of the *avant-garde*. On one side were those who worked within the plastics or fine arts; these, he suggests, followed the formalist path, and include the classic *avant-garde* of Le Jeur, Eggeling and Brakage[37]. The main concerns of this group were the formal issues within the arts. On the other side were a smaller group, whose work attempted a critique of the dominant modes of experiments with not only the formal properties of film but also film understood as a mediator of social and political concerns. These were made up of analytical *avant-garde* film-makers such as Vertov, Eisenstein and, later, Goddard and Straub, whose references take in aesthetics but through the filter of notions of the social and political. The two groupings can be further divided into sub-groups; the significance of this approach is to create a tool that can be used to reassess the claims of modernism in the films of the *avant-garde*. Some of the differences between the two groups were largely due to their backgrounds; the first group came from painting, the second group from theatre (Eisenstein) and futurist sound poetry (Vertov). Wollen states[37]:

> Painting, I think it can be argued, played the leading role in the development of modernism in the other arts. The innovations of Picasso and Braque were seen as having an implication beyond the history of painting itself. They were intuitively felt, I think, very early on to represent a critical semiotic shift, a changed concept and practice of sign and signification.

It is this philosophy that the painter film-makers brought to their use of cinema and that led to the production of work which, although of significant value in the history of the development of a modernist theme in film theory, has had little effect on the development of a modernist perspective in mainstream cinema. The impact of *avant-garde* ideas from the world of visual art has ended up pushing film-makers into a position of extreme purism or essentialism. Ironically anti-illusionist and anti-realist, it has ended up with many preoccupations in common with its worst enemies. André Bazin argued that the ontology and essence of film was its photographic reproduction of the natural world. This, Wollen explains, offers two perspectives from which to approach film – an extroverted and an introverted ontology of film, one seeking the soul of cinema in the nature of the pro-filmic event, and the other in the nature of the cinematic process, the cone of light or the grain of silver. The Wollen approach to the *avant-garde* film is useful because it enables the movement to be considered as separate influences upon the course of modernism, in the first place in an attempted displacement of the hegemonic, fictional models by a broader and more fragmented set of types and genres. This fragmentation leads to a blurring of the parameters between film and the other arts. Secondly, it allows the group to be researched not only from the modernist preoccupation with new subject matter but also with the processes and apparatus of sign production, which lead to the classic *avant-garde* controversies in modernism over form and content. Thirdly, the social practice of film practices must be considered. Since the period of the *avant-gardes* the breach between film and experimentation has become increasingly wider, with transitions from the experimental fringe to commercial success being regarded as betrayal. Thus, when Fritz Lang's *Metropolis* (1927) – which developed modernist themes such as the city, the machine and the problem of capital versus labour – received critical acclaim in both Europe and the USA, its *avant-garde* credentials were questioned. But the irony is that while much of the mainstream film has kept pace and remains a true expression of many of the aspects of modernism, the experimenters seem ever more lost in a time warp, looking back to the 'good old days' when *avant-garde* film was potentially a significant force in modernism.

6.7 The age of fragmentation

In 1986, Jean-Francois Lyotard described post-modernism in terms of the universalists' ideas of progress and rationality. He also produced a defence of the *avant-garde*, and proposed an historical reading of the term 'post' in post-modernism. He suggested that we live in a post-modern era that has three separate strands; that the ideas of progress, science and rational thought, which had for 300 years given credence to a western modernity, were no longer applicable[38]. His main reason was that they took little or no account of otherness and its cultural differences. There was, he said, no confidence that high or *avant-garde* art or culture had any more value than popular or low culture. He also concluded that the possibility of separating the real from the copy or the natural from the artificial in a situation where the technologies used to produce and reproduce information have so much reach and control is limited. His argument of the opposition between post-modernism and modernism uses a basis of architectural theory that points to the fragmentation of the various sources which architects draw on to fulfil their roles. This fragmentation, or bricolage, uses quotations from previous styles and periods, classical or modern. This bricolage, Lyotard suggests, condemns post-modern architecture to generate a multiplicity of small transformations in the space it inherits and to give up the project of the last rebuilding of the whole space occupied by humanity. He contends that the universal is no longer applicable to modern culture. There is, he says, no longer a horizon of universalisation.

Against this, Lyotard proposes an objection to the historical understanding of 'post' in post-modernism. He points out that 'post' in the term post-modernism is to be understood as a simple succession, a diochrony of periods, all of which are distinct and identifiable. He suggests that this way of looking at progress intimates that there is a conversion in history, and that it succeeds in producing a new direction after a previous one. This concept, he points out, is modern, and belongs to Christianity, Carthesianism and Jacobinism[39].

The concept of modernity is closely related to this principle – that it is possible and necessary to break with one tradition in order to begin a new way of living and thinking. He suggests that we can presume that this breaking is rather a matter of forgetting or repressing the past. We do not overcome the past, but rather we repeat it.

However, it is mainly in his questioning of the idea of progress that Lyotard begins to uncover a theory for post-modernism. He states that the idea of progress as possible, probable or necessary had its beginnings in the belief that progress in the arts and science, knowledge and freedom would be profitable to mankind as a whole. However, he points out that after two centuries we are more aware of the opposite; neither economic nor political liberalism nor the various Marxisms emerged from the sanguinary of the last two centuries free from the suspicion of crimes against mankind. The development of techno-science has become a means of increasing disease, not fighting it. He says this form of development can no longer be called by the old name of progress; it is not a response to the demands and needs coming from human beings but quite the opposite, and humanity (individual or social) seems always to be discomforted by the results of this development.

He points to Theodore Adorno, who cited Auschwitz in his example of the use of science to subject mankind to horror. Mankind is divided into two parts; in the first world he is confronted with the complexities of modernity, and in the other (the third world) it is the terrible task of survival that is the primary factor. This, he suggests, is a negation of the modern project[39].

In his book *The Coming of the Post-Industrial Society*[40], Daniel Bell posits that society can be divided into three parts; the social structure, the polity and the culture. The economical, technological and occupational system comprises the social structure. The conflicting demands and claims of the individual and group, which regulate the distribution of power, is signified by the polity. The realm of expressive symbolism and meanings is represented in the culture. Social structure operates economically, which is a way whereby the resources can be allocated according to such factors as the cost, substitutability, optimisation, maximisation and participation, some- times mobilised or controlled. Self-fulfilment, a desire, is recognised in culture.

Bell suggests that post-industrialism deals mainly with the social structure and its changes – the changes in the economy and in the area of occupation. It also operates in the relations between theory and empiricism, particularly science and technology; the management problems posed by changes in social structure for the political system means that society is increasingly conscious of its future and necessarily seeks to control its own fate. The political order becomes the prime mover; with the increasing importance of the post-industrial society, the components of knowledge and technology force what Bell calls the 'hierophants' of the new society (the scientists, engineers and technocrats) to either compete with politicians or become their allies.

Culture is challenged by the primacy of cognitive and theoretical knowledge. Bell draws attention to five specific dimensions of the post-industrial society. In the first, he suggests that the change from a goods producing to a service economy and the change in the mixture of the three economic sectors – the primary = agriculture, the secondary = manufacturing or industrial and the tertiary = services – are grouped within the economic sector.

The growing importance of the professional and technical class he groups in the occupational distribution sector. Centrality of theoretical knowledge, in that post-industrial society is organised around knowledge for the purpose of social control and the organisation of innovation and change, he calls the axial principle. The decline of the industrial worker relative to the non- production worker in the factory (that is, the control of technology and technological assessment) he lists under future orientation. Intellectual technology, which he describes as the decline of inherited power and the rise of the manager, meant that power passed into the hands of a technical intellectual elite, including corporate managers, and this he groups under the heading of decision-making.

The main significance of the post-industrial society is the strengthening of the role of the cognitive and scientific values as basic institutional necessities of our society; the bringing of decisions into the technical and scientific area gives the scientist or economist more direct access to political power. By increasing the existing tendencies towards the bureaucratisation of intellectual work, he says it creates a set of strains for the traditional definitions of intellectual pursuits and values. It also creates a dichotomy between the technical and literary intellectual, the technical intellectual achieving the power and influence that the literary had in the past. He says that post-industrialism brings into question issues such as the distribution of wealth, power and status that are central to any society. The changes he attributes to the seeking of these values are that they are no longer dimensions of class, but have become values sought and gained by classes. There is no continuity of power; power drifts and changes depending upon two major axes of stratification – property and knowledge. The political system that is reflected in post-modernity manages the two and gives rise to elites, which are temporary in that there is no necessary continuity of power. As Bell says, there is no continuity of the family or class through property and the differential advantage of belonging to a meritocracy.

How do the products of the mass media industry reflect the changes in society broadly described with the term 'post-modernism'? Norman Denzin takes the film *Blue Velvet* and suggests that it can be read as a cultural statement that locates within the small American town all the terrors and simulated realities that Lyotard and Baudrillard see operating in the late post-modern period. He suggests that the film offers clarification of the sociological, aesthetic and cultural meanings that the term post-modernity describes. It is the two features of Jameson's perspective of post-modernity that Denzin describes; the effacement of the boundaries between the past and the present, signified in the forms of pastiche and parody, and the concept of the treatment of time, which locates the viewing subject in the perpetual present. He says that it is these films that describe a post-modern nostalgia, bringing the unpresentable in front of the viewer in ways that challenge the boundaries that separate private and public life – the sexual violence, the brutality, the insanity, homosexuality, the degradation of women, the sadomasochistic rituals and the drug and the alcohol abuse he cites as subjects being brought to the forefront in these films. He points out that the late post-modern period is all at once fearful and drawn to the concepts and ideas of sexuality and violence that these films represent, and the forms of freedom and self-expression demonstrated and presented in them. Gender stratification is decidedly pre-modern, with the denigration of women and the signifying of women within two categories – those of the respectable middle-class marriage or the disreputable occupational and sexual categories. In *Blue Velvet* the women are treated as traditional sexual objects and recipients of sexual and physical violence. These films do not simply reflect an attitude of nostalgia; they bring the past into the present. Denzin, quoting from Jameson, suggests that they 'make the past the present, but they locate terror in nostalgia for the past'[39].

In these films, signifiers of the past (such as 1950s and 1970s rock music, the signs of destruction in a Lyotard sense) mean that these films wage war on nostalgia. They signify two types of nostalgia; the safe and the unsafe. In the first place they create a comfortable illusion of adult middle-class life, which is connected to the past in an unbroken chain. These films take rock and roll, the music of youth, and suggest that if it is carried into adulthood then it leads to self-destruction and violence. By projecting two versions of the past (the one sacred and the other profane) into the present, the film *Blue Velvet* extends the boundaries of now further into the future, where the unreal and hyper-real are always real and not possibilities.

These films bring the margins of society into the centre of a safe, middle-class world. The dope fiends and sex perverts portrayed represent the violent margins; they are now placed in small towns next door to middle- or lower-class Americans who are attempting to live safe, respectable lives. Denzin suggests that films like *Blue Velvet* echo and reproduce the tensions and contradictions that defined the late 1980s. These texts locate strange, multifaceted, violent, timeless worlds in the present; they make fun of the past and they keep it alive. Their main function is to present new ways of presenting the unpresentable, so as to break down the boundaries that keep the profane out of the everyday. They take conservative stances, while they appear to exploit the radical social margins of society; with the post-modern eye they look fearfully into the future and observe the technology, uncontrolled sexual violence and universally corrupt political systems. Presented with this world they attempt to find safe regions of escape in the form of nostalgia and fantasies of the past. The small town in the USA is no longer safe in these films; the fantasies of the past have become the realities of the present.

These films make the global village even smaller; they present a landscape populated by people filled with hope who in their schizophrenic attitude know that in the end everything will turn out all right, the villains die or are reformed, male heroes transgress moral boundaries but come back home to mother and father, etc. In the end these films are about individuals and their fantasies, and by portraying individuals they keep alive the middle-class myth of the individual; the post-modern person still confronts the world through the lens of nineteenth and early twentieth century political ideology. This appears to be the chief function of these 1980s nostalgia films, for it seems that as the world political systems turn ever more violent and conservative, the need for textural texts that sustain conservative political economy increases. As Denzin says[39], 'it seems that post modern individuals want films like *Blue Velvet* for in them they can have their sex, their myths, their violence and their politics all at the same time'.

6.8 References

1. Charters, W. W. (1966). *Motion Pictures and Youth*. Reprinted in: *The Reader in Public Opinion and Communication*, 2nd edn (B. Berelson and M. Janowitz, eds), p. 383. Free Press.
2. Blumer, J. G. and Gurevitch, M. (1982). *The Political Effects of Mass Communication*. (1982). In: *Culture, Society and the Media* (M. Gurevitch, T. Bennett, J. Curran and J. Woollacott, eds), p. 261. Methuen.
3. Charters, W. W. (1966). *Motion Pictures and Youth*. Reprinted in: *The Reader in Public Opinion and Communication*, 2nd edn (B. Berelson and M. Janowitz, eds), p. 385. Free Press.
4. Cantril, H. (1940) *The Invasion from Mars*, p. 198. Harper and Row.
5. Dembo, R. (1973). Gratification found by British boys. *Journalism Q.*, **50(3)**.
6. Gerbner, G. and Gross, L. (1976). Living with television; the violence profile. *J. Communication*, **26(2)**.
7. Berelson, B. (1949). Communication and public opinion. In: *Mass Communication* (W. Schramm, ed.), p. 500. University of Illinois Press.
8. Burch, N. (1978–79). Porter, or ambivalence. *Screen*, Vol. 19, No. 4, p. 91.
9. Burch, N. (1978–79). Porter, or ambivalence. *Screen*, Vol. 19, No. 4, p. 97.
10. Burch, N. (1978–79). Porter, or ambivalence. *Screen*, Vol. 19, No. 4, p. 94.
11. Thompson, K. and Bordwell. D. (1983). Linearity. *Wide Angle*, **5(3)**, 8.
12. Thompson, K. and Bordwell. D. (1983). Linearity. *Wide Angle*, **5(3)**, 14.
13. Staiger, J. (1980). Mass-produced photoplays. *Wide Angle*, **4(3)**, 14.
14. Staiger, J. (1980). Mass-produced photoplays. *Wide Angle*, **4(3)**, 21.
15. Demetz, P. (1967). Letter to Starkenberg, 1894. In: *Marx, Engels and the Poets*. University of Chicago Press.
16. Craig, D. (ed.) (1975). Letter to Minna Kautsky. In: *Marxists on Literature*, p. 267. Penguin.

17. Craig, D. (ed.) (1975). Letter to Margaret Harkness. In: *Marxists on Literature*, p. 269. Penguin.
18. Dudley Andrew, J. (1976). *The Major Film Theory, An Introduction*, p. 46. Oxford University Press.
19. Vertov, D. (1972–3). Film directors: a revolution. *Screen*, **14(4)**, 289.
20. Vertov, D. (1972–3). Film directors: a revolution. *Screen*, **14(4)**, 284.
21. Radak, K. (1977). *Maxim Gorky et al. Soviet Writers' Congress 1934. Debate on Socialist Realism and Modernism in the Soviet Union*, p. 151. Lawrence and Wishart.
22. Radak, K. (1977). *Maxim Gorky et al. Soviet Writers' Congress 1934. Debate on Socialist Realism and Modernism in the Soviet Union*, p. 157. Lawrence and Wishart.
23. Crafts, S. (1976). Ideology and form: Chapeyev and Soviet realism. *Film Form*, **1**.
24. Turvey, G. (1936) (reproduced 1982). The culture of the popular Front and Jean Renoir. In: Media, Culture and Society (M. Gurevitch, T. Bennett, J. Curran and J. Woollacott, eds), p. 355. Methuen.
25. Brecht, B. (1971). Against Georg Lukacs. *New Left Review*, **84**.
26. Bazin, A. (1958). William Wyler, or the Jansenist of mise-en-scene (translated from *Qu'est-ce que le Cinema?*. Editions du Cerf.
27. Walsh, M. (1981). *The Brechtian Aspect of Radical Cinema*, p. 130. BFI.
28. Benjamin, W. (1992). The work of art in the age of mechanical reproduction. In: *Film Theory and Criticism* (G. Mast et al., eds), p. 675. Oxford University Press.
29. Richter, H. (1986). *The Struggle for Film*, p. 62. Wildwood House.
30. Drummond, P. (1979). *Notions of Avant-garde Cinema Film as Film*, p.10. Arts Council of Great Britain.
31. Marinetti, F. T. (1973). The Futurist cinema 1916. *Futurist Manifestos* (A. Umbro, ed.), p. 207. Thames and Hudson.
32. Tisdell, C. and Bozzollo, A. (1977). *Futurism*, p. 150. Thames and Hudson.
33. Kracauer, S. (1992). The Cabinet of Dr Caligari. From Caligari to Hitler. In: *Film Theory and Criticism*, p. 27. Oxford University Press.
34. Kracauer, S. (1992). The Cabinet of Dr Caligari. From Caligari to Hitler. In: *Film Theory and Criticism* (G. Mast et al., eds), p. 30. Oxford University Press.
35. Benjamin, W. (1985). Surrealism; the last snapshot of the European intelligentsia. In: *One Way Street*, p. 236. Verso Books.
36. Kracauer, S. (1960). *Theory of Film*, pp. 186–7. Oxford University Press.
37. Wollen, P. (1975). Two *avant-gardes*. *Studio Int.*, **180**, 172.

38. Lyotard, J. F. (1993). Defining post-modernism. In *The Cultural Reader* (S. During, ed.). Routledge, p.170.
39. Denzin, N. K. (1992). Blue velvet: post-modern contradictions. In *The Post-Modern Reader* (C. Jenck, ed.). Academy Editions/St Martin's Press.
40. Bell, D. (1973) *The Coming of the Post-Modern Age: A Venture in Social Forecasting*. Basic Books Inc.

6.9 Further reading

O'Sullivan, T., Hartley, J., Saunders, D., Montgomery, M. and Fiske, J. (1994). *Key Concepts in Communication and Cultural Studies*. Routledge.

Cobley, P. (ed.) (1996). *The Communication Theory Reader*. Routledge.

During, S. (ed.) (1993) *The Cultural Reader*. Routledge.

During, S. (ed.) (1993). *The Cultural Studies Reader*. Routledge.

Jencks, C. (ed.) (1992). *The Post-Modern Reader*. Academy Editions.

Part 2

Management theories and applications to the media industry

Chapter 7

The growth of business in the audiovisual industry

7.1 Summary

How any new business is established and thrives is the subject of many management theories and textbooks, and a copious number of case studies. How businesses are established, expand or decay in the audiovisual industry is also a subject of much debate, although unfortunately not often analysed objectively and critically enough to try and clarify why one business succeeds where another one fails. It is difficult to think of any other industry whose very structure and inception is devised and controlled by a government – an industry that would without doubt fail if government and international bodies did not reach some level of agreement in trade and technology, through EU regulations, directives, GATT and bilateral agreements. The BBC was incorporated by Government Charter in 1926, and Channels 4 and 5 were established by the Government. The structure of the original regional franchises provided the framework for the establishment of the independent television companies (ITV). Whilst the principle is one of 'at arms length', the tension between state control and interference *vis-à-vis* the free market remains.

In the UK, the growth of the independent production sector (IPS) flourished with the establishment of Channel 4 in 1982. Enormous changes and opportunities for the IPS came about because the Thatcher Government put a legal requirement on the BBC and the independent franchise companies to contract out a percentage of their work. In essence, the audiovisual industry is highly volatile, regulated by government, and dominated by media conglomerates. For the small firm, success or failure can turn on the opportunities of a single production. As we move into the twenty-first century, with the impact the number of digital channels will have on the consumer, we may get the final shake-up in the still relatively 'cosy' media environment that is the UK broadcast industry.

The questions this raises are:

- If, to date, Government regulation of the television industry had been as loose as that of the film industry, would the UK have a television industry as vibrant as it is now?
- In addition, would the UK television industry be struggling to survive in the same manner that the film industry seems to be?

This chapter begins its examination of the growth of the media company with a discussion on innovation and the role of the entrepreneur. The Greiner Growth Model is used as a means of explaining the structure of the individual production firm. In Chapter I we took a macro approach to the IPS, a consequence of government policy and technical changes. This chapter takes a micro-view as to the growth of the media company. We will consider the small and medium-sized enterprise (SME), and review the buyer–supplier relationships in the British audiovisual industry.

It has been said that there is no business like show business; the issue for many struggling in the audiovisual industry is whether there is any business at all.

7.2 Objectives and key issues

The key objective of this chapter is to examine the role of the entrepreneur within the start-up mode of a small production company. It is our intention to give some insight into the key issues that beset the growth of an independent production company. These are:

- Survival in a chaotic environment – what is the entrepreneurial spirit?
- What are the drivers for innovation and creativity?
- Management control in company growth
- The buyer–supplier relationship in the media industry.

7.3 The independent industrial scene

Chapter I took a brief macro approach to the growth of the independent production sector (IPS). This chapter takes a micro approach to explain the growth of the IPS from a commercial entrepreneurial perspective.

As stated in Chapter 1, at the start of the 1980s there were relatively few small and medium-sized companies (SMEs) of any consequence in the broadcast television industry; about 350 in total. Many of these independent companies, 'indies' as they have become known, had been formed to help the careers and promote the talents of presenters and TV personalities. Michael Rodd (*Tomorrow's World* etc.) formed Blackrod. Other independent programme-makers concentrated on education and training. One of the most famous of these companies, Video Arts, was formed by a partnership that included John Cleese, and employed many well-known comic performers such as Eric Idle, James Bolam, Rowan Atkinson, Richard Wilson, Dawn French and Jennifer Saunders (the last two formed their own production company). These SMEs and their counterparts in other sectors of the audiovisual industry were viewed as pleasant backwaters in the audiovisual industrial landscape, and generally they were not considered to be important in the provision of broadcast programmes.

The first Thatcher administration considered SMEs across all industrial sectors to be the springboards to the regeneration of the British economy. At the time, there was a general collapse of many of the larger, heavy industries. More specifically, the SME sector of the television industry was given stimulation to grow by the 1980 Broadcast Act and the creation of the first publisher–broadcaster; Channel 4. The invigorated independent production sector was financed by the redundancy monies of ex-broadcast staff (the BBC and ITV companies were in the process of shedding staff), and by banks and suppliers who were willing to lend to media companies against relatively limited security in this buoyant market. The independent production sector was viewed as a good investment for risk capital.

The environment of IPS company growth during the 1980s provides background reference material to this chapter. Here, we examine theories and models of management, business and economics as a means of explaining what is actually going on within the IPS. Of special interest is the start-up phase of media companies, designated here as very small independent production houses (VSIPH). The Channel 4 producer's guide identified these businesses as 'the proverbial man, dog and answerphone' (*sic*). The current huge expansion of the Internet and the associated start-up companies in many ways repeats the IPS boom period of the 1980s.

7.4 The role of the entrepreneur

... look, you're a painter, and a good one. I happen to have a little drive. That's a good combination, besides you have to face the critics some time.

Spoken by Nina Foch, the wealthy socialite to Gene Kelly's struggling artist in the film *An American in Paris* (1951).

According to Bengt Johannisson[1]:

An entrepreneur is an individual who personifies and orchestrates the creative process through which a new venture is realised in the market place.

The owner or director of the VSIPH is being creative on two levels:

- in the establishment of the new enterprise
- artistically, in applying their craft skills on each new production project produced.

Continuous creativity is at the very core of the company; if the creativity fails, the company will fold. They must be innovators and not adapters (these terms are measurable attributes applied in some psychometric tests). They must also function in the area of ambiguity and uncertainty that Stacey[2] suggests must be present when managers practice extraordinary management. The VSIPH have no tangible products; only a history of past successes to convince the new client or broadcaster that the new, non-existent product will be the same (quality and production values) but different (innovative, novel and stimulating).

Johannisson suggests that the 'entrepreneurs usually have limited owner-controlled resources ...'[3]. Many owners and managers of VSIPH recognise that they are under-financed and consequentially vulnerable to deficits in cash flow.

Almost by definition, the 'good' television programme has to obey the rules of production and what is referred to as the grammar of television, and yet break the rules sufficiently so that something innovative and new emerges whilst still being a consumable product. This reinterpretation of the paradoxical dynamic that demands change with stability, as identified by Johannisson, is one of the essential problems of the audiovisual industry. Who holds the power to make decisions, the creative programme-maker or the accountants? This was not a problem that had to be faced by the in-house director or producer in the BBC or ITV company until the early

1980s. Yet finding the balance between creativity and financial prudence becomes an essential requirement for the independent programme-maker.

Many owners or managers of VSIPHs do not actually address this issue. They retreat into a fantasy world of not even attempting to run an effective business, but believe that the next commission will be the big break to sustain the company and put it on a high plain of success. This lack of commercial focus is often lost in the other drivers to success that motivate the production company owner. The strength of these individuals is their tenacious spirit and positive attitude towards risk. Research conducted at the University of Hertfordshire examined the attitudes of the owners of small production companies, these were typified by quotes such as[4]:

> ... a staggering amount of hard work and a total refusal ever to accept defeat.

In Chapter 8, we will look at the characteristics of the individual and their impact on production teams. Here we take a holistic approach, and look at the observed attributes of the entrepreneur or artisan and professional as identified by Johannisson. In Table 7.1, reproduced from Johannison's work, we see the suggested attributes attached to each role. The interest for us in the audiovisual industry is that many individuals start their media careers in artisan roles, seek opportunities to become entrepreneurial, and possibly

Table 7.1 The personal attributes of the entrepreneur, artisan and professional manager

	Entrepreneur	**Artisan**	**Professional**
Mission	Urge to create	Independence	Company career
Guide	Vision and action	Action	Planning
Environmental orientation	Interaction	Reaction	Proaction
Risk orientation	Ambiguity management	Risk avoidance	Risk reduction
Time orientation	Synchronisation	Time as a buffer	Time management
Focal resources	Social	Physical	Financial
Generic competence	Intuition	Imitation	Professional experience
Education/training	Organic, qualified practice	Formal and practical	Institutionalised

(©Professor Ralph Stacey 1993. Reprinted by kind permission.)

end up in the professional mode as their business or company reaches or maintains a degree of stability. However, it is clear that new non-artisan entrants to the industry join it as entrepreneurs seeking a new venture or adventure, whilst experienced professionals will tend to enter the industry or company at a later stage of its development or maturity. This is when non-specific industry skills are required to help manage the organisation or the infrastructure that supports it. If in any doubt as to the validity of this argument, read *Who's Who in British Television*[5] and take a look at the percentage of senior managers and managing directors who have come up 'through the ranks' of the media industry.

To summarise, entrepreneurs:

- have an innate need to launch ventures
- have the ability to combine visionary thinking and concrete action
- cope with their environments by interactively redefining them wherever possible
- regard risky ambiguous situations as providing a potential for imposing their own ideas on others
- combine internal and external resources flexibly through networking
- consider financial surpluses to be an indicator of capability in the marketplace
- base their competence on intuition, experience and the ability unconsciously to refine the environment in which they work
- identify new niches and disobey established industry references or formal training.

At the beginning of this section there is a quotation from *An American in Paris*. It is suggested that programme-making often requires the innovative skills of the entrepreneur and the creative skills of the writer and/or director. As the line from the film suggests, these are hard to find in one individual. With these thoughts in mind, we now go on to look at the growth of a company, irrespective of the individual or individuals that have set out to establish it.

7.5 Greiner's development model

Greiner's model of company development (Figure 7.1) is of interest because it seeks to explain the stages of company growth as generalised phenomena. If a company is to grow successfully then, according to Greiner, it must pass through the five stages of growth followed by a defined crisis. He also

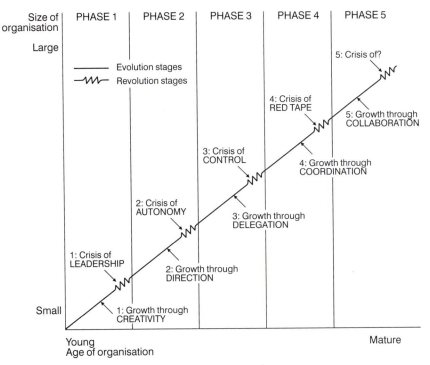

Figure 7.1 Greiner's model of company development[6]. (©Harvard Business School Publishing 1972. Reprinted by kind permission.)

suggests that 'A company's past has clues for management that are critical to future success'[6].

The five stages of growth with their associated points of crisis are:

1 Creativity followed by a crisis of leadership
2 Direction followed by a crisis of autonomy
3 Delegation followed by a crisis of control
4 Co-ordination followed by a crisis of red tape
5 Collaboration followed by a crisis of ? (the unknown).

The two elements of growth and crisis form a stage in the organisation's life. Greiner also suggested that specific elements of management organisational practices are present during each phase. Those of phase 1 and 2 are reproduced in Table 7.2 as they characterise the management behaviour of the owner or manager of the VSIPH.

There is evidence to suggest that the VSIPH oscillates between these two first phases of a company's growth. The audiovisual company that has no

Table 7.2 Business behaviour of small enterprises

	Phase 1	Phase 2
Management focus	Make and sell	Efficiency of operations
Organisational structure	Informal	Centralised and functional
Top management	Individualistic and entrepreneur	Directive
Control system	Market results	Standards and cost centres
Management reward emphasis	Ownership	Salaries and merit increases

(©Harvard Business School Publishing 1972. Reprinted by kind permission.)

current commission functions as in Phase 1. When there is work, a more defined structure comes into play and the company progresses to Phase 2. The problem for the company owner (and entrepreneur) is that the skills needed to acquire and complete the contract stage of a commission are often very different to those that are needed to manage the production phase.

Here are a few further commentaries from company owners[7]:

> Periods (of no work) where we are effectively forced to 'hibernate'.
>
> Small core staff ... who employ others as and when needed by production.
>
> When there is work, a more defined structure comes into play.
>
> Production teams with overlapping responsibility.

While the first commission is in progress and going into production, the company owner/manager has to seek new projects. If the contract is complete and the company has not secured another commission, the company falls back to the Phase 1 mode of operation. The team created to produce the programme is lost, and so are the shared skills that may differentiate the company from the competition. The cycle then repeats itself. This pattern of work shows itself with freelance staff as well as small businesses. The successful company is one that can look to the future and develop strategies that can cope with the almost destructive crises that will impact on the firm. As Ralph Stacey points out, '... creativity is closely related to destruction'[8].

7.6 The role of the SME in the industrial reorganisation of the UK film and television industry

With the decline of much of the heavy industry during the 1960s and 1970s, the Thatcher government looked to the small and medium-sized enterprises to regenerate the economy. In some regions this was because they were the only 'green shoots' of economic growth that used redundancy monies and provided local employment. In some of the industrial sectors, they were seen as the catalyst to industrial change. The television industry was an example of this philosophy. The independent production sector provided the lever to change the British television industry.

Hilbert, Sperling and Rainnie[9] suggested that:

Broadly, the craft-based SMEs specialise in diversified and customised products and services which are of high quality and which are produced by a high proportion of skilled workers; they are, to a certain extent, able to act strategically in their special market segments.

The SME in the television industry (and the UK film industry) to a great extent match these features.

Storper examined the reorganisation of the American production companies. His findings are similar to those found in the UK[10]:

Many of the firms in the expanding entertainment business service sector are small and specialised. They typically subcontract their services on a project-to-project basis.

He argued that this reorganisation was an example of the shift from mass production to flexible specialisation, where the industry is fragmented with flexible disintegrated firm structures and production organisation. There is a parallel with the British audiovisual industry, although the validity for the UK industry may yet be relatively short-lived. The industry has reshaped itself contrary to the Conservative (1979–1997) government's wish to maintain a large IPS, into a few powerful independent programme-makers. Many of the VSIPHs were forced into bankruptcy or voluntary liquidation as the power base shifted. Despite the government's intention, it would seem that unless there are true market forces at work an industrial sector will tend to reform the boundaries of the firm. The sector will establish an economic structure that provides the most efficient system to conduct business and minimise transaction costs. Now the requirement for the broadcasters to contract out 25 per cent of new productions to the independent sector has become a problem as 'independents' become owned by other, larger, media conglomerates.

7.7 The boundaries of the firm

Like trying to describe an elephant (we all know one when we see it), defining a firm and its function is more complex than an initial intuitive response would suggest. Much of this chapter has been about the shifting nature of the firm as VSIPH establish themselves, grow and become one of the large players in the industry, or remain small and in many cases decline and become another bankrupt organisation.

In a seminal work on the nature of the firm[11], Coase suggested that it is the suppression of the price mechanism that determines the boundaries of the firm. Within the firm, the role of the entrepreneur is to organise, co-ordinate and direct the process of production, and by doing so simplify the role of the price-dependent exchange transactions. Consider the example of the BBC (see Chapter 1), where the price mechanism is no longer suppressed and each area has a charge code for internal transaction costs. This delivered the infamous internal market with, for example, the BBC internal CD library costing up to three times more than the amount charged on the open market.

Coase suggests that many attributes of the firm are constructs within a social framework. The theme of 'efficiency' that the 1990 Broadcast Act sought to impose on the BBC and ITV companies was part of the government's strategy to a more 'effective' television industry. These terms are only valid if the outcome is understood. We have to agree as to what is 'efficient' and what is 'effective'. As Coase succinctly puts it, 'Efficiency is contextual'[12].

The vertical integration of the broadcast television industry prior to Channel 4 defined the boundaries of the firm, BBC or ITV company. The script or idea was the input, and the completed transmitted programme as the output. The Peacock Report and the 1990 Broadcast Act required the broadcast companies to redefine the boundaries of the firm by separating the means of production from the control of transmission.

If efficient, this new construct would have flourished and become the most effective means of organising transactions within the market. However, there is much evidence to suggest that this new imposed system was not 'efficient', and that small companies are no longer providing the seed corn of innovative programmes.

7.8 The relationship between the supplier and buyer

It is only in a very few market structures that the government does not seek to control or regulate the behaviour of firms. If the market power of one firm becomes too great, then it is referred to some form of monopolies or mergers commission/board or, in the UK as of 1 April 1999, the Competition Commission. This states:

> The word 'monopoly' has a special meaning under the Fair Trading Act (the FTA). For the precise legal definition please refer to sections 6 and 7 of the FTA. Broadly speaking, the Act provides for two different kinds of monopoly situations: scale – when an individual or a single company, or companies within the same group, accounts for at least 25 per cent of the supply or acquisition of particular goods or services; and complex – when individuals or companies, which together account for at least 25 per cent of the supply or acquisition of particular goods or services, follow a course of conduct, by agreement or not, that prevents, restricts or distorts competition. The FTA does not presume that it is wrong to be a monopolist, but recognises that a monopolist may be in a position to act against the public interest and that a monopoly situation may need investigation

(see www.competition-commission.gov.uk)

Firms which have a very strong market position may abuse that position by imposing high prices or by giving poor service. They may also use unfair tactics to keep other companies out of their market, or distort the market in their favour.

The 'concentration ratio' of buyers or sellers is one that the government uses to monitor and test whether a firm's actions are against the public interest. Pappas et al. have examined the work of Sosnick, and have extracted certain key factors in the structure of a free market in what they call 'workable competition'[13]. These are reproduced here, since they serve as a useful benchmark in the performance analysis of the audiovisual industry. More specifically, they indicate the relationship between the independent producer and the media conglomerates or broadcaster by which any government action in the twenty-first century should be measured.

1 *Structure.* There should be:
  (a) a sufficient number of independent sellers
  (b) no artificial barriers to entry or exit from market
  (c) moderate and price-sensitive quality differentials.
2 *Conduct.* Firms should:
  (a) act as rivals without collusion
  (b) not shield inefficient producers or customers
  (c) avoid persistent harmful price discrimination
  (d) avoid misleading sale promotion activities.
3 *Performance.* Could lead to:
  (a) efficient production and distribution in terms of resources use
  (b) a level of profit which is just sufficient to reward efficiency and induce investment in innovation
  (c) output levels and quality features that are responsive to consumer preferences
  (d) exploitation of new technology, resulting in new processes and products
  (e) a reasonable level of sales promotion expenditure.

The model, when applied to the buyer–supplier relationship between the IPS and the broadcasters, highlights some of the anomalies of the current industrial structure. For example, 3(b) (level of profit) is often set by the broadcaster, who cash flows the project so, in effect, no true competition can exist.

The company that wins the contract has to:

1 Produce the programme to the budget agreement
2 Accept the 'profit' that the broadcaster allocates to them.

James Hogan summarised the buyer supplier relationship thus[14]:

> The bulk of the independent community is made up of tiny companies which are little more than conduits for freelance producers ... They are, in truth, very *dependent* on the power and patronage of the broadcaster, who has the daunting task of sorting through thousands of programme proposals every year and choosing, at best, approximately four per cent.

How can we characterise the audiovisual industry? It is volatile, unpredictable and unforgiving. The entrepreneur can, as John Ellis describes, find him or herself in a 'precarious and marginal' environment. The paradox for all in the industry is that the fragmentation of the market can only increase the uncertainty, but may also offer more opportunities to reach an audience.

7.9 References

1. Johannisson, B. (1993). 'Organisational networks and innovation' in *Strategic Thinking and the Management of Change – International Perspectives on Organisational Dynamics*. (R. Stacey, ed.), p. 57. Kogan Page.
2. Stacey, R. D. (1992). *Strategic Management and Organisational Dynamics*, p. 112. Pitman.
3. Johannisson, B. (1993). 'Organisational networks and innovation' in *Strategic Thinking and the Management of Change – International Perspectives on Organisational Dynamics*. (R. Stacey, ed.), p. 57. Kogan Page.
4. Block, P. L. (1996). *Strategies for Survival – The Small Television Production Company*. University of Hertfordshire.
5. Coopman, J. (ed.) (2000) *Who's Who in British Television*. Profile Media.
6. Greiner, L. E. (1972). *Evolution and Revolution as Organisations Grow*. Harvard Business Review, July–August.
7. Block, P. L. (1996). *Strategies for Survival – The Small Television Production Company*. University of Hertfordshire.
8. Stacey, R. (ed.) (1993) *Strategic Thinking and the Management of Change – International Perspectives on Organisational Dynamics*. Kogan Page.
9. Hilbert, J., Sperling, H.-J., and Rainnie, A. (1994). *SMEs at the Crossroads – Scenarios on the Future of SMEs in Europe*. Future of Industry Paper Series, Vol. 9, p. 15. Commission of European Communities.
10. Storper, M. (1985). *The Changing Organisation and Location of the Motion Picture Industry – A Research Report*. UCLA Publishing.
11. Coase, L. (1937). The nature of the firm. In: *The Economic Nature of the Firm (A Reader)*, p. 79. Cambridge University Press.
12. Coase, L. (1937). The nature of the firm. In: *The Economic Nature of the Firm (A Reader)*, p. 79. Cambridge University Press.
13. Pappas, J. L., Brigham, E. F. and Shipley, B. (1983). *Managerial Economics*. Penguin, Cassell.
14. Hogan, J. (1997). *From Demi-Gods to Democrats? The Television Revolution 1976–1996*. London School of Economics Working Paper WP6.

7.10 Further reading

Ellis, J. (1992) *Visible Fictions*. Routledge.
Horrie, C. and Clarke, S. (1994). *Fuzzy Monsters: Fear and Loathing at the BBC*. Mandarin.
Pascale, R. (1989). *Managing on the Edge*. Penguin.

Chapter 8

Behaviour in media organisations and organisational behaviour

8.1 Summary

There is a dynamic and a tension between the individual and the organisation for which he or she works. It can be a virtuous or a vicious circle, reinforced through positive or negative feedback. Therefore, the individual's behaviour within the dynamics of a business environment is a key determinant to the success or failure of the individual and, by extension, the firm. This chapter considers and reflects on the attributes of the individual and his or her behaviour within an organisation. By so doing, we attempt objectively to examine the needs of the individual and the wants of the organisation.

Whilst we might crave a sense of belonging, most of us would also like to think that we are special and unique. To an extent this is true, but to others we are identified by the following classes and associated sub-groups:

- Gender – male, female
- Intellect – nature, nurture (the mental models we maintain)
- Temperament – personality (specific, inherited, learned)
- Culture – ethnic group, religious group, national, organisational
- Social – family, location, education, work, pastimes
- Health – age, social, genetic, social group, lifestyle, occupation, and all of the other classes above.

There are many systems to code these differences quantitatively. Academic exams and IQ tests attempt to differentiate intellect. Social scientists examine values, beliefs and buying behaviour. In international sport, we are even tested for our sex.

These measures enable others to sell to us, select us, predict our buying behaviour, and indicate national trends etc. Business managers and recruiters apply the techniques of psychometrics to aid the selection process for recruitment and succession. Sociologists and psychologists look for patterns, similarities, correlation and significance in the data produced between individuals, within groups and between groups.

It is important for the manager within the audiovisual industry to have an insight into individual and group behaviour. Management is not just about the process of production; it is as much to do with managing people. It is important to understand the range of personalities and temperaments that are found within production groups. Many have argued that to do so effectively, you also need to understand yourself. We need to be aware that there are identifiable attributes, values and beliefs that individuals share, and others that they do not share. Do production managers or researchers or engineers share more than just a job specification? This knowledge may enable you to manage yourself, individuals and teams more effectively. The significance for individuals is to gain some insight into their personal profile; it may even help them determine whether they are the right person for the audiovisual industry!

This chapter, whilst based on theories of behaviour, does wander into the realm of industrial relations and human resources. We begin by examining some of the theoretical models of individual personality and temperament taken from Maslow and Jung, and then move on to consider how they might apply to the individual working within the audiovisual industry. Finally, we consider the dynamics of groups by reviewing the work of Belbin, and W. R. Bion gives us some insights into conscious and unconscious behaviours.

Modes of employment within the television industry have changed profoundly in the two decades leading up to the millennium, from secure employee status to short-term contracts. From its earliest days, film production has been a model of mixed employment that includes casual and freelance workers, short-term projects, short-term contracts and full-time retained staff. The entire audiovisual industry remains a precarious occupation. Most production staff would agree that you are 'only as good as your last job' in the negotiations to secure the next one. Reputation, networking, contacts, word of mouth and sheer bloodymindedness in persistent pursuance of individual aims lead to success within the business.

An understanding of organisational behaviour has become key to management strategy. It is also an ally to effective human resource management. Since the day that the artisan moved from working autonomously within a village environment to being part of organised labour, observers have taken an interest in the behaviour, attitudes and values of the individual or the group within the organisation. Some have examined the mechanistic actions of the individual or the group. This was seen as a means of making the working environment more efficient (Taylor, *Scientific Management*; Fayol, *The Function of Management*). Others have been interested in the values and attitudes imparted to the individual by the organisation (Mayo, *Human Relationship Movement*; Moss Kanter, *The Post-Entrepreneurial Corporation*).

More recently, writers on management issues have taken a close interest in the psychodynamics of groups within organisations (Argyris, *Organisational Learning*). The models devised attempt to explain aspects of human behaviour, such as the individual's 'theatre of the mind' and shared 'mental models'. These behaviours have an impact on how groups, once formed, storm, norm and ideally perform — become a functional, not a dysfunctional, team or group.

After considering individual differences and behaviour and group dynamics, we go on to look at organisations in more detail and consider organisational culture. This culture is made up of company practices, communications, physical structures, and the common language and jargon that make a business function as an entity in its own right (Handy, *Understanding Organisations*; Morgan, *Images of Organisations*).

If you need no other reason to examine individual or group behaviour, just consider characterisation in any dramatic work. The believable well-rounded characters have many dimensions to their personality. In essence, these are modelled on the attributes listed at the start of this summary. It is the craft of the writer to create the characters (Reel One), and set the challenge or crisis for them (Reel Two) so that we can possibly empathise with the dilemma of the character and, by our understanding of them, know when they might 'act out of character'. The writer has taken us on this journey so that we may share the emotion of the closure at the end (Reel Three) of the work. In our work or social environment, we continually make assumptions about and respond to other people's behaviour. The more we understand the 'character' of our colleagues and ourselves, the better the chance of managing more effectively.

In *Cultures and Organisations*, Hofstede quotes from *Twelve Angry Men* by Reginald Rose (the 1957 film starred Henry Fonda). He does so to illustrate individual differences between a European immigrant watchmaker and a New York garage owner, and their behaviour patterns that undermine their ability to discuss the guilt or innocence of the accused[1]:

> Eleventh juror (rising): 'I beg pardon, in discussing ...'
>
> Tenth juror (interrupting and mimicking): 'I beg pardon. What are you so goddam polite about?'
>
> Eleventh juror (looking straight at the tenth juror): 'For the same reason you're not. It's the way I was brought up.'

8.2 Objectives and key issues

The main object of this chapter is to introduce the concept of human behaviour and how it manifests itself in organisations.

By reading this chapter we expect you to:

- recognise individual differences and the sources for these differences
- gain an understanding of these differences through the works of leading writers on organisations
- gain an awareness of group behaviour and behaviour in groups
- have some insights into the relationship between the individual, the team and the organisation.

The issues addressed are drawn from the needs of the audiovisual industry. Being a member of a team in the media production environment has special demands. Usually teams are not big enough to enable an individual to hide in the shadow of someone else doing similar work. Some of the tasks performed at the first instance may appear trivial, yet they are vital elements in the process that produces a successful production. Individuals have to take ownership and control of the activity to which they have been allocated. There is a dynamic interaction between the needs and wants of the individual, and the requirements of the organisation.

Production managers expect their staff to act positively by looking for how they can add value to their role and to the project as a whole. For them, good productions are made up of people who are not content with 'this will do' and 'this will suffice'. Good productions are made up of teams of people in which each individual not only does the job allocated, but also thinks about that extra 10 per cent he or she can bring to the role. That is what managers seek from staff and colleagues who work for them and alongside them when trying to get a project completed successfully, with the right quality, to the right cost, and on time.

This chapter considers the attributes and values of the individual. We ask the question, who wants to be in the audiovisual industry and why? We do so by considering the personality and temperament of the individual, and look at some of the models of character and temperament types. This is followed by some of the ideas on learning and behaviour in groups, conscious and unconscious. This then gives us a framework on which we may consider some of the concerns of teams and team memberships. How effective can they be? We have made the case so far that the media industry is essentially a project-based enterprise. In Chapters 13 and 14 we will illustrate how important the team is to the successful completion of the production project.

Observers of the media industry have stated what many in the industry would have considered implicit; that it is an industry of long hours, job insecurity and unknown elements in terms of training and career development. There has only really been one period post-Second World War (1957 to the early 1980s) in which workers in the UK television industry have been in the enviable position of being in paid, secure posts. Some argued that this was due to disproportionate union power. It was the Thatcher Government of 1979 that attacked 'this last bastion of restrictive practices' (*sic*), and the result has been an industry with labour even more fragmented than in the pre-Second World War period. Training has become a second best option, while the skills pool of existing personnel trained by the BBC and ITV remain in employment or are available as freelance staff.

As we move into the twenty-first century, these skilled members of staff (the youngest of whom are in their mid-forties) will retire. An even greater skills gap will emerge, and although industry observers and government are aware of this they are unable truly to address it. The solution seems to be as below:

> One woman, one camera ... is this the future of TV? (London Weekend Television's The Lab is the nerve centre of a revolutionary training project that will change television production techniques forever. Stephen Pile reports from inside the heady world of multi-skilling)

(*Daily Telegraph*, Saturday October 23, 1999)

The latest camera is now so small, so cheap and so easy to use that it has revolutionised the way we make TV programmes …

This removes the distinction between amateur and professional

(Marcus Plantin, director of programmes at London Weekend Television).

The Lab 'delivers' the promise of the single-person production house, from Graduate media trainee to broadcast director in 6 months.

8.3 The employment landscape

From an industrial perspective, the audiovisual sector is part of the entertainment industry. Despite the opinion expressed by many programme-makers and commentators that media products are cultural artefacts, the sector operates in a highly competitive market place. In the UK, there are just over 1000 organisations that operate within the audiovisual industry. Some, such as the BBC, are considered to be large organisations, with 20 000-plus staff, whereas others are considered to be large only inasmuch as they are a division of a much larger organisation, multinational or conglomerate. There are currently about 50 production houses in the UK that could just about qualify for being called medium-sized enterprises.

With varying degrees of success, the rest of the organisations are:

- Sole traders – freelance staff working under their own name or business name and providing craft skills purchased at an hourly/daily/weekly rate.
- Very small companies – individuals registered as companies selling more than just the craft skills. They may own cameras, lighting and transport, and provide the subcontracting package deal for, say, a location shoot. They also contract in other very small companies and sole traders to build the crew and service offering.
- Small production companies – these have a staff of between 10 and 20 people, and could typically be production houses with project-driven staff needs. These expand and contract as required. They have a relatively low capital value, and are typically start-up film companies formed to exploit a project. They could also be niche programme providers for a programme strand.
- Small facility houses – these provide equipment and services to the industry, and are often proprietor owned. Two of the biggest equipment and service providers, Optex and Samuelsons, began in this manner.

- Facility houses – these offer a range of cross-media services; studio space, editing and equipment hire. A high level of investment is needed to maintain the business at the 'cutting edge'; some are proprietor owned whilst others have been taken over by media conglomerates to provide a wider portfolio to potential clients – the 'one-stop shop'.
- Larger production houses – these have a mixed profile of broadcast, corporate and industrial programmes, although their broadcast work is not quite 'A' list.
- Agencies – these provide crews, performers, locations, accounting services etc.

There has been a huge expansion in the range of opportunities for working in the audiovisual sector. The divergence of channels and the convergence of needed technological skills have provided opportunities for cross-media work for multi-skilled staff. Yet it has been reported by union and industry bodies that the total number of employees actively working in the sector has if anything gone down, with the exception of the multimedia industry.

A feature of the audiovisual sector is that although the total number of organisations and enterprises involved in the sector remains in total relatively stable, the churn (reforming into new companies or associations) is high. Despite failures or successes within a particular production or facility house, individual staff members tend to maintain their relationship with the sector by returning to freelance work or by joining another business – the name changes, but the game remains the same.

Two expressions to describe the economic model can be applied; the 'portfolio worker' and 'flexible specialisation'. For the individual worker in the audiovisual industry, a list of credits and a show-reel was essential. Now this has to be accompanied by a range of transferable skills – a portfolio of past work, and also a willingness to perform a wider range of production activities.

Companies supplying to the large production houses have to provide a flexible and adaptable offering within their area of specialisation. A portfolio and flexibility has been implicit to the working practices within the audiovisual sector from its earliest days, but the impact of digital technology has radically changed the industrial landscape for worker and employer (see The Lab, p. 178).

The audiovisual sector is project based. Unless the project is given the production go ahead, no more than one or two core members of staff are needed to manage the production. In most small production houses there is not the throughput of work to retain a full production crew. In most countries, bar the USA and India, there is not a critical mass of activity to guarantee that as everyone finishes one job they can move effortlessly to the next. 'You are only as good as your last job' remains a key determinant of future employment.

To negotiate the next contract, individuals carry their portfolio of past successes around with them as a showreel to prospective production partners or employers. Freelance workers have to be able to function successfully in the job they are doing and negotiate for new opportunities whilst the current project is still in progress. This is reflected in the claim that the film and television industry had one of the highest take up of mobile phones in the early 1980s. It was seen as a key tool to negotiate the deal (and it looked good!). It is still quite usual to observe the crew during production breaks, Palm Pilot or Filofax in one hand, mobile telephone in the other, discussing with their various contacts the next project on which they are anticipating employment.

The casualisation of staff has ebbed and flowed in both film and television industries. A stable model for the ever-growing and changing multimedia industry has yet to emerge fully. In the 1940s and 1950s, Hollywood moved from employing hundreds of staff, including the performers, to a model of flexible specialisation as described by Michael Storper[2]. This model, now inherent in the television sector in the UK, relies upon specialist subcontracting organisations to provide the skills needed by the main contractor or producer. In addition, the UK television industry has changed from having sufficient permanent staff on standby to meet all the needs of production (in the vertically integrated production model) to a business that retains only a few key members of staff. These staff are those required in highly specialised areas.

In the mid 1980s, several of the larger studio facility houses in London and the home counties sacked most of their camera crews. The decision to do this was taken because there was no longer a need for the camera operators to understand the idiosyncratic aspect of camera technology associated with a particular camera and its manufacturer. As technology has converged, first by analogue techniques and more recently by digital techniques, the differences between cameras, vision mixers and VTRs have become negligible – notwithstanding the personal preferences expressed by operators and the technical crew. Modern digital cameras are 'point and shoot'. They no longer require complicated and complex line-up procedures that need two or three technicians just to ensure that cameras match each other in a studio environment. This market place has made it tougher for all concerned. At one time in the larger production houses there was a clear division between the technical infrastructure and the staff needed to maintain it, and project-based production staff. Now machine operators have become interchangeable.

The advances in technology have eliminated the need to provide a management structure and hierarchy for technical services. With no technical continuity and specialist skills required, training has also been degraded.

The BBC took this to its logical conclusion by removing the heads of craft departments. Their role was to train and develop the careers of new camera operators, editors, sound recordists etc. They were replaced by resource allocators, who hold an administrative role.

With these changes to working practices and technology in mind, let us consider one group of individuals in the UK TV industry; broadcast engineers. In the early days (1920s–1950s), the BBC engineers were drawn from a traditional technical background. They joined the organisation with an engineering career in view and, in the first instance, not really with an interest in the programme-making as such. (This statement has not been subjected to academic rigour; this attitude has been reported by several 'second cohort engineers'.) It was not until the early 1980s that ACTT had its first requests for a freelance engineering grade in the union.

The 'three cohorts' of engineer in the broadcast industry could be presented in the following manner:

1 Cohort 1 (1920s–1950s). These were the engineering production staff who joined the BBC and stayed with the organisation from its very early days, circa early 1930s, through to 1957, when the first franchises for the independent companies were released. Their electrical and electronic skills were based on City & Guilds, HNCs, HNDs and degrees in the subject area, and not on television as such. They were trained further by the BBC.
2 Cohort 2 (1950s–mid-1980s). This cohort is typified by those engineers and production staff who left the BBC to join the independent companies. By doing so, they earned considerably better salaries. They were also in a position to train and educate those members of staff who were direct entrants to the independent sector. Thames Television was one of the few independent production companies to run a formal (albeit short-lived) graduate entry programme and training scheme. Thames was also (to its credit) the first independent company to explicitly take on women as trainee camera operators and film editors.

3 Cohort 3 (1980s–to date). Government policy and changing technology brought about:

(a) The creation of Channel 4, which stimulated the growth in the independent production sector and many more facility houses to support this sector.

(b) Recording and camera technology that provided, for the first time, portable and 'lightweight' location equipment. High Band U-matic gave the opportunity to record, on a cassette format, a broadcastable image that was acceptable for news or current affairs.

(c) A more cost-driven (though not quite yet least cost) producer working environment in the television industry.

These factors shifted the requirement for the broadcast companies to retain engineering skills within the firm. From an operator's perspective, equipment technology has converged and is inherently more reliable. The professional engineer has returned to the equipment manufacturer.

Who has the skills – film to tape?

In the late 1970s and early 1980s, a major row blew up between studio-based camera operators and film crews. Until that time television cameras were not just earth bound, but literally bound to a large truck with lots of technology and a very heavy length of cable to send the video signals from the camera to the VTR. The introduction of a cassette format and lightweight cameras enabled a crew of two to record news items or documentary material in what the industry terms a 'film-style shoot' – with a single camera. Prior to this date, a crew of 10 did the same job.

The argument that ensued was about whose skills were most appropriate to use this new equipment. Was it the technically competent camera operators who had so far been studio-bound or part of heavily engineered outside broadcasts? They had the technical competencies. Or should the work go to film camera operators, who knew how to work on location with a single camera in the film-style technique?

It took many months of negotiation with ACTT to find a formula that all sides – film, studio and management – agreed upon. Meanwhile, engineers were learning how to use cameras that were almost obsolete before they were used.

Given the inherently unstable working environment for all in the audiovisual industry the question posed is; who wants to be in the industry?

First let us examine the options available. Places to work include:

- The UK film industry.
- The BBC.
- Independent television companies.
- Channel 4.
- SC4 (the Welsh fourth channel).
- Independent television news.
- Channel 5.
- Cable and satellite companies.
- New media.
- Multimedia, cross-media, world-wide web.
- Independent production companies.
- Facilities houses (studios, editing suites, recruitment agencies).
- The corporate sector, for example Barclays Bank, Shell International, Unilever, BP, British Gas – these businesses and many more like them have had a long history of high quality production work using staff broadly drawn from the film and broadcast industry to produce their in-house communications and training programmes.
- Equipment manufacturers – throughout the UK many people with an engineering background have found themselves becoming involved in the television industry in the fields of designing camera, mixers, light filters, lighting systems, generators, camera technologies. Some of these businesses, like the very successful Optex and Samuelsons, were formed by operators who saw a need in the market for better support services for their colleagues in the industry.
- Education – joining the Open University production centre was at one time a path to mainstream production and working with the BBC. Now many more universities and colleges are using television cameras as part of their training remit. They use the systems with their own staff and students, and in some cases produce distance learning packs as part of their own ambitions in the national and international education marketplace. The reduction in start-up costs has enabled them to try and compete in reselling class-based materials. The Mori poll of 1999, conducted for the British Council, showed that to the rest of the world the UK education sector is considered second only to the American. As technologies change, the growth in this sector through distance learning and franchised opportunities will offer opportunities for those who want to join the audiovisual industry.

- Analysis – government, consultancy, accounting, legal. This is more difficult to define, and could be considered peripheral to the main thrust of the industry. However, just check the CVs of the main players in the industry!

Given the industrial landscape, how do we match the person to the possible job options?

8.4 Who wants to be in the media industry?

The statistics are grim in this highly casualised industry. Current figures suggest that up to 70 per cent of all staff within the UK audiovisual industry are freelance, a high percentage of whom are unemployed at any one time. Those in employment are on short-term contracts with no guarantee of their next assignment. To understand what might motivate people to work within this sector, we first need to consider the concept of human motivation. Abraham Maslow, dubbed as 'the father of humanist psychology'[3], suggested that we have seven innate needs:

1 Physiological – what our bodies need to physically survive (water, food, sex)
2 Safety – this is a physical security need, so that we can maintain a secure and safe environment from predators (both human and animal)
3 Love – often considered the basic social need, for relationships and a sense of belonging
4 Esteem – some have described this as the need to satisfy the ego by social standing and peer group recognition
5 Self-actualisation – a sense of self-fulfilment
6 Freedom of enquiry and expression – this may be a more nebulous need, but includes a sense of fairness, honesty and ethical dealing
7 To know and understand – to fulfil the need to satisfy an enquiring mind that is curious and wants to learn and explore.

This 'hierarchy of needs' is often represented in a simple form (Figure 8.1) as a set of steps or blocks. As one level is satisfied, the individual can go on to the next – in absolute terms, we would agree that the need to eat is a rather greater priority than a career goal. However, this diagram doesn't really explain the more complex behaviour in relatively stable modern economies, or the paradox of how people behave in relatively unstable industries within these economies, such as the audiovisual sector.

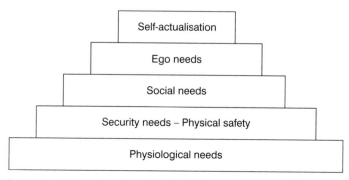

Figure 8.1 Maslow's hierarchy of needs – simple form.

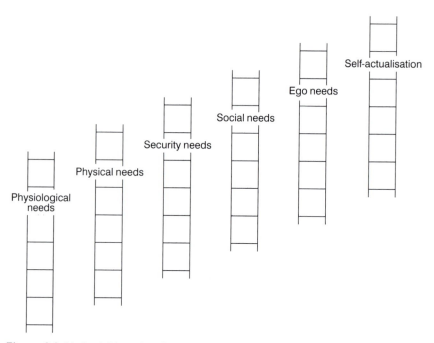

Figure 8.2 Maslow's hierarchy of needs – complex form.

Given the complexities of the modern industrial working environment, it is probably more useful to envisage Maslow's hierarchy as less a series of stepping stones and more a continuum of overlapping ladders that might be traversed by the individual (Figure 8.2). This model gives an indication of the behaviour of workers in the audiovisual industry. They operate not with a strict hierarchy of needs, but with an expectation of future promise. The individual who can see future opportunities that might lead them to a point of self-actualisation is often more than willing to put up with short-term hardships.

There has been a tradition in the audiovisual industry to appoint new joiners as runners. The tasks they are given are often trivial and sometimes demeaning compared to their intellect and qualifications. Whatever their motivation or ambition, they are party to an industry that gives them the promise of future opportunities and self-actualisation. There is an expectation that if they can see themselves through this period of initiation, then somehow their talent will be recognised. In Hollywood, 'every taxi driver has a script in their back pocket or is an out of work actor'.

While a film producer was casting roles for his next film, a carpenter working nearby was making too much noise and had to stop work. To pass the time, the carpenter read the roles with the performers who were being auditioned. The carpenter got the role. The producer was George Lucas, and the carpenter was Harrison Ford. Ford, even though an actor with some credits to his name, worked as a carpenter for approximately 10 years before this break.

In *Organisational Behaviour,* Huczynski and Buchanan quote Maslow[4]:

> ... a musician must make music, an artist must paint, a poet must write, if he is to be ultimately happy. What a man can be, he must be. This need we may call self-actualisation ... it refers to the desire for self-fulfilment, namely to the tendency for him to become actualised in what he is potentially – the desire to become more and more what one is, to become everything that one is capable of becoming.

A key driver for the motivation of those in the audiovisual industry is to express a sense of creativity as embodied by the term self-actualisation. Many would recognise that the path to this self-fulfilment will be a rocky one. It is a high profile industry in which creativity, innovation and the potential to earn a great deal of money may be achieved. The freedom of opportunity and choice coupled with financial security is nice work – if you can get it! However, high expectations of success and a limited number of opportunities to fulfil that expectation come with a high degree of failure.

Workers in the media industry are not part of a homogeneous group, and there are some indicators to suggest that a broad picture of three points of entry emerges; technical, entrepreneurial and creative/artisan. These strands are defined as much by the job specification as by individual differences or drivers for career goals.

The convergence of the technological platforms has reduced the need for highly qualified engineers and their associated skills in the production chain. There has been a clear shift in the need of engineering competencies from the production chain to the equipment manufacturers. Equipment has become more reliable, and maintenance contracts more dependable. The demarcation line between different craft skills competences have virtually disappeared through multi-skilling requirements.

Multi-skilling and a willingness to be flexible in employment contracts and terms of engagement has removed the once perceived control of the trade union movement. Witness L!VE TV and its employment strategy[5]. This station relied to a great extent on untrained junior staff with almost no production skills to produce the programmes. In the 1960s and 1970s governments were concerned about union power, and in the 1980s the Thatcher government made radical changes to the industrial relations landscape, shifting employment control mechanisms from national collective bargaining into the hands of the employer and the local contracting companies.

To date, papers written about the employee in the UK audiovisual industry have tended to focus on processes and outcomes, and not on the attitudes and values of the individual. In psychological terms, they have tended to take a behaviourist approach by examining the inputs and outputs to organisational structures within the audiovisual industry along with the impact of government legislation. They have seen these macro factors as the key influences on the behaviour of the individual within the industry. As a general point it has been argued that by maintaining a degree of uncertainty in the industrial landscape, an employee's compliance is assured. An alternative view is that individuals choose the audiovisual industry knowing that ambiguity and uncertainty go hand in hand with a creative working environment; they embrace the industry for that very reason. Would the sort of individual who is attracted to the audiovisual industry want a stable and predictable environment? Would you? An evocation of this attitude is the role of the media entrepreneur (see Chapter 7).

The shift in responsibility for skills acquisition has moved from the employer to the employee. Even so, there has been a tradition within the film industry of 'learning on the job'. With these boundaries of external control, uncertainty and instability established, how would you test whether you or others would be able to cope with this working environment?

A final factor in setting the scene for the worker in the audiovisual industry is some consideration of how effective they may be at working in teams, and possibly leading those teams.

Employers will almost always look for a good fit between job specification and person specification. There are many tools by which researchers attempt to code individual differences. Business managers, recruiters and careers advisors seek some form of quantitative data to attach to the individual – if it could be shown that most film editors were better than average at crosswords, then it might form part of the basis of selection for a new editor. Qualitative data is harder to gather, and open to greater challenge. We could stray into the dangerous waters of causal, significant and relevant relationships, viz. storks, Stockholm and birth rate. If this is relevant to you, then its significance is assured; if not, read *Simple Statistics* by Clegg[6].

Whether you are a prospective employer or employee, and whether or not you share or see the value in these processes of modelling attitude and behaviour, forearmed is forewarned. A useful starting point would be to examine one's own temperament and that of those with whom you are likely to work.

Jung (1875–1961) suggested that each individual has a preferred way of processing information from their internal and external worlds, and these differences between people help to explain the variety found in human behaviour. It was during the 1920s and 1930s that Jung established a set of paired scalar temperaments that could be used to indicate a preferred style or temperament profile for an individual. This was incorporated by Myers and Briggs, who developed the Myers–Briggs Type Indicator (MBTI) personality inventory. By the use of a questionnaire and score-sheet system, people are placed at a point on each of the four scalar paired personality types:

- Extraversion (E) vs Introversion (I)
- Intuition(N) vs Sensation (S)
- Thinking (T) vs Feeling (F)
- Judging (J) vs Perceiving(P).

You should note that each of these terms has a specific meaning different to everyday usage. To use one of the scales as an example in the workplace, 'Js' like structure and closure, whilst 'Ps' like flexibility. Unless these differences are understood, conflict can result – for example, 'Js' may interpret flexibility as procrastination, whilst 'Ps' may find structure confining and feel controlled. It is important to recognise the limitations of tools such as the MBTI. Useful as they may be, the human personality is far too complex to fit into a particular set of definitions. However, they can be a starting point in gaining an understanding of yourself.

Use of the MBTI is not readily available to the general public. *Please Understand Me*[7], written by David Keirsey and Marilyn Bates, provides an introductory text to this method. The reader completes a questionnaire from which the answers are coded on a scorecard. From this, an indication of an individual's temperament on the four scales is measured – more extrovert than introvert, more feeling that thinking, etc.

From the coding, the four pairs of preferences create 16 possible temperament types (e.g. ENTP – extrovert, intuitive, thinking and perceiving). Because some of these pairs can be numerically balanced, up to a further 32 combinations can be included. These combinations have been defined in four broad personality types:

- Dionysian (SP) – not to be tied by routine, focuses on the present, seeks action, impulsive
- Epimethian (SJ) – dutiful and wants to be part of an organisation, careful, thoughtful and accurate, a giver not a taker
- Promethian (NT) – power, control, predictability; avoids personal and emotional involvement and wants to be seen as confident and in charge
- Apollonian (NF) – intuitive decision-makers, wants to be unique, finds it hard to take criticism.

For example, the Apollonian (NF) group is strong on the intuitive/feeling scale, and it is suggested that these people tend to pursue extraordinary goals. To illustrate this, Keirsey and Bates[8] quote from 'Kubrick's Grandest Gamble' (*Time*, 1975)[9]:

> As for Kubrick, he is still working eighteen hours a day overseeing the final fine tuning of the soundtrack ... there is such a total sense of demoralisation if you say you don't care. From start to finish on a film the only limitations I observed are those imposed on me by the amount of money and the amount of sleep I need. You either care or you don't, and I simply don't know where to draw the line between those two points.

The NF personality is a driven individual who can act unreasonably and be demanding, both on themselves and on others around them.

The importance of personality and temperament type goes beyond just an expression of individual differences or a means of indicating a personal preference for working in one industry or another. In the audiovisual industry, the majority of the work is a team process. How often have we heard the expression 'all chiefs and no Indians'? It has been shown that groups made up of different personality types can function more effectively than a group made up of all the same types of people. Groups made up of people with no similarities at all can similarly be dysfunctional. Let us go on to consider group behaviour as examined and illustrated by Belbin.

8.5 Group behaviour

In 1981 Meredith Belbin expanded on the Jungian approach to personality and temperament by applying the technique to management and project teams. In examining the work of teams in action, his research identified eight roles within a team structure:

1 The chairman – calm, co-ordinating and controlled
2 The shaper – directive, creative, and a balance to the chairman
3 The plant – creative, often an 'off the wall' thinker, sometimes a little tangential to the needs of the team at that time
4 The monitor/evaluator – the person to bring the plant down to earth and provide some critical thinking on the ideas that have been brought to the forefront
5 The company worker – the backbone of a good team, providing stability and solid work for the team's function, gets the job done
6 The teamworker – good at bringing the team together, but may not be a great decision-maker
7 The completer/finisher – conscientious, often meticulous, keeps the team focused on what has to be done, deals with outcomes and (awful jargon) 'deliverables'
8 The resourcer/investigator – a great starter, full of enthusiasm, an extrovert keen for a challenge who, once the challenge is being met, often loses interest in the work that needs to be completed.

Few of us would want to be labelled as totally matching any single one of these roles, but as you reflect on your own behaviours you may recognise some of these attributes in your own role in a team. Belbin's work did show that most managers or project workers adopt one or two of these roles with a high degree of consistency. Again, some degree of sensitivity in interpretation is required; an individual's role in a group is also bounded by the job specification imposed on them and shaped by the perceived attributes that historically the individual has been shown to exhibit. We know little of the 'hidden talents' an individual may have. It has been argued that the job specification will have as much impact on the role and direction your job will take as any personal temperament preferences and style of working might suggest. Does the worker fit the job, or the job the worker?

Belbin's work suggested that, by using psychometric tests, it was possible to predict the role an individual could take on within a team. According to Belbin, a team will perform more effectively and be more successful if all of the eight group member role behaviours are covered by members of that team. To do this, Belbin devised a team role inventory; on the basis of answering a series of multiple choice questions from a set of seven, a team role style would be identified for each team member. Many texts offer an opportunity to fill in the inventory as devised by Belbin, including the Organisational Behaviour Workbook[10] by Huczynski and Buchanan.

An understanding of the personality and behaviour of the individuals with whom we work is vital to the success of the project, the quality of the work produced and, in no small measure, to the work experience. Recognising the kinds of behaviours that could be manifested by colleagues – and possibly more importantly by yourself – might lead you to think a little bit more not only about the conscious behaviours that we manifest, but also about the more unconscious behaviours of which we are not aware.

The interactions we have with others are underpinned by individual attributes (gender, intellect, culture, etc.). Some of these behaviours will

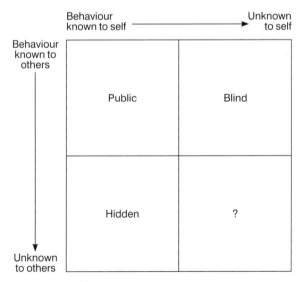

Figure 8.3 JOHARI window[11].

manifest themselves in a conscious and public manner, and others we will not be aware of.

W. R. Bion suggested that four behaviour models manifest themselves as outcomes of known and unknown behaviours, and illustrated them in the JOHARI window (Figure 8.3). The behaviours are explained as follows:

- Public – this is behaviour known to oneself and also apparent to others
- Hidden – we knowingly hide some of our behaviours in certain situations
- Blind – we also know or may have discovered that on many occasions others have recognised behaviours and traits in ourselves that we have not been aware of until that moment; we have been blind to those behaviours and may remain so
- Unconscious – behaviours unknown to ourselves and, on the face of it, unknown to others manifest themselves by having an impact on either the public, blind or hidden areas that we might present; these may not necessarily be rational or irrational behaviours, and may be something that others consider 'out of character'.

Organisations such as the Tavistock Group have worked with individuals and companies to show how some of the unconscious behaviours inform our conscious actions. For example, in personal relationships a member of the family, a friend or a colleague will finish a relationship with person A and then strike up one with person B. To others (us) he or she will express a view that A and B are completely different individuals, yet to you, as an observer of your friend's choice of new partner, it seems that A and B are remarkably similar. Not only are they similar as individuals, but the patterns of behaviour that your friend is exhibiting appears to be a repetition of the previous relationship. Meanwhile, the individual in question is oblivious to these behaviours. This has sometimes been labelled the 'theatre of the mind' – we play out the same scenes with new people. What about your own repeated patterns in both social and the work environment? In the film *Groundhog Day*, our anti-hero, Bill Murray, is condemned to relive the same day over and over again. It is only when he has learned new behaviours and gained an insight into his behaviour that he is able to progress. In doing so, he gets the girl and breaks the cycle of events. The vicious circle has become a virtuous one reinforced through positive behaviours.

This leads us on to exploring the concept of the 'mental model'. In becoming an adult, we create a framework of the world within which we can successfully operate. We do this by creating a multiplicity of mental models that at any particular point in time help us to make sense of our environment and allow us to function at all, and ideally, effectively. We have mental models of social interaction as well as those of a more mechanistic nature. These allow us to function in the social and work environment, and govern our expectations of how all systems work. The danger for each of us is that there is a tendency to throw away or reject new information if it doesn't fit the current model.

At one time, the physical model for the world was that it was flat and the sun went round it. To disagree with that model was an act of heresy. Gallileo confronted the conventional wisdoms of the day by suggesting that the earth went round the sun. By doing so, he not only undermined the current laws of nature and science but also challenged fundamental religious beliefs. He was offering data that did not fit the current model.

This aspect of human behaviour has been known for some time. The allegorical tale of Plato's Cave provides a philosophical approach. He asked us to imagine the following scenario.

Some people are chained up within a cave and have no knowledge of the outside world. The only light available comes from a fire at the mouth of the cave. They cannot see the fire, but they see the shadows formed from people and other objects going by outside. Those chained to the walls of the cave believe that the shadows are the reality, and give

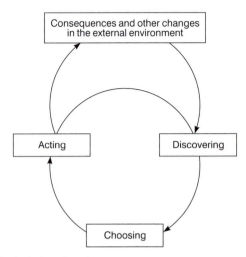

Figure 8.4 Simple single-loop learning.

meaning and essence to them. One of the cave dwellers escapes, discovers that the shadows are a mere artefact of a larger reality, and realises all is not as it first thought. He returns to the cave to inform the other inhabitants. Like Gallileo, he is ridiculed for what he suggests. The cave dwellers have devised and maintained a mental model of the world around them, based on the knowledge that they had available to them to that time. When new information comes along they have a choice – to change their mental model, reject the new data or possibly, as Alexander the Great is reputed to have done, 'shoot the messenger'. This model of behaviour has been described as single-loop learning (Figure 8.4). If the new data do not fit the existing model or paradigm, they are rejected.

Complex or double-loop learning (Figure 8.5) requires the individual to question the existing model or paradigm and change it to account for the new data. This is a difficult task, because it makes the assumption that we need to test and question every new piece of data that comes to us. In fact, once established, single-loop is not really learning any more. In more recent times, Einstein's work had a similar impact on Newtonian physics. It is alleged that Einstein was quite disparaging towards some of his predecessors, especially Max Plank, for not seeing the 'new model'. Double-loop learning is the cornerstone to innovation and creativity; it requires us to question and revise our mental models. This has often been called a 'paradigm shift'.

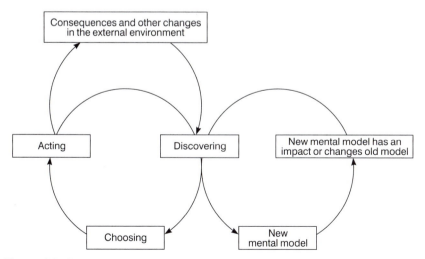

Figure 8.5 Complex double-loop learning.

8.6 Innovation and creativity

Once we have identified individuals who function well in teams and offered them an opportunity to work in an innovative and creative environment, there are still the wider organisational constraints that might limit the ability of the team to function effectively. It has been suggested that one of the major threats to innovation is a sense of job insecurity and lack of safety at work (see Frederick Hertzberg's work on 'hygiene factors'). In production teams, if all the members feel that they are truly part of the team and are participating in the production process, there is much evidence to suggest that the project will be more successful. A good project manager who gives continuous feedback and fosters a sense of belonging in members of the team will have a powerful effect on improving the team's performance. Here we reach a conundrum. Many of the texts that deal with motivation and the actions of an entrepreneur could be seen to be at odds with the requirements for an innovative environment. An entrepreneur is a risk taker. However, this might explain why we need a director and a producer to bring a production project successfully to its conclusion. The entrepreneur could be seen as the individual who manages the risk on behalf of the creative team.

It might be suggested that the role of the entrepreneur/producer or the proxy, the project manager, in fostering innovation is:

1 To identify the staff who are likely to be innovative
2 To establish an innovative climate
3 To promote innovation amongst all staff
4 To promote innovation among teams
5 To promote innovation within the work organisations.

Made in Japan

In his book Made In Japan[12], Akio Morita suggested that he created an atmosphere in Sony that allowed people to fail. He says: 'Once you have a staff of prepared, intelligent and energetic people the next step is to motivate them to be creative'. He goes on to say:

Our brilliant researcher, Nobutoshi Kihara, came up with the system that did away with the blank spaces between the bands of recorded material on regular videotape. These empty bands (called guard bands) were placed there to avoid interference or spill over as each band of programme material is recorded and played back. This meant that half the tape was going unused … Why not record onto the empty spaces, greatly increasing capacity and avoiding interference by using two recording reading heads and angling the heads at about 90° from each other, so that each head could not read or interfere with the recording track next to it? A new revolving head drum had to be designed and a different mechanism developed, but after many months of testing, his group produced a new system that worked beautifully, and we have built a brand new video system for home use with the picture yet attainable.

Sony called this Betamax, because 'beta' is a brush stroke in painting or calligraphy, and it is also is similar to the Greek letter beta and sounds scientific. In engineering terms, Betamax was far superior to and came out before VHS. However, due to clever marketing the VHS format swept away Betamax in the domestic environment. Again creativity came to the fore in Sony, with some modifications the Betamax quality was considerably improved and it became the first true broadcast-quality cassette videotape recording format. Sony has dominated the world of professional video recording ever since.

By creating a working environment in which people could fail, Sony allowed them to succeed. In doing so, Sony fostered an environment in which enormous leaps in technology were possible. Current wisdom suggests that innovation and creativity is possible if the following factors are taken into account:

- a balanced team, as recommended by Belbin, is formed
- individuals are trained and developed
- the team is given a clear goal – the making of a television programme or a film certainly focuses the mind
- tasks and targets are clear – most jobs in the television industry are very clearly identified
- the team has a motivating piece of work to do, such as a film or a television programme; this gives the team a sense of cohesiveness
- members of the team feel they are part of what is going on
- there is a high level of participation, which also ensures a high standard of work and quality of innovation
- challenges to the team are made within a safe environment
- the crews' opinions on work are canvasses

- the production manager, director or producer has good communication skills, which will bring the best out of the members of the crew
- individuals are respected and given a great deal of autonomy in the work they do.

8.7 The culture of the organisation

When many people first learn that organisations have a definable culture they are somewhat surprised. Up until that moment, most people would have considered culture only as a social or national artefact – this manifestation of culture being determined by race, religion, location in the world and other aspects of the social order. All of these attributes are present within the business environment, but in addition to any national social culture there is a unique business culture relating to that organisation. This will include formal and informal business structures – how people dress, how they behave, how they refer to one another. Do they call the boss 'sir' or 'madam', or refer to them on first-name terms? Is it jeans and T-shirt or a three-piece suit dress code? It is stated that today is 'smart casual' or 'dress down' (at Levi's in San Francisco, the corporate dress is jeans). Is it a conservative or liberal working environment? Is it expected that you turn up at 8.30 am and do not leave until 8.30 pm? Is there an understanding that to do your job well you are not necessarily bound to your desk? There must be many more organisational behaviours of which you are aware.

The elements of organisational culture can be presented in three groups:

1 Company practices, typified by rights, ceremonies and rituals
2 Company communications, such as stories, myths, sagas, legends, folk tales, symbols and slogans
3 Physical cultural forms, including artefacts, physical layout, national and international teams, common language comprising of industry jargon, company-specific jargon, dominant culture jargon and in-jokes.

The resultant behaviours, whilst making those who are part of the organisation feel inclusive, are also barriers and exclusive. Unless you understand the jargon, the acronyms and the shared behaviours, it is almost impossible to penetrate and understand what is going on easily and quickly. The next contract of the media production programme-maker may depend on the ability to deconstruct these behaviours and reflect them in any production submission.

The cultural conditions of an organisation also have an impact on the mindset of the individuals within the organisation, in the shared mental models of the way things are done. In many instances this allows the business to function but also, probably in just as many instances, it is actually disables free thinking in an innovative, creative environment. Sometimes expressing a new view in the wrong format can cause it to be dismissed because the mode of presentation does not conform to the cultural framework. The corporate culture is not necessarily in harmony with the formal company management structure. To an extent it reflects and impacts on the formal hierarchies of the business. Charles Handy, in *Understanding*

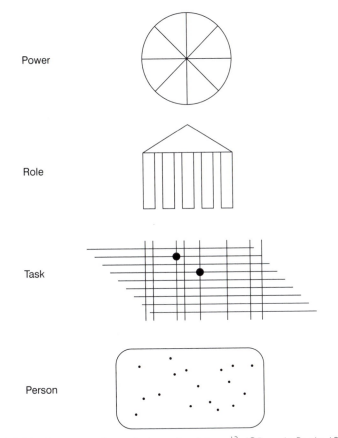

Power

Role

Task

Person

Figure 8.6 The four types of organisation cultural forms[13]. (©Penguin Books 1976, 1981, 1985, 1993. Reprinted by kind permission.)

Organisations[13], suggested that there are four types of organisation cultural forms (Figure 8.6):

1 The power culture
2 The role culture
3 The task culture
4 The person culture.

Of the four cultures described, the power culture and the task culture have the strongest resonance in the audiovisual industry. The power culture is found in the small entrepreneurial organisations typical of many small audiovisual businesses. There is a central figure who controls the whole aspect of the business. It is suggested that we can visualise the structure as being similar to that of a spider's web. Whilst the business is small, the individual at the centre of the organisation controls all of the activities of the organisation (see Chapter 7). It is a somewhat Machiavellian type of organisation, inasmuch as the end usually justifies the means. 'It'll be alright on the night' is a strong driver within this kind of business.

The role culture image is that of a Greek temple. The pillars represent the departments; specialisations or silos of activity support the centre. The capping stone sits on top of these functional areas, being symbolic of the infrastructure and management of the business.

The task culture is project driven; the image is that of a fishing net. Where the strands intersect, there lies the power in an organisation. It is based on teams getting the job done with a high degree of autonomy. The control is maintained by the managers through resource allocation. The current status of the BBC is a model for this type of organisation. Producers have a degree of autonomy and power with a clear line to the audience, and management exercise control over this power by allocating financial material resources.

The person culture is a little bit more of an amorphous mass, often made up of a group of individuals who need some form of administrative and management support to enable them to do their professional tasks. A doctors' group practice, a law firm or any team of professionals who feel they have equal standing in the community and amongst their peer group are examples of this type of organisation. To an extent, it is a self-limiting group.

Tom Burns carried out a study of the BBC and suggested that the BBC was a very segmented organisation, both horizontally (by departments) and vertically (where as you move through the grading structure you lose contact with your professional or craft skill roots). He goes on to suggest that 'in this situation the career and the political systems can become more important than the formal task system'[14].

To an extent, these cultural forms are implicitly built upon and in some cases shadow what might be set up as a formal structure to the business. It may be true that within the power culture a formal system may exist. However small the company may be, there might be heads of department (such as an editor in post-production) plus a couple of assistants, a sound recordist and editor, and a computer graphics group with 2D and 3D capabilities.

If the owner and director of the company behave as if they are directing a production, they will still be the key decision-makers within the company. To an extent, the behaviour of the company will be an extension of the behaviour of the person at the centre of the business. His or her personality, temperament and leadership style will have an infectious, formal and informal impact on everyone else within the business.

Charles Handy suggests that organisational issues can be divided into three groups:

- People – motivation, needs, level of energy, career/experience, age, individual skills and abilities, pay, personalities, training, role
- Power – groups, the leaders, inter-group relations, type of influence, leadership style, rewards and punishment, responsibilities, control systems.
- Practicalities – the environment, the market, philosophies, values, norms, goals, objectives, ownership, history, career structures, size, structure, change, technology.

There has been a great deal written about organisations and the behaviour of organisations in terms of how they manage staff and people internally, and how the organisations faces the external environment. The scope of this book does not offer us the opportunity to explore these many topics in any great detail. As an introductory text, we have concentrated on the role of the individual within the business environment. We have also tried to introduce some of the issues regarding group dynamics that we find in Charles Handy's classification of organisations. Other aspects of media management, such as control systems, are found in Part 3 of this book, where we look at media production management in more detail.

The legitimate use of authority within an organisation is the accepted form of power within an organisation. It is recognised and bestowed upon the individual as part of the formal structure of the business. The legitimate power encapsulated in authority gives the individual, whether the managing

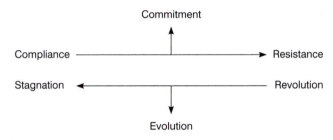

Figure 8.7 Compliance, commitment and resistance.

director, the line manager or head of the team, the opportunity to delegate tasks to others. In a successfully functioning organisation, this delegation of roles will be seen as a way of giving opportunities to members of staff. In some dysfunctional organisations, it is seen as a way of pushing the workload onto those at the bottom of the organisation.

Figure 8.7 shows a simple illustration between compliance, commitment and resistance. You gain commitment from the staff when they are fully engaged with and part of the decision-making process. You obtain compliance from the staff when they feel they have no choice but to do the work as required. Resistance and possibly revolution, or at least a strike, is shown to occur when those being given tasks to perform feel that they are not being consulted on the decisions made as to why they should be doing those particular jobs.

Professor Ralph Stacey suggested that in any large organisation there is a whole range of interactions taking place. He suggests that there is a complete shadow organisation by which communication takes place and cultural forms are devised. Figure 8.8 indicates that although there is a 'rational loop' of business behaviour, there are at least four other interlocking behaviour models that will impact upon the dynamics of the organisation. How often have you heard it said, if you want to gain insights into the values and attitudes of the managing director, make sure you have a good relationship with his or her assistant or secretary? Influence is the handmaiden to power.

For Stacey, strategic management education and business behaviour models have tended to be about organising the business in stable equilibrium conditions. He suggests that our real task as managers is to cope with the uncertainty of an unstable future – it is our ability to adapt to a changing environment that will enable one organisation to survive while another

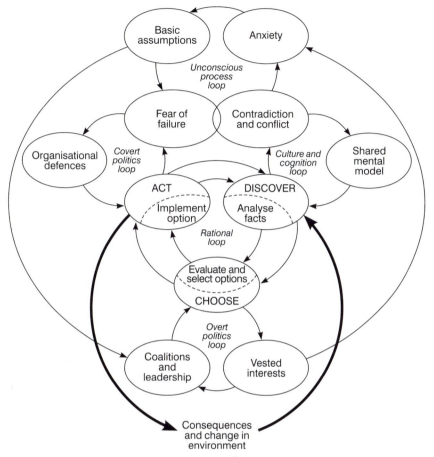

Figure 8.8 The self-organising form of control[15]. (©Pitman Publishing 1993. Reprinted by kind permission of Pearson Education Limited.)

perishes. His models are of particular interest to media managers. By definition, we work in an unpredictable and chaotic working environment. His views about the behaviour of organisations are worth considering. Two of his points are[16]:

> Organisations are characterised by fundamental contradictions: stability and instability; the need to differentiate and the need to integrate; the need for rule-based negative feedback control systems, and the need for flexible amplifying systems to deal with unforeseen, unseeable change which are impended by the negative feedback systems.

> People operating in complex systems might easily develop trained incapacity and skilled incompetence. If they are to combat this they

need continually to question existing mental models and develop new ones to cope with the unfolding future of the organisational system they operate in. They need to think in system terms.

Chapter 7 looked at the growth of businesses within the media industry. The four cultures described earlier and the Greiner development model all come into play in trying to describe organisational culture. Organisations not only change their structure as they grow, but they also change their cultural form. Most will start as a power culture. Video production companies will then tend to shift into a task culture, where small project teams are producing the work required. As they grow they will inevitably become a role culture type of organisation, when a more rigid structure and reporting system is put in place (see the first two stages in the Greiner model). As a business expands, not only do the owners and managers need to understand the culture of organisations within one national boundary, but they also need to have some sense of cross-cultural sensitivity in international markets and be able to achieve a more understandable form of cultural mis-match. The attributes of the individual and the attributes of the organisation all come into play, with even more complex circles of confusion.

One of the most widely read commentators on cross-cultural issues is Geert Hofstede[17]. He identified four dimensions to classify differences in cultural forms between countries:

1 Power versus distance
2 Collectivism versus individualism
3 Femininity versus masculinity
4 Uncertainty avoidance.

Whilst Hofstede applied these dimensions to nation states, in many ways it is a useful structure to help define the internal cultural form of an organisation as well.

Within organisations, power/distance is about the relationship in the chain between owner, director, manager and staff. A collectivist approach is about consensus; Japan has often been referenced as the archetypal collectivist society. The USA personifies the individual, yet it is a highly conformist society due to a high level of uncertainty avoidance by minimising future risks. It seems that the Anglo-Saxon nature is a wish to control the future. Being willing to show the feminine side of one's nature within the work environment might not be well received in some Middle East countries. This gender scale is not just concerned with the male–female dimension, but also with the quantity (male)–quality (female) aspects of life – what some firms have characterised as the work–life balance.

This chapter has sought to set the agenda for analysing the individual, the group, the organisation, the industry, and the national and international cultures in which we find ourselves. You might now not only look at the behaviours of others, but also reflect on your own behaviour in the social and organisational environment. Remember, how others act towards us is, to an extent, dependent on our own complicity actions and behaviour.

8.8 References

1. Hofstede, G. (1994). *Cultures and Organisations*, p. 3. Harper Collins.
2. Storper, M. (1985). *The Changing Organisation and Location of the Motion Picture Industry – A Research Report.* UCLA Publishing.
3. Kennedy, C. (1991). *Guide to Management Gurus*, p. 95. Century.
4. Huczynski, A. and Buchanan, D. (1991). *Organisational Behaviour*, 2nd edn, p. 59. Prentice Hall.
5. Saudella, C. (1998). *The Importance of L!VE TV as a Part of Mirror Group's Diversification Strategy.* University of Hertfordshire.
6. Clegg, F. (1984). *Simple Statistics: A Course Book for the Social Sciences.* Cambridge University Press.
7. Keirsey, D. and Bates, M. (1984). *Please Understand Me; Character and Temperament Types.* Prometheus Nemesis.
8. Keirsey, D. and Bates, M. (1984). *Please Understand Me*, p. 65. Prometheus Nemesis.
9. 'Kubrick's grandest gamble' (1975). *Time*, p. 78. December 15.
10. Huczynski, A. and Buchanan, D. (1991). Belbin's team role theory. In: *Organisational Behaviour Workbook*, 2nd edn, p. 76. Prentice Hall.
11. Stacey, R. (1996). *Strategic Management and Organisational Dynamics*, 2nd edn, p. 193. Pitman Publishing.
12. Morita, A. (1987). *Made In Japan*, p. 160. Fontana.
13. Handy, C. (1993). *Understanding Organisations*, p. 180. Penguin.
14. Burns, T. (1979). *The BBC – Public Institution and Private World.* The Macmillan Press Ltd.
15. Stacey, R. (1996). *Strategic Management and Organisational Dynamics*, 2nd edn, p. 289. Pitman Publishing.

16. Stacey, R. (1996). *Strategic Management and Organisational Dynamics*, 2nd edn, Pitman Publishing.
17. Hofstede, G. (1994). *Cultures and Organisations*. Harper Collins.

8.9 Further reading

Handy, C. (1993). *Understanding Organisations*. Penguin.
Huczynski, A. and Buchanan, D. (1991). *Organisational Behaviour*, 2nd edn. Prentice Hall.
Kennedy, C. (1992). *Guide to the Management Gurus*. Century.
Keirsey, D. and Bates, M. (1984). *Please Understand Me; Character and Temperament Types*. Prometheus Nemesis.
Morgan, G. (1986). *Images of Organisations*. Sage.

Chapter 9

Strategic management

9.1 Summary

Strategic management as presented in this text examines a generic set of management models. By definition, they have application to any organisation or industry. In this chapter, we look at how these strategic management tools and techniques can be of value in considering management issues in the audiovisual industry. Johnson and Scholes[1] define strategy as:

> the direction and scope of an organisation over the long term: ideally which matches its resources to its changing environment, and in particular its markets, customers or clients as to meet stakeholder expectations.

Strategy is essentially about the big decisions that owners, directors or managers might make; for example:

- which products to make and services to offer
- how they (owners, directors or managers) see their company in the marketplace
- how they analyse their own internal and external competitiveness
- how they can be a more effective company or firm in the future.

Strategic management starts by analysing the business environment, and we suggest a few tools and techniques to help that task. An organisation's managers can consider the options based on this analysis by, say, scenario planning and risk analysis. Then they have to consider how to apply the

choices available. Finally, the management team develop the implementation plan and tactics to match this strategy.
This process can be summarised as:

- analysis
- choice
- implementation.

In the last 50 years, many strategic theories have come and gone, along with the popularity of the professors of various business schools or management gurus who propound them. In this chapter, we present tools and techniques that will allow any competent manager, irrespective of the particular strategic model favoured, to analyse the economic and business environment in which he or she operates.

The audiovisual industry is highly volatile and unstable. The churn rate of SMEs (small and medium enterprises) listed in media trade directories is high. Many UK film production companies are formed for a single production. Others, such as Goldcrest[2], go from being lauded in Hollywood to receivership within just a few years. 'The British are coming' said Colin Welland, actor and scriptwriter, at his Oscar acceptance speech for the screenplay of *Chariots of Fire* in 1982. The British might be coming, but just as many are going.

As earlier chapters have indicated, management strategies in the audiovisual industries are often underpinned by government policy. In the UK there is currently controlling regulation for television and a minimalist intervention policy for film. The business environment of the media company (see Introduction, Figure I) was devised to show some of the interlocking, complex and circular relationships with which the media manager has to deal. Imagine the media manager at the centre of this space; every one of these relationships will influence the decisions of the media manager – decisions that cannot be made without recognising the paradoxes that beset a manager in the audiovisual industry:

- balancing creativity with project control
- managing a chaotic and unstable business environment
- coping with change or an increasing rate of change
- dealing with an ever-changing technical platform.

This chapter has been devised to introduce you to how you might deconstruct, understand and possibly act more effectively in organisational management.

9.2 Objectives and key issues

As we enter the twenty-first century, strategic management has gathered much critical comment – often not particularly complimentary. The last 50 years have witnessed the expansion of business schools such as Harvard and London in their mission to educate and train the business elite. The MBA qualification has become an almost essential requirement for new and aspiring fast-track managers. More recently, there has been a proliferation of management courses at almost every university and college. Of late, somewhat unfairly, strategic management skills have been dismissed as a mixture of 'consultant speak' and business school jargon.

The media business model for this book (Figure I) shows the media company positioned in the middle of many concentric and interlocking circles, and business owners or managers need to make sense of what is going on within these various spheres of influence. Whatever one's personal view on the matter, strategic management is a core skill that any manager, even a media manager, should acquire in order to help them understand these complex relationships.

The objectives of this chapter are to make the potential media manager aware of strategic management, what it means, and its use to the manager and decision-maker. It is anticipated that the knowledge gained from this chapter will give you:

- an awareness of some management tools and techniques
- knowledge of how a manager might apply these tools and techniques.

9.3 Introduction to strategic management

Set out below are two seemingly contrasting but remarkably similar tasks that a manager (or a potential manager) might undertake.

Case I

You have been asked to provide an analysis and appraisal of the media production group within the multinational for which you work. This film and video unit, comprising about 20 people, has been producing corporate training, PR and communication products for the last 50 years. It is part of the infrastructure of the business and generates little capital. It is well respected within the film and video industry, and its programmes are used widely by schools and other educational establishments. However, it is a period of cost cutting, and senior management have turned their eye on this group as an expensive luxury that the business can no longer afford.

Your task is to conduct a business analysis into the value of the unit.

Case 2

You and two associates have hit upon a good idea; a new method for producing computer graphics, both faster and cheaper than traditional methods, or so you believe.

How do you go about testing this in the market place, and how do you decide whether you have a viable business or not?

Before you read on, make some notes as to how you might go about exploring the issues in these cases. Where would you start? What information would you need; What is relevant? Who would you talk to? Why would you talk to them? When would you stop the research and start the writing? How would you structure the report?

Whatever you do, both cases require a clear and cogent argument to explain what is going on. You need first to tell the story of the events, to create the narrative, by possibly using the seven questions given above. By doing so, you clarify the issues for yourself and for those who will be influenced by and then make decisions on the basis of the report you produce. In Case 1, the report will be aimed at senior business managers and ideally produced in partnership with the production team. In Case 2, it could be aimed at potential business partners, shareholders or a finance manager.

In this chapter, we examine methods by which we may structure our strategic analysis, choice and implementation to provide a pathway through the complex issues that surround any decision made in an organisation. The steps are:

1 Analysis – explain what is going on
2 Choices – examine options then select and devise a strategy
3 Implementation – recommend and act on the chosen course of action.

The term 'strategy' comes from the Greek *strategos* – the art of the military general. In recent years there has been much debate about what strategic management actually encompasses, but essentially it is still about the main objectives or goals of an organisation. Many businesses try to capture this objective in a mission statement. This attempts to provide a point of reference for all of those involved in the business, both those employed by it and those possibly buying or using goods created by it. The strategy for a business is something that sets up the policies and guidelines for that entity. Throughout the rest of this chapter, we will use the term 'organisation' to represent any business entity or enterprise. Strategic management can apply to almost any organisation; after all, an individual could set out a strategy to become the British Prime Minister. Their tactic could be:

1 Become a lawyer
2 Join a political party
3 Get voted into local government
4 Become a member of the Shadow Cabinet
5 Become elected leader
6 Get voted in at the next election.

Thus we have defined the strategy and the tactics; the only hurdle is the implementation. There is often little point in suggesting 'get yourself a job and you'll no longer be impoverished' to someone who is impoverished and unemployed. The strategy might be sound, but the tactic has little chance of implementation. The second point to make, then, is that strategies have to be effective and achievable.

The strategy challenge

- You're running a small company that is successful in providing services to a particular part of the media industry, and you make extensive use of computers.
- The particular skills that you've been applying to support the industry are no longer required – technology has changed and the particular area of support is no longer needed.
- The repair and maintenance skills of your team have grown greatly over the period – you are a good team.
- Is it a viable strategy to become a repair and maintenance company?
- Is that in the mindset of yourself and your colleagues?
- Would such a strategy work?

Strategy is also about trying to build in a position or posture for the unpredictable or unknowable. This often comes down to devising a set of scenarios – the 'what ifs' – but if it is *truly unpredictable*, then by definition at this stage it cannot be predicted. Yet any manager should consider the extremes in future possibilities. For example, in Case I the future for the film and video group could be:

1 There is no video group within the business – all work is contracted out
2 The group is expanded to take on all sorts of areas of work – not only internal but external contracts – to become self-funding.

Therefore, if a strategy is devised it should be cohesive but also testable. The definitions of what can be tested and how are often reflected in key performance indicators (KPIs) or benchmarks. These measures, along with the organisation's reports and accounts, define how the business has met its strategic goals.

Strategic management has been summarised and expressed by Ralph Stacey[3] as the five 'P's. These are:

- Plan
- Position
- Ploy
- Perspective
- Pattern.

By keeping these factors in mind as you go forward in making a more detailed analysis of the strategy as a potential strategic manager, you will maintain a clear view of the objectives of that strategy.

In *Exploring Corporate Strategy*[4], Johnstone and Scholes devised a summary model for the elements of strategic management. Figure 9.1 provides a framework and a model from which a manager may structure strategic decisions. It is a generic model that can be used to interpret the inter-relationships of the media firm (Figure I). It is one of the strategic models that will be suggested throughout this text as a means of analysing the working environment within which managers find themselves.

Comprehensive management texts tend to take a historical perspective when reviewing strategic management and management theories. We recommend that the student of strategic management in the media industry should take some time to look at the work of those who have shaped modern concepts and terms of management. Carol Kennedy's *Guide to Management Gurus*[5] provides a succinct text on the subject.

Figure 9.1 A summary model of strategic management. (©Prentice Hall Europe 1988, 1993, 1997, 1999. Reprinted by kind permission of Pearson Education Limited.)

These thought leaders have come from widely diversified backgrounds – engineering, psychology, sociology, economics etc. Included in the book are many of the names that, even with the most superficial of management reading to date, a manager would have come across –Ansoff, Taylor, Maslow, Herzberg, Handy, Peters, Fayo, Drucker, Weber etc. These people, along with many others, have conducted research and provided theories that have shaped and modified management behaviour over the last 100 years.

We now consider some of the management tools that can assist you to make effective strategic management decisions. This chapter will reference aspects of the models and theories by some of the leading authors and writers on management.

9.4 The company audit

Many books that introduce the concept of the company audit using a SWOT (strengths, weakness, opportunities, threats) and PEST (political, economic, social, technical) analysis usually fail to suggest methods by which the results could be assessed and measured. Often the reason for this is that it suggests a degree of ambiguity in the models outside the scope of the text. Any form of assessment (and this is especially true in strategic management) has with it a degree of ambiguity. This ambiguity should be translated into some form of risk measurement.

Decision-making is about risk assessment. Almost every decision we make has an element of risk attached to it, some of which is bounded by experience, intuition or a *true* risk assessment. Risk assessment is difficult, and often not well judged. Consider an individual's fear of flying. It is well known that we are more at risk in the taxi driving us to the airport than we are in the hands of the airlines, yet for many otherwise rational individuals the fear persists. We make more risky yet rational assumptions about the environment in which we work. Our analysis for simple tasks, such as arriving at work on time, is often rational but more risky. Many people will catch a train that gets them into the office 5 minutes before the daily deadline although, knowing the vagaries of the UK transport system, an error of margin of 5 minutes on a train journey of, say, 45 minutes is probably cutting it fine. A risk aversion approach would be to catch the earlier train in order to reduce the risk and the margin for error. The reasons we don't do this are many (crowded trains, time between service, lift to station etc.). It would also be true to say that life would be unmanageable if we operated at all times by a total risk-aversion philosophy. The risk of the train to work being late could be moderately high, but the impact on lifestyle or career quite low. However, on an interview day we will catch the earlier train. Under these circumstances, we try to minimise the risk.

We therefore do have an appreciation of the chance or level of risk and the impact that risk will have. These two variables, level and impact, become the axes on a risk analysis chart. It is not a trivial task to quantify this risk. In general, the best we can do is to assess the level of risk as low (L), medium (M) or high (H), and similarly assess its impact as L, M or H (see Chapter 14 for more details on risk assessment). Suffice to say at this stage that should any element in an audit or SWOT or PEST analysis throw up a great many Ms and Hs in the analysis, further work is needed.

The new business idea

At their simplest, SWOT and PEST analyses provide an opportunity to list all the issues that affect the organisation.

Consider Case 2. Here we list some of the business factors involved:

1 Strengths
   - new idea
   - requires little specialist equipement
   - profit/unit very attractive; could become a cash cow for the company.
2 Weaknesses
   - undercapitalised
   - partners have no business track record
   - why would buyers take the risk?
3 Opportunities
   - key market segments not currently addressed
   - initial potential customers well known to business
   - partner with a market leader to shelter company and product growth
   - other ideas ready to explore.
4 Threats
   - current market leaders will adopt the idea
   - other start-up companies with similar ideas might exist
   - current market changes very quickly; only have 12 months to market.

The two (albeit basic) tools of SWOT and PEST analysis, used in conjunction with an external audit, can provide a comprehensive review and evaluation of the organisation's business environment.

Below are some of the elements considered in an external audit of a media company. As an example, the macro economic environment has some further detail included.

1 Macro economic environment
   (a) Government policies – UK offers 100 per cent capital allowances write-off in the first year for any qualifying film costing up to £15 million. If a film costs more than £15 million, the production costs can be written off over 3 years.

(b) Social/cultural – demographics (age distribution, potential audience), location of population, wealth distribution, social attitudes (say, towards health) or other elements within.

(c) Political/legal/fiscal – in this particular area one would look at the nationals, internationals (EU), government buying and multinationals. All of these elements will have an impact on the behaviour of the business.

(d) Economic – what is the current stability of the economic environment in which the business is functioning? Is it stable? Is it going through a boom cycle? Depression? What fluctuations, interest rate, price control, credit controls, tax rates will have an impact on the business to date? For example, government tax breaks introduced in 1997 meant that British films could write off 100 per cent production costs.

(e) Technological – most commentators on the film and television industry suggest that it is one of the most technically driven industries there is. In fact, one of the major criticisms of some of the programmes in recent years has been that it is all technology driven with no content.

2 Market environment
  (a) Total market profile – for example the segment size and potential growth.
  (b) Market characteristics – trends in buyer behaviour and development in products related to technology or customer behaviour.
  (c) Buying characteristics – customer profile.
  (d) Features of products available.

3 Competitive environment
  (a) Competitor market shares.
  (b) Marketing skills.
  (c) Marketing mix.
  (d) Product features, prices and conditions.

4 Distribution methods – method and extent of promotion.

5 Industry structure.

6 Industry practices.

7 Barriers to entry and industry profitability.

Most of the above has been elegantly presented in Michael Porter's five forces model. Porter[6] suggests:

> To establish a strategic agenda for dealing with these contending currents and growing despite them a company must understand how

they work in the industry and how they direct the company in a particular situation.

He goes on to say:

The essence of strategy formulation is coping with competition.

9.5 Porter's 'five forces' model

In *Competitive Strategy: Techniques for Analysing Industries and Competitors*[7], Porter sets out what has become known as the 'five forces model'. In the first instance, he posed five key questions. These were:

1 How can I reduce the bargaining power of my customers?
2 How can I reduce the bargaining power of my suppliers?
3 How can I reduce substitutes for my product or services?
4 How can I limit rivalry in my industry?
5 How can I prevent new entrants from coming into my industry?

This rather hard yet objectively rational approach to business management became encapsulated in the five forces framework (Figure 9.2), where a more general model is presented as:

1 Buyer power (bargaining capability)
2 Supplier power (bargaining capability)
3 The threat of new entrants (to the market)

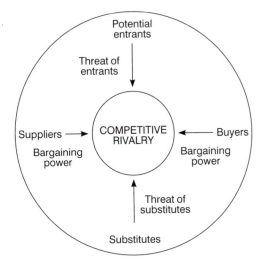

Figure 9.2 Porter's five forces model.

4 The threat of substitution (of products and services)

5 The nature of rivalry (between existing firms).

As with the SWOT and PEST analyses, it is a useful tool to analyse the business environment. To see how this may inform our assessment, let's examine just one of these forces, the threat of new entrants, in more detail from a media company perspective. The threat of a new entrant to an industry will be determined by what Porter labels as the barriers to entry, of which there are seven:

1 *Economies of scale.* The media industry, even at its most mechanistic, Fordist level, has been considered a cottage industry. A telephone, a fax machine, an address in Soho, London (the heart of the film and television industry) and now an email address are all that are required to turn you into a production company. At one time, to be effective in terms of production a facilities house required huge capital investment. Now editing can be completed off-line on the most modest of domestic PCs. Armed with master tapes and an edit log, this can then be conformed to a broadcast or broadcastable format within an on-line studio using virtually the same computer software.

2 *Product differentiation.* This operates at many levels within the media industry. Differentiation is the process by which one production company differentiates its offering from that of another, by which one facility house identifies its skills and techniques from another and, at the 'top' level, how the consumers are persuaded to make choices as to whether to watch BBC1, BBC2, ITV1, ITV2, Channel 4, Channel 5, or one of the cable or satellite offerings.

3 *Capital requirements.* The capital cost of a feature film can be enormous. The struggling film industry within the UK in the late 1990s looked to the Department for Culture, Media and Sport to provide support and assistance. Government tax breaks introduced in 1997 provided British films with an allowance to write-off 100 per cent of production costs over 1 year. This is applicable on films costing up to £15 million. Many smaller films that have been made in the UK in recent years have been funded by paying basic union rates even to star performers, and deferred payments to performers and technical crew.

4 *Switching costs.* This is the cost attached to changing suppliers or buyers. Retooling for an alternative video format due to supplier or client preferences carries capital and operational costs. New software tools for production or administration will require staff to be trained. The 'experience curve' requirement will determine how viable this switch is for the business (see below).

5 *Access to distribution channels.* Since its very inception, the UK film industry has been dominated by American distributors. One of the major complaints by British film-makers (and indeed other European film-makers) has been access to these potential markets.

6 *Cost advantages independent of scale.* In an industry that is still largely freelance and essentially contract- or production-based, being a name in the market place is vital to continued success. Whilst the well-known phrase 'You're only as good as your last production' is true, with no production track record the chances of breaking into the market place are small. The number of potential entrants into the market are enormous. Those who want to break in to the film and television industry are willing to do 'almost anything' to succeed. The learning curve, reduced cost per unit of output or, as Johnson and Scholes express it, 'the experience curve'[8] is a key determinant of company profitablity when product price is inflexible. If a small, experienced production team deliver the programme on time and to budget, then their costs will be contained and their retained profit as predicted (see Chapter 14).

7 *Government policy.* Policy has a major impact on the behaviour and action of players in the media market, especially film and television. It is by government edict and action that the radio and television market exists at all in any structured form in the UK. In the run up to the year 2000, Chris Smith (Heritage Secretary in the Labour Government of 1999) set out the agenda for the transfer to digital transmission. At the RTS conference in October 1999, he said: 'In a word, there's a revolution going on in TV technology; and Britain is at the forefront of change. I want to keep us there and press home our global advantage.' It is the government who therefore establish the regulations by which the media companies operate.

Expected retaliation

Although not one of the listed seven barriers, the expected retaliation to a new entrant has to be considered. Quantel, the broadcast computer graphics manufacturer, took legal action in the late 1980s against several smaller innovative computer graphic companies. The impact was to stop the new companies from trading. Quantel, the market leader, put the smaller companies out of business. Some years later, when Quantel took the same action against Adobe, they lost. Adobe has the funds to fight the case. Some small comfort to the directors of the start-up companies!

Overall, this more detailed analysis can be performed on the other four forces of Porter's model. The outcome from this process is an anlaysis of the media business environment from which the choices for action can be drawn.

When a company examines its business processes, ideally each stage should 'add value' to the product. The value chain (Figure 9.3) is a model to put internal processes to the test.

9.6 The value chain

Two terms that are bandied around with a great deal of sloppiness by some managers are 'added value' and 'value chain'. The term 'added value' is one that has been applied by almost every analyst who looks at the way a business behaves and makes a statement regarding that organisational entity and how they 'add value' to a production chain or product lifecycle. If a business entity or organisation can add value to the product lifecycle, then they have something for which they can charge. Supermarkets take lettuce from the producer, wash it, chop it up, combine it with other salad ingredients, and put it inside a plastic bag for the consumer to open and eat. If the customer accepts the 'value added' by purchasing the end result, then the supermarket has created 'added value' for which they can charge. They have become more that just a reseller with a mark-up in the transaction chain; rather, a manufacturer. If by suppressing transaction costs between stages of production this added value can be managed efficiently and passed to the customer, added value becomes added profit.

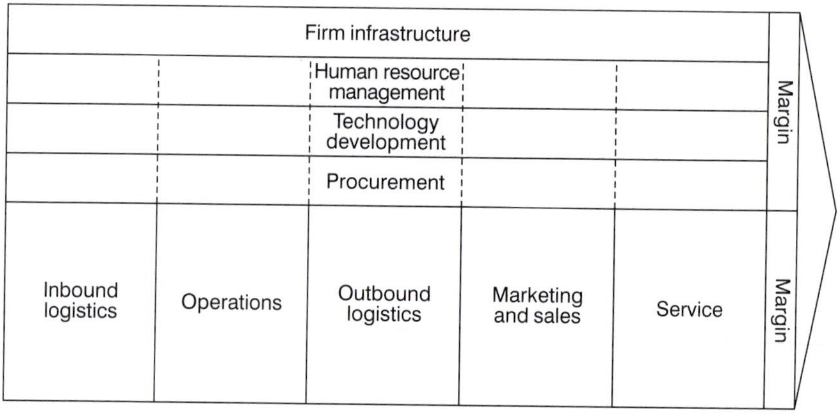

Firm infrastructure					Margin	
		Human resource management				
		Technology development				
		Procurement				
Inbound logistics	Operations	Outbound logistics	Marketing and sales	Service	Margin	

Figure 9.3 The value chain.

The value chain is used to show where costs are being incurred, where the margin is being made (where the value is being added), and where the organisation can and should make decisions as to whether to buy or build at a particular stage in the manufacturing or production process. Possible results could be the make or buy decision or outsource, or share production or other forms of partnership with other organisations. This model can be and has been used in a variety of ways:

- To analyse the internal processes of an organisation
- To establish theoretically the processes an organisation might put in place, or that a new business might construct for its business processes
- As a means of assessing the competitive advantage of the competition.

The outcome can be a rethink of company processes. As with any aspect of management decision-making, it must be placed within the overall strategy of the business. A singular model of decision-making can lead to prescriptive strategies, such as total internal markets that cut across the remit of the organisation and the culture of the business. At the BBC, where financial models have been the key drivers, the evidence suggests that the total internal market, through producer choice, has created a flawed system (even to the current Director General) with many anomalies (see Chapter 1).

At this point, you might like to go back to the two Case study questions posed at the beginning of this chapter and apply the value chain analysis to them as a means of extending the analytical processes.

9.7 The Boston Box

The Boston Consulting Group devised a model for assessing a company's portfolio of products, and this has become universally known as the Boston Box (Figure 9.4). In keeping with many other models, in its simplest form it can be a useful shorthand by which managers can encapsulate a particular market offering.

The axes on the grid are scaled in percentage values of market share and market growth. The four product identities within the grid define the attributes of the product or service. These are known as:

- cash cows
- stars
- question marks
- dogs.

Figure 9.4 The Boston Consulting Group matrix.

The term 'cash cow' has almost passed into common language to define a low-growth, high-share product that requires little effort to generate income for the business. Stars products are those that have fast growth and a high market share. As they mature, they 'fall' and ideally become cash cows. The question products are often new and with great potential. Will they become stars? Dogs, products at the end of their life, are retained to complete the portfolio or support a maintenance agreement.

At a more complex level, the Boston Box can be an illustrative model by which the analysis can lead to options for strategic choices. This can be achieved by considering what is required in a particular situation to shift a product around the grid to become, say, the star performer. For example; a small production company may have several department teams involved in the production process – graphics, post-production, production and location work. If we were to take a holistic view of the company and to say that overall, as a single entity, it was profitable, then that would be sufficient justification for each division to be maintained.

However, if we were to do a value chain on each step through the pre-production, production and post-production process, we may find that the post-production suite was a very expensive area to manage. This facility, comprising of equipment, maintenance charges, air conditioning and the rental for the room itself, is a fixed cost to the business. The staff editor is well respected in the industry, but is only employed on in-house productions. Would it be cheaper to move offices and work near an edit facility house than to maintain an expensive edit suite that is being under utilised? Should the editor be 'released' to go freelance?

Applying the Boston Box method, we might say that the editor was a questionable star performer but not being fully used. The edit suite with the editor could be marketed as a separate unit in its own right. This could be an effective and potentially profitable area of business, perhaps becoming a cash cow to the business. Many production companies do just that; they market the services of each department to increase the utilisation of resources.

Of course there are many issues that influence the business decisions, but the evidence suggests that many small companies don't even start that debate in a structured manner.

9.8 Forecasting and scenario planning in a chaotic environment

To forecast or predict future trends, whether or not through any of the given analytical tools, is key to successful strategic management. In the history of strategic management, a key factor post-Second World War and into the mid-1970s was the concept of the 'one best way' for any given organisation to work. This assumed a controllable, stable business environment. It does not require strategic analysis to reveal that the media industry is a highly volatile, highly unpredictable industry.

During the 1945–1980 period, the concept of corporate planning for the short, medium and long term were essential elements of the strategic manager's tool kit. Today, the rate of change in the working environment has devalued central corporate planning as a strategic tool. Theories on chaos, managing in chaotic environments and planning for the unknown have become more prevalent. Current strategic management models reflect many of the changes that have shown the shift from stable and known environments to unstable and unknown working environments.

A leading exponent of chaos theory is Professor Ralph Stacey, who challenged the traditional 'rational approach to strategic management'[9]. Stacey argues that to succeed in uncertain environments, we need to work in different methods and learn from chaos theory. This perspective is of particular value to the media manager, and will be referred to in a later section.

Tom Peters and Robert Waterman, in their book *In Search of Excellence*[10], identified eight characteristics that were shared by 43 of the most successful companies in America in 1977. These eight well-known characteristics have become linked with what one may call the *one best way* for a business to function, and include:

1 A bias for action: getting on with it
2 Being close to the customer: learning from the people they serve
3 Encouraging autonomy and entrepreneurship: fostering innovation and nurturing 'champions'
4 Achieving productivity through people; treating the rank and file as a source of quality
5 Being hands on, value driven: management showing its commitment
6 Sticking to the knitting: stay with the business you know
7 Having a simple form and lean staffing: some of the best companies have minimal headquarters staff
8 Having simultaneous loose and tighter properties: autonomy in shop floor activities plus centralised values.

It is also now well known that only 5 years after the book's publication, two-thirds of the companies who revealed these characteristics had a range of economic and structural problems. Which leaves us with the question – is there one best way, and can we plan?

Meanwhile, during this period, companies both small and large were maintaining their strategy of producing corporate planning documents with newly defined mission statements as a means of inspiring their shareholders, staff, bank managers and potential investors. These well-researched and glossy documents sometimes found their way into the managing director's office and were placed in a filing cabinet, never to see the light of day again.

Igor Ansoff, who wrote the seminal work *Corporate Strategy*[11], said of strategic planning that remained to be implemented that businesses were often suffering from 'paralysis by analysis'. Many of the current texts on strategy are a distillation of the work first put forward by Ansoff.

From his work, five key themes emerge:

1 There is no universal success formula for all firms
2 The driving variable that dictates the strategy required for success is the level of turbulence in the firm's environment

3 A firm's success cannot be optimised unless the aggressiveness of its strategy is aligned with the turbulence of its environment
4 A firm's success cannot be optimised unless management capability is also aligned with the environment
5 The key internal capability variables that jointly determine a firm's success are cognitive, psychological, sociological, political and anthropological.

You may wish to reflect on these themes, and consider them in terms of your own experiences within a firm to date.

9.9 Choices and options

Gathering data and market intelligence is just the first stage in formulating a strategy. If we assume that strategic decisions are an iterative process, in as much as there is continual feedback from the market place or from within the business, then the strategic analysis and monitoring is constantly informing the choices and options that the business leaders make. Of course, at different times in a business lifecycle these can and will be fundamentally different. Shall we start a business? How shall we improve the business? How do we move into new markets? When should we close the business?

In the previous section, we looked at the tools you could apply to help gather and organise the data needed to make informed choices. Financial and accounting data offer quantifiable measures of the organisation's performance. Year-end accounts tell how well the company did, management accounts tell how you're doing, financial analysis tells how well you're doing compared to others.

Management accounting data give company-specific information such as:

- the balance sheet
- profit and loss accounts
- the worth of work in progress
- the value of plant and machinery
- the status of the cash flow
- utilisation of resources
- current bank balances
- how often your staff are on chargeable projects
- project budgets
- the balance between fixed and variable costs
- above the line and below the line costs.

These internal measures can then be used to assess the organisation's performance on previous years, and the financial performance compared with competitors can be established from media market sector financial data.

In Chapters 8 and 9 we tried to give you some insights into the range of organisations that exist within the media industry and the individuals that the industry attracts. Notwithstanding any seemingly irrational behaviour about decision-making, how would we make sensible decisions from the data so far received? Many large organisations, especially international businesses, have whole departments dedicated to scenario planning and future planning – with, it must be admitted, varying degrees of success. Management texts are littered with case study analyses of these groups in action. So, how do you move from analysing the environment to making choices using the available data to substantiate and underpin the decisions you make? At this stage, there is a huge amount of data that needs to be filtered and evaluated.

The start-up business

How many times have you walked down the high street, looked at a new shop opening up and wondered, why on earth are they running that particular business in this particular location? It is fairly certain that in a shopping centre you know well you will have noticed that many shops open up, only to close down within 6 months to a year. Over 90 per cent of all start-up business fail within a few years. What was the 'rational' argument or case for starting this business? Who lent them the money? Why did they get funds to allow them to embark upon such a venture without due process taking place? Was it down to a plausible business plan presented to a local bank manager, or with monies from a retirement fund? Somewhere within a family or a group of associates, this foolhardy business adventure began. However, if all business analysis was predicated on the good offices of the company accountant, then nothing innovative would ever take place. Risk aversion is high on the accountant's shopping list.

Look back at Chapters 7 and 8. The criticism of many entrepreneurs is that their filter can be a little bit 'rose tinted'. This is what we might call the 'high street shop' view of business strategy – you only need to open the shop and put up a banner, and people will flock to buy the product.

9.10 Mental models and business behaviour

In Chapter 8, we considered the concept of 'a mental model'. How does this relate to one's own business endeavours? Simply this, the reason why so many businesses fail is that business managers have a fixed mental model about the nature of the business and the work they are trying to do, irrespective of the market intelligence, financial models and other data being offered. If it doesn't fit their current mental model they will reject it, either irrationally (because they will say they do not like what they are hearing) or rationally (by saying the data are wrong).

We know from our own experiences that the action of monitoring an event or a condition gives us information to allow us to act. In the jargon, this is known as a 'feedback loop'. Negative feedback acts as a controlling mechanism; a thermostat on a central heating system provides negative feedback inasmuch as when the temperature rises to a fixed point, it then shuts down the boiler. Similarly, the governor on a steam engine, whether in a science museum or in a still-working model, acts as a release for the pressure to maintain the boiler at an acceptable fixed pressure level. Positive feedback would amplify and exacerbate these particular circumstances. Consider the image of an army troop marching across a bridge and having to break step so that the rhythm of their marching feet does not act as an amplifying effect on the bridge and make it fall down, or the new footbridge over the Thames that closed a few days after opening because the swaying rhythm of the bridge made the pedestrians fall into step, which further amplified the swaying. Feedback is all about providing the mechanisms of control with information from the environment. These feedback loops are just as important in the business environment. The key model for this book (Figure 1) shows cyclical events and interractions; these are essentially a whole series of feedback loops.

As Chapter 8 suggests, complex learning is all about being able to change the mental model, the frame of reference, paradigm or mindset of the individual or the organisation. It is an essential stepping stone in the ability to manage and control business processes. This ability to shift the frame of reference keeps an organisation agile enough to cope with change yet still function effectively. There are many theories and illustrative industry case studies of how companies lock themselves into ways of working that become routine and predictable.

Given the level of uncertainty, it is particularly difficult to gain insight into the business behaviour of people in the audiovisual industry. The most satisfactory interpretation of those involved in creative endeavours seems to be found in chaos theory.

Chaos theory – always on the edge of catastrophy?

A scan of the literature of personal memoires and 'war stories' of media moguls reports a working environment dominated by egos, ambitions and intuitive (irrational?) behaviours. John Harvey Jones, in a special edition of his *Trouble Shooter* programme, suggested that the UK independent television industry was 'not a business at all'[12]. The audiovisual industry requires people to be creative and innovative, and this has to take place within the bounds of a system that requires a product to be completed and distributed. The dynamic between a stable and unstable environment requires managers to provide 'bounded unstable' working conditions for their teams. A highly stable, routinised environment does not lead to creativity, and a highly unstable yet energised creative environment will probably not lead to a completed product. The idea of bounded instabilty has its basis in chaos theory. The principle is that of hidden order in a seemingly random and uncontrolled environment. These hidden patterns provide the controlling mechanisms to differentiate a system from a purely random association.

To illustrate this concept, consider a jazz group. They begin the piece with written music, they then move into known patterns and 'riffs', and the virtuosos then improvise for a period. As the improvised sessions come to a close, the group (without a conductor or obvious signals) come together to finish the piece. All the musicians taking part know what is happening, and the audience hears more than a random sequence from a group of musicians. There is hidden order through time signature, key and repeated riffs or patterns. The piece remains a whole, even though some elements might be a unique offering on the day. The ideal production environment should provide this mix of creative control.

9.11 Corporate finance and the media industry

We often read articles in the media trade press, or in the media or business sections of the broadsheet papers, reporting the share price, current profits, price earnings ratio etc. of companies in the audiovisual industry. How are we to interpret this information? As employees or potential investors, we may want to understand more about the performance of a particular media company listed on the stock exchange. Financial advisors use the performance of companies listed on the stock exchange as an indicator of the health of a sector as a whole. This may have an impact on the opportunities of even the smallest company to borrow money or negotiate with venture capital. Should a small company grow big enough to offer shares more widely, the price set will be determined by comparison with the performance of those companies listed on the stock exchange. It is therefore important to have an understanding of the market mechanism and the performance of companies beyond the balance sheet and the profit and loss account. These measures have implications for all players in the media industry – employees, freelancers, subcontractors, and those who own companies.

In the past, the small investor was key to a company owner's ability to raise capital. This role has diminished over the past few decades. The private investor's percentage of total share holdings declined from approximately 66 per cent in 1957 to 21 per cent in 1989. It is the institutions that have become the important investors on the stock market. This has had a significant effect on the style of investment portfolios as the power shifts from many small investors to key personnel managing investment portfolios for insurance companies, pension funds and financial institutions.

The current status of the media companies listed on the stock exchange is printed each day in the *Financial Times* (FT). They represent a cross-section of media-related industries, from print, packaging, publishing, photography and entertainment to broadcast television companies and the larger production companies. These companies are used as a benchmark to the health of the media sector as a whole. The performance of companies such as Carlton, Pearson will more specifically provide an indication of the trend in the television industry. There are other sources of financial information that give more details of a company's performance. These sources can provide data on the performance of the media sector as a whole, or a more defined sub-section of it.

To be able to measure comparative business performance requires an analysis that is independent of the balance sheet numbers. There are several financial tools used to convert balance sheet figures as published by a company, and this is known as ratio analysis. Some of the important ratios are as follows.

Profitability

The *return on capital employed (ROCE)* is the key profitability ratio. It is a measure of the profit compared to the capital invested, and is therefore a measure of the capital efficiency of the company.

The ROCE = profit/capital × 100%

If a project cost £250 000 and the profit was £40 000, then ROCE = 16 per cent.

Investment

The *price earnings ratio (p/e)* ratio is simply the ratio between market price and earnings per share, expressed as:

p/e = market price per share/earnings per share (eps)

For example, if the market price of a share is £1 and the eps is £0.50, then the p/e ratio is 2. To think of this in another way, it will take 2 years to recover the capital investment in this £1 share. It is also a way of knowing the interest payment on the share. In this case it would be 50 per cent; an extremely good return in the current market with bank interest at about 6 per cent.

When examining the performance of a company that is not listed on the stock market or has not provided a listing of the p/e ratio in the year-end accounts, we can establish this figure for ourselves by finding the earnings per share.

The *earnings per share (eps)* is given by the accounting profit per share after all costs have been deducted. This should not be confused with the actual dividend per share, which is the payment per share voted by the company board. The eps is the amount of money available to the board to offer to the shareholders. It is a measure of the overall profitability of the share base, and is shown by:

eps = net profit/number of shares

For a company with a current share issue of three million shares, a net profit of £0.9 million before dividend payments and a share price of £2:

eps = £0.9M/3M = 30 p

Using the eps and knowing the market values of the share, the p/e ratio can then be calculated, given that:

p/e ratio = market price per share/earnings per share

The p/e ratio is therefore 6.6.

It would be helpful to establish what the p/e ratio actually means to the market and to the company. The purpose of this ratio is to be able to compare the relative performance of shares with one another without having to consider the absolute value of the share. The range of the p/e ratio is therefore crucial to the analysis of the relative merits of a share within its sector, or between one sector and another.

From these and other ratios, we can interpret the reported accounts of the company. Does the current share price undervalue the company? Do the performance indicators across the sector inspire speculative investors? The current p/e ratio could indicate that the future earnings for the group are expected to be good; it could also mean that the market will expect a good performance in the future and that the share price will continue to rise.

Theoretically, for all companies the choices of what to do with profits are:

1 Issue a bigger dividend up to the maximum eps
2 Invest more.

Either could encourage investment. If there was a sudden shift to a larger dividend that could not be sustained in the future, then the danger is that the share price will fall substantially due to lack of confidence in the future performance of the group and the board's ability to manage the company.

The answer could be to offer a dividend in line with the investment strategy and allow the 'efficient market' to decide and thus regulate the share price.

The *dividend yield (DY)* shows the shareholder the return on the investment, and is calculated as:

DY = dividend per share/market price per share

The *capital gearing* is the relationship between what the owners of the company have invested in the company and what the bank or other third party investors have invested. The company will be considered highly geared if there is a high proportion of preference shares and long-term loans (from third parties) compared to the money invested by the shareholders. High gearing, along with high risk, with unknown profits, makes for a very nervous bank manager. This is often typical of the small production company. When two or more people come together to make a film or video production, they are often advised to form a limited liability company; hence many media companies are really a collection of projects organised and managed by the same core team. The smallest company is then a single project, and the rules that apply to the company performance as a whole can be applied to the single project or contract.

$$\text{Capital gearing} = \frac{\text{preference shares and long-term loans}}{\text{shareholders' fund}}$$

9.12 The role of the manager

No study of strategic management can be complete without considering the roles and responsibilities of those given the task of planning the organisation's strategic approach. Henry Mintzberg, the Canadian Professor of Strategic Studies in Organisations at Miguel University, came from an engineering background, and made his reputation in two key areas; how strategy is made, and how managers use their time. Mintzberg studied the behaviours of managers and identified 10 principal managerial roles, which he grouped into three areas – interpersonal, informational and decisional:

1 Interpersonal
   - figurehead
   - leader
   - liaison.
2 Informational
   - monitor
   - disseminator
   - spokesperson.
3 Decisional
   - entrepreneur
   - disturbance handler
   - resource allocator
   - negotiator.

He stated that[13]:

> To much analysis gets in our way. The failure of strategic planning is the failure of formalisation. We are mesmerised by our ability to programme things.

In exploring the relationship between strategic management and those who are going to formulate the strategy of the organisation, Mintzberg said:

> Effective strategists are not people who extract themselves from the daily detail, quite the opposite; they are the ones who immerse themselves in it, while being able to abstract the strategic messages from it.

These managerial roles are influenced by the personal attributes explored in Chapters 7 and 8. An individual's style of management in the roles described by Mintzberg is underpinned by his or her personal profile, which will make some inclined to focus on some of the tasks in the list above in preference to others. A challenge for all managers is to play to their strengths and recognise their weaknesses.

9.13 References

1. Johnson, G. and Scholes, K. (1993). *Exploring Corporate Strategy*, 3rd edn. Prentice Hall.
2. Eberts, J. and Ilott, T. (1992). *My Indecision is Final: The Rise and Fall of Goldcrest Films.* Faber and Faber.
3. Stacey, R. (1996). *Strategic Management and Organisational Dynamics*, 2nd edn. Pitman Publishing.
4. Johnson, G. and Scholes, K. (1993) *Exploring Corporate Strategy*, 3rd edn, p. 23. Prentice Hall.
5. Kennedy, C. (1993). *Guide to Management Gurus.* Century.
6. Porter, M. (1980). *Competitive Strategy: Techniques for Analysing Industries and Competitors*, pp. 9–13. The Free Press.
7. Porter, M. (1980). *Competitive Strategy: Techniques for Analysing Industries and Competitors.* The Free Press.
8. Johnson, G. and Scholes, K. (1993) *Exploring Corporate Strategy*, 3rd edn, p. 130. Prentice Hall.
9. Stacey, R. (1996). *Strategic Management and Organisational Dynamics*, 2nd edn. Pitman Publishing.
10. Peters, T. and Waterman, R. H. Jr (1982). *In Search of Excellence.* Harper and Row.
11. Ansoff, H. I. (1965). *Corporate Strategy.* McGraw Hill.
12. Harvey Jones, J. (1993). *The Trouble Shooter – On the Treadmill?* BBC television special on independent production for Edinburgh Television Festival (not broadcast).
13. Mintzberg, H. (1980). *The Nature of Managerial Work.* Harper and Row.

9.14 Further reading

Kennedy, C. (1993). *Guide to Management Gurus.* Century.

Chapter 10

Introduction to media law

10.1 Summary

The primary objective of this chapter is to introduce some of the basic facts of the English legal system you may encounter. It also sets out to highlight one or two of the major areas of law that lie outside what is generically referred to as 'media law', but are of fundamental importance in the commercial world.

10.2 Objectives and key issues

There is no getting away from the fact that the law will touch every part of a media manager's work, and that some knowledge of it is therefore essential. Basic managerial tasks will be governed by contract law, employment law, health and safety law, and the law of tort. More specialist media work will require knowledge of the law that regulates the media industry and places controls upon the content of media productions. This book can only hope to cover in bare outline the basic legal background to any media management position, and the more specialised media law can only be thinly covered. However, such a limitation is not necessarily a major disadvantage – a person with a clear idea of general principles may be more likely to spot potential legal problems than a person encumbered with several textbooks of undigested law. It is the ability to spot legal problems that this chapter hopes to develop.

10.3 Introduction

An introductory guide to the English legal system is both the first and the last thing needed by a media manager – the first thing because it serves to provide both general knowledge and a guide to basic legal terminology, and the last thing because it is the system into which one is drawn when there is a problem, usually when something has gone wrong.

10.4 The English legal system

10.4.1 Legal actions in practice

Ignorance of or disregard for the law will inevitably lead to an experience which is universally regarded as one of life's little lowlights – a meeting with a lawyer. Lawyers may emerge from the in-house legal department, or they may be summoned from the pages of a legal directory (if the needy party wants to ensure an appropriate specialist) or a business directory. They may be solicitors, barristers, legal executives, or even para-legals. Your briefing should then prompt the next stage in the process – the giving of legal advice.

If the matter is so far only a proposed course of action, such advice will usually concentrate on the possibilities of whether it is actionable and/or criminal. The responsibility for the decision as to whether to go ahead, given the risks of prosecution or other legal action, will be the relevant manager's (who could be you).

However, if the legal problem is one that already exists as a result of action or inaction on the part of you or your staff, the legal advice will concentrate on what the next move should be. The advice may be to do nothing and hope that no-one finds out. However, if the problem is one of civil law, the next step is usually to attempt to settle the dispute through an exchange of correspondence. This may be followed by the settlement of the problem without resort to law (the cheap and preferred option). Only when such attempts are unsuccessful or one party wishes to adopt a tougher stance is it usual to try and obtain satisfaction through the issuing of a claim. Bear in mind that limitation periods mean that legal claims must be made within the specified time limits or be lost, with only a possibility of being revived. For example, you must bring a libel action within 1 year of first publication, and a personal injury action within 3 years of knowledge of the potential action.

From the issuing of such claims, there is a set timetable regarding responses and counter-responses, the gathering of evidence and the passing of it to the other side, and the readying of the case for trial. Such a timetable can impose obligations to act, which must be observed. For example, if you receive either a County Court or a High Court claim form, you should reply within 14 days or you may find that judgement has been entered against you. However, such a timetable can always be terminated by settlement of the case prior to the accumulation of exorbitant legal fees.

If the problem is a matter of criminal law, possible advice might include one's rights in the face of investigations (such as whether the police have the right to seize footage to be used as evidence) and the preparation of a defence in the event of a decision by the authorities to prosecute.

Decisions taken based on such advice can be entirely pragmatic. For example, the publication of security-sensitive information may without question be an offence under the Official Secrets Act, but it may be felt that the attendant publicity and the nature of the public's interest in publication would make any prosecution, except of the discloser, very unlikely (this was so in both the Clive Ponting and Sarah Tisdall cases). However, the publication of perfectly true information about a public figure may be decided against because of the threat of a libel action that would involve great expense and/or might expose an informant to retaliation.

10.4.2 A legal who's who

1 *Solicitors and Barristers.* These are the two distinct branches of the legal profession. Put simply, it is the solicitor who will deal directly with the public, whilst the barrister offers specialist advice and presents the case in court. However, this distinction is in the process of disappearing via government-inspired reforms of the legal profession. Moreover, members of both branches of the profession may be found in in-house legal departments.

2 *The Attorney-General.* This is the government's chief legal adviser. Some criminal prosecutions can only be brought with his consent, notably for contempt of court and for some offences under the Official Secrets Act, the Public Order Act, and the Race Relations Act. This fact therefore gives a measure of additional protection to the media – the Attorney General will only permit prosecutions to be brought if they are in the wider public interest. He or she can also take over private prosecutions brought by private individuals, and then bring them to a halt if it is judged that this would be in the public interest (e.g. the Attorney General stopped Mary

Whitehouse's private prosecution of the people responsible for the play *The Romans in Britain*).
3 *The Director of Public Prosecutions*. This is the head of the Crown Prosecution Service, who is responsible for bringing most criminal prosecutions.
4 *The Lord Chancellor*. The Lord Chancellor is responsible for appointing the judiciary and initiating legal reform, and is also a judge in the House of Lords and the Speaker of the parliamentary House of Lords.

10.4.3 Types of law

There are two basic categories of law; criminal and civil. However, it is useful to treat administrative law as a further separate category. Criminal law is self-explanatory in its subject matter, with a court imposing a fine, community sentence or a term of imprisonment on those who are found guilty beyond reasonable doubt. Civil law covers such areas as contract law, employment law and the law of tort, and cases must be proved on the balance of probabilities. The usual remedies awarded against the party found to be liable are damages and/or an injunction (an order for one party to act or to stop acting in a particular manner).

Administrative law, *inter alia*, deals with the making of challenges to the decisions of public bodies, commonly called judicial review. These are made not on the grounds that the decision was wrong, but on the grounds that the decision-making process was in some way flawed. The common remedy is for the public body to be forced to reconsider its decision.

All three types of law are relevant to the media environment. For example, contempt of court and blasphemy are criminal offences, along with transgressions of obscenity and indecency law and some types of copyright infringement. A breach of contract, a libellous broadcast or an intellectual property infringement may all give rise to a civil action by the victim. Finally, a challenge by means of judicial review might be used if a broadcasting license-holder objected to a decision of the ITC to withdraw the license because of quality failings, or to a decision of the BSC to uphold a viewer's complaint of infringement of privacy.

Another issue that needs to be addressed in relation to the classification of the law must deal with the question of different national jurisdictions. Technically speaking, what follows is the law of England and Wales, although the law of both Scotland and Northern Ireland does not differ significantly in the subjects covered. However, the fact that there are differences even between the laws of the 'home nations' serves as a good introduction to a further limitation in the scope of these chapters. Media managers who intend that their company's product should be supplied to an international market must be aware that a different legal environment exists in each and every country that makes up that market. Moreover, even if media managers decide that the product is destined solely for the national market, they cannot ignore the international dimension. A success may prompt half of the world to try and 'buy the rights', and the other half to copy the ideas that made the product such a success. Such matters should not be neglected in the initial setting up of any media production.

10.4.4 Sources of law

1 *Parliament*. This is the supreme law-making body of the United Kingdom – even European law is only applicable because Parliament has passed a law that says it should be. The basic framework of law is provided by Acts of Parliament. However, the vast majority of legislation is delegated legislation – it is made by ministers under powers conferred by Acts of Parliament, and does not need to pass through Parliament via the House of Commons and the House of Lords.
2 *The Courts*. The English legal system is a common law system, and this means that much law was not introduced by Parliament but was evolved by judges. Although judges are today reluctant to evolve new law, it is still possible that significant legal change can originate with them rather than with Parliament. Of more everyday significance is the fact that judges are responsible for the interpretation of Acts of Parliament.
3 *European Union Law*. One of the consequences of membership of the European Union is that its law is supreme over domestic law in those areas with which it is concerned. The law derives from the furtherance of the treaty obligations agreed by members, and is implemented in the form of directives and regulations. It is enforced by the European Court.
4 *The European Convention on Human Rights*. In 2000, this was incorporated into UK domestic law by virtue of the Human Rights Act 1998. It contains important guarantees of rights that are fundamental to the work of the broadcast media. These can then be cited before an English court and domestic law must be interpreted so as to comply with the convention if possible. Where there is direct conflict, the court must uphold English law over the convention. However, the new Human Rights Act 1998 has introduced a Parliamentary fast-track procedure for altering such law.
5 *Treaties*. International treaties are domestic law once incorporated into UK domestic law by an Act of Parliament.

10.4.5 The court structure

1 *Tribunals and other quasi-legal bodies.* Tribunals are often the courts that will deal with important matters. For example, employment law, social security law, and immigration law have a tribunal as their court of first instance.

2 *Magistrates Courts.* These mainly deal with criminal matters – in particular, mode of trial proceedings and summary trials (i.e. trials without a jury). Their civil jurisdiction includes domestic/family proceedings and some licensing matters.

3 *County Courts.* These deal with a wide variety of civil matters, usually those where the matter under dispute has a value of less than £25 000. If a claim is for less than £3000, it will be referred to the informal Small Claims Procedure (where it is unusual to have legal representation).

4 *The Crown Court.* This deals with criminal matters, usually in jury trials. Its civil jurisdiction includes licensing appeals.

5 *The Divisional Court.* Among its many functions, this court deals with judicial review of the decisions of public bodies.

6 *The High Court.* This is predominantly a civil court. It deals with higher value claims, including most with a value over £50 000.

7 *The Court of Appeal.* This has two divisions, one criminal (headed by the Lord Chief Justice) and one civil (headed by the Master of the Rolls).

8 *The House of Lords.* Technically the Judicial Committee of the House of Lords, this is the highest domestic appeal court.

9 *The European Court of Justice.* The decisions of this court are binding in English law when they deal with the interpretation of European Community Law and how it must be implemented by member countries.

10 *The European Court of Human Rights.* This should not be confused with the European Court of Justice, and owes its existence to the European Convention on Human Rights. Individuals within countries that have signed the convention can challenge domestic law before the court on the grounds that it breaches their fundamental human rights.

10.5 A brief guide to commercial law

10.5.1 The law of contract

Contract law textbooks are not particularly amenable to the sort of crash diet that the writing of a brief summary would impose on them. It is therefore proposed instead to give a few basic practical hints as to what to look out for when negotiating a contract. However, further reading is highly recommended in this area – a basic knowledge of the outline contract law is almost indispensable.

Contracts may be agreed verbally, but for certainty's sake it is wise to record what has been agreed in writing and get it signed by both parties, even if the only paper to hand is the proverbial back of a beer mat. Always read the small print, and make sure that you know just what version of the terms has been agreed.

To find out all the terms of a contract, it may be necessary to look beyond the terms as recorded on the document (compare what is on a railway ticket with the terms and conditions under which it is actually sold). For example, there may be such clauses as 'subject to our normal terms and conditions', and references to collective agreements (as negotiated by trade unions such as Equity).

When negotiating a contract, always be aware of time limits by which an offer must be accepted, and the form in which that acceptance must be communicated (letter, email, fax, telephone, or in person). For example, if prescribing the limits yourself, always specify the date by which a letter etc. must be received, and the location at which it should arrive.

Be aware of clauses that attempt to limit liability for breach of contract or for torts. Consider whether they are fair and within the law, and whether the risks they refer to are or should be covered by insurance (and who should be under a duty to arrange that insurance).

Think carefully over the implications of every contract term. For example, both George Michael and the 'Artist formerly Known As …' have found that guaranteed financial rewards were no compensation for restrictions placed on their artistic freedom (in the form of obligations to deliver a specified number of albums).

Above all, when negotiating a major contract such as a management contract or a production agreement, get legal advice. If this is impossible, think very long and hard about what the contract is supposed to achieve, what its subject matter is (including what rights are acquired and for how long), and what obligations and royalty rates it imposes. Then get legal advice.

10.5.2 The law of tort

A tort is a civil wrong for which the victim may wish to seek compensation or other remedy at law. The law of tort regulates where an action lies for those who suffer such a wrong, what they must show to succeed, and what remedy they will achieve. Below is a brief list of torts that may be applicable to the media manager. Note that the principle of vicarious liability means that in general the employing organisation will be liable for any torts committed by the workforce in the course of their employment. Moreover, employers' liability insurance is not only highly desirable but also for some matters a legal requirement.

1. *The tort of negligence.* Damage caused by the negligence of one party is only actionable if that party owed the victim a duty of care. Among the relationships within which a duty of care exists are employer/employee, road user/other road users, doctor/patient, professional advisor/clients, and parents/children.
2. *The tort of nuisance.* This tort exists to provide a remedy for the occupier of land whose enjoyment of possession of that land is being unreasonably interfered with. Common examples include regular excessive noise and other forms of pollution. Note that creating a public nuisance can be a criminal offence, and that such a nuisance can be created by obstructing a public highway in some way. It is also important to note that landlords can in some circumstances be liable for the nuisance created by their tenants.
3. *Occupier's liability.* The occupier of premises owes those who lawfully come onto them a duty of care. A more limited duty of care is also owed to those people who come onto premises unlawfully.
4. *Breach of statutory duty.* The most important area covered by this tort is civil liability for any breach of health and safety law. Any breach of health and safety law is also a criminal offence.
5. *Trespass.* Both trespass to the person (e.g. assault and battery) and trespass to land are actionable under tort law. Although any trespass (however minor) is in theory actionable, it should be noted that the doctrine of implied consent allows normal life to carry on without constant recourse to law. Otherwise, every person approaching your front door could be sued once they had set foot on the front path (and can still be sued if you have put up notices denying them entry).

10.5.3 Employment law

Like contract law, this is an area that really demands further reading. Subject areas a media manager should have some familiarity with include:

- Avoiding racial and sexual discrimination, both direct and indirect
- Ensuring compliance with the law on equal pay for men and women doing equivalent jobs

- Implementing the Working Times Directive
- In the event of any sale of the business, compliance with the Transfer of Undertakings regulations
- Collective bargaining
- Lawful and unlawful industrial disputes
- Avoiding unfair and constructive dismissal, which can generally be achieved through proper treatment of the workforce and, in the event of disciplinary offences, observance of due process.

10.6 Further reading

Adams, A. (1996). *Law for Business Students*. FT/Pitman.

Chapter 11

Principles of media law

11.1 Summary

This chapter contains a brief overview of broadcasting law and intellectual property law, together with a rather unsavoury mix of obscenity, indecency, blasphemy, libel and slander, contempt, and flagrant infringement of privacy.

11.2 Objectives and key issues

The essential purpose of this chapter is to give a brief overview of the legal issues that may arise in relation to the contents of media products. The key objective is for the media manager to be able to recognise potential legal issues, and also to be able to begin to make judgements as to the risks and benefits of a particular course of action in the light of the degree of threat of legal action.

11.3 Introduction

For an understanding of the nature and function of media law, it is very useful to have some grasp of the policy issues that underpin it. The central justification for legal protection of the media is that it is now the essential forum in which the fundamental human right of the freedom of speech is exercised. Indeed, a free and healthy media is a necessary guarantee of democracy – perhaps the best legal news the media have had for a long time came in the 1999 Albert Reynolds libel case, when the House of Lords recognised the vital function of the media as the eyes and ears of the public. To this end it held that, as long as the media performed its activities with appropriate levels of professional care and attention, it should be afforded some defence against libel actions.

In essence, though, the structure of the law derives from the eternal conflict between the necessity of protecting the personal rights of individuals, and the necessity of providing protection of the rights of the community as a whole (and thus in turn the rights of the individual). This conflict is enshrined in Article 10 of the European Convention on Human Rights, which, although the media's guardian angel in its dealings with the law, is only a conditional guarantee of the freedom of expression. It recognises that a state may still allow the proportionate restriction of the freedom of expression in order to protect such rights and interests as 'the reputation and rights of others ... the prevention of disorder and crime ... the protection of health and morals ... the prevention of the disclosure of information received in confidence' and the maintenance of the 'authority and impartiality of the judiciary'.

Following its incorporation into UK domestic law by the Human Rights Act 1998, the European Convention on Human Rights is becoming increasingly influential in how the courts create, interpret and apply the law as applied to the media. The media industry will increasingly rely on Article 10 as a tool with which to defend actions and challenge restrictions. On the other hand, Article 8, which guarantees the individual's right to privacy, and Article 6, which guarantees the right to a fair trial, will increasingly be invoked to challenge certain aspects of media behaviour.

However, the broadcaster (and possibly, by analogy, the Internet provider) has also to bear in mind an extra set of principles (see, for example, The Annan Committee Report on Broadcasting, 1977, Cmnd 6753). These assert that we are all potentially weak-minded individuals who fall instant prey to every malign influence that television deliberately or inadvertently throws up. Our children are on the one hand innocent victims to be protected from all corruption at all costs, but on the other are manipulative in obtaining any end that TV portrays as desirable. Sex and violence are equal menaces that deprave and corrupt, and result in dangerous copycat behaviour.

Such are the principles, albeit exaggerated, that have driven the regulators to impose detailed rules relating to taste and decency on the broadcast media in this country. Television is the guest in the home with a pervasive impact on its viewers; the codes tell it how to behave so that the vulnerable, and in particular children, are protected from its possible excesses. The cinemas are by and large seen as more protected arenas from which the vulnerable can be excluded if a film that would adversely affect them is showing. However, the video is an even more dangerous guest in the home – one that will not only say or do naughty things, but will say or do them repeatedly on demand and without regard to the age of the audience.

11.4 Broadcasting law

At present, the primary sources of broadcasting law are the Broadcasting Acts 1990 and 1996. These set up the mechanisms for the structure and regulation of independent television services, including domestic satellite services and digital television. Their general effect is to place responsibility for the administration of independent broadcasting on the ITC.

This section will focus on the mechanics of content regulation, but media managers must also be aware of other matters dealt with by these acts. Foremost among them are the systems by which licenses are awarded for both terrestrial and digital television franchises. Others include the restrictions placed on cross-media ownership (which have been relaxed as the media industry looks for ever more necessary economies of scale), and the regulations in place to ensure that nationally important sporting events remain available on 'free-to-air' television services.

11.4.1 Domestic television and radio services

Regulation of UK domestic broadcasting services is in the hands of three bodies; the BBC, the Independent Television Commission (ITC) and the Broadcasting Standards Commission (BSC). However, the government has retained a small degree of direct control in that the Broadcasting Act 1990 gives the Home Secretary limited powers to order that things should or should not be broadcast. Such powers are most likely to be used in the case of war or national emergency, but were also invoked to enforce the controversial Sinn Fein broadcasting ban.

There are several common principles that are applied to all domestic broadcasting services. These range from the fundamentals (that all programme services should not offend against good taste and decency, should not incite crime or lead to public disorder, should not be offensive to public feeling, should be accurate and impartial in presenting news, and should be impartial on matters of political and industrial controversy) to such peripherals as the ban on subliminal messages.

The BBC

The BBC is governed by two documents, the Charter, and the License and Agreement. Both of these are renewed periodically by Parliament, and contain terms relating to content regulation. However, the primary responsibility for programme services is with the internal management structures of the BBC, with ultimate responsibility lying with the Board of Governors. The BBC has its own programme standards code, and is also subject to the BSC code (there is also an argument that it is subject to the ITC code).

The ITC

The 1990 Broadcasting Act included a major shake-up of ITV. The ITC is now the regulating body, and is responsible for both licensing and regulating programming. It is no longer considered to be the broadcaster, and therefore individual companies have responsibility for their schedules and the contents of the programmes broadcast as part of them.

The ITC has a statutory duty to draw up, review from time to time and enforce both a programme standards code (on matter such as taste and decency, privacy and editorial impartiality) and an advertising standards code. Enforcement is backed up by the ITC's power to levy fines and review licenses. Regular reports of adjudications on complaints made by the public are published, and serve as an important guide as to how the various programme codes are applied. However, the ITC will also initiate investigations in appropriate cases. Its jurisdiction includes the examination of programme services as a whole, as well as problems with individual programmes. For example, it gave a warning to *Good Morning* television that its programme standards were below what was acceptable – too many cheap cartoons and not enough quality television. Behind this lay the important matter that GMTV had had to pay a high price for its franchise, and was therefore more restricted on what it could pay for programming. Possible solutions were a reduction in the fees to be paid to the ITC for the franchise (unrealistic, although a policy consideration was raised which would need to be taken into account during the next round of franchising), or a merger with another franchise holder to achieve economies of scale (which eventually took place).

The BSC

Under the Broadcasting Act 1996 (which predominantly dealt with the introduction of digital television), the Broadcasting Standards Council merged with the Broadcasting Complaints Commission to form the Broadcasting Standards Commission. It now has a combined remit – the BCC's jurisdiction to investigate complaints of unwarranted infringement of privacy and unjust or unfair treatment, and the BSC's jurisdiction over programme standards in general (including the drawing up and enforcing of a programme standards code). Its sanctions are more limited than those that can be imposed by the ITC – the broadcasting of a report of an adjudication, with in some cases payment for publication of the report in the national press.

11.4.2 International satellite television

Domestic satellite television is regulated by the ITC, and any signals that are received by a broadcasting organisation and rebroadcast are also subject to the ITC control. However, satellite channels beamed directly to the home from outside the UK are subject to regulation via European law. There are essentially two sources of controls placed on transfrontier broadcasting in Europe:

1 The 1989 Directive on Transfrontier Broadcasting, which is aimed at ensuring uniformity of regulations in 'up' states. The most detailed regulations concern the frequency, placing, and types of advertisements.
2 The 1989 Council of Europe Convention on Transfrontier Broadcasting, which is similar to the EU directive but applies to members of the Council of Europe, including many non-EU countries.

Although regulation is a matter for 'up' states, it is still possible for a receiving state to try and control reception in the home. Transfrontier broadcasters tend to make their money from encrypting their broadcasts and then selling decoders. If the sale of a decoder is banned in a particular country, that country will effectively have prevented reception by the majority of people. Although such a ban would in most cases be against European law, the British government has successfully banned the sale of decoders for pornographic channels under an exception to the law that allows such bans in order to safeguard the heath and moral wellbeing of a country.

11.4.3 Advertising

Advertising in the UK media is regulated by:

- the Advertising Standards Authority, which is responsible for the control of advertising in the printed media and in cinemas, and which publishes and enforces its own code of practice

- the Independent Radio Authority, which regulates radio advertising and promotions
- the ITC, which regulates advertising and promotions on domestic television.

The ITC code regulates advertising on the broadcast media. It contains detailed rules relating both to misleading claims and to the projection of undesirable images. It gives particularly strict guidelines for advertisements promoting such products as alcohol, slimming aids and medicines, or that feature or are aimed at children (see also the list given below for the ASA code). It also imposes controls on the techniques used by advertisers – for example, no advertisement should portray or refer to a living individual without that individual's written permission (with the exception that a product such as a newspaper advertising its contents may do so if the reference is fair). There are regular reports of its adjudications on complaints made by the public, which serve as an important guide to interpretation of the code.

The Advertising Standards Authority

This has no jurisdiction over the broadcast media. It has its own code of practice, but its enforcement does not have the force of law behind it. However, it can take effective sanctions within the industry.

The main tenets of the code are that advertisements are:

- legal, decent, honest and truthful
- prepared with a sense of social responsibility (considerations include privacy, antisocial behaviour, excessive smoking and drinking, children)
- conform to fair competition rules (no denigration or abuse of rivals and their businesses)
- pay particular attention to special care categories (children, hair and scalp products, slimming products, health products, cosmetics, job advertisements, mail-order, alcohol and tobacco).

A word should also be said about promotional activity on the broadcast media. Competitions for prizes must involve an element of skill, however illusory – if you know that the capital city of France is Paris and not Trumpton or Milton Keynes, and can ring a premium-rate phone line for long enough to register your brilliance, you have exercised sufficient skill to appease the regulatory authorities. Such competitions must always be free to enter; the cost is in sending/calling in the free entry.

11.5 Other media: film and video law and the Internet

The content of films intended for release through cinema and video is naturally subject to the general criminal law – blasphemy can in theory be prosecuted, whilst obscenity, indecency with children and incitement to racial hatred (to name but a few offences) will almost certainly be so. However, there is an extra hurdle that also has to be cleared; submission to the British Board of Film Classification (the BBFC). Its power to demand that a film be cut comes from two distinct sources: its role in the regime imposed by the Cinematograph Acts and its statutory powers under the Video Recordings Act 1984.

11.5.1 The Cinematograph Acts and the BBFC

The fact that a film does not have a BBFC certificate for cinema release is not, in theory, of binding legal significance. However, it becomes so because of the way in which the law controls the public exhibition of films in cinemas. Public cinemas have to be licensed, and the licensing body is the local authority. Under the terms of the model Home Office license, it is a condition of the granting of the license that a cinema only allows the display to particular age groups of films certificated by the BBFC as being suitable for them. A BBFC certificate is the evidence that is used to determine the suitability of films for particular audiences. Hence, the BBFC has the power to demand cuts in a film by virtue of the certificate's ability to control the audience for a film – if a film-maker wishes his film to be seen by people over 12 years of age, he or she must comply with all the cuts demanded by the BBFC if it is to grant a 12 certificate. For the film-maker to refuse to comply may be to damage the economic viability of a particular film. In effect, therefore, the BBFC may delay, prevent or restrict the release of a film by virtue of its refusal to grant a particular certificate.

It should be noted that a local authority may refuse to allow the cinemas in its area to show a film regardless of whether a certificate has been granted. The cinema licensing rules still include a power to preview a film and decide whether it should be shown in the area under the authority's jurisdiction. This power was exercised, for example, with the films *The Last Temptation of Christ* and *Crash*.

The BBFC must also, when considering the granting of a certificate, have regard to whether or not a film could be prosecuted under the general law. If prosecution is a possibility, then the film will have to cut the offending

249

scenes or be refused a certificate (see, for example, the sections below on blasphemy, cruelty to animals and indecency with children).

11.5.2 The Video Recordings Act 1984

Under this act, it is illegal to offer a non-exempt video for sale without it having been submitted to the classification body for classification. A video must therefore be submitted to the BBFC unless it is of a type that is exempt. Exemptions are given for videos that are designed to inform, educate or instruct, those concerned with sport, religion or music, and for video games. However, exemption is denied any video which depicts 'to any significant extent' human sexual activity, torture or extreme violence, or human genitals or urinary or excretory functions.

With any non-exempt video, the classifications are the same as for cinema. Films classed as 18R must only be supplied through a licensed sex shop. Because videos are viewed and available in the home, more cuts are demanded than would be the case for the cinema before a particular certificate will be granted.

11.5.3 The Internet and other sources of computer images

There is as yet no specific statutory or legal framework that has been created for the Internet or such media sources as CD ROMs etc. They are therefore subject to the provisions of the general law. Notable problems include tracking down the party responsible for any material that infringes one's rights, and bringing legal action against parties such as the Internet provider, who might be outside the jurisdiction.

11.5.4 Potential criminal liability of the media

The Official Secrets Acts 1911 and 1989

The passing on by the media of information supplied in breach of the Official Secrets Act can be an offence. However, prosecutions of the media are rare because of the political sensibilities involved. In a number of cases, the government has proceeded by getting a court order for the recovery of the material that has been passed to the media, and using that material to identify the person responsible for the leak. Prosecution of that person has then followed.

The Obscene Publications Act 1959

The obscenity laws have as their focus not the nature of the material *per se*, but rather the likely effect it will have on those who view it – the basic definition of an obscene publication or broadcast is that it tends to deprave and corrupt the audience at which it is aimed. Such a definition covers not only sexually explicit material, but also includes anything that encourages violence and drug taking. It also establishes different thresholds for obscenity depending on the audience – acceptable adult material when aimed at a child audience may well render a publication obscene.

It is important to realise that potentially obscene subject matter (for example, scenes of drug taking) may not render a publication obscene if it is depicted it in a way that is either negative or if it is a responsible exploration/portrayal of the issues. There is a defence if the portrayal creates an aversion to the activity being shown (known as the aversion defence), and a defence of public good if a publication is in the interests of science, literature, art, learning or other objects of general concern. However, there will be levels of obscenity that are too extreme to be covered by these defences.

These rules apply (with minor variations) to film, video, television and theatre. They are obviously subsumed within Broadcasting Standards Codes, and the BBFC will censor any film that, in its view, could be prosecuted under the Obscene Publications Act. However, in other media an unsuccessful prosecution for obscenity can be a marketing triumph – witness the success of *Lady Chatterley's Lover.*

11.6 Blasphemy

Blasphemous libel is a common law offence that makes it a criminal offence to blaspheme against the Christian religion. That it is confined to the Christian religion was established with the failure of the private prosecution brought against Salmon Rushdie's *Satanic Verses* for blasphemy against Islam.

It is highly unlikely that the DPP would bring an action for blasphemy, and the refusal to extend the action to Islam arguably reflects a pro-freedom of speech approach rather than one that is hostile to other religions. However, there have been convictions for blasphemy in recent times (e.g. R v Lemon and Gay News Ltd (1979) AC 617).

Of greater significance is the fact that the BBFC will take into account the possibility of a prosecution for blasphemy in its decision to grant a certificate. In recent years this gave rise to the *Visions of Ecstasy* saga, when a blasphemous film was denied a certificate unless cuts were made, and the film-maker's challenge to this decision failed in front of the ECHR.

11.7 Racial hatred and public order

The Public Order Act 1936 s.5A, as substituted by the Race Relations Act 1976, makes it an offence to publish or distribute material that is racially threatening, abusive or insulting, or to incite racial hatred by words in a public place. This includes such material in a play, film or broadcast. For any prosecution to be successful, it must be shown that there was either an intention to incite racial hatred or a likelihood that such hatred would be stirred up. Such a requirement offers some protection to a film-maker who wishes to tackle racial issues in a responsible manner.

11.8 Indecency

It is an offence to display (or allow to be displayed) indecent matter in public. Although broadcasts, displays in art galleries, plays and films are all excluded from the general provision, there are no such exceptions for the taking or distributing of indecent photographs (including films) of children. Note that an indecent photograph here is one that is indecently posed or contrived by way of sexual indulgence, and therefore depictions that some might feel are indecent will not be offences if the purpose is legitimate.

An important consequence of this is that the BBFC will refuse a certificate to any film that includes dramatic reconstructions of scenes of indecency with children, unless it can be shown that the actor/actress shown in the scenes is actually 16 years of age or more.

11.9 Protection of animals

The laws laid down for the protection of animals must be observed in the making of a film; there are no exceptions, even if the infliction of suffering is for a film. The BBFC will censor any scenes that involve cruelty to animals in their making, even where the film is an overseas product whose making conformed to the law in its country of origin.

11.10 Defamation

A man commits the tort of defamation when he publishes to a third person words or matter containing an untrue imputation against the reputation of another.

(P. Milmo Q.C. and W. V. H. Rogers, *Gatley on Libel and Slander*, 9th Edition (1998) Sweet & Maxwell, London, page 4.)

The publication of defamatory words and matter can be a highly expensive mistake. It can take one of two basic forms; defamation in a non-permanent form (slander), or defamation in a permanent form (libel). Of these, it is libel that is of paramount importance to the media. The common conception that slander is defamation by the spoken word is not correct – Parliament has now decreed that defamation on television or radio is libel rather than slander (s.1 Defamation Act 1952), and that defamation from the stage during a theatre performance is also libel if it is part of the performance (Theatres Act 1968). Slander is now in effect restricted to what is said by one party to another in the hearing of others, and therefore its restrictions on the recovery of damages will not benefit the media.

11.11 Libel

11.11.1 The game

Libel is a game in which wealthy people gamble large sums of money to correct and gain compensation for the slurs cast on their character by the media. The first move is made by the media – it must make the decision whether to publish/broadcast material that may be considered defamatory of an individual. That decision may be made with no awareness of potential trouble, especially when the publisher does not realise that there is any identifiable subject of the allegation/material. However, more often than not the publication relates to some story or piece of investigative journalism that contains a defamatory allegation. When this is the case, factors to be taken into account may include:

- Whether the allegation is true. This is of only secondary importance, but it may be that the nature of the allegation means the publisher feels it is important that it is brought out into the open, even at the risk of a libel action.
- Whether the allegation can be proved to be true. This is the primary consideration prior to publication, and may involve judgements not only on whether there is enough evidence to prove the allegation, but also on

whether that evidence can be used in court. If your only evidence comes from an informer who has risked his or her job or even life to give you information, can you risk exposing the informer through a court battle?

- Whether the subject will sue. Even if the allegation cannot be proved, it may be that the subject is unlikely to sue. This may be because of a lack of funds, although such an individual may still make a complaint to the relevant regulatory body and may even bring a malicious falsehood action (and there is now the possibility of a 'no win no fee' libel action). There are also individuals who, because of their position, may not wish to bring an action, the usual example being members of the royal family.

If the outcome is favourable and the publication/broadcast goes ahead, the next move falls to the subject of the allegation. He or she must make the decision as to whether to sue. Factors that might influence this judgement include:

- Whether the allegation is true, and whether it can be proved to be true. The truth of an allegation may not deter the start of a libel action; the threat of such an action may be enough to force the publisher to back down (and may even be used to deter publication if the individual finds out prior to it taking place). Moreover, it may be that the nature of any likely evidence is so weak that, even if the allegation is true, it may still not be provable (or able to convince a jury).
- Whether there is adequate funding in place to commence an action, and if necessary to take it all the way to court.
- Whether the whole allegation is so serious that fighting it is worth several years of misery.
- Whether the resulting media attention might not cause more damage and embarrassment than the original publication, and in particular whether it might provoke further investigation that may uncover facts better kept secret.

If the individual takes the decision to sue, then there follows a period of legal manoeuvring in which offers to settle may or may not be made. If no agreement can be reached, and if the proceedings are not struck out for some reason, the case will end up in court.

11.11.2 The law

This procedure is all well and good, but before it is embarked upon there should be some judgement as to whether a case in libel can actually be made out by the subject of the material. A case is made out if the claimant can show three things: that there was a publication; that it was of defamatory words or matter; and that the claimant was identifiable as the subject of that publication.

Publication to a third party

Generally speaking, this will not be at issue in any action involving libel within a media product. Moreover, at any stage within the production of a media product that includes a libel there is probably publication to a third party – for example, when a libellous script is read by a producer, there is publication. The mere fact that the libel has not been released to the public does not affect the question of whether or not there is a libel, but it is of obvious relevance to whether the producers have any liability for the libel (in effect, their liability will only begin once they have published it to another third party), the degree of damage caused by the libel, and whether the subject ever finds out that the libel has indeed been published.

Note also that all involved in the distribution of a libellous media product can be held liable for the libel, although this is subject to the defence of innocent dissemination (i.e the distributor did not know and had no reason to know of the libel contained in the product).

Defamatory words or matter

The essence of a libel action is that defamatory words or matter have been published. It is therefore important to establish just what is defamatory material. There is no absolute definition of what is defamatory; the classic formula is that it damages a reputation by exposing the plaintiff to hatred, ridicule or contempt. However, this is now too narrow and has been replaced by variations on the theme of lowering the reputation in the eyes of reasonable people generally.

From the outset, it is also important to realise that truth can be defamatory unless it can be proved to be true, and that falsehood is not necessarily defamatory unless it satisfies the definition of what is defamatory. For example, it would not be defamatory to claim falsely that a business rival has died (although such a claim would be actionable as malicious falsehood), but it may be defamatory to say that he or she died from a sexually transmitted disease.

Classic examples of what may or may not be defamatory include the following cases.

Berkoff v Birchill. Repeated assertions by a journalist that an actor was hideously ugly were held to be arguably libellous, because such a person made a living in a way that was connected to his personal appearance. Note that usually gratuitous personal abuse will not be libellous unless it carries some specific allegation.

Donovan v The Face. Allegations that the singer was gay, and was a hypocrite because he had denied it, were found to be libellous. The question of whether saying someone is gay should be libellous is highly contentious, because it concerns the question of whether society should think less of people because they are gay. Most such cases now rely heavily not on the allegation of being gay, but on the allegation of hypocrisy implicit if the subject has denied being gay.

Cassidy v Daily Mirror. This is the classic case illustrating that publishing a libel quite innocently might still render one liable. A photographer took a picture of a man ('the general') and his escort attending the races, and was told by the general that his companion was his fiancée. When the newspaper published the picture it was successfully sued for libel by the general's wife, who claimed that the caption implied moral laxity on her part to those who knew that she and the general had been living together as man and wife.

Byrne v Deane. The Court of Appeal held that it was not libellous to allege that an individual had informed the police about illegal gambling, even though this may in fact have brought the individual into hatred and contempt. The court commented that a right-thinking member of society would applaud such behaviour, and libel actions must be judged by this standard, and not according to how society had in fact viewed such behaviour.

Tolley v Fry. This case illustrates how something that is not in itself libellous will be defamatory if a section of the public viewing it possesses knowledge that would render the material defamatory. In the case, an advertisement featured the photograph of an amateur golfer without his permission. This was not in itself defamatory; however, the fact that a number of people seeing the advertisement would have known that he was an amateur and that accepting money to appear in it would have breached the amateur rules meant that the picture was in fact libellous.

Hayward v Thompson. This illustrates how two publications, neither of which in themselves are defamatory, may be read together and be found to be defamatory. In the case, a Sunday newspaper published a front-page story that the Liberal Party had one individual millionaire backer, and named him. The next week, their front-page story made allegations about the role in the

Jeremy Thorpe affair of an unnamed millionaire backer of the Liberal Party. It was held that the two publications would be read together such that people would understand that the second publication referred to the individual named in the first.

Charleston v News Group Newspapers. This illustrates that potentially defamatory material will not be held to constitute defamation if it is accompanied by sufficiently prominent material that negates the defamatory meaning. The case involved the presentation of a story in the *Sun*, which had involved a large picture showing the apparently naked plaintiff actor and actress in a sexual embrace, together with the headline 'Cor! What is Harold Up to with our Madge, then'. It was accompanied by text explaining that this picture was an example of Internet pornography in which famous heads were superimposed on indecent photographs. The argument that many readers would only flick through the paper and would therefore be left with a defamatory impression was rejected; the material should be read as a whole, and as a whole it clearly was not defamatory.

Identification

The third element necessary to establish a libel action is that the plaintiff must be identifiable as the subject of the defamatory matter by a relevant section of the public. If a section of the public believes that the individual referred to is the plaintiff, that is enough, and it is irrelevant that such an identification was unintended. For examples, see: *Hulton v Jones* (a lawyer with same name as the subject of a skit could sue as people believed it referred to him); the Stoke Newington police case (a news item on police corruption included footage of the plaintiff walking out of the police station); and *Youssoupoff v MGM* (a fictional portrayal in a film of the seduction by Rasputin of a princess whose husband had later murdered him libelled the wife of the Prince who in reality had actually killed him).

To make an allegation against an unnamed individual may not be any protection if the publication specifies a narrow enough group to which the subject belongs. The actual effect will be that all the members of that group will have been libelled. For example, in the Banbury CID case, an allegation made against one unnamed person within the CID led to 10 of the 11 members successfully suing for libel. Judgement of the size of the group to which this applies is difficult; a common example is that an allegation against an unnamed member of the cabinet would libel all members of the cabinet, but an allegation against an unnamed Member of Parliament would not libel all MPs.

A public body cannot bring a libel action, although an individual within that organisation identifiable as responsible for the subject matter in question might do so.

11.11.3 Defences

Defamation is a strict liability tort. Hence, once the three above elements have been proved, the defendant is liable unless it can be shown that one of the following defences apply.

Justification

A defence is made out if you can show that the material and the facts upon which it is based are true. There is one notable exception under the Rehabilitation of Offenders Act (you cannot refer to someone as a convicted criminal after a varying period of time if his or her sentence was less than 30 months). Note that under Section 5 of the Defamation Act 1952 (DA 1952), only the sting of the libel need be shown – for example, allegations of drug taking and heavy drinking might be successfully justified if the drug taking allegation was true but the heavy drinking allegation was not.

Note that to report a libellous rumour as a rumour, even if you deny its truth, is to publish the libel and render oneself liable. For example, when the *New Statesman* featured an article that cited as an example of ridiculous Westminster gossip a rumour that John Major had had an affair with a Number 10 caterer, they laid themselves open to a libel action.

Fair comment

To succeed as defence to libel, the material claimed as fair comment must be on matters of public interest, based substantially on true facts, and not made with malicious intent. Within these bounds, it can be fairly robust. For example, see the Charlotte Cornwell case (criticism that 'she can't act, can't sing, and has the sort of stage presence that jams lavatories' went beyond fair comment) and the Derek Jameson case (the satirical portrayal of a newspaper editor as stupid and illiterate, with an editorial policy of 'all the nudes fit to print and all the news printed to fit' was fair).

Absolute privilege

This applies to statements made in parliamentary and judicial proceedings, and fair and accurate reports of the latter when made contemporaneously.

Qualified privilege

This applies to fair and accurate reports of parliamentary and judicial proceedings, matters in S.7 and the schedule of the DA 1952 (mainly reporting the proceedings of official enquiries and tribunals), and reports of information made under a legal, moral or social duty (i.e. informing to the police etc.). The House of Lords recently considered the extension of this defence in relation to publications on matters of political/governmental importance. They were unwilling to grant a blanket exemption to all publications on such matters, but did say that where the media had exercised its powers fairly and reasonably in compiling a publication on such matters, it would be entitled to a defence based on its responsibility to exercise the public interest in monitoring the activities of government.

The Defamation Act 1996 has introduced a new defence based on responsibility for publication (Section 1), replacing the defence of innocent libel. It is a defence to libel that:

- the person in question was not responsible for the defamation, and that he was not the author, editor, or publisher of the statement complained of
- the person in question took reasonable care in relation to its publication, *and* did not know, or had no reason to believe, that he or she was causing or contributing to the publication of a defamatory statement.

This defence applies to printers, distributors, retailers, legitimate copiers (as in the making of videos etc.), most Internet providers, and the broadcasters of live programmes. However, the defence may be withdrawn if this is justified either by the circumstances of the publication or by the character of the person primarily responsible. For example, if you invite someone onto a live programme who is notorious for an extreme or libellous point of view on the subject under discussion, you may not be able to avail yourself of the defence.

11.11.4 Remedies for libel – injunctions, damages and costs

An injunction against repetition of the libel will only be granted if the plaintiff has an almost infallible case. There will be no injunction if the defendant intends to plead the defence of justification.

Note that the size of damages awards is on the way down. In *John v MGN*, the Court of Appeal held that the jury should be directed with reference to personal injury damages when considering the level of damages for hurt feelings alone (although compensation for actual loss remained unaffected by the judgement). This will have the effect of substantially reducing the level of damages.

The Defamation Act 1996 has introduced several important new provisions, although most have not yet come into force. They include a new defence of 'offering to make amends', a new procedure for summary judgement, and new provisions relating to absolute and qualified privilege.

An offer to make amends will be a defence to a defamation action if it is refused by the victim, and if the publisher had offered to publish a correction and apology as soon as the defamatory nature of the statement was pointed out and to make appropriate recompense. If the offer is accepted, then the actual terms can be negotiated between the parties or settled by a judge.

Summary judgement will help to cut costs in low value claims by dismissing weak claims or weak defences, and giving judgement at an early stage in the proceedings.

The most important feature of the new rules relating to the defence of privilege is that qualified privilege will not be available to the defendant when a request was made by the plaintiff for the publication of a correction or explanation and refused by the defendant.

A criminal libel action will only be allowed in serious cases, where it is felt that the conduct in question is such as to render it necessary to bring criminal sanctions. In *Goldsmith v Pressdram*, a repeated false allegation in *Private Eye* that Goldsmith had helped Lord Lucan to escape was held sufficiently serious to allow such an action to be brought. Note that such actions have to get leave to proceed from courts if taken against newspapers. In all probability, every such case is now likely to be a private prosecution brought by the victim rather than a public prosecution.

11.12 Privacy law

There is no legal right of privacy in English law at the present. However, the privacy interests of individuals must still be considered for three reasons:

1 The Broadcasting Codes include privacy provisions
2 Many other countries have privacy laws that must be taken into account should a media product be sold abroad
3 English law may very well develop a legal right of privacy within the next few years.

11.12.1 Regulation by code

The main privacy concerns of the Broadcasting Codes are the portrayal of real people and real events as news and entertainment.

The Broadcasting Standards Commission code contains provisions including the following that relate to the reporting of current affairs:

- Any infringement of privacy must be justified by an over-riding public interest in disclosure of the information (e.g. when it is in the interests of detecting crime and/or disreputable behaviour, exposing misleading claims, publicising significant incompetence in public office etc.).
- Care must be taken with situations of bereavement and personal distress, and with the interviewing of children.
- Consent must be obtained: to film in a school, factory or other closed institution; to include people in such situations where use is not incidental; from responsible persons in the event of interviews with incapacitated persons; to record telephone conversations; and to use recordings of individuals in public places when words and actions are not sufficiently in the public domain.
- Secret filming and recording is only acceptable where necessary for a story that is strongly in the public interest (usually in connection with investigative journalism).

The ITC Code gives the following rule relating to the portrayal of real persons and events as part of a 'docudrama':

Where innocent parties are portrayed as central figures in recon-structions of a crime or other momentous event, special care should be taken not to portray them in an unfair light. Producers should use all reasonable endeavours to contact them at an early stage, and to give due consideration to their perspectives on the production. The same applies to the immediate family of principle characters who have died. Producers should also use best endeavours to inform such people of the times of intended transmission ... and the programme trails ...

The essential question that should be addressed by the programme-maker is whether the degree of public interest (NOT public curiosity) in the making of the programme outweighs the likely distress to the family (which can be judged by factors such as distance of time from the event, nature of event, extent of other coverage and nature and extent of proposed coverage).

11.12.2 Rights in other jurisdictions

Privacy rights can be found in many other jurisdictions, including the USA, Canada, France, Germany and other European countries. Although the basic principle may vary from country to country, the usual interests that privacy law protects can be summarised in the four torts which collectively constitute the right of privacy under American law:

1 Physical intrusion into the private life of an individual, for example by means of telephone tapping or long-lens photography
2 The publication of true but embarrassing facts, for example the details of an individual's private life
3 Publicity that places an individual in a false light, for example by misrepresenting his views or actions (commonly by suggesting that the individual agreed to some publicity)
4 The appropriation of personal identity (name and likeness), for example by using it in an advertisement without permission.

It should be noted, however, that the exercise of such rights in relation to media products is always subject to the public interest in the freedom of speech.

11.12.3 English privacy law

At present, English privacy law is not based on any single principle that protects privacy, but is a collection of disparate types of specific legal action together with regulations imposed by such bodies as the Advertising Standards Authority, the Broadcasting Standards Commission, the ITC and the Press Complaints Commission. It therefore does offer protection from some of the wrongs listed above, but in the form of libel, malicious falsehood, breach of confidence or breach of regulation.

Malicious falsehood

To publish false information about someone is not necessarily defamatory (e.g. falsely to report someone's death in order to steal custom from them). Malicious falsehood was developed to protect businesses from such activity, but it has also recently been used as an alternative to libel because legal aid is available (see *Joyce v Sengupta*, which concerned an allegation that P, a maid, stole love letters written to the Princess Royal). It therefore can provide a remedy against the publication of false information about an individual, but with the limitation that it can be used only when the plaintiff can show actual or likely financial damage.

Breach of confidence

Breach of confidence makes it actionable to disclose information with the necessary quality of confidence which has been communicated in circumstances implying an obligation of confidentiality, and unauthorised disclosure of which has caused or will cause detriment to the plaintiff (see Sir Robert Megarry in *Coco v Clark*). It has been used to prevent the publication of such material as marital secrets, the details of a lesbian affair, and etchings made by members of the Royal Family.

As well as privacy, this law has been used to protect trade secrets and 'national security' (see the *Spycatcher* litigation). The reason for its use by the government is that a court will grant an injunction to prevent publication whatever the information as long as it is confidential, whereas Official Secrets legislation only allows the restraint of publication if there is damage to national security. Recent developments within this action may lead to it becoming very close to a right of privacy (see *Hellewell v Chief Constable of Derbyshire*), which appears to say that the publication of pictures of a private nature taken with a telescopic lens would be an actionable breach of confidence. In *Creation Records v News Group Newspapers*, it was used to prevent the *Sun* selling copies of a poster which used a photograph taken from the same position as one used on an Oasis album cover. The grounds were that the security precautions used to keep the media out of the area of the photo shoot had imposed an obligation of confidence on any person entering.

However, there are some current developments that may or may not lead to such a general right becoming part of English law:

1 The courts are developing a common law right of privacy through the law of breach of confidence. This may yet grow into a more fully-fledged model.
2 The Human Rights Act 1998 has now incorporated the European Convention on Human Rights into UK domestic law. Article 8 of this gives a right to private life, which may be developed into a right of privacy. However, there remains a question mark about whether, and in what form, this will happen.

11.13 Contempt of court law

Contempt of court is not a very easy concept and it is difficult to give a simple definition – it is basically the law that punishes individuals who obstruct or interfere with the administration of justice. Contempt is a criminal matter, and sanctions include heavy fines and even imprisonment. However, imprisonment of members of the news media is likely to be very rare, and individual journalists will often have their fines paid by their employers – such fines are often viewed as a cost of good investigative journalism. The media is also protected by the requirement that the Attorney General must consent to any prosecution of the media for contempt, and his or her decision should be made with the interest of freedom of speech firmly in mind.

Why do such laws exist? The key reason is that if the media directly discusses a matter that is the subject of court proceedings, this may prejudice the basic right of an individual to a fair trial (a right guaranteed under Article 6 of the European Court of Human Rights). For example, such coverage may influence the opinions of the jury deciding the case. Hostile press coverage may also have the effect of deterring an individual or organisation from asserting the right to have a hearing in court. There is also a risk that, whatever the verdict of the court, the individual may still be judged to be guilty in the public eye.

However, the public interest demands that there must be a right both to discuss issues of legitimate public interest and to indulge in fair criticism of people prominent in these issues. Incidental prejudice to a party in court proceedings should not be punished as contempt if it is as a result of the exercise of such rights.

There are two main situations in which the media will risk being in contempt of court:

1 When there is failure to obey a court order. To report matters that are the subject of either a statutory restriction or a reporting restriction imposed by a judge is a criminal offence. It can also be contempt of court for a journalist to refuse to disclose information needed as evidence to a court.
2 When it broadcasts or publishes material that has the effect of prejudicing legal proceedings. This may occur through the publishing of articles, the broadcasting of programmes, and even the presentation of musicals that deal with subject matter which is, or is about to become, the subject of legal proceedings.

The Contempt of Court Act 1981

The core law is at present to be found in the Contempt of Court Act, 1981. This provides that contempt of court is a strict liability offence – if you publish an article or broadcast an item that could prejudice legal proceedings, you can be guilty regardless of whether you had any intention to prejudice proceedings (subject to a defence under Section 3).

Whether broadcast or publication of material is prejudicial is judged with reference to the stage of the legal proceedings and the degree of risk that the broadcast poses. There is strict liability only if proceedings are active. Criminal proceedings are active in the following circumstances:

- if there is an arrest without a warrant
- when a warrant or a summons is issued
- on the serving of a paper specifying a charge
- on an oral charge being made (not Scotland).

Civil proceedings (e.g. libel) become active when arrangements are made for a hearing, usually when the case appears in court lists.

The biggest risk of prejudice is in cases involving a jury trial because it is felt that juries are very susceptible to the influence of media publicity. Factors that will determine whether there was a risk of prejudice include such obvious ones as geographical proximity (a story in a regional paper is unlikely to prejudice proceedings in another region). Time before the trial may also be a factor in cases where the behaviour did not pose a serious risk. For example, it has been held that the mere repetition of allegations that were to be the subject of a libel trial did not justify a contempt action when there was still a year to go before the hearing. There was no likelihood that a jury would be more likely to believe in their truth by their repetition so long before the trial.

The publication of a photograph of the accused may be contempt if identification is an issue. There have been two cases where the publication of the photo of the accused on the day of an identity parade has been punished by heavy fines. However, the publication of a 'wanted' poster is unlikely to be contempt.

The most extensive contempt of court saga of modern times concerns the trial of the Maxwell brothers. In one case, an injunction was issued to stop *Maxwell the Musical* appearing on the London stage; its portrayal of Robert Maxwell as a crook was felt to create in the public mind too strong an impression that the associated business dealings were criminal. Likewise, a 'knowing reference' to the trial on *Have I Got News For You* was held to be contempt, because it could influence those watching into believing that those 'in the know' all knew that the brothers were guilty.

Restrictions on behaviour in court

It is well known that physically to disrupt proceedings in court is punishable as contempt. It is also contempt to tape record proceedings without leave, or to film, photograph or even draw proceedings – those sketches used in the news must be drawn outside the courtroom.

On a related matter, it is important to realise that to reveal details of the jury's deliberations in a case is contempt. This is an essential protection to stop every verdict being questioned because of the unorthodox thought processes of the jury. If a jury member reveals that they found the defendant guilty after tossing a coin, to report such a travesty of justice would risk prosecution. However, it may be felt that the public interest in revealing the outrage might outweigh any contempt consideration, and also make it unlikely that a prosecution would follow.

Journalist's privilege

As a general rule, it is contempt to refuse a court order, and so a witness summoned to give evidence can be guilty of contempt if he or she refuses. It can also be contempt to refuse to answer a question, and this can lead to particular problems for a journalist who has obtained information in confidence. Section 10 of the Act says that the refusal by a journalist to disclose sources is only contempt if disclosure is necessary in the interests of justice or national security, or to prevent disorder or crime[a].

An important additional restriction on journalists is the power of the police to seize journalists' material under the Police and Criminal Justice Act 1984. Permission is needed from a county court judge; nevertheless, this will not be refused in circumstances in which the information is vital for any police investigation of serious crime. The police have seized news footage from both the BBC and the ITN under these powers.

[a]For how this provision has been applied, see *Defence Secretary v Guardian* (it did not protect journalists when they held information that could identify the source of a Ministry of Defence leak) and *X v Morgan Grampian* (it did not protect a journalist who had the source of a leak of information relating to the restructure plan of a company). However, the European Court of Human Rights has recently overturned part of the decision in *X v Morgan Grampian* – it held that the disclosure order was unnecessary because injunction against the publication of the information was enough protection for the company.

Defences

According to Section 3, it is a defence to a prosecution that you did not know, and had no reason to suspect, that proceedings were active. Note that this defence has to be shown by the defendant. Moreover, for a news organisation to be able to make such a claim may be difficult – the topicality of an issue will often relate to such proceedings being active. Even where this is not the case, knowledge that such proceedings were contemplated should put the organisation under notice that it should at least check the stage they have reached.

According to Section 4, it is defence, subject to s.4(2), if the complaint refers to the publication of a fair and accurate report of public proceedings made contemporaneously and in good faith. However, Section 4(2) makes one proviso; that it is still contempt of court to publish a fair and accurate contemporaneous report of proceedings if the court has made a postponement order.

According to Section 5, it is a defence that any prejudice to proceedings was merely the incidental product of a general discussion of a matter of public interest. A major law case will often make the issue it involves a major matter of public debate. Section 5 means that such debate will not be contempt as long as it does not directly try and influence the result of the case (e.g. by mentioning the case and discussing the facts in any critical fashion). It should be noted that Section 6 specifically removes this defence where any prejudice was intentional, even though it was an incidental result of a public interest discussion.

A good example of this provision at work is *Attorney General v English* (1983). A newspaper published a by-election address made by a candidate sponsored by the Society for the Protection of the Unborn Child at the time of the 'Dr Arthur' murder trial. This trial involved issues relating to the unborn child – issues that were also the subject of the address. It was held that the publication of the address was not contempt by virtue of s.5.

Reporting restrictions

Court reporting by the media is seen as an important guarantee of the principle that justice must not only be done, but must also be seen to be done. However, there are situations in which other interests outweigh this rule, and either statutes or court orders restrict the reporting of legal proceedings; these are listed below:

1 In committal proceedings (i.e. when an individual is committed for trial) the media can only report the name, address and age of the individual, the details of the charges (NOT the evidence), any decision and arrangements for future hearings made, the names of solicitors and barristers, and other administrative details.

2 There is a common law power to go 'in camera' (i.e. to exclude the public and the media from the proceedings) which can only be exercised in the interests of justice – see *R v Malvern Justices* (the order made because the defendant would be very upset was overturned). The usual reason for exclusion is to protect security-sensitive information; note that this will not be the case to protect the identities of witnesses, who can be protected using screens and specific reporting restrictions.

3 Reporting restrictions orders can be made under s.11 and s.4(2) – orders can be made on a wide definition of 'in the interests of justice'.

4 More common are the situations in which proceedings are held in the judge's chambers. Most of these deal with pre-trial applications, but cases can concern the following, all of which have restrictions placed on their reporting:
   - matters relating to the care of children (adoption, wardship, maintenance, custody, access etc.)
   - Mental Health Act proceedings
   - national security, secret patents or trade information
   - matters on which the court has placed a prohibiting order.

5 Other restrictions include:
   - a statutory prohibition on the publication of indecent matter forming part of the evidence
   - statutory restrictions on the reporting of divorce and family proceedings
   - prohibitions on the identification of young offenders and the victims of rape or serious sexual assault.

11.14 Intellectual property law

The acquisition, exploitation and protection of intellectual property are fundamental to the activities of any media-related business. To avoid the infringement of the property rights of others is also of high importance. This section is aimed at giving you a basic knowledge of the law as it relates to these issues.

11.14.1 What is intellectual property?

Intellectual property rights are statutory property rights created by the law to enable the protection of intangible property, such as the technological innovation behind an invention, the creative effort behind an original work ('creative' in the sense of bringing to creation, rather than being novel and inventive), and the business reputation and goodwill belonging to an undertaking (an inclusive term designed to cover various forms of commercial and charitable organisations and individuals). With their introduction, the law imposed a number of major restrictions on the mode of expression available to others, both in respect of how they could present their business to the outside world and in what could form the content of their media products. However, such restrictions can be justified in the public interest for both of the two basic types of intellectual property.

Rights are granted by statute to encourage creativity (and hence progress) by securing for the creator an exclusive right to profit from the exploitation of the creation (e.g. patent, copyright, industrial design, performing rights).

Rights are granted to protect businesses and the consumer from fraudulent attempts to pass off usually inferior products as those of another (e.g. trademarks, the tort of passing off).

In this section, it is proposed to concentrate on copyright and other rights that relate to the products of personal creativity. However, it is also necessary to have a brief look at trademark law.

11.14.2 Trademark law

A trademark is the sign by which an undertaking distinguishes itself from other undertakings[b]. By implication, it is also the sign which indicates to the

[b] To be registered under the 1994 Trademarks Act, a trademark must be 'any sign capable of being represented graphically which is capable of distinguishing goods or services of one undertaking from those of other undertakings'. Examples given include words (including personal names), designs, letters, numerals, or the shapes of goods and their packaging (the famous Coca Cola bottle is now capable of registration; under the old Act, it was not). Geographical names are now capable of registration. Recent applications have included the exclusive right to use certain colours – e.g. BP green. Trademarks can only be registered for particular categories of goods. Multiple registration is possible, but it costs extra for every category in which a trademark is registered, and failure to use the trademark for a particular category of goods will lead to the registration becoming invalid. It is therefore advisable to register trademarks only in those categories in which they will be used.

consumer that a particular undertaking has some commercial involvement with any product on which that sign appears as a trademark. If one undertaking, X Ltd, applies the trademark of Y Ltd to its products without permission, it is making the false representation that the product so marked has some trade origin with Y Ltd. Consumers looking to buy a product made by Y may buy the false product, with the result that Y loses revenue in the form of a lost sale. Moreover, if that product is in any way substandard or deviates in some essential way from the qualities to be expected from the original brand, the consumer will think badly of Y and its products may become less desirable. Both the consumer and the trademark owner will therefore have lost out. It is the function of the law that protects trademarks to protect the interests of both the owner of the trademark and the consumer. Any business, whether it is a company, a pop group, the maker of a film or even an author, must therefore be able to protect its business reputation through the right of exclusive use of its own trademark. If other businesses were free to use that trademark, its function as an indication of origin would be lost, and with it would go all its ability to indicate quality and positive reputation to the consumer.

There is infringement of a trademark if there is use of the same or a similar mark on goods of the same category as those for which the mark is registered. If the mark is used on goods of a different category, there is infringement if there is a likelihood of confusion with the registered mark (and hence as to the manufacturer). An important qualification to the scope of the protection of trademarks is that there is only an infringement if the use of the trademark is in the context of trading in goods or services. For example, a book published with the trademark name 'Wet Wet Wet' in its title did not infringe the trademark, because it referred to the contents of the book and did not indicate any involvement of the group with the product. By the same token, the title of a film or a TV programme should be able to include a trademark name as long as it is a genuine use for the purposes of describing the subject matter.

In addition to the system of registered trademarks, there are two other branches of trademark law. The tort of passing off is generally said to protect unregistered trademarks. However, it is fairly flexible in form; it merely makes it actionable for a trader to make a misrepresentation to the consumer that damages the business of another trader. In effect, this means that it is actionable for one trader to annex the commercial reputation of another for its own ends, and this may be done without appropriation of a trademark. For example, ASDA was found liable for passing off when they marketed their 'Puffin' chocolate biscuits in a similar packaging 'get-up' to that of 'Penguin' chocolate biscuits. The essence of the wrong was that ASDA's actions were felt likely to lead the consumer to believe that there was some sort of commercial link between 'Puffins' and 'Penguins'.

The third branch of trademark law has already been mentioned in the context of privacy law – the tort of malicious falsehood. In its original guise as the tort of trade libel, it existed to stop the intentional or reckless making of false statements which damaged the business interests of individuals and undertakings. For example, it would be actionable under malicious falsehood falsely to tell various concert venues that a musician was too ill to perform (thus causing them to cancel concerts) or falsely to tell various production companies that a particular producer was already committed to another project and therefore should not be considered for work.

Because they embody an undertaking's business reputation and are used by consumers to ensure that they buy the undertaking's products, trademarks are among the most valuable and jealously guarded property belonging to any undertaking. The basic message here for media managers is therefore not to mark your products with trademarks that belong to other undertakings. However, trademark law is also of relevance because of the issues of the derogatory treatment of trademarks, product placement, and character merchandising.

11.14.3 Character merchandising

Character merchandising is the practice by which products are sold using designs derived from media products in order to increase their consumer appeal. A successful TV series or film will create a number of instantly recognisable names and characters with ready-made public images, and in many cases a demand for souvenirs and products that relate to that film/programme. The rights in these images will suddenly assume enormous value – for example, it is a well-known fact that the film *Star Wars* made more money from the spin-off merchandise than it did at the cinema. The producer of the media product should have already taken steps to secure agreement over character merchandising rights by the time the media product reaches the public. Every contract involving the acquisition of intellectual property rights in relation to a media production should include provision for character merchandising rights; if this is not done, it is likely that the rights acquired will not cover all the activities that character merchandising can involve. Merchandising rights acquired during the production phase will inevitably be acquired more easily than merchandising rights relating to a programme that has suddenly become the latest craze.

The status in English law of this important area is still uncertain. Recent decisions involving the Tellytubbies and Elvis Presley have both cast doubt on whether the tort of passing off can prevent the use by others of characters as designs for or on products. It is therefore important to secure copyright protection for such characters, and to pursue the registration of character names and images as trademarks.

11.14.4 Product placement

Another important implication of trademark law for programme-makers is the capacity for featuring specific brands of goods within the programme. The prospect of such featuring can often attract payments to secure such publicity – the practice of product placement. Even where such overt practices are disapproved (for example at the BBC), it is still possible that corporate donors may be generous in letting film-makers have free use of branded items needed as props.

11.14.5 Derogatory treatment of trademarks

The other aspect of product placement is the possibility that trademark owners might object to any derogatory treatment handed out to their goods. A recent example in the USA is the action brought by the makers of Spam against the latest Muppet movie for their naming of an evil pig character as Spa'am (although this action was not successful). A more serious example might be if in the needs of drama a feature film shows a particular make of car bursting into flames after a minor crash. If those watching are left with the impression that such a make of car is not as safe as they would like it to be, the demand for that car may well fall, and an action for derogatory treatment of the trademark might follow (in the UK this action would probably be for malicious falsehood).

11.15 Copyright and related rights

11.15.1 Copyright

Copyright is the name given to the legal rights granted to the owner or creator of a qualifying work. It exists in any work automatically upon its coming into existence; there is no need for registration, although it may be a wise precaution in some circumstances – especially in relation to music – to be able to prove the date of creation. Copyright is now governed by the Copyright, Designs and Patents Act (CDPA) 1988 (as amended in 1996).

It is traditionally said that English law does not grant copyright for an idea, but only for the expression of that idea. Recent ideas that have failed to obtain copyright protection include a film-editing technique (see Norowzian v Arks Ltd, 1998, concerning a short film call *Joy* whose innovative technique was later copied for a Guinness advert) and an arrangement of objects deliberately contrived for the purpose of an 'artistic' photograph (Creation Records v News Group Newspapers, 1997, which featured an array of objects – including a Rolls Royce in a swimming pool – posed for an Oasis album cover). It is therefore arguable that copyright law may need to be revised in the light of what is now considered to be 'art'.

Copyright is the exclusive right to do or permit the following acts in relation to a work: to copy it; to issue copies of the work to the public; to perform, show or play the work in public; to broadcast it or include it in any cable service; and to make an adaptation of the work (including a translation)(section 16 CDPA). It is infringed if any of these is done without either permission or valid defence.

11.15.2 Types of work that qualify as copyright works

There are nine types of copyright work. These are: *original* literary, dramatic, musical or artistic works; and sound recordings, films, television and sound broadcasts, cable programmes and the typographical layout of published works.

- *Literary works.* Almost any words written down or recorded will qualify as a literary work; there is no requirement of quality. Timetables and lists therefore qualify, as do TV schedules (although the Broadcasting Act 1990 stipulates that they must be made available to other publishers at least 2 weeks in advance if a fee is paid). There must be some degree of skill and labour in the production of the work for it to be protected; therefore individual words and some phrases are too short to attract copyright (e.g. a 'made-up' company name such as Exxon). Computer programs are protected as literary works.
- *Dramatic works.* These include plays, choreographed work, mimes, and scenarios and scripts for films. Programme formats can be so protected, but they have to have sufficient distinctive features to qualify for protection. In *Green v. New Zealand Broadcasting Co.*, it was decided that *Opportunity Knocks*, essentially a talent contest judged through audience reaction, was too general a programme idea to qualify for copyright protection. The basic idea behind most quizzes and game shows would be

unlikely to be protectable as a dramatic work, but a more detailed treatment of the programme format, including its different stages and unique characteristics, might be. To be protected, it is necessary that the dramatic work must be recorded in appropriate form. It has recently been held that it is enough if the work has been recorded on film.

- *Musical works.* To attract copyright protection, these need to be written down. Lyrics are separate literary works. Great care has to be taken when there is arguably multiple authorship; it is easier if ownership of joint compositions is governed by some prior agreement.

- *Artistic works.* These include paintings, drawings, sculpture and photographs. To qualify, skill and labour must have gone into their production, but there is no quality requirement.

- *Films.* Copyright in films has recently undergone a major upheaval. There were previously separate copyrights for the sounds and the pictures, but the film soundtrack is now to be treated as part of the film itself. Copyright has also been changed in a way that partially reflects a film's status as an artistic work rather than just a financial interest. Although overall copyright still belongs to the producer, the duration of the right is now linked to the life spans of the director and the writers of the screenplay, music and dialogue. Although a film is now the subject of a single copyright, it is the product of a number of people's work, all of whom have a separate copyright in that work. It is up to the producer to make the necessary arrangements to obtain the necessary copyright to use these elements through the contracts that commission the work.

- *Others.* These exist to protect the financial interests of those responsible for them, and exist in addition to other copyright interests. For example, copyright in a sound recording is separate to copyright in either music or lyrics. Copyright in a broadcast is separate to copyright in the material broadcast; the broadcast of a live sporting event will attract copyright in the broadcast only, but the broadcast of a pre-recorded programme might involve copyright in the music, the story, the script, the sets, the music, the film itself and the broadcast. There may also be performing and moral rights at issue (see below).

11.15.3 Ownership of copyright

For literary, musical, dramatic and artistic works, the owner is normally the author, although it can be the employer if the work is produced in the course of employment. It may, however, be the person responsible for the recording of the words etc. – e.g. the journalist who records what is said at a public meeting (note the rights to their words of those who speak, etc.), or the ghost writer who has an autobiography dictated to him. The author has to be human; there is no copyright in randomly generated numbers (e.g. newspaper bingo, the national lottery numbers), although there may be copyright in the way they are presented. The photographer is the owner of copyright in any photograph he takes, although where he is commissioned to take photographs (e.g. family portraits) there is a moral right for the subjects to object to the photographer exploiting that copyright.

Copyright in both a sound recording and a film belongs to the person who made the arrangements for it to be made; copyright in broadcasts belongs to the broadcaster. Although copyright in a film belongs to the producer, its duration is related to the lives of those artistically responsible for the elements of the film – the principle director, the author of the screenplay, the author of the dialogue and the composer of music specifically created for and used in the film.

Ownership is naturally subject to contractual variations, and it can also be bought and sold as property. Note that it is separate to the physical existence of the work.

11.15.4 Infringement

The primary infringement of copyright is the copying of a substantial part of a copyright work. This is satisfied if the part copied is significant or distinctive – for example, copying the first few notes of Beethoven's Fifth would be infringement (if copyright actually existed in it). Hence sampling using the distinctive hook of other songs is probably breach of copyright. Secondary infringements are concerned with commercial dealing in infringing products.

11.15.5 Defences to infringement

Fair dealing

It is a defence to an infringement action that the use of parts of a copyright work was fair dealing for the purposes of reporting current events, or for the purposes of criticism or review. There must be acknowledgement of the original work for the dealing to be fair, although this does not apply to television and radio reporters in their reporting of current events.

Beyond this, there is no exact definition of what is fair dealing. Fairly extensive extracts of a book may be used if you are writing a book that challenges its philosophy. However, if you are merely planning to 'spoil' a rival's exclusive rights to extracts from a book, the amount that may be quoted for the purposes of fair dealing may be limited. For example, Channel 4, without any permission, used extensive extracts from the film *A Clockwork Orange* in a half-hour programme as part of their *Banned* series. The programme discussed the impact of the subject matter, and in doing so showed many of the 'juicy bits'. This use was held to be fair dealing.

If it is thought that a parody has borrowed from the original work such as to constitute copying, it will still be a possible defence that the use was for the purposes of criticism or review. The extent to which parodies are infringements of copyright is unclear. The purpose of the parody will be relevant – the parody of a song as part of an advertisement was held to be an infringement of the literary copyright in the lyrics, but a parody for the purposes of political or humorous comment would be likely to be treated more leniently. However, a parody must be careful to avoid passing itself off as the work of the individual being parodied – in the 'Alan Clarke diaries' case, the *Evening Standard* was found liable because it did not sufficiently make clear that Alan Clarke was not the author.

Others

It is a defence that the copying of the work was pursuant to a 'permitted act'. It is permitted to make a copy of a limited part of a book etc. if it is for the purposes of private study. There are also defences if the material is to be used in judicial proceedings or their reporting, and if the material is of a type that is open to public inspection under statute.

There are also detailed rules relating to educational purposes and libraries. The legality of much of the copying that takes place in such circumstances will depend upon both obtaining and the specific terms of a copyright license for a specific type of use.

Much use of copyright work is done via copyright licenses. However, the existence of a license will only be a defence if its terms are strictly adhered to and the required fee is paid to the correct organisation.

It is possible in some cases that it may be a defence that no copyright exists in a work as a result of public policy. The original decision that came to this conclusion related to an immoral 'novel' by Eleanor Glynn, and so would not apply today (even video 'nasties' have copyright protection), but it was suggested in the House of Lords that *Spycatcher* would not be protected by copyright such as to reward Peter Wright for his breach of confidence.

Incidental inclusion of a copyright work within a film or photograph is also a defence. For example, news footage of a procession which includes a band will not infringe the copyright of any music the band might be playing, and the inclusion of a publicly displayed sculpture in a film will not infringe the artistic copyright in the work. However, it should be noted that the inclusion of any music in the sound track of a commercial film or programme would be unlikely to be regarded as incidental.

11.15.6 Duration and remedies

For literary, dramatic, musical and artistic works, the term of duration is for the life of the author plus 70 years, except where the work is computer generated (it is then 50 years). For films, copyright lasts until 70 years after the death of the last of the four people with an interest in the film. For sound recordings and broadcasts, the term is 50 years from the end of the year in which they were first released/broadcast (or from the year in which they were created if they have not been released). The one exception is the copyright to *Peter Pan*, which was extended because it had been left to Great Ormond Street Hospital for the benefit of the children treated there. It should also be noted that, for authors who are not nationals in a European Economic Area state, the copyright period to be applied to works created outside the EEA is that of the country of which the author is a national, provided that it is not longer than the protection granted under English law. For sound recordings and broadcasts, it is only the nationality of the author that is relevant to determining the applicable law.

The remedies for breach of copyright are normally damages and an injunction. An award of damages may be reduced if it is felt that the defendant was acting out of laudable motives. Damages are only available against a defendant who knew or should have known that he or she was infringing the copyright in a work; however, once an innocent infringer has notice that the copyright is being infringed, damages will be available against the infringer if the infringing acts continue. Under the CDPA, it is also possible to obtain the delivery up of all infringing copies so that they can be destroyed.

11.15.7 Performing rights

These were created to protect both a performer's right in live performance and the rights of those who have signed an exclusive recording contract with him or her. They are infringed both by recording a performance without permission, and by dealing in that recording. Infringement can lead to both civil and criminal action. In addition, you cannot show or play a recording in public without permission and/or the payment of royalties (to the Performing Rights Society).

Perhaps the most notorious case involving what were to become performing rights involved the last Inspector Clouseau film, *The Trail of the Pink Panther.* Peter Sellers had contracted to appear in the four previous films under terms that specified that the right to use any footage of his performance was limited to that film alone. When the fifth film was compiled from out-takes from the previous four, it was held to be an infringement of his performing rights.

11.15.8 Moral rights

Moral rights include the following:

1 The right of the author to be identified as such. This includes the directors of films. It does not apply automatically, but must be asserted by the author. It does not apply to articles and reports for newspapers and magazines. Damages are obtainable for consequential financial loss.
2 An author, artist or director can also object to the false attribution of work to him or her. This right has recently been used to bring an action against a parody of the author's work that did not make sufficiently clear that it was a parody (the Alan Clarke case). Moreover, it can be used to inhibit the making of unauthorised film biographies of an individual. Prior to its filming, the makers of the Francis Bacon biopic *Love is the Devil* were presented with the problem that they could not use extensive quotations from interviews given by the painter, because that would be an infringement of the copyright in the interviews. However, if they decided to use any piece of fictional speech long enough to constitute a literary work if recorded, there was the possibility that it would constitute the false attribution of authorship of the speech to the person portrayed making it.
3 There is also a right to object to derogatory treatment of one's work. The usual example quoted is the successful action taken by Terry Gilliam to stop an American network removing all the animations prior to the broadcast of *Monty Python.*
4 A person who commissions a photographer to take his or her photograph has the right to object to any unauthorised use of the image by the photographer.

All of the moral rights survive death, and will pass to the personal representatives.

11.15.9 Intellectual property (IP) right protection bodies

For ease of administration, the enforcement and exploitation of the various forms of copyright work is often undertaken by centralised bodies. Important examples are the Performing Rights Society (songwriters, lyricists, and publishers controlling public performance and broadcast of their work), Phonographic Performance Limited (controlling the public performance of a sound recording), and the Mechanical Copyright Protection Society (copyright owners controlling who can first record and manufacture their work).

There are also several bodies that protect the wider interests of potential copyright owners, notably the Directors' Guild of Great Britain, the Musicians' Union, Equity, the Writers' Guild of Great Britain, and BECTU.

11.15.10 Copyright exploitation agreements

This section is intended to serve only as a rough guide to the contents of agreements for the filming and broadcasting of copyright works. Such agreements can involve a complex assortment of different rights, such as rights of performance, broadcast and adaptation, and must cover important issues such as the period of time and geographical extent of the rights concerned. The Writers' Guild and the Society of Authors have negotiated collective agreements dealing with the commissioning of original works and the adaptation of existing works. Similar agreements exist with respect to music. The exploitation of a work as a film or television programme can add substantially to an author's income, but all the risk and outlay involved will devolve onto the producer. As a result, it is often the practice that a producer will negotiate a right to a share of these increased royalties. However, it is also common practice for an author to negotiate a share in the future profits of the film, etc. The size of this will vary depending on the reputation of the author.

Potential issues include:

1 *Character merchandising rights.* These are protected in English law by copyright, trademark law, and the tort of passing off. The latter two depend on registration and use in a commercial context. Copyright will

belong to both the creator of the characters and the producer of the film from which they take visual form. Failure to agree who should register and license trademarks, and how the copyright interests should be divided and licensed, could lead to expensive and messy legal battles. It is in all the parties' interests that these matters should be settled in the contract between the writer and producer. Normally, the responsibility for character merchandising will be undertaken by a third party, who will then pay all the parties an agreed level of royalties.

2 *Rights acquired.* These can vary according to the individual contract and to the nature of the project. For example, UK television production companies will often only acquire the exclusive right for 2 years to broadcast a performance of the script on domestic television. This period can be extended (to 3 years), and once broadcast is made further rights are triggered – for example, the right to unlimited repeat transmissions within the UK subject to the payment of an appropriate fee (which may vary according to the time of the repeat), rights to sell the programme abroad (again subject to the payment of royalties to the writer), an option to acquire the rights to issue the performance of a script on video, exercisable within 7 years of the first broadcast (again subject to fees being paid).

Contracts usually also provide for additional media rights (i.e. satellite, cable, video, and public showings of television programmes). Again, a royalty fee is payable. It will be a term of the contract that the script does not infringe other copyrights (unless permission has been obtained) and that it is not defamatory (although the writer will not have to reimburse the payment of damages if the defamatory matter was not included negligently or maliciously). This is a warranty.

The contract will often make credit provisions – in particular, it will provide for how the writer will be mentioned in the credits of the programme.

BBC contracts provide that for a year following the first broadcast, a writer must consult the BBC before allowing any other publication. Unless expressly dealt with by the contract, no right of publication passes to the television company.

Rejection, revision and payment are also covered in the contract. Naturally, there should be provisions in any contract dealing with when and how a writer should be paid, and what the consequences are for both parties in the event of the rejection of a script. For film scripts, there are standard form contracts that deal with the rights at issue at each of the following stages of production: treatment, first draft, second draft, and principle photography script. There are undertakings on the writer's part to attend meetings, and to avoid the infringement of other copyright works. The agreement will decide the allocation of the copyright interests, and will deal with the rights of additional exploitation.

11.16 Further reading

Barendt, E. M. (1995). *Broadcasting Law – A Comparative Study.* Clarendon Press.

Barendt, E. M., Lustgarden, L., Norrie, K. and Stephenson, H. (1997). *Libel and the Media.* Clarendon.

Crone, T. (1995). *Law and the Media*, 3rd edn. Focal Press.

Fazzani, L. and Hart, T. (1997). *Intellectual Property Law.* McMillan Law Masters.

Robertson, G. and Nicol, A. (1992) *Media Law.* Penguin.

Welsh, T. and Greenwood, W. (1999). *McNae's Essential Law for Journalists*, 15th edn. Butterworths.

Chapter 12

Media ethics

12.1 Summary

The audiovisual industry is a high profile business sector in modern society. Film, television and other media communication channels have had a profound effect upon society within modern western culture. Watching television is a major pasttime for many people. It has been accused of being a key influence in aspects of antisocial behaviour, and of being the underlying reason for obesity in children and teenagers of the 1990s. In the near future it will have an even more profound effect upon people throughout the rest of the world, as greater opportunities to view become available. Most texts on media ethics have been concerned with the controversies of the day and the representation of individuals and organisations through news or documentaries. There are many high profile examples across the media, from the paparazzi following Princess Diana to Carlton Television being creative with the facts regarding a documentary on drug-running.

In this chapter these controversies are not overlooked, but should be implicitly included in all media managers' analyses of their work and ethical policies. For people working in the media industry there is a special responsibility over and above those that any individual or organisation might have.

Business behaviour has become a subject hot debate for all the stakeholders of any organisation. These stakeholders include employees, buyers and suppliers, the community within which the business works and the government, in addition to the traditionally accepted interested parties of owners and shareholders. Whilst business ethics may often be considered an oxymoron, many would suggest that media ethics as a subset of business ethics doesn't even get to the starting gate.

Ethical issues within the audiovisual industry fall into two main areas of concern; internal systems and external impact. Internal systems refer to the ethical environment within the business, while external impact considers the audience that consumes the media product and the role of the media company in the wider socio-economic framework. All media products will have some ethical issue attached to them. There are high profile areas of intense debate, such as representation, pornography and violence, that attract scrutiny from many organisations. In addition, there are many decisions and actions taken by seemingly less controversial programme-makers that influence the audience. The simplest task of modifying an edit point within a production can profoundly change the meaning and construct that the audience might infer from the work. In the UK, a television advertising campaign for the *Guardian* newspaper showed how, by viewing an event from differing angles with different edit points, new interpretations can be made. Editorial decisions are being made every day in studios throughout the world to help convey or reposition a message to a wide range of audiences.

This chapter introduces the reader to the debate about possible ethical frameworks within which decisions can be made. It has been suggested that ethics is the science of morality. Many would see the words 'ethics' and 'morality' as interchangeable. Both terms concern themselves with the expected code of conduct for an individual within a particular social group.

If you agree that ethics is indeed the science of morality, then the two main schools of philosophical thought are attempts at codifying this science into some acceptable reference framework.

The first two sections of this chapter consider the framework of ethics from a personal and organisational standpoint. We then examine business ethics, corporate governance, reputation management and international business ethics.

This approach should enable the reader to consider and find a satisfactory process to resolve contemporary ethical debates that have an impact on the audiovisual industry.

Organisational ethical debates will occur internally due to:

- company structure
- working practices
- staff relations
- new technologies
- codes of conduct

or externally through:

- buyer and audience relationships
- supplier relations
- sales management
- choice of production projects undertaken
- codes of business behaviour.

All of the above will generate potential issues and debates that will have an impact on colleagues and staff within the audiovisual industry for whom you may have a responsibility.

In his first month as Director General of the BBC (February 2000), Greg Dyke set out 'the most comprehensive code of ethics in broadcasting'. Although you may never run the BBC, you do need to have a process by which you too can deal with potential ethical issues and debates.

12.2 Objectives and key issues

The key objective of this chapter is to introduce readers to methods by which they can make decisions within their working environment. These decisions cannot be made without an understanding of the internal and external ethical environments surrounding decision-making. This ethical framework provides a filter by which decisions in management are processed.

In Chapter 9, it was suggested that decisions follow the following simplified format:

- Discovery
- Choices
- Actions.

The choices available are made on the basis of the paradigm (the mental model) that the individual or the organisation holds at the time of decision-making. An understanding of ethics, and more specifically business ethics, can provide individuals or managers with a framework by which they can literally 'frame' and bound the choices available. The consequent actions of these choices are filtered by the process of an ethical code of conduct.

The route to this objective is provided by:

- considering and evaluating personal ethical behaviour
- applying it within an organisational and social environment

- placing your own business ethics within this template of organisational and social responsibility
- considering the wider impact of business behaviour from an ethical perspective, both in corporate governance and international business dealings.

With the theory and options for ethical business management set in place, the reader is asked to consider some of the ethical debates within the audiovisual industry. In reading this chapter we would therefore ask you to reflect on the following:

1 What is your moral or ethical frame of reference?
2 Is there a role for ethical behaviour in business?
3 If so, how do you or will you handle ethical dilemmas within the business environment?

12.3 Introduction to ethics

Initially this chapter began out of a need to find a better method for analysing and describing the impact and consequent organisational changes new technology brings to the media industry. New technology is a main driver for change within mature media production markets. Describing the web and its functional form, or digital television and its capability and effectiveness in being able to produce cloned copies of a tape, leaves us with only a description of bigger and better, or smaller and faster. The nagging feeling remains – so what? Do we make 'better' programmes? What does this mean for the programme-maker and the audience. Will the medium remain the message?

Marx suggested that rapid progress occurs in the infrastructure, the economic sphere of activities which then supports the superstructure. This superstructure or secondary level is the social sphere of art, politics, law and prevailing traditional attitudes. He suggested that the superstructure evolves more slowly and is more resistant to change than the economic infrastructure, especially in the modern industrial age of advanced capitalism. To rephrase the point, we are always looking to develop and work on technologies for which we have not yet developed systems and techniques for coping within society. The ethical application of new or contemporary technology within the media industry is clearly party to this process. Do we have the moral and ethical tools to deal with these rapid technological changes? Many think not. The scientists plead that they are not the moral guardians of their research; it is for society to decide. From the steam train and the spinning jenny to atomic energy and the human genome project, society has had to grapple with the consequences of technological advances, often not very effectively.

Individuals implicitly or explicitly make decisions within a moral framework; it just might not be one shared by others. This chapter offers the reader some points of reference by which the debate on shared moral and ethical structures can take place. By considering technology as the herald for change, we see the enormous impact it will have upon the following:

1 Working practices within the industry
2 Time taken to produce a product
3 Ownership and control of that product
4 Re-purposing of the raw assets (how they may be used, re-used and manipulated for other means)
5 The channels to the marketplace (the audience and the consumer)
6 The level of distribution control over those assets (tagging the material and therefore licensing its use).

Call centres have become synonymous with new technology. In *Notes from a Big Country*, Bill Bryson writes that he cannot cope with the simplest of questions being asked by a 20-year-old who requires a 10-digit number before help can be offered. Meanwhile that 20-year-old is armed with a script to answer calls, and the call conversation and the time to resolve the problem is being monitored by management. Technology has not freed the individual but has rather given greater control to the employer.

In the last quarter of 1999, the media industry reached the seemingly much desired position (sic) where an individual researches, writes, presents, records and edits an insert to a broadcast programme. A media manager's dream come true? Low wages and possibly low skill is part of the media ethics debate.

If, for the moment, we maintain the idea that new technology is the main driver for change in the media industry, the following need to be considered:

1 Why use it? Because it is more reliable, cheaper, faster and more efficient. In the case of portable broadcast cameras, the lighter body meant that the issue of physical strength became an irrelevance. Another gender barrier was broken, as it was argued at one time that only men could be camera operators.
2 What price digital technology? It was suggested by Chris Smith, the Culture and Heritage Secretary in the UK in 1999, that the transfer to digital

technology would take place over 10–12 years (by circa 2010). Already this has been brought forward to, possibly, 2005. The caveat is that he wants to know that 95 per cent of the UK population are in a position to receive digital transmission before the analogue signal is turned off. Despite this, it seems doubtful that the government will wait until this figure of 95 per cent is met before the analogue signal is switched off.

Taking the team with you

You are an experienced media manager and producer, and for the past 2 years have been working with Company A as the line producer. The production director is not only a working colleague but also a close friend. You have together built up a successful team. You are then offered a new post as production manager for Company B. The work is broadly the same as in your current occupation; the advantage is that you will be offered some equity in the new firm, and a broader remit for the role with hire and fire responsibilities. Part of your remit in the new firm will be to build up a new production team. Ideally you would recruit the members of your old team with Company A to join you in the new venture. What would you do? You might like to bear in mind that the media industry is relatively small. Your old boss in Company A is a well-respected member of many of the guilds and trade associations. If you were to poach staff from your old company, do you think it would have an impact on your reputation within the industry? Should you consider the financial implications for the old company?

12.4 The underpinning debate

Ethics is concerned with the role of human nature and conduct; it is the values or standards by which we would see something as being correct or right. An individual's set of values has much to do with cultural background, religion, education and other social attributes. These factors would predetermine many of the constructs that an individual puts in place from a moral point of view, and therefore be axiomatic to any ethical decision-making.

At the extremes of human behaviour there are common actions that most people would recognise as being moral or immoral. The debate also concerns the actions a society will take to keep an individual within the boundaries of moral behaviour for that society; to punish or reform – retribution or rehabilitation. Where any society has difficulties is with what might be called the 'boundary conditions', where the dilemmas are at their greatest and the answers not clear-cut. The majority of the population does not have to operate under these circumstances. We abdicate our responsibility to the government, police, judges, doctors, teachers, business leaders etc. Many make or allow others to make decisions for them by default. We do not even vote in large numbers. The 'floating voter' determines the election outcomes. Most of us do not have to function on the boundaries of ethical decision-making.

Let us first establish the moral landscape. It has been suggested that our ethical frame of reference is taken either from a predominantly religious viewpoint or from a scientific/secular viewpoint. Ronald M. Green states that[1]:

> … the major ethical teachings of most religious traditions are largely compatible with various secular or rational ethical views. Religious traditions typically prohibit forms of conduct that secular culture also views as morally wrong. Almost all religious codes condemn violence against innocent persons, theft, and dishonesty.

Green is suggesting that the secular view is essentially a sub-set of any religious perspective. The religious point of view is based upon a set of beliefs taken from, for example, the Old Testament, the New Testament or the Koran. These are a set of God-given rules, or dogma. The scientific or secular point of view suggests that by deconstructing an issue into its component parts, a true statement will emerge by which the individual can arrive at an ethical and moral standpoint. Many have argued that these viewpoints can coincide happily within the one individual. Can someone be deeply religious and profoundly scientific, and not have conflicts over their moral set of values? It has been suggested that we could have an internal 'god' that helps us make decisions that seem right. Or is it just our conscience?

From the opening discourse on ethics and morality, we have to consider the formal and contemporary expression of morality and ethics in society – the law. A prime role for government is to protect the population, providing a safe environment against external forces and internal disorder. To do so requires an army, a police force and laws. The legal framework is usually an evocation of the moral and ethical standpoint of a particular society at a moment in time; it reflects the consensus of what is deemed good and right behaviour. Those who don't believe in it, or who agree with the consensus yet transgress, meet a set of criteria for punishment and retributions administered through the judicial system.

The law is a shifting framework. What was an appropriate law in the fifteenth and sixteenth centuries is clearly not an appropriate law in the twentieth and twenty-first centuries. At the beginning of the twentieth century, it was considered an appropriate law in the UK not to let women vote. More recently in the UK, in the early 1990s, the Thatcher Conservative government considered it appropriate to have a new property law, the community charge that became known as the poll tax. It was highly controversial, and resulted in riots in central London.

How individuals and communities respond to laws to which they object will be determined by the level of democratic engagement they believe is available to them. It may not be about the action they actually take. When, for whatever reason, people feel that law is bad *and* they feel that the democratic system or the legal framework does not give them any redress, there is the potential for revolutionary change (as opposed to the democratic and evolutionary change that might take place over time). Clearly, in reality the process from dissaffection to revolution is a complex path.

The framework of law is only a function of society's values at the time. Some laws are a government's response to a media campaign event or events that have put issues into the public mind – such as the Dangerous Dogs Act 1991 (see www.hmso.gov.uk/acts). This was a response to a series of tragic high profile incidents with guard dogs and savage 'pets' that had maimed or killed children. The statistics did not bear out this 'sudden' rise in dangerous dogs. Prior to the campaign there were the same number of dogs doing harm to children. Due to public (or was it tabloid newspaper-led?) outrage there was a need to have a law that was seen to be responding to this problem. Laws can be instigated by a subsection of society, especially if supported by the national press. In the military, judiciary and the clergy, we have the three elements of what has been termed the state. Whilst any government is made up of ' here today gone tomorrow' politicians, the state remains. So does the media, labelled the fourth estate due to its influence and power.

Non-government organisations (NGOs) and pressure groups tend to act on the boundary conditions of society. They may oppose current legislation for many reasons. Consider the matter of clean water. Pressure groups such as Greenpeace may say that the water companies are not providing clean water. The water companies will dispute this; they are adhering to the legal framework and are allowed to dump chemicals x, y and z to a certain level within the watercourses. The counterargument is that the companies don't know what the cocktail of those chemicals is doing to the environment, even though each one in its own right may be below European or UK regulations. Due to legal interpretation and possible ambiguity, pressure groups believe that corporations often hide behind the rule of law (e.g. legal levels to dump chemicals) as much as they adhere to the spirit of the law (e.g. we don't contaminate the water at all). This is why it is argued there that there is a need for a code of business ethics that extends beyond the strict legal framework of business behaviour.

The above illustrates the two broad schools of ethical philosophical thought. These are identified as denotologists (who have a rules-based approach) and consequentialists (who believe the outcome is key).

Denotologists argue that an action is inherently right or wrong, irrespective of its consequences. This approach has its basis in Judeo-Christian beliefs, with a clear evocation of the Ten Commandments. It is also manifest in the UK legal tradition of rights and duties. These are set against the obligations the individual has to society. The principle rests on the notion that an action should only be judged as right or moral if it conforms to an agreed set of rules by which the individual decision and resulting action may be tested. There is no reference to the final outcome of this decision.

This theory suggests that if you create enough rules within a system, you can deconstruct a dilemma into a hierarchical flow diagram by which you define your decision methodology. The final outcome is reached by satisfying the rules of the system. There are many that would endorse this theory. The difficulty arises when challenged by something unknown, outside of the rules to date. It requires a new subset of rules.

Company owners/managers devise mission statements, and from mission statements they create codes of practice, or business principles. As new business activities fall outside those existing business principles, another element or rule is added. We arrive at 'Business Principles, revised edition, version 4'. The problem is solved until the next ambiguity. A rules-based system may deal with those conditions within some understood or known boundary very well until something new comes along to challenge the *status quo*. In other words, a denotological approach provides a set of codified structures that equips us with answers to everyday decisions within a known environment. This will be explored a little further in the section on business ethics.

An understanding of the consequentialist approach requires two steps. The first is to note that there is a philosophical school of thought that suggests a judgement as to whether an action is right or wrong can only be completed if we consider the outcome of such an action. The second step is to note that there is a particular version of this approach known as utilitarianism. Some commentators present utilitarianism as 'the greatest good to the greatest number'; others as the 'greatest happiness to the greatest number'. Good and happiness are clearly not necessarily the same thing. For example, within a religious context 'good' is interpreted as that which 'God approves'. This analysis is not necessarily a God-given one.

Each of the groups – denotologists, consequentialists and utilitarians – believe they are looking for the 'greater good' as a means of identifying the most appropriate or ethical behaviour that will sufficiently solve the problem. As with the management theories of the 1970s, there is an implication that there has to be 'one best way'.

In the first instance, the problem associated with the utilitarian point of view concerns the method to quantify the greatest good or happiness. What is the *utility* of the outcome? Here we stray into the realm of cost–benefit analysis and having to put a price on all potential outcomes. Does the Machiavellian maxim 'the end justifies the means' give us sufficient cause for a course of action? This would allow us to justify slavery if a small number lived in terrible conditions whilst the rest lived very well – in this case the condition of greater good for the greater number has been satisfied.

The inherent conflict in ethical approach can be further illustrated by a recent case study. The oil company Shell International Exploration and Production's activities in the decommissioning of the North Sea oil platform Brent Spar received a great deal of press attention. Brent Spar had reached the end of its useful life, and Shell's intention was to dump the platform in a deep-water trench in the Atlantic. There was a great deal of adverse publicity, highlighted by the actions of Greenpeace occupying the Brent Spar facility. At the time, several television programmes followed the events that took place. Viewed relatively dispassionately, both sides were behaving within a set of criteria in an honourable manner. Both parties were assessing the issues, yet they were coming to very different conclusions.

On one hand, a set of engineers and scientists within Shell were looking at the problem from a rules-based system. Their approach was, here's a piece of ironmongery, what's the best way to deal with it? They looked at the options in order to arrive at the best solution, financially, and ecologically. They looked at the situation in terms of its engineering needs, health and safety, and the least harm to people, and they came to the conclusion that the best thing to do was to find a big hole and dump it. That seemed a sound solution for Shell from a rule-based denotologist's point of view[2]:

> Shell says it has always adopted an ethical approach to business and that all its actions are based on a comprehensive statement of business practice which is continuously updated. 'The statement is based on our core values of honesty, integrity and respect for people,' says spokesman Mark Wade.

Greenpeace entered the fray and argued that dumping is not the way to behave, because the outcome of Shell's actions is one that sends the wrong signal. It is just wrong. The Greenpeace position is that you do not dump anything at sea.

The response from Shell was to offer a list of options and criteria for disposing of Brent Spar for all stakeholders to analyse. If the option to break up Brent Spar were chosen, it would actually create more greenhouse gases than if it was just dumped in the sea. Greenpeace's response was to express the view that there was something fundamentally wrong with the Shell analysis. They argued that society should not dump its scrap cars in the village pond, even if it is a deep one.

Greenpeace argued that the consequences of the actions were inappropriate, irrespective of how the rules-based system might suggest an outcome. The public debate ebbed and flowed for some time. The adverse publicity, especially in Germany, had a strong commercial influence in Shell. In the end, it was agreed that the platform would be broken up to form part of a harbour in Norway. Shell's case remained that Brent Spar's net contribution to greenhouse gases would be greater than disposing of it at sea.

Consequentialists (Greenpeace) not only see that the issue at the time is at stake, but also take a view on the overall outcome. Greenpeace argue that your actions today send signals to others about the correct ethical and moral stance to take beyond the immediate decision.

This case also illustrates that when a NGO such as Greenpeace, who have a consequentialist point of view, try to debate with a denotological group such as the Shell, who use a ranking of rules, they cannot communicate. Their mental models are profoundly different.

This case study also indicates that an understanding of an organisation's approach to ethical issues is essential if you want to be effective in business negotiations. In the relatively mundane matter of negotiating contracts, there is a need to understand the interests of the other party. Negotiating may be about understanding how your own interests are best served, but if you don't understand the moral and ethical framework of the person or organisation with whom you are working, you are left on the wrong foot in terms of how to negotiate. Having an insight into a company's business principles will help you to understand some of their negotiating terms of reference.

12.5 Personal and social responsibility

Most people remain within an ordered social framework most of the time; rarely do we have to make profound moral or ethical decisions. Ethical constructs and ethical systems are not explicitly addressed in educational systems, and therefore it is when we are confronted with moral uncertainty that our ability to deal with problems becomes harder. We are not equipped with the necessary tools to consider the ethical boundary conditions. We either avoid that kind of decision-making, or we make disastrously wrong decisions. It is only occasionally that we really have to cope with profound moral and ethical dilemmas.

Our challenges occur when we have to draw the line between personal responsibility and the demands of society – when we have to resolve the obligations we have to family and friends with those of the wider society and organisations with which we may be involved. This is no longer at the basic level of how we determine right and wrong. If we can determine that individuals can assess right from wrong, can we go on to defining and determining their level of responsibility? Can someone be responsible if they are ignorant of the facts? This becomes even more complicated when it comes to organisational responsibility.

Knowledge and power

At one time in the field of medicine it was suggested that the doctor knew best – 'Trust me, I'm a doctor' was the standard watchword, now a much devalued term. In their book of the same name[3], Doctors Phil Hammond and Michael Mosley severely criticised medical practices of the past. They and others have shown that the more information patients have, the more effective and informed choices they can make. It has also been argued that the more patients are engaged with the treatment, the better the prognosis for their recovery. Is this a pointer for all who have to make decisions that will have an impact on others – give those who have an interest the facts?

12.6 Business ethics

In *Capitalism and Freedom*, the economist Milton Friedman states[4]:

> ... there is one and only one social responsibility of business – to use its resources and engage in activities designed to increase its profits so long as it stays within the rules of the game, which is to say, it engages in open and free competition without deception or fraud.

If we refer back to the introduction to this chapter, the limitations of the rules-based system presupposes that we know all the rules. Responsibility must depend on knowledge and intent. This becomes more complex in large organisations when we try to assess collective responsibility that is dependent on the actions of its individual members. Should the head of a hospital resign:

- If a junior technician sets a dial for radiation therapy too high?
- When a patient dies due to a doctor's negligence?

Could the first be considered to be about the quality of training and understanding, whilst the second concerns an individual's professional misconduct? Or was the doctor just too tired to function properly? Any organisation has to define the concept of responsibility. Only then can it be clear in attributing responsibilities to each of its employees. To date, the legal system has found it difficult to identify individuals in senior positions directly responsible for an organisation's misdeeds. The organisation might receive a very large fine, but the operative will lose his or her job.

Whatever the codes of practices that are in place, the level of acceptance and compliance by individuals within the organisation will be determined by how adherence is demonstrated by the directors of that organisation. There should be no gap between espoused values and the values in action. The responsibilities of directors must be tightly linked to the actions of the firm. We might look to the Institute of Business Ethics for a guide to modern business behaviour[5]:

> Rapid changes in the technology, methods and scale of business raise ethical issues to which legislation and experience cannot provide all the answers. Society is increasingly concerned and there is growing involvement with business ethics in political, academic and theological circles. Business must be seen fully to share these concerns. There is also the need to promote practical solutions which combine social responsibility with efficient operations. Otherwise business can find itself fighting constant rearguard actions against well-meaning but inappropriate solutions proposed by people not directly involved.

Our business lives cannot be isolated from our personal moral norms.

So far, we have presented the theoretical models of ethical behaviour. Business ethics can be analysed on three levels:

1 The individual
2 The organisational
3 The national and international.

Each has an inpact on the other; the inter-relationship between the individual, the organisation and the wider economy completes a complex feedback system. People working within an organisational context are influenced by their working environment, by its rituals and practices (see Chapter 8), as they are by their social environment.

The Institute of Business Ethics outlines 12 steps for implementing a code of business ethics[6] to support this tripartite relationship:

1 Integration: produce a strategy for integrating the code into the running of the business at the time that it is issued.
2 Endorsement: make sure that the code is endorsed by the Chairman and CEO.
3 Circulation: send the code to all employees in a readable and portable form and give it to all employees joining the company.
4 Breaches: include a short section on how an employee can react if he or she is faced with a potential breach of the code, or is in doubt about a course of action involving an ethical choice.
5 Personal response: give all staff the personal opportunity to respond to the content of the code.
6 Affirmation: have a procedure for managers and supervisors regularly to state that they and their staff understand and apply the provisions of the code and to raise matters not covered by it.
7 Regular review: have a procedure for regular review and updating of the code.
8 Contracts: consider making adherence to the code obligatory by including reference to it in all contracts of employment, and linking it with disciplinary procedures.
9 Training: ask those responsible for company training programmes at all levels to include issues raised by the code in their programmes.
10 Translation: see that the code is translated for use in overseas subsidiaries or other places where English is not the principal language.
11 Distribution: make copies of the code available to business partners (suppliers, customers etc.), and expect their compliance.

12 Annual report: reproduce or insert a copy of the code in the annual report so that shareholders and a wider public know about the company's position on ethical matters.

Even if you accept that the 12 steps above can provide the required infrastructure, this will not resolve the moral dilemmas confronting the individual. A set of guidelines will only prove their worth when individuals find themselves involved in some action on behalf of the organisation that is at odds with their personal moral framework. Can they use the system above or have they to whistle-blow?

12.7 The media debates

As stated at the beginning of this chapter, organisational ethical debates impact on the individual as well as on the organisation for which they work. Throughout this book, issues of government policy, business management, team management etc. have had an ethical dimension. For the media industry, some special concerns arise. These include:

1 Ownership and control
   - let the market decide
   - EU and UK legislation and regulations
   - global ownership.
2 Professional behaviours
   - codes of conduct
   - professional bodies with ethical policies
   - enforceable rules
   - representation.
3 Exploitation
   - of issues and events
   - of staff
   - of new joiners
   - of people of conscience.
4 Digital processing
   - images manipulated, edited, perfect 'copies'
   - data on individuals no longer text-based
   - intellectual property rights.

Whilst the main debates in media ethics will remain those of accuracy and representation, you may like to consider the chapters covering UK media policy, given the ethical approaches suggested in this chapter. Does the legal system outlined in Chapters 10 and 11 provide a suitable framework to support government policy? Is the ethical dimension addressed?

12.8 References

1. Green, R. M. (1994). *The Ethical Manager: A New Method for Business Ethics*. Macmillan.
2. White, D. (2000). Ethical policy can bear fruit. *The Sunday Times Business File*, 19 March.
3. Friedman, M. (1962). *Capitalism and Freedom*. University of Chicago Press.
4. Hammond, P. and Mosley, M. (1999). *Trust Me (I'm a Doctor)*. Metro Books.
5. Extract from the *Policy Statement* (2000). Institute of Business Ethics.
6. Le Jeune, M. and Webley, S. (1998) *Company Use of Codes of Business Conduct*. Institute of Business Ethics.

12.9 Further reading

Allinson, R. E. (1993). *Global Disasters: Inquiries into Management Ethics*. Prentice Hall.
Gordon, A. D., Kittross, J. M. and Reuss, C. (1996). *Controveries in Media Ethics*. Longman.
Hartley, R. F. (1993). *Business Ethics: Violations of the Public Trust*. John Wiley & Sons.
Singer, P. (1996). *Practical Ethics*. Cambridge University Press.
Smith, K. and Johnson, P. (eds) (1996). *Business Ethics and Business Behaviour*. International Thomson Business Press.

Websites

Institute of Business Ethics – www.ibe.org.uk
Professor Tom Cannon, article on business ethics – http://www.bbc.co.uk/knowledge/business/tradesecrets/theme9a.shtml
BBC Code of Ethics – http://www.bbc.co.uk/info/news/news222.htm
Greenpeace – http://www.greenpeace.org

Part 3

Media management in action

Chapter 13

Production

13.1 Summary

An audiovisual production project follows the classically understood model of any project; it has a beginning, a middle and an end. This defines and differentiates a project from a manufacturing process. Somewhat light-heartedly, people have referred to the Hollywood film and TV studios as factories, yet each programme or film within that factory still conforms to a project format.

Any activity defined as a project has the control process of quality (q), cost (c) and time (t) imposed upon it. The demands on the production manager are to keep the costs down, maintain the quality and deliver on time. In an ideal world these three elements would be independent variables, but they are interdependent.

This chapter explores the theoretical processes and models that a production manager has to consider in order to be effective in production management. It examines some of the issues in project and production preparation, and looks at some of the factors that impact on project management rules.

We introduce the concept of the production project cycle (PPC). This chapter establishes the theory of project management and should ideally be read before Chapter 14, where we examine production management in action. Chapter 8 provides a useful precursor to production management because it examines team membership and individual differences.

A comment is needed regarding names and definitions. We use the generic term 'project manager' to represent the individual who has overall responsibility for the entire project. This is akin to a line producer in an audiovisual production project. The term 'production manager' used here refers to the individual who has prime responsibility for the project from the planning stage through to post-production and preparation for delivery. The word 'production' (and by extension 'production manager') has often been the overarching term for all stages of a programme made within the audiovisual sector. This is because historically the main focus has been on the creative elements of the project, and not on examining the production process as a whole from initiation through to completion. This is especially true where the subject is taught academically.

Workers in the media industry often wish to emphasise the creative elements of the work they do. Quite understandably, the mechanisms used to manage the process of bringing the programme to the audience are often overlooked.

We will examine details of project team structure and project membership, and how roles and responsibilities might be assigned, irrespective of the form of media production the project manager may be undertaking.

Many organisations are adopting a project-orientated approach to 'getting work done'. This methodology (however poorly achieved) has been implicitly applied in the audiovisual industry from its earliest days. The audiovisual industry may yet be able to teach other industries a few lessons in this area.

13.2 Objectives and key issues

This chapter is built on the assumption that any media production is a particular example of project management. We set out some of the processes and systems by which a media production project should be managed. The terms 'audiovisual production' and 'media production' are interchangeable, and are applied in turn to make the text easier to follow. (The term 'audiovisual' is applied by the European Union to describe any mono- or mixed media programme that has a time-based dependency. Media production is a less rigorous term applied to all forms of media; print, still image production, video, audio etc., but is widely used in the industry. Web and CD-ROM projects receive a wide range of labels, in most cases dependent on their source material.)

The key objective is to define what project management is and, more specifically, how a production project can be organised using the production project cycle (PPC). It is anticipated that the potential production manager will be able to use this outline as a method of good production management for any form of media project. We intend to show that the PPC has clearly defined stages that embody standard project management methods. The model also segments the areas of responsibility into managerial themes, within which tasks in the project reside.

This chapter therefore sets out to explain:

- What a production project is
- Why it is worth using the PPC
- Who does what task and when (the where will depend on production strategies; see p. 309).

Chapter 14 expands on the how of the PPC, with some suggested practical templates and guides.

13.3 Introduction

In different industries, project management definitions and terms have been used to describe essentially the same project process. In this chapter, we have applied terms familiar to the audiovisual programme-maker. The production project cycle (PPC) illustrated in Figure 13.1 is outlined in this

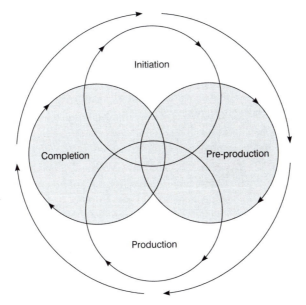

Figure 13.1 The production project cycle.

chapter, then studied in more detail in Chapter 14. The PPC has four stages of operation, and within each one there are two or three steps that need to be successfully completed for the project to proceed.

The four stages and associated steps are:

1 Initiation – ideas, assessment and evaluation
2 Pre-production – definition and planning
3 Production – media production and post-production
4 Completion – delivery, distribution and wrap.

A production project is essentially a linear process with a start, a middle and an end. Complexity is introduced such that each of the four stages has steps that in themselves are iterative. They can require several revisions to refine the task in question by testing both concepts and technologies. Thematic pathways are defined to indicate areas of overall management responsibility and project focus throughout the project lifecycle (Table 13.1). In addition, steps overlap and feedback components will have an impact on the success of each stage and therefore on the final outcome of the project.

For example:

1 During the initiation stage, the evaluation of risks and rewards will have an impact on the outcome of the assessment process. This will then be fed back to influence and modify the initial ideas.
2 During pre-production, further assessment takes place as the project is scoped. As the project becomes more tightly defined, production budgets and contracts are devised; these too will impact and re-shape the initial ideas.
3 In production, the monitoring and control systems give the assurance of successful delivery by maintaining the feedback path. Completion will be influenced by the distribution deals and the requirements of the agent for, or owner of, the programme.
4 A website can all too easily be 'tinkered' with – the project never ends. The end of the project has to be defined by the scope and contract terms defined in the initiation and design stages.

Overall, a production project is governed by the rules of quality (q), cost (c) and time (t), as in any project. These three factors have an impact at all stages of a production.

Consider the relationship: quality $\times$ time $\sim$ cost. If the time increases, then costs go up unless quality goes down

Table 13.1 Management themes of the production project cycle

Management theme	Initiation			Pre-production		Production		Completion		
Project stage → Step	Ideas	Evaluation	Assessment	Definition	Planning	Media production	Post production	Delivery	Distribution	Wrap
Organisation	▓	▓	▓	▓						
Client/Owner/Sponsor	▓	▓	▓							
Investors – investment	▓									
Global project issues	▓			▓						
Risk management				▓						
Legal and finance		▓								
Project processes (internal)					▓	▓	▓			▓
Supplier relationships					▓	▓				
People					▓	▓		▓		
Asset management						▓	▓	▓		
Quality Assurance				▓	▓					
Technical				▓		▓	▓		▓	▓
Feedback										

Table 13.2 Production project cycle – the route map

Management responbility	Initiation ideas, evaluation and assessment			Pre-production definitions, design and planning		
Project path				PPC		
Organisation **Client/owner/** **sponsor**	investment proposal	value chain	commitment	marketing strategy		
			commitment	sign-off forms at each stage		
	Producer's guidelines (CH4, BBC etc.)	Guide to project				
Global project **issues**	champion	director/writer	commitment	scope & objectives		
	initiator	decision models	first draft script or treatment	international project teams		
	producer	suitability check	content collation and management	communication systems		
Risk management		PEST	audit (int/ext)	content management tool (CMT)		
		SWOT	risk models	rights and rewards matrix		
Project processes **Internal to project**	brain storming	request for proposal (RFP)	initial project workplan	formal project workplan	project responsibility chart	
Internal to production company	consult with potential client and share with potential production team	project decision models	internal kick-off meeting – with supplier if working on staged prototype	micro design & storyboards	technical prototype specifications for suppliers	
				facilities bookings		screen tests and voice over artists/actors tests
Supplier relationships	suppliers' guide	tender boards	select key suppliers	select key suppliers (if not already done so)	content collation & scripts contracts	system flow charting and navigation
Legal & finance	confidentiality agreements	provisional budget model	IPR framework	legal checks	detailed budget	copyright clearances and licensing
General project events/actions	mind maps			production kick-off with workplan 'handover' to supplier	look & feel design with supplier	
Technical	scope of technical needs: 3D, VR studios, animation, etc.	macro template and design	advise IT of project start-up (if part of infrastructure)	draft technical framework established and 'tailoring' of universal installer	Tec Spec and Standards confirmed with supplier	IT project manager
Technical testing (web/CD)	determine scope of multichannel offering			establish product database for errors, revisions and review	clarify any new elements, password, streaming video, etc.	IT to raise any tech issues and concerns
Project **management tools**	budget models	project workplans		content management	risk management	
People	producer/director	production/project manager	relationship manager(s)	key team	mentors	
	production assistant	SME(s)	suppliers	shadow roles	coaching	
	content manager	external consultant(s)	client	team (F, N, S, P)	team meetings	test group assigned
	others	technical director	production designer	steering group		
	script writer(s) & editor	financial controller				
Feedback		financial/budget tools	project status reports			
			refining plans			

Production — media production and post production			Completion — delivery, distribution and wrap			Notes	Management responsibility
						highlighted sections show core activities for the period of the project	**Project path**
			final sign-off on the programme and project budget				**Organisation Client/owner/ sponsor**
							Global project issues
						risk monitoring continues throughout the life of the project	**Risk management**
...agement and	shooting schedule	voice over schedule	pass to delivery managers	launch dates to global markets IT support aware	project review		**Process**
...on cycle	release of prototypes, alpha, beta and final according to contract		marketing launch			detailed media production methods are not included here	
collation and	costs	invoicing and logging	contracts review and sign-off			contracts can sometimes take the life of the project to complete. Co-productions and co-marketing deals add complexity	
					quality, cost time constraints achieved		
prototype ...for IT	sign off on install, impact on Desktop and IT support script	error log on alpha and beta versions sign off and action	multi-channel offering	pilot roll-out if required		revisions to product as scope demands and funds allow	
tests by ...and ...on teams IT ...nts for help	feedback from IT to internal team and suppliers on impact and support issues	soak and stress tests data throughout, downloads, media players, etc.	external verification of product by appointed third party test company		issue 1 pressing		
g design and ...s	risk management	content management	second (or additional) feedback from IT				
	video production crew					the point at which to hire staff is always open to interpretation. Shadow or training roles (super-numery as they used to be called) are important but often overlooked securing a key performer may be the most important factor	**People**
ers secured							
and design ...feedback	media production raw material / external testing agency feedback / IT technical testing feedback	beta stage pilot testing	post-production pilot testing / technical testing / focus groups		recommended changes to the system / performance review / monitoring of help line and e-mail to add to log		**Feedback path**

307

If the quality (production values) increases, then costs must go up and time may also increase.

If the cost is capped or reduced, then either the time is reduced and the quality suffers, or the quality is reduced irrespective of the time left.

Sometimes, if the time decreases then the costs go up as overtime payments are made to meet deadlines whilst maintaining the quality.

In most audiovisual productions, time is the constraint that determines the other two components. The budget becomes the element debated by the production team, irrespective of its impact on the quality.

How do the key players view this situation?

- Producers and backers believe quality and value for money is paramount.
- Production companies are concerned with how to deliver on time to budget and still make a profit.
- Freelance and subcontractors are concerned with whether the work can be completed before their next contract – all their activities come at a cost to the programme-maker for the time slot allocated.

It is into this environment that the production manager steps. Within the PPC, the role of production project manager is to:

- establish primary planning tools for the rest of the PPC
- allocate tasks to team members
- monitor progress
- co-ordinate production meetings
- manage client, sponsor, producer, stakeholders or whoever else has appointed them as production project manager.

Traditional project management is a method or a technique used to 'get a job done'. It is a mechanistic system often presented graphically as a chart or, as it is sometimes called, a route map to guide you through the project management process (Table 13.2).

Every project is unique, and production projects have some special requirements that the PPC accommodates. It may seem a paradox that we apply such a mechanistic system to manage the development of what is often considered an artistic, creative endeavour. Consider; would Hitchcock or Scorsese have found this a useful process? Maybe not – but modern audiovisual projects are complex, and often have to operate across all media production processes and techniques.

If managing a media project is about managing creativity, then it is also about managing the people who embody that creative spirit. A particular style of project management is known as 'goal-directed project management' (GDPM)[1]. This approach to project management is meant to develop people's involvement and commitment to the project. It does so by making stronger reference to people, systems and organisation. Media projects are about the creative skills and talents of the people on the project; this approach, what the GDPM authors call 'a PSO way of thinking' (PSO stands for people, system and organisation), is devised to have improved outcomes not only for the project itself but also for those individuals involved in the project. The production project cycle uses some of the PSO techniques and incorporates them into the project management plan.

The overall purpose of the PPC is to provide a template by which the programme-maker can effectively manage all the resources needed to complete a project. A challenge often made to media producers is, 'Was the money on the screen?' To which, by using the PPC process, you as the audiovisual production project manager can say, 'Yes it is!'

13.4 Production strategies

Before considering detailed methodologies to manage an individual production project, we need to be aware of the management environments within which an audiovisual production might reside.

Within the media industry, there are many methods and systems by which a programme can be created and distributed to the target audience. If you have read earlier chapters in this book, you will be familiar with the production model established by the BBC. This vertically integrated model (now going through many changes due to producer choice) embodied all stages of the production process, from staff writers who presented the initial idea through production and broadcasting to print and distribution channels. This all embracing model is now complemented by the provision of the BBC Online services on the Worldwide Web.

At the other end of the scale we have the model of the traditional book or print publishers. They receive a completed manuscript from the author, which, assuming approval takes place, is edited, typeset and printed. The distribution channels of wholesaler to retail outlets ensure that the product reaches its potential readership. This approach was first applied in the UK television industry by Channel 4, and is known as the publisher–broadcaster model (embodied in the 1980 Broadcasting Act).

Producing media products has become a more complex process in the last few years. The distinctions between the fully integrated broadcast company and the traditional arm's length publisher have become blurred. This cross-media complexity has impacted on any media project that we might manage.

Given the complexities of processes and management models, a media or contracting company may choose any one of the following options to organise its business and therefore manage its projects:

1 *Full vertical integration.* The production broadcaster has complete in-house control of production methods, systems and processes; this would include script writers, content editors, subject matter experts, graphic designers, production tools and technologies in video, print and multimedia, and possibly web design, through to packaging and distribution capability (à *la* old BBC).

2 *Partial vertical integration with opt-out capability.* This is in-house production management with production services available internally. These internal services are purchased across the business infrastructure. This is the current model applied by the BBC and known as 'producer choice'. All content is managed internally, with various degrees of subcontracting as required. The media industry in the UK, although called a 'cottage industry', has a wide range of specialist agency firms. Facility houses offer editing, filming, location finding, voiceover artists, specialist catering services (the honey wagon!) etc. Many are based around key media industry centres such as Soho in London, Manchester and Bristol. (See Michael Porter's work on fragmented industries[2] and on industrial clusters[3], and then Michael Storper's commentaries on flexible specialisation[4].)

3 *Publisher–distributor.* Here, there is in-house capability mixed with a certain level of subcontracting; all content is managed internally, possibly programming, with various levels of subcontracting adopted as required – video production, audio production, graphics and computer programming. This model is prevalent in the new media arena, and is illustrated by companies such as Dorling Kindersley. Despite changes in the industrial landscape, it maintains an in-house multimedia capability. The company is well known as a publishing house of print materials; hence its capability of managing its own distribution network chain for new media products.

4 *In-house management and in-house prototyping.* This option requires external suppliers to carry out a very precise set of operations to a clearly defined set of objectives. The production is managed by the internal team who have set and scoped the project.

5 *Retained subcontractors.* In this case, a variable degree of control inside the business is maintained. Accredited companies are held on file as a competent selection of companies who can make the programme. These would include, for example:
  - a video company
  - a print production company
  - several programming companies with web design, DVD design or CD ROM design capability as required in different market sectors, possibly focusing on marketing skills, communication background and education
  - production and post-production facilities.
6 *The publisher–broadcaster.* Here, production is abdicated to the third party. At its most basic, a strategic view is taken. The supplier then scripts, designs and completes a project to those parameters. It is virtually a 'pay and expect delivery' type of programme. Many old-style corporate films and videos were made in this mode, before the days of the corporate communications managers who now manage such projects. Channel 4 illustrates this approach. The station maintains its public service broadcasting requirement through its commissioning editors, and they in turn contract independent production companies to make the pro-grammes by an invitation to a tender round process (See Channel 4 website for independent producers' guidelines).

Irrespective of the overall strategy applied to manage production projects, the stages and tasks in the process remain the same. What does change is the location and environment of the individual or firm managing or executing the specific task. The theory of project management will now be looked at in more detail.

13.5 The characteristics of a project

It has been proposed that all projects have a number of common characteristics:

1 Projects have a beginning, a middle and an end. Production projects usually have defined start and finish dates. The official start is often determined by the day the commissioning editor, sponsor, producer or studio releases the initial tranche of cash. The finish date is usually set by the day of transmission or agreed screening or commercial release for the programme. Media production projects are almost always constrained by time.

2 Projects are unique. Although any film, musical event, multimedia programme or website will have many shared characteristics with other films, musical projects or websites etc., many aspects of the production will differ.

3 Projects are team events. Production projects pull together a wide range of skills and expertise across the audiovisual industry. A director or producer will often request a particular camera operator, sound recordist or lighting camera operator etc. This is true both within the framework of a large organisation, such as the BBC, and where a producer selects key personnel from a pool of freelance staff. A continuing concern of the media industry is that the new shared knowledge, skills and expertise are often lost once the production is complete. Somehow this experience needs to be transferred to new joiners and the wider media community. There are few formal opportunities to share this knowledge. It is usually restricted to celebrity sessions at the NFT, or master classes held by trade associations or conferences attached to exhibitions.

4 Projects are driven by quality, cost and time. This is a well-known homily to those who have been involved in project management, but is nonetheless true. It doesn't matter whether it is £200 million plus spent on *Titanic* (1999), or (the alleged) fraction of that spent on the *Blair Witch Project* in the same year. The producers and directors of both had set out to produce a style of film in a certain time with a defined outcome, but at a very different cost and quality of production. What these projects share is the unpredictable outcome in the form of financial rewards to those who backed the films. The money made as an outcome of the film sometimes bears little relation to the money spent in the first place. Hollywood, being risk-averse, looks to the formula film (*Lethal Weapon 2, 3* etc. or, for example, a film starring Meg Ryan and written by Nora Ephron, such as *When Harry met Sally, Sleepless in Seattle* and *You've got Mail*). Read *My Indecision is Final – The Rise and Fall of Goldcrest Films*[5] for an insight into risks and rewards in the film industry. The multimedia industry has suffered from some very bad business economics that have led to some very public company disasters (e.g. First Information Group and many others).

The Association of Project Managers defines a project as '... a temporary endeavour undertaken to create a unique product or service'. By now you might be thinking, well, what isn't a project? The other question often asked is, does it help to define things as a project in the first place? As we go through this chapter, these questions will be addressed and answered.

13.5.1 When is a project not a project?

If you were to undertake to design and build a house, it would be defined as a project. Once you were living in the house, it would no longer be a project; it would become routine. Within an industrial setting, the process of setting up a production line to build vehicles would be a project. Once the production line was running and cars were rolling off the production line, this would no longer be a project. A production line, once functioning, is a manufacturing process and can no longer be defined as a project. If we were to apply the Fordist industrial metaphor to the Hollywood means of production, it could be suggested that the studio complexes are a manufacturing process. The individual film is but one programme or product coming off that production line. In its own right, each film is a project.

The many texts that have been written on project management suggest that projects can be grouped into the following categories:

1 Engineering and construction projects, often defined by location and large amounts of capital
2 Manufacturing projects, in which some piece of equipment or hardware is produced
3 Management projects, which requires the management and co-ordination of some set of activities of which the end result is not a construction or a piece of machinery.

From these groupings and definitions, we suggest that a fourth category emerges. A production project is an amalgamation of a management and manufacturing project. This is because the project management involved in film or media production is in the main the management of human resources. The outcome, one anticipates, is a finished product of some form, viewed or used by an audience whether as mass media or as a more narrow cast presentation.

13.5.2 The zero-value media project

A unique aspect of a media production project is the value, or lack of value, that a media project (whether film, music or multimedia) has until it is viewed by an audience or paid for by the client. Even after the main photography has been completed, and possibly even after the first edit, the project is still a high-risk enterprise – unless the programme is accepted by the producer or sponsors of the programme, it could be cancelled. In this aspect, media productions squarely fit within the definition of a project. Many media projects have been wound up because they could not meet the objectives of the programme-makers. If each one wasn't a project and unique, it would be possible to adopt a new set of objectives and continue the work.

As defined earlier in the chapter, this feature of a project is controlled by the three variables of quality, cost and time. Time is often fixed, usually by the end of the assessment and evaluation stage (as defined in the production project cycle). This may be determined by, say, the programme's transmission date, or by the presentation date at a shareholders' meeting. Therefore, any audiovisual production will have its scope defined by the transmission or viewing date. Programmes can be delayed, but these delays will increase the costs of the production and may result in those who have invested in the project withdrawing their funds.

Costs are the truly dependent variable, and are determined by the time taken on the project and the quality required. Close monitoring and control are vital in good project management. Quality will also be determined by how much time you have and the funds you have to spend in that time. It will also be determined by the skills and creativity of the team involved in the project.

Whether the project is a feature film for Hollywood or an industrial training video, the quality of the narrative will set the agenda for the rest of the project. No wonder scripts are called 'the property'! The three factors of quality, cost and time have been called the eternal triangle of project management. A truly efficient and effective project manager keeps the project to time and controls costs, but keeps the quality at its highest possible level. The production project cycle (PPC) incorporates these project characteristics.

13.6 The production project cycle (PPC)

The production project management method presented in this book is aimed primarily at the new entrant to media management. We have applied terms that will be familiar to people who have studied and applied traditional project management techniques. For those who come from the background of media, we have also incorporated terms such as pre-production, production and post-production into the processes and terms applied by the wider project management community. Hence we have come up with the production project cycle (PPC). In doing so, we have slightly bent the rules by including elements that some would say fall out of the strict definitions of the project management process. Within this model, each step has a set of activities to be completed and each stage has some defined sign-off points. For example, during the commitment stage a risk management analysis will have taken place. At the end of this stage, business commitment and supplier contracts will have been agreed and signed off. What follows is a more detailed explanation of the route or pathway through the four stages of the model.

13.6.1 Initiation: ideas, assessment and evaluation

There has to be a concept, a requirement, some form of inspiration to start the need for a production. It could be that a potential film-maker decides that a book, an idea or a storyline is something he or she wants to try out and exploit, to turn into a film. It could be that the BBC, Channel 4 or any other publisher–broadcaster has decided to offer a tender to independent production companies, of which you are one. A corporate media group may have distributed, through their known supply channels, a request for proposals from potential supply companies for a training video or a corporate communication piece of work. Companies seek contractors for any project that requires a media element requiring skills and techniques outside those available in their own particular organisation. In this initiation of project stage, the idea(s) thus produced have to be assessed and the viability of the project evaluated. These three activities form the steps within this stage. The optimum outcome of this stage of the project is commitment and funding.

13.6.2 Pre-production: definition and planning

This stage has two steps; definition and planning.

Definition sets out the project's scope and objectives, some initial assessment of cost, and who will actually carry this work out. Although a project has a start, a middle and an end, it is an iterative process. Therefore, several cycles of events take place within the project. There is a refining and redefining that takes place throughout the life of each phase of the project. This can have an impact on the earlier steps and stages of the project. Good project management should allow each step (the sub-sections of one of the four stages) to be sufficiently clear to minimise the risk of redefining earlier elements of the project plan. It is important that later steps don't create a ripple effect back through the project. This is also the step at which some of the key contracts are set in place between the pre-production staff and crew and the contracting companies.

Production projects can often be determined by availability of the key players, and not by the content of the material itself. Establishing detailed time lines that are dependent on their availability can be difficult.

At the planning step, more detailed planning and design work takes place. This is also where, in the terms of traditional project management, 'chunking' takes place. Chunking describes the process of breaking the project down into manageable elements and assigning responsibilities to each person. It defines what work needs to be done and the resources that will be allocated to the task, and provides a more detailed analysis of time-scales and budget. It is at this time that most of the project tools used in production planning are initiated. It is also probably the most labour-intensive element for the production manager. This is where the overall plans that will determine the ultimate success or failure of the project are made.

13.6.3 Production: media production and post-production

This stage of the PPC incorporates the key production areas of media production and post-production. By now final scripts, if they haven't been done, are being completed. Principal photography takes place. The graphics are being developed and music written. This is when production managers discover whether all their efforts in co-ordinating, say, a location shoot have paid off. Now many aspects of the project come to life, and the monitoring process is at its most critical. It is at this stage that the vision of the director, sponsor and/or client will become a tangible resource. The shared vision that has to date been only talked about may now come to life.

13.6.4 Completion: delivery, distribution and wrap

Completion is where the project comes to a close. In 'production only' projects, the work is completed at the delivery of the edit master. If a commissioned project, whether industrial, commercial or broadcast, the obligations of the production project manager will end. There may be a requirement that the programme itself must be tested before the final handover. This could be through:

- market testing – even though screenings have taken place at several stages in a production (rough cut etc.)
- focus groups – before the release of the programme

- checking that it functions technically – even though the content is good for a multimedia programme
- acceptance tests by the owner of the product.

If distribution management is required, then the project manager may have to negotiate with various distribution channels – managers of cinema chains, commissioning editors for broadcast television programmes, or even owners of record stores – especially if they are on the Web. Supervision of print materials, packaging and shipping could also be required prior to project closure. As with the other phases of the project, all these tasks need specialists on the project management team.

Completion would not be effective without analysing what has taken place. The wrap stage examines not just whether the product has fulfilled all its needs as a piece of work but also how well the project was managed. So, apart from the post-production party, some other thoughts worth considering are:

- Was it successful – did it meet its objectives?
- What went well?
- What went badly?
- Should it be done differently next time?

There are always things to be learned from a production project, for the project team, the organisation who set it up and the individual who has been working on the project. A difficulty with many media projects is that many productions are short engagements, typically 2–12 weeks in length. The crews come together, do their job, walk away with a sigh of relief that they have been paid, and look for the next production. It is important to establish how the knowledge gained from a particular project can be encapsulated and retained for others to use in the future. This is a major challenge to a fragmented industry, and to the workforce. Time should be found to pass on this knowledge.

13.7 Why bother with planning?

If you have been reading this text in a reasonably diligently manner, by now you might be thinking, 'This is ridiculous for a simple video production – all this planning, all this organising – it'll probably take longer than running the project itself'. This is a view shared by many, including, at one time, the author of this chapter. Yet experience over many years of running productions has shown that the 'let's get through, muddle through, everybody will pull together' approach just doesn't work.

With good planning:

- thousands of pounds can be saved
- the right people, the right tools and the right equipment will all turn up at the right location with everything ready for the shoot
- the crew and the performers will feel confident that you know what you are doing
- the backers, sponsors, financiers will be impressed by the level of detail you are giving them, and that you are keeping them informed about what is going on
- everybody's confidence is maintained.

For simple shoots it is a simple plan, but it is a plan nonetheless. Any system, once understood and applied, can become second nature to the user and also becomes an effective tool.

By getting the project definition step sorted out clearly and unambiguously, you are establishing clear boundaries for the project. Then, in partnership with the planning step, roles and responsibilities for those involved can be assigned. The production team can then proceed confidently to the production stage, clear about the main production goals.

13.8 Project fatigue

At the beginning of a project there is a high degree of enthusiasm and optimism. Figure 13.2 shows how, as the project proceeds, this enthusiasm wanes as the reality of the challenge becomes clear. The task of the project manager is to minimise this by good planning and process control.

However meticulously and carefully you have planned your production project, production project fatigue can creep in. There are a number of reasons why this may happen:

1 *Creative challenges.* Despite the project manager's best endeavours to control stakeholders (the interested parties), they continually change their minds about what is required. This can have an enormous impact on the morale of the people doing the graphics, programming or filming, even though they may be paid to continue the work. There is a level of team spirit within media projects that requires a certain respect for the creative flair of those involved. Even if a team is being completely reimbursed for all the

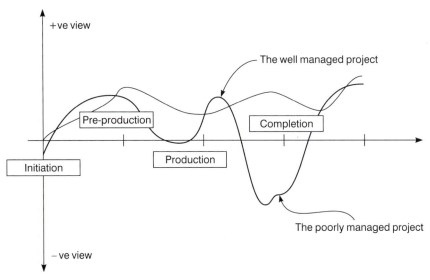

+ve view

The well managed project

Pre-production

Completion

Production

Initiation

The poorly managed project

−ve view

Figure 13.2 Project fatigue.

effort and energies required to change a project, enthusiasm will fail. As far as we know there is no empirical evidence for this, but it is an observed phenomenon within the creative industries. It occurs because the creative personnel take personal ownership of the element of the project for which they are responsible, and it is often quite hard for them to cope with their creativity being challenged. There appears to be two reasons for this; creative disfunction (i.e. good ideas wrongly applied) and external disruptive factors (seemingly arbitrary budget or content changes, stakeholder reviews that change programme focus). Budgetary concerns are a secondary issue at this stage. It is important for a project manager to recognise the signs of project fatigue, and look for ways to give energy back to the team and to the project itself.

2 *Poor communication.* This happens because there are not enough team meetings, or because there are too many team meetings. The need is for an appropriate level of coaching and mentoring of team members. It is important to keep the number of meetings to a minimum yet maintain team communication. At times of pressure it is especially important to find a balance between talking and doing. Collective experience has shown that in media projects the first tangible product, such as the first rough cut edit, print proofs or alpha CD, will suddenly change any sense of despondency within the team. Look for small successes, or just take everyone out for a meal!

3 *People management* – inter- and intra-relationships. Look at the dynamics of the team and get an independent view. Trust and partnership are vital. Don't belittle even in jest; tease with care; support your team and encourage them; let them take the credit. If you do need a particular solution let the team find it with you or, better still for you, even if you already have the answer, the 'straw-man' approach offers a potential solution for the rest to demolish, and from this can come an agreed outcome.

The traditional roles of media pre-production and post-production have changed. The audiovisual industry has moved from a mono-media domain into a multiple cross-media process. Media productions are never finished, and web-based multimedia projects can always be modified. We know that 90 per cent of a solution is obtained in 50 per cent of the time available, and the final 10 per cent of the solution in the other 50 per cent. It is always a mixture of pragmatism, quality, cost and time that will determine that the project can be completed and delivered. In media and audiovisual projects we know we have been successful in completion of the project when the programme is transmitted, the brochure is distributed or the CD is in the shops. The next chapter looks at the tools and techniques to use as part of the PPC approach to media project management.

13.9 References

1. Andersen, E. S., Grude, K. V. and Haug, T. (1995). *Goal-Directed Project Management*. Kogan Page.
2. Porter, M. E. (1998). *Competitive Strategies: Techniques for Analysing Industries and Competitors*, pp. 191–214. Free Press.
3. Porter, M. E. (1998). *Competitive Advantage of Nations*. Macmillan Press.
4. Storper, M. (1985). *The Changing Organisation and Location of the Motion Picture Industry – A Research Report*. UCLA Publishing.
5. Eberts, J. and Ilott, T. (1992). *My Indecision is Final: The Rise and Fall of Goldcrest Films*. Faber and Faber.

Chapter 14

Production project management in practice

14.1 Summary

Once the decision has been made to produce the programme, it is the role of the project manager to take the production project successfully from initiation through to delivery. In partnership with the production team, he or she has to have a clear view of the entire project from start to finish. A successful project is dependent upon each step being completed successfully. This can only be achieved by negotiating with all parties, keeping to the original scope and timetable, and being able to track all elements within the project lifecycle.

This chapter gives an overview of project management in practice using the production project cycle (PPC) approach, and sets out the key stages and steps with the associated production tools and techniques. The practical issues that concern production project management are also addressed. Whilst theories and processes may appear very lucid and clear on paper, in practice (as most experienced production managers would report) there is always an element of ambiguity and risk involved. The true skill of the experienced production manager is to be able to note and recognise the 'pinch points' at which risk is at its highest. The production manager then has to make decisions that are the most effective in overcoming them. However many systems you put in place for signing off, for defining terms, for agreeing methodologies and procedures throughout, audiovisual projects are high-risk endeavours. If the client or producer doesn't like the outcome at a particular stage, the production manager will still be the person to take the responsibility (and probably the blame) for the mismatch between vision and reality. The experienced production manager is able to review the project at each step, recognise most if not all of the issues and, working with the producer, suggest already developed alternative scenarios for completing the stage of the project successfully. The production management templates presented and discussed in this chapter are offered as guidelines to assist the production manager; the rest is down to experience.

If we apply business analysis terms to this process, it could be said that a successfully completed programme is the strategic intent of the project. Production management is all about the tactics to achieve this outcome.

Included in this chapter are matters relating to negotiating, managing meetings, having answers, checking credentials, scripting terms of reference and budget analysis. The precursor to this chapter is Chapter 13. Discourses on human resource matters are found in Chapters 7 and 8. Legal matters are referred to, but details can be found in Chapters 10 and 11.

14.2 Objectives and key issues

The key objective of this chapter is to illustrate how the production project cycle (PPC) can be used to manage media projects. We illustrate this with examples taken from hypothetical projects. We would like to think that you, the reader, might apply the PPC technique to a project you are currently managing or are considering managing in the near future.

A second objective of this chapter is to establish the idea that formal project methods are essential tools in managing media projects. The more detailed aspects of project management are discussed as they would often naturally arise within the project lifecycle.

14.3 The PPC in practice: introduction

If you accept the concept and framework of the PPC as a useful device for production project management, then this chapter provides some of the tools and techniques that support that process. In themselves, these tools are not unique and have been applied across many project management applications. Here they have been adapted to serve as templates for the PPC model.

If challenged on the effectiveness of this seemingly mechanistic approach to production project management, the retort has to be: 'What can you offer instead?' To paraphrase another management system, it offers a disciplined environment in which to be creative. This chapter takes you through the PPC using the illustrative template guides that can be applied by the reader. More detailed versions can be downloaded from the associated website for this book (www.mediaops.net).

14.4 Initiation: ideas, evaluation and assessment

14.4.1 Ideas

Ideas for potential productions can come to the media producer from many sources. Whether from musings on a Sunday afternoon watching an old black and white film on television, a walk through the back streets of the city to gain inspiration, team brainstorming or the need to communicate a new industrial technique, they all need evaluation and assessment. You will need to convince someone that this project is worth doing, even if only yourself. Several models can be applied to make this initial evaluation and assessment. In this model, the evaluation step attempts to frame the project in the broadest terms. Assessment tests its viability.

14.4.2 Evaluation

Start by applying SWOT (strength, weaknesses, opportunities, threats) and PEST (political, environment, social, technical) analyses to the idea. This could or should be done to shape some of your thoughts about the idea and the project. Then get a group of people together who can help you 'brainstorm' the ideas you have had to date. Though a much-derided technique, it is still very useful to bring people together to discuss what is going on. One person needs to co-ordinate the session; it is important to have one person able to drive the debate and help generate an outcome. Get a piece of paper and do a mind map (see Glossary) to scope out all the potential links to the idea of the project.

14.4.3 Assessment

This step of the production project is all about assessing the opportunity. It is about setting boundaries and clarifying the impact of the risks involved. It is the output of the assessment step that produces:

- an assessment of the opportunity
- the response to the proposal
- the tender proposition for risk assessment
- the level of commitment
- the range of costs and pricing
- resource implications.

All of the above become an input to the pre-production stage, should the project go forward. It would be a very foolish production house or project manager who had not made some form of initial evaluation and assessment prior to the commitment required of the pre-production stage. A production company could find themselves in serious trouble if they submitted budgets devised without a clear policy and process of evaluation and assessment. The reality could be a contract awarded by a BBC, Channel 4 commissioning editor or a corporate producer for a high-risk project with a poorly crafted budget.

In *Global Television and Film* Hoskins, McFadyen and Finn[1] say of film production: 'A high degree of risk translates into a high rate of failure.'

14.4.4 Risk and impact assessment

The level of risk in any project has to be assessed. A basic form of assessment lists all people, processes and activities associated with the project. Often project workplan (see later) tasks can form the basis of this list. These elements can be divided into internal and external influences, and then further subdivided into manageable/controllable and unmanageable/uncontrollable components. Table 14.1 illustrates how some estimate of the risks attached to a media project might be displayed for consideration.

Another technique is the risk cluster grid (Figure 14.1). A grid is devised that places probability along the y-axis and the possible impact on the x-axis. How finely divided these axes are or what scales are used depends on the amount and detail of data available to analyse. As with the media project risks shown in Table 14.1, we are often limited to guesses that fall in the broad range of low, middle and high.

Using the media project risks, all known contributing factors to the project are listed. Once done, we examine the possible chances they might occur and consider the scenarios for action should this happen. The gap in all risk assessment processes is finding the unknown!

Table 14.1 Media project risks

Project stage	Risk element	Internal	External	Controllable	Uncontrollable	Risk level low	Risk level middle	Risk level high	Action	Status	Contingency plan
Initiation	When the business framework of the project is agreed		X					X			
	When scope and delivery methods are agreed										
	When outline design is agreed										
	When initial plan is agreed										
	When investment proposal is approved										

Possible impact on success of project

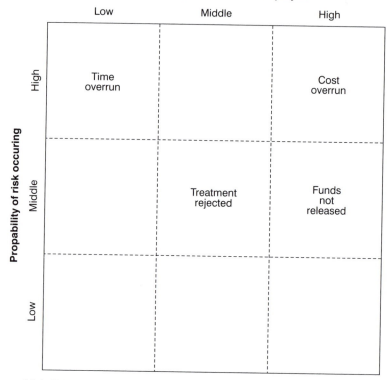

Figure 14.1 Risk cluster grid.

The risk cluster grid does more or less the same task, but by clustering the issues graphically sometimes a class of risk becomes apparent. These relatively simple exercises can form the basis of a team discussion on how to manage the risk and develop a contingency plan.

The production team can then decide:

- how they might shift the probability of the risk factor occurring
- how they might minimise the impact
- how to modify the scope of the project.

With the ideas discussed, the business case established and the risks assessed, a framework for the project can be agreed:

1 You have gathered the key personnel to form the core members of the project team.
2 There is a general statement about the named project.

3 Some form of treatment, script or storyboard has been devised as a working document.
4 Some aspects of the risks and the rewards have been addressed.
5 Those who manage the finances have been approached and have enough information to commit funds, subject to the details of the definition and planning stages. Sometimes final agreement only comes after the planning stage, but at this time pump priming or prototyping funds should be made available.
6 There is some form of consensus of understanding between the stakeholders and project team regarding what the project is trying to achieve.
7 There is commitment.

14.4.5 Selecting the supplier

Where exactly in the PPC the supply company or companies are appointed is dependent on many factors. These factors can be summarised as:

- the company's production strategy as (see Chapter 13)
- the production framework
- the clarity of the project (at this stage)
- business requirements (tender round as part of business process)
- the relationship with the retained subcontractor
- the partnership arrangements
- the style of prototyping options (several companies could be tested)
- the time to do any of the above
- the stability of the project, the budget
- assessment of risk by the project manager
- obligatory subcontracting arrangements (the advanced partnership arrangement of, say, having staff in both offices).

The task of selecting the main subcontractor and other suppliers should start at the beginning of the pre-production stage. If there is no real clarity of content or the script is still very much in an embryonic stage, there is little point in lining up production companies to carry out the work. You and your team need to be clear as to the scope of production work that actually needs to be done.

If a company has one or two retained subcontractors, this allows the producers to work on various prototypes or pilots to test out the idea. If a high degree of technology and technology prototyping is required, then some budget will have to be allocated to test these concepts.

If there is some ambiguity in the budget, then the only way forward is to try and get funds allocated to test out some of the issues and processes. Ideas for storyboards, animations or other visual techniques have to be shown or demonstrated to the stakeholders as a means of explaining what can be done. In multimedia production, it is very easy for a great deal of misunderstanding to take place. A demonstration Director Movie (a multimedia authoring software tool) can shift the understanding and appreciation (perception) to a point where meaningful decisions can be made.

14.4.6 The selection (or tender) board

Managing a tender round carries a great deal of responsibility. Commissioning a programme could require you to invite up to 10 companies to bid for the work. This means that you will be asking a number of staff across these companies to commit and potentially 'waste' between ten (one day each) and hundreds (a team is allocated to bid for the project) of days in preparing a proposition. Usually no payment is made for this process. The media industry recognises, therefore, that all buyers pay for this in the end by increased fees and supplier overheads. This 'sunk cost' is a high-risk factor for the companies who intend to make the pitch. Though a much maligned and debated process (independent production companies through PACT – Producers Alliance for Cinema and Television – have campaigned for alternative models for years in their bids to the broadcasters), the tender board is often the only real opportunity for new entrants to the industry to bid for work. A favoured alternative option is to maintain a set of retained subcontractors who will automatically receive the next project work as it comes to the production stage.

The objections to this approach are:

- How does a company get onto the list?
- Fresh ideas and approaches are not easily brokered
- All parties can become complacent
- It is anti-competitive.

On the other hand, the advantages are:

- Faster development
- The supply company is more willing to test ideas prior to contract
- A reduction in the negotiated charge-out rate
- Production planning of resources is possible
- Trusting relationships are developed.

Whatever model you apply, managing suppliers (whether freelance or large enterprises) demands integrity and a strong ethical approach to the process. It has been suggested that some of the larger players in the film and television industry do not subscribe to a clear ethical policy when dealing with potential suppliers.

To help you through the tender process, here are a few steps you might like to apply in running a tender board:

1 Contact the possible candidates who may be to invited to tender. Informally explain to them the scope of production project. Identify the kinds of responses you expect. Establish and clarify their interest in the project and their wish to be considered for the tender round.
2 By a defined date, issue treatment, prototype, storyboard or whatever is needed to explain to the contracting companies what the contents of the project are actually going to be.

Companies that offer submissions to the tender board will require:

1 A terms of reference document that will set up the context in which the programme will be used.
2 A product or programme overview.
3 The criteria under which the bids will be judged.
4 To know what company credentials are required (you don't want to see 50 VHS video tapes with all their past programmes. If you've done your homework, you should know whether the companies are capable of doing the job in the first place).
5 Tender bid materials – this might include a written expression of interest from the company, any initial contractual arrangements such as signed non-disclosure agreements and ownership, their proposal for the programme or project and how it might be achieved, any unique or innovative features they think they can bring to bear and, finally, the kinds of costs that they believe the project will entail.
6 The time for the production and the expected production values.
7 Occasionally, the expected price range.
8 Contract terms – this would express standard project milestones and payment periods, asset and product ownership.

It is important that companies are not persuaded to waste their time. Often companies are approached to bid as 'make-weights' to the tender round. It has been said that a good idea submitted to Channel 4 on a double-sided A4 sheet of paper would be sufficient to secure a contract. Few companies have ever believed that to be true. Even so, it is important for you as the potential production project manager to establish a clear and open relationship with supply companies.

Sometimes companies get in touch with you during the first phase of the bid round with questions requiring clarity on the original documents. If you are inclined to answer their questions (assuming that they are reasonable ones to pose), it is incumbent upon you as project manager to share the reply with the other bidding companies. As a precursor to the written documents, there could be a presentation session. At this session the producers/ production contractors present to the potential bidding companies an outline of the programme or project they hope to produce. The value of these sessions is very dependent on the clarity of the original concept and completeness of the tender documents. The greater the ambiguity of the papers, the more useful the presentation session to both contractor and potential supplier.

Once the bids have been received, the next step is to select two or maybe three companies who will present their programme proposal. This initial selection should be based on the criteria stated in the tender document. With these companies, the project is discussed in more detail. The tender board does inevitably become 'a beauty parade'. You need an agreed day and slot for each company selected, and this is their opportunity to present programme ideas in some more detail. If this is managed with any sense of commitment to the companies, your own company and your colleagues who may be sitting on the panel, you should not attempt to see more than four companies in one day. This will give each company 30–60 minutes to make a presentation, with a further 45-minute question and answer session, and allows the team the opportunity to discuss the supply company's proposition for about 30 minutes before the next presentation is due to start.

Companies must be assessed on the previously established set of criteria. Although it may seem obvious, number one on the list should be that the tender response answers the programme brief. Often project bids do not. What follows is a list of possible criteria you might like to include:

1 Creative contribution
2 Innovative ideas
3 Cost-competitiveness – how sections of the programme are cost-balanced against the proposed production values applied
4 Technical competence – relevant to whichever arena of media you are working in
5 Their own project management resources, if they are taking on a substantial element of the production.

There will then be company credentials which, if this particular company is a new joiner to the industry, you will need to check:

1 Other product competencies – does the company have a proven track record in the area of the media industry in which you are working?
2 Does it have named individuals who will provide quality and add gravitas to the project you are working on?
3 Does it have the critical mass and resource bank and the capacity to undertake the work without the stability of their company being at risk? Many a media company has been known to go into receivership whilst in mid-project. If the project has been a speculative pitch, what level of financial exposure has the supply company got at this stage?

Once all these criteria have been assessed and, if necessary, given appropriate weighting in your deliberations, a company should be chosen as swiftly as possible and this communicated to them. It is just as important to let those who failed know why they failed and to discuss the project with them. There should be a commitment on behalf of the project team to make sure that this task is completed in a timely manner.

The selected company now becomes a partner in the project.

14.5 Pre-production

The pre-production stage has two steps; definition and planning.

14.5.1 Definition

There could be some uncertainty as to which elements of the project are approved or signed off by the start of the definition step. One way or another, certainly by the end of the definition stage, all these elements need to be in place. A key factor is whether the money has been approved. A formal request for investment may not have taken place until the definition step is over, or it may have been approved prior to the definition step on the basis that the project is clear and unambiguous.

The definition phase is where the full scope of the production project is defined. This includes:

- the reasons why you are doing the production
- who the audience are
- why there is a need for the project
- some idea of the contractual obligations and implications
- more detailed planning

- an outline of the timetable
- resource implications.

14.5.2 Production team meetings

There is no right or wrong time to assemble the production team. Budget is often a determinant (to delay recruitment), and any cost savings have to be balanced with time saved in having a more effective team. This has special relevance if there are members of the team with no media project experience. For those new to a media project, much has to be taken on trust. These initial sessions are as much about team building and developing partnerships with all concerned as they are to do with project methods.

The first task is to make sure that all those party to the project understand what the team is trying to achieve. Obvious? Not so! Try some of the techniques set out in the assumptions test and the paired list (see boxes) to examine the assumptions team members have made about the project. These 'games' are a useful and non-confrontational method by which you can check that all in the team have a shared understanding of the project. If the diversity often revealed by these exercises is a concern, then just consider how different the views of suppliers might be to the 'clearly defined project'.

The assumptions test

There are many techniques that project managers can apply to help clarify the terms of reference for members of the team on the project.

Suggest that each member:

- gives the project a working title
- defines five benefits for the business
- defines five benefits for the audience
- defines five outcomes from the project.

Select a style approach from a given list. This is often presented as a paired list (see below).

Write a 25–50 word (or the shortest) description of the programme for a marketing exercise. Reduce the limit by five words, and do it again and again.

What you actually use is not really important. What is vital is that the session establishes a consensus on what the product actually is. This should help make sure the specifications are agreed by all.

The paired list

This 'game' helps flush out attitudes of the core production team and their vision for the production. Each member is given this list or an equivalent and asked to scale the paired attributes. This technique can be used across all media and the list is not aimed at any one channel; it is a thought-provoker to generate discussion. If a master chart is then presented on which members explain their choice, you are guaranteed an interesting debate!

Simple	⟵⟶	Elaborate
Restrained	⟵⟶	Electric, visually loud
Monochrome	⟵⟶	Multicolour
Land Rover	⟵⟶	Volvo saloon
Practical	⟵⟶	Conceptual
Constable	⟵⟶	Salvador Dali
Herbal tea	⟵⟶	Double espresso
Ben Elton	⟵⟶	Laurence Olivier
Perrier	⟵⟶	Gatorade
Earthy	⟵⟶	High-tech
Visceral	⟵⟶	Exploratory
Frank Sinatra	⟵⟶	Frank Zappa
Homely	⟵⟶	Night club
Safe	⟵⟶	Dangerous
Fantastical	⟵⟶	Realistic

14.5.3 Project specification

The project specification becomes the blueprint against which the project may be measured. The specification is the final outcome from the definition step in qualitative and quantitative terms.

It might include the following:

- scope of the project
- reasons for the project
- objectives for the project
- time-scales
- staffing
- capital cost
- preliminary design.

14.5.4 The planning step

Project planning is all about what needs to be done. In media projects, it is vitally important to know who should (or will) do what. Standard texts on planning set out five elements to the planning process that can be applied to any project. These are:

1 Set clear objectives
2 Clearly define the scope of the project
3 Break down the work into smaller tasks and activities (known as chunking)
4 Devise an outline schedule for the whole project
5 Prepare a detailed plan for each stage.

The initiation stage of the PPC has dealt with the first two elements. Stage two, the planning step of the pre-production stage, now tackles the remaining three elements.

With this five-element planning technique in mind, it is probably more advantageous to look at the types of tools available to the project manager than to go through a detailed analysis of the technique. These elements are embodied in the PPC. If you refer to Figure 13.2, you will see that the four stages of the project are subdivided into themed strands, or areas of management responsibility, such as risk, legal, technology and people. As the project progresses, the concerns of the project manager move from the strategic (business, stakeholders, risk, legal) to the operational and tactical (production processes, people, quality assurance and feedback). During the planning stage, we are particularly interested in organising the production process and the people engaged in the project.

14.5.5 Project workplan

The production project cycle (PPC) itself is the first tool that you would use in planning a project. It provides an overall model for the development of the media project.

Project planning can be paper-based, but it is now fairly common practice to use some form of computer-based project workplan tool. One of the most widely used software packages for the non-specialist project manager is Microsoft® (MS) Project. This is relatively straightforward and easy to use. Given the current state of affairs in the PC market, its advantages are that it is compatible with all other Microsoft products, and it can probably be shared with most of the people with whom you work.

ID	❶	Task Name	Duration	Start	F	S	S	M	T	W	T	F	S	S	M	T	W	T	F	S	S	M	T	W	T	F
								03 Jan '00							10 Jan '00							17 Jan '00				
1		production name : PPC	10 days	Mon 03/01/00																						
2																										
3		initiation	3 days	Mon 03/01/00																						
4	▣	ideas	1 day	Mon 03/01/00																						
5		assessment	1 day	Tue 04/01/00																						
6		evaluation	1 day	Wed 05/01/00																						
7																										
8		preproduction	2 days	Thu 06/01/00																						
9		definition	1 day	Thu 06/01/00																						
10		planning	1 day	Fri 07/01/00																						
11																										
12		production	2 days	Mon 10/01/00																						
13		media production	1 day	Mon 10/01/00																						
14		post production	1 day	Tue 11/01/00																						
15																										
16		completion	3 days	Wed 12/01/00																						
17		delivery	1 day	Wed 12/01/00																						
18		distribution	1 day	Thu 13/01/00																						
19		wrap	1 day	Fri 14/01/00																						

Figure 14.2 The production project cycle workplan (a typical screen from Microsoft® Project)

Figure 14.2 shows a typical screen from this software. Here the PPC is illustrated, with one day allocated to each task associated with the four phases of the PPC.

MS Project provides the options to:

- set start and finish dates
- list all the activities that need to take place
- identify those that have to happen before another (precedence)
- establish the resources that will be required to carry out those particular tasks (video directors, programmers, script writers, graphic artists etc.).
- modify the time allocated to each task to assess the impact on the overall project.

By setting out the workplan in this manner, whether as a paper-based flow chart or using MS Project (or an equivalent package), the project manager can establish time, resources and complete budget projections for the whole project.

14.5.6 Source of funds – managing the budgets and making the money

Let us be clear on this; in a commissioned programme, it is probably in the last 20 per cent of the project that 100 per cent of the profit is made. This is why it is so important to get the funding formula for productions right, whether commissioned by a commercial organisation or by a broadcast company. How the budgets are managed is a crucial element in the success or failure, not only of the production, but also possibly of the company itself.

A funding formula for a video production could be as follows:

- one-third on script acceptance
- one-third on completion of the principal photography or commencement of the initial (rough cut) edit
- the final one-third on delivery of the completed programme.

During a 9-month project, this establishes a reasonable cash flow for the programme-maker at 3-monthly intervals. Many production companies attempt to cover all direct costs (known as 'above the line') over the first two elements of payment. The overheads are recovered and the profit acquired at the end of the final period. If for any reason the final product is rejected, with this model of payment the production company has at least covered its running costs. Figure 14.3 illustrates the cash flow waves through the life of the project. This simplified model shows how financial exposure and risk increase towards the end of each production period. The shorter the time between payments, the smaller the deficit on the project. As funds

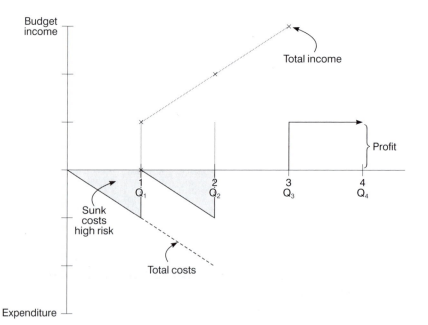

Figure 14.3 Production project cash flow.

are released at the end of each completed project period, ideally finances become balanced once more. If a project is being fully funded by a broadcast company, then agreed funds can be released on a monthly basis into a production acoount. These funds will be based on the final production budget model.

With retained subcontractors, a more complex model can be applied. Tranches of money are allocated according to the step reached in the production. This can sometimes even be before the staged work is completed. For example, 'pump priming' funds might be released before formal contracts are issued to provide the cash for a development prototype.

The amount of these funds might be based on:

- a percentage of the total budget anticipated
- the time and materials required for this stage (should be used with some care)
- a fixed price prototype project that will be written off against the full contract – whereby payment for this work is only due if the full contract does not materialise.

In a high-risk industry, these three strategies are contained approaches and relatively low risk. However, projects do over-run or have delays for which the suppliers are not responsible, and strategies for accommodating these eventualities are needed.

The options given above are based on a negotiated fixed-price model of subcontracting. In principle, if all runs to time there will be no overheads or over-run costs to be considered.

There are four other models that can be used in contracting freelancers or subcontracting companies. In each case, the exact scheduling of payment is open for further negotiating and approval by both sides.

The five models of contracting are:

1 Negotiated contract – as previously discussed
2 Time and materials, plus agreed expenses – the contract job
3 Bracketed time – a defined product
4 Fixed time – an ambiguous product
5 The fixed price 'buy out' deal – the production catch-all.

Let's consider models 2–5 in more detail.

Model 2, the time and materials model, is often used for individuals with whom you have contracted to do a defined task. This is usually over a known period, although there may be over-runs. For example, you might hire a director for a specific number of days for location recording (the same could be true for a sound recordist or camera operator) where overtime agreements have been made for the work.

Model 3, the bracketed time model, is often used with writers, graphic artists and possibly storyboard artists. It is for a defined product, but the full scope is unclear; it could be reworked and refined. You know there is going to be a minimum contract time for the project and a maximum over which you will not go. With a good relationship with these individuals, you will both be seeking to minimise cost and keep the number of days down on this project. The anticipation on the supplier's side is that there will be more projects in the future, and that this work is part of an ongoing relationship.

Model 4, the fixed time model, is a useful production method when the scope of work to be done is ambiguous. The expectation is to see 'what can be delivered' in the time available. It does not necessarily require the work to be done in one go, and an overall time frame can be set. For example, a script budgeted as 5 days' work could be delivered in 1 month from the commissioned date. It enables the freelancer or subcontractor to feel confident of a minimum number of days over the working period. There is a strong possibility that both parties may need to negotiate more time. By being open with the suppliers, you are giving them the opportunity to plan their working schedule.

Model 5, the 'buy out' deal, is usually applied to those members of production who are working on the project for a reasonable length of time. This approach is decried by the media trade unions. They view the approach as an inevitable consequence of production costs being driven down. The option is used for many reasons:

- it is a way of offering a package price with no overtime or weekend payments involved
- the team works as agreed and when the production demands
- it is a way of providing secure staff costs over an agreed period
- contracts do not have to be renegotiated at every new step in the project
- it gives good budgetary control
- it is not explicitly time-driven, but implicitly there is a time cap (certainly in the view of the subcontractor).

In all of these options, if overtime rates can be negotiated out of a project then greater control can be maintained over the production finances.

However, this should not be achieved at the expense of losing the goodwill of all working on the project.

There are other ways of funding projects. Low-cost British films have been funded by deferred payments, profit shares and any other method that postpones or removes actual cost to the production. However, the only comment we can make regarding these options is – seller beware!

14.5.7 Budgeting tools

As with the project workplan, there is a range of computer solutions for budget management. Project management budgeting is an iterative and dynamic process. It is a method by which you can:

1 Prepare a preliminary budget based on best-guess values. This can be initially set by averages based on past projects. As the project proceeds, these figures are replaced by the final agreed costs and then by actual payments.
2 Predict costs.
3 Track costs.
4 Manage the cash flow for the project.
5 Warn of overspend or, more unusually, underspend on elements of the production.
6 Apply and maintain any of the standard business financial ratios that will help the stakeholders or sponsors understand how the money is being spent. (It is sometimes difficult to clarify how financial ratios will assist the producer of an internal project, but they can prove useful for comparative studies – for example, a production company's average location shoot costs.) Key performance indicators (KPIs) in analysing the budget include the following:
   - fixed costs
   - variable costs
   - above the line costs
   - below the line costs
   - the percentage spend on each aspect of the project (writing, storyboards, video shoot, graphics etc.)
   - overheads
   - profit (to date and predicted).
7 Track staff utilisation; to gauge effectiveness and how to allocate staff resources in the future.
8 Note when to invoice in accordance with the cash flow or staged payment model required by the sponsors or programme-makers.

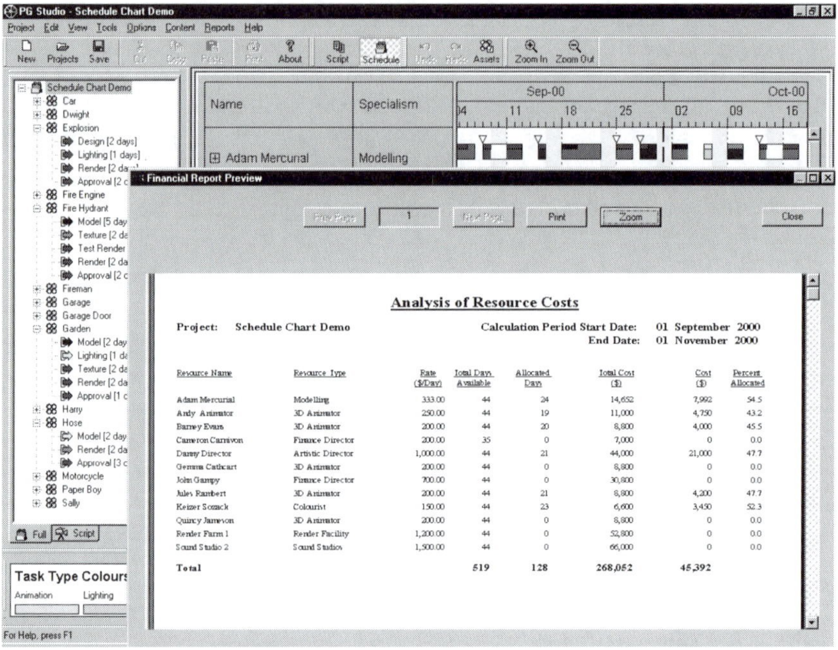

Figure 14.4 Budgeting software: typical screen shot (PG Studio Copyright 2000, Pepper's Ghost Productions Limited).

9 Compare project performance against given budget models.
10 Produce tailored reports for the producer, project managers, heads of department etc.

Budgetary control has to be applied irrespective of the department or organisational managerial framework around the project. It also enables the project manager and producer to plan and change resource management across the production by applying 'what if' scenarios.

A fully integrated budget should track the time that individuals have put into the production. This could be by timesheets, invoices or by 'call off' (the term used to describe a form of model 4 contract where time and costs have been agreed but the actual days/hours are requested as required by the project). All of the above form essential management information for the business or sponsors who are the overall management stakeholders for the production. Any organisation that is funding (see references to British Film Fund and other funding bodies) or underwriting by Completion Bonds will want regular and pertinent workplan and budget data.

14.5.8 Project responsibility charts

The project responsibility chart (PRC) is based on the concept applied in goal-directed project management (GDPM)[2]. A project workplan is defined by milestones; these are points at which it has been agreed that an aspect of the work should be completed. The philosophy behind GDPM is not to define a series of tasks, but rather a series of outcomes. It is true that the end results should be the same, but there is a conceptual difference between the two project management methods. Tasks define what needs to be done (processes); outcomes define what needs to be completed (deliverables).

Whichever way you feel most comfortable, in determining and defining the project workplan there is still the need for a PRC to accompany it. To an extent this can be worked into the project workplan layout. It has been done using Microsoft® Project, with mixed success.

Table 14.2 illustrates this approach as applied to the PPC workplan set out in Figure 14.2. The PRC shows the key personnel and companies who are part of the project. In this simplified illustration, we have identified just the broad areas of responsibility. For example, milestone 6 (M6) is complete when project definitions have been agreed. A series of letters (explained in the accompanying legend) define the roles and responsibilities. So for M6, the work is managed (P) by the production project manager, and executed (X) by the manager with the writers, directors and subject specialist. The internal stakeholders are consulted (C), as is the key supplier. All stakeholders will take joint decisions (d) to approve the steps completion. Others with an interest are informed (I) of progress. As the production becomes more detailed, so the value of this model in clarifying roles and responsibilities becomes an essential tool to effective project management.

The project responsibility chart explained

In Table 14.3 we have highlighted a small segment of a project responsibility chart (PRC) to illustrate this in more detail.

Table 14.3 shows a hypothetical segment of a PRC for one episode of a broadcast comedy drama programme. This is shown just to illustrate the concept; we do not suggest that this is what actually took place in the production. The diagram indicates that the writers made the decision about the story line and then had to write it.

Table 14.2 Project responsibility chart for the PPC

M#	High level milestones	All milestones and some activities	PLAN dates	Comments	External stakeholders: usually finance	Producer(s) production project stakeholder(s)	Internal project manager	Writer/ content owner	Specialists on topic	Director	Media production manager	Key supplier	Other sub-contractors	Marketing/ packaging	Audiovisual producers	Graphics designer	Software	Notes	#
M1	when initiation phase complete																		1
M2		when ideas have been formulated			C	D	P/X	X	X	C		C							2
M3		when evaluation has been completed		the sub tasks of risk vs. reward and other strategic business analyses have taken place	d	d	P/X	X	X	X	X	C	C						4
M4		when project assessment has taken place		this usually implied that funds have been allocated and that there is commitment to the project	d	d	P/X	C	C	d	C	I	I	C					3
M5	when pre-production phase is complete																		5
M6		when project definitions have been agreed		scope, reasons, objectives, timescales and initial design	d	d/C	P/X	X	C	X		C							6
M7		when all planning tools have been initiated		budget, workplan and PRC are completed	d	d	P/X		C	C									7
M8	when production phase is complete				I							X							8
M9		media production		this will become a more detailed area once project workplan has been completed	I	C		C	C	C	A			P	X	X	test CBT training		9
M10		post production		rough cut, alpha, beta, or print copy	C	P/d/X		d	d/X	X	d			d	C	C	measure stakeholder satisfaction		10
M11	when completion has been signed-off													A					11
M12		delivery		has been shipped to agents or supplied direct to customers/clients		P			C	X	A						produce packaging		12
M13		distribution		when product has been exhibited and viewed/used by audience	d	P			C	X	A						produce packaging		13
M14		wrap		when review of project has been agreed and all accounts closed															14

X = Executes the work. D = Takes decisions solely. d = Takes decisions jointly. P = Manages progress. C = Must be consulted. I = Must be informed. A = Available to advise.

Table 14.3 Segment of a project responsibility chart

	High level milestone	Detailed milestone		Mr B Elton	Mr R Curtis	Producer	Director	Project manager	Mr R Atkinson: Blackadder	Mr T Robinson: Baldrick	Mr S Fry: Col Melchit	Other members of cast	Comms/Distrb. team
M10	When script is finished		This might change up until location recordings have finished										
		storyline/storyboard		d/x	d/x	I	I	I	–	–	–		
		script		d/x	d/x	c	c	I	c	c	c		
		script edit (before or after read through)		d/x	d/x	d/x	c/d	P	c	c	c		
		shooting script	the script is prepared for recording – tests make changes necessary	c	c	c	x	P/x	c	c	c		
		location changes	although the director decided on location the actors may assist	I	I	I/d	D/x	P/x	c/d	c/d	c/d		

x = executes work; D = takes decisions solely; d = takes decisions jointly; P = manages progress; T = provides tuition on the job; c = must be consulted; I = must be informed; A = available to advise.

> At the script edit stage, there are joint decisions made between the writers and the director. The writers still execute the work, yet consult the producer. The project manager, who is also consulted, is managing the progress of the whole production. By the shooting stage, some script changes may have to be made. The writers do that task in consultation with the producer. By this time, the key performers have been given a copy of the script and they may make comments. Star performers are inevitably consulted about their role.
>
> Once on location, the project is in the hands of the director, who will make decisions on how to interpret the script. The performers will execute the script that they have been given, and this is managed by the production manager. If required, the producer is there to advise, and both writers are consulted on changes that might be made to their work. This will vary from project to project, and is dependent on the role and influence that the writers have on the production – in the case of this example, probably quite a lot.

The importance and use of a PRC cannot be overstressed. It will:

- determine roles and responsibilities for every step of the project
- define the particular tasks for each project member
- set out the relationship between the team members and the task
- clarify who the decision-makers are at each milestone.

By applying this technique, everyone knows 'where the buck stops' before actions and decisions are taken.

14.5.9 The critical path and shooting schedule

In a drama production, the availability of a key performer will be a main determinant of a programme's production timetable. This is an example of a project dependency, known as the critical path. Other time-dependent activities, such as filming the opening of Parliament, recording the fireworks for Labour Day or having to record someone turning on a gas pipeline, will impact on the project workplan. In a multimedia project, the video shooting schedule is only part of the larger planning process; it forms only one element (however vital) of the whole project.

Critical path analysis (CPA) is built into planning tools such as Microsoft® Project. For example, the marketing and packaging of a film can only really begin once some principal photography and graphic design for the entire project have been completed. The conflict occurs because a product mock-up will be required for the marketing campaign some months before the production is complete. This requires images, designs and typographical layouts to be planned and completed. The packaging mock-up will enable those in the marketing department to make a start on their campaign. They will want to release flyers or other marketing collateral to distribution agencies. With the use of proper project planning, these critical path dependencies can be factored into the production.

If the planning has been conducted successfully, you should be in a position where:

- the overall scope of the project is known
- budgets are established
- contracts have been issued
- key production staff and crew have been contracted
- the key performers are cleared and available
- the script/narrative has been completed
- all technical strategies and processes have been set in place
- subcontractors are standing by.

The project is now ready to run.

14.6 Production

We are now at the production stage of the project cycle. Tasks have been allocated and people deployed to their allotted roles within the team. Rigour, routine and monitoring help the project manager to keep control of the project's progress. Some of the tools that will help you through this process are described here.

14.6.1 Status reports

At the end of agreed periods, status reports are provided by the project manager. On short run projects of, say, 12–16 weeks, an ideal situation could be that the production team meet at the beginning of the week to:

- look back on the previous week's achievements
- consider the project plan and how well the project is staying on track
- look forward to the coming week and consider the activities (maybe just the highlights) that the team is going to undertake
- examine the status of any identified risks on the horizon.

At the end of the week, the project manager issues a status report. Different organisations use differing reporting processes and techniques, but whatever system is chosen it should be clear, concise and understood by all. Be sure that team shorthand and acronyms, if there are any, are understood by all who might read the document. This can be distributed through email, group management software, Lotus Notes Databases, or by placing data on a shared website. Whatever method you use for distributing it, the most important things to be clear on are that information is:

- accurate
- pertinent
- told in time, and
- appropriate to those who need to know.

It should also highlight the strengths and weaknesses of the project to date.

By making succinct reports a feature of the project process, and by explaining this process to all concerned, as project manager you will be able to:

- keep people up to date with the achievements so far
- identify any drift in the project at the earliest possible opportunity
- keep all team members aware of their responsibilities and tasks for the project
- track and report changes in areas of risk, whether lower or higher.

If kept simple, status reports can be very effective.

Once the project manager has the process methods clear, the human factors become a prime concern. The relationship between team members is a vital element to the success of a project. Chapter 8 considers organisational behaviour and explores some of the issues regarding:

- team behaviour (forming, storming, norming, performing)
- cultural variations and issues
- global projects and teams
- the organisational culture
- networking in the media industry.

Managing creative teams will always remain the most challenging task for the media project manager.

14.6.2 Asset management

Most productions acquire a range of materials and resources, digital, analogue and physical in nature. These could exist in a physical form as location master tapes, pre-edits, alpha and beta copies of CD ROMs, word documents, voice-over tapes, DAT recordings, logos and graphics. Other resources will only exist in an electronic form. In addition, script and project documents will have several versions throughout the life of the project. A means of tagging and organising the assets is vital to the smooth running of a project.

Whether the resources are physical or electronic, the first task is to build some form of spreadsheet that identifies the asset by:

- what it is
- when and who generated it
- the version number
- the current location (if physical)
- the current user (if electronic).

After this, whether you apply the technique of the 'job bag' used in the print and publishing industry or whether it is just in a box somewhere is not significant; the important aspect is to be able to track the materials. On even the simplest of video shoots, it is possible to misplace one of 10 Betacam tapes. Tapes are often in transit – between off-line and on-line editors, on their way back to directors for reviewing or turning into burnt-in time code (BIT), or for copying to a VHS tape. With electronic documents, the problem is not owning a copy, but rather maintaining control of the version being edited.

Let us deal with version control first. Start by giving the file a name that is meaningful to the project, for example b_adder v1.doc. This becomes the first script version for this particular programme. As the script goes through edit cycles, each individual who is performing the edit can do so in whatever way they wish but must change the file name by putting their initials within the file name – for example, b_adder(BE)v2.doc means that one of the scriptwriters has edited the script and it is now in its second version. Some agreement as to how the team tracks document changes must be applied. Effective use of editing techniques in word processors helps to identify those parts of the script that have been changed from previous versions.

Where a production group all works within one company, they can share either the email system or hard disk space for resource management. This becomes more complicated when people are working not only in different companies but also across the world. Many organisations can now use the Internet or an Extrant as a means to store shared data. Project files, asset databases and spreadsheets on a password-protected website can provide an

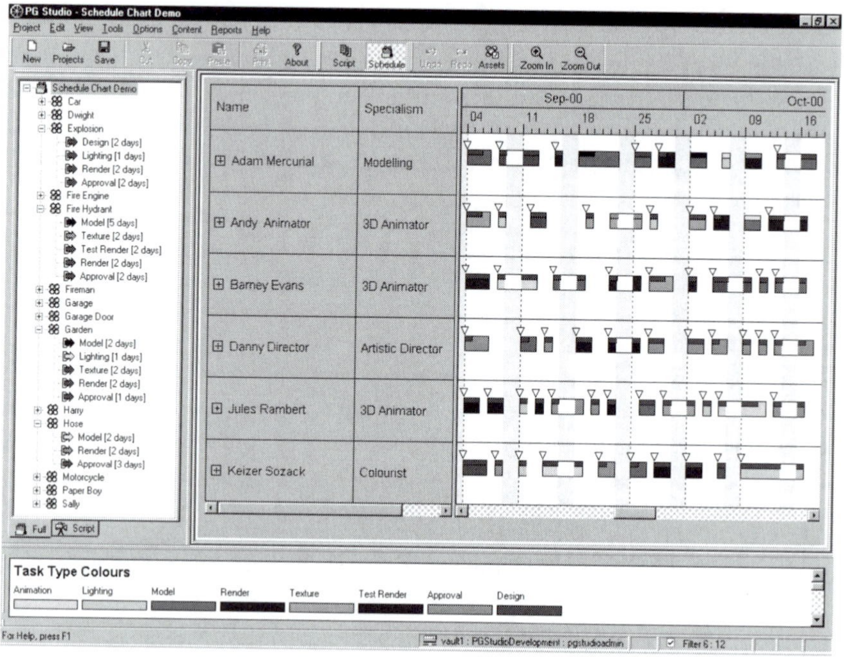

Figure 14.5 A project team tool (PG Studio Copyright 2000, Pepper's Ghost Productions Limited).

effective resource management tool. In this way individuals share project communication and work lists (Figure 14.5), and they can download project files. Depending on the configuration of the website access rights, team members can upload revised documents. Alternatively, they may have to send them to the site web master to co-ordinate new versions being uploaded.

14.6.3 Negotiating

Production managers are called upon to negotiate at almost every stage of the PPC. From the start they will be negotiating with the 'ideas generators', who are very enthused about the project. Their team members will have sensitive blind spots about the weaknesses of their proposals and insights regarding the production. Tailoring their proposals without curtailing their enthusiasm whilst still meeting the business need can require careful handling. Making ideas applicable to a budget that the project can stand and defining a programme that can be feasibly filmed and recorded is all part of the project manager's remit. The project manager will also be called upon to allocate tasks to the project team. If done in a rather cavalier manner without understanding the needs and wants of the individual, this can lead to problems in the medium and long term. Contracts and terms of employment have to be agreed with subcontractors and freelance staff. All these activities require some form of negotiation. Given the type of companies and individuals one is working with on creative projects, it is important to build a high degree of trust and commitment on all sides. The endeavour to complete the project as efficiently as possible should not be sacrificed for price at the expense of performance. If you enter any negotiation with this policy of openness and even-handedness, most individuals in organisations will respond favourably.

Given the nature of the audiovisual industry, two expressions embody the outcomes from successful negotiation with subcontractors or suppliers; partnership sourcing and obligatory subcontracting. In both cases, the outcome is to derive a mutually beneficial relationship based on respect and trust. Both terms imply an open approach in all matters. Partnership sourcing is about building relationships with key suppliers who will support all the projects your team undertake. Obligatory subcontracting may be for a single project, but the contracting parties have representatives working in one another's firms. They cross the barrier between the financial entities to enhance mutual understanding and speed the production process.

Negotiating: hints and tips

Let us never negotiate out of fear. But let us never fear to negotiate.

(John F Kennedy, inaugural address, 20 January 1962)

If you want to pay too much, settle for too little and give in too soon, then don't prepare for negotiating. If you want none of the above outcomes, then consider the following.

There are three main environments that typify negotiation:

1 To explore and create a new relationship
2 To examine and redefine the current relationship
3 To analyse and recover the damaged relationship.

Whichever of these environments you might find yourself in, negotiating skills can be broken up into four themes: strategy, issues, behaviour and outcomes.

Strategy
First you need to establish whether you should be negotiating. If you have nothing to negotiate with, your position is very weak. Ask yourself, is there flexibility and/or ambiguity in any aspects of the deal on matters such as:

- contract?
- quality, cost, time?
- terms and conditions?
- reciprocal arrangements?

If so, you can negotiate. If you are only considering the price, it is bartering.

Be prepared. Have a checklist. What you need to know, with a few amendments, is drawn with permission from *The Leadership Toolbox*[3]:

1 What is it I want? Know what you need to achieve; otherwise you could end up giving away the very thing you need to keep.
2 What is it they want? Know what your 'opponent' is after and what realistically you can afford to give.
3 With whom do I have the pleasure? Find out if you're talking to decision-makers or messengers; you need to know if they can close the deal; get to know them and what makes them tick.
4 What are my options? Work out your BATNA (best alternative to the negotiated agreement); don't go in fighting with one arm tied behind your back; know at what point your alternative kicks in.
5 What have I got to trade? Make sure you have a few cards up your sleeve – these are your bargaining base; both sides must be seen to make some concessions, so know how high/low you can go.
6 Do they trust me? Build that trust; call when you say you'll call; if you agree to bring Tom, Dick and Harry, don't turn up with Tom, Dick and Joe.
7 Do I trust them? Find out as much about them as possible; check the information they give you; test their reliability; ask someone else who's been in your shoes.
8 Is this just about price? Take away the price to see what is left; is there anything else of interest? If it comes down to price, you're buying/selling, not negotiating.
9 Take their side. To reach a reasonable understanding of the other party's position, it can be useful to put yourself in their shoes. First figure out your own position, and then try putting yourself in theirs.

If you just busk it, think on your feet and haven't analysed what is best for all concerned, your advantage in dealing with the detailed issues will be lost.

Issues

Be clear on your position over the issues; the earlier risk analysis should have identified the specific concerns regarding this project. Do not fall into the trap of persuading suppliers to over-scope, only to have them under-deliver. Specifics will fall into one of the three aspects of project control; quality, cost or time. You might like to refer back to the section on tender documents – the criteria list (page 330) provides a useful starting point for further detailed analysis.

Behaviour

Skilled negotiators check that they've understood what is going on. Some expressions you might use include:

- to summarise: 'just to recap where we are …'
- asking for reasons: 'how can you justify that?'
- asking for terms: 'what would your ideal volume be?'
- creating doubt: 'have you considered the implication for …?'

Poor negotiation can be revealed when you:

- want something too much and are too keen; people who look like they want it least get the most – desperation shows
- think the opponent has all the power (this gives them the upper hand) and don't realise what they have to gain from you
- get hung up on one issue, fail to see the big picture and get bogged down in detail; the result is winning the battle and losing the war
- have no alternative and go in to bat with no other options to fall back on, putting all your eggs in one basket so you have to get a result no matter what
- compete and don't negotiate, taking a win or lose approach where the aim is to score points; your victory will be fleeting and their revenge, when it undoubtedly comes, will be sweet.

Effective negotiators:

- ask more than twice as many questions
- give 40 per cent less factual information
- do more than twice as much testing, understanding and summarising
- use fewer support arguments, sticking to one or two good reasons rather than a whole string of excuses, which will weaken their case.

Research shows that skilled and average negotiators devote the same amount of time to preparation; the difference is in how the time is used. Average performers spend the vast majority of time gathering data and working out the numbers, while their more skilful counterparts spend much more time considering soft issues and strategy, and working out what the numbers tell them.

Outcomes

Even with the best preparation, the actual process at the table can still be a fraught experience. Overall, it's best to aim for a win–win outcome and resist the urge to beat the other side. Remember, the other side probably knows all the tricks you do, and sensible negotiators quickly put the game playing to one side.

Do:

- start high – it raises the perceived value of what you have to offer
- take plenty of breaks – pauses can be used to take control
- separate fiction from fact – beware of bluffs and beware bluffing yourself; you can lose credibility when found out
- be generous at the end – let them leave feeling as good as you do; offer something of value to them and of little consequence to you
- learn to lose face early – if you forget this point and are faced with the choice of losing face or losing money, you'll surely lose money; be seen to back down with grace.

If negotiations have broken down and the other side has said 'no', find out what this really means. It could be that they:

- need more information to decide
- cannot afford it at that price
- do not trust you – yet
- cannot justify the current outcome to their boss
- find you (as an individual) difficult to deal with – remember Prime Minister Thatcher's famous expression of Mikahail Gorbachev: 'we can do business together' (from the *Times*, 18 December 1984)
- do not understand the terms etc.
- cannot say 'yes' without losing face.

Do not:

- concede – trade instead, and give them what matters to them and what doesn't matter to you
- pick on the person – probe the problem and avoid getting personal
- aim to get even – in anger, you'll make the best deal you'll ever regret
- assume – ask
- react – respond
- side step – ignore attacks and move onto a new topic
- burn boats – build bridges
- make it difficult for the other side to change their mind – disarm them; nodding and niceties can do the trick
- reveal trump cards until absolutely necessary.

A special note on when you have to negotiate at times of failure

You may be arbitrating between a supplier and one of your staff, between team members, or having to act on behalf of the production management team in discussions with stakeholders and backers. The issues can range from personality clashes to fundamental matters of the project's integrity.

This is another occasion when the perception of one individual, team or supplier is quite different from that of another individual, team or supplier. In all cases, it is important to start by taking a history of what has occurred. Take a status report from each side. Explore the outcome that each side requires in order to continue the work. Always seek to establish a high degree of commitment and trust. As indicated earlier, try to deal with the issues and not the individual.

Negotiating does not necessarily require formal meetings. Should a meeting be required, set out a plan for the session and clarify what you intend to cover and what outcomes you hope to achieve. Explain this to all parties before the meeting begins. It may prove advantageous to have an independent facilitator to lead the event. If no consensus emerges, give everyone a cooling off period of, say, 24 hours. If necessary, start again and set smaller goals. Look for the small gains and areas of agreement. Eventually a decision will have to be made, possibly by you. Be clear on the basis of this decision. Negotiating is not an easy task but, if you use the guidelines suggested, you will have a framework with which to work.

14.6.4 And finally . . .

There is a risk that once the resources are deployed and the production teams busy doing their allotted tasks, the production project manager will, or can, to an extent, relax. Not so. You can never assume that all is going well. In a creative and high-risk industry you are up against people, technology, logistics, the weather and financiers. Each conspires to behave in an irrational manner. This is where you have to think, often literally, on your feet. Don't lose track of all the project planning tools you have put in place. There was no point in drawing up all these models, spreadsheets and workplans if you don't use them. Similarly, status reports are a living document telling you where you have got to and where you intend to go. You have to maintain the commitment and the trust of all concerned. If you have made good choices in the personnel in your core team and the subcontractors that you are working with, then the programme, CD-ROM or website should come together in a relatively trouble-free manner.

The Further reading section of this chapter lists some of the standard texts on production methods to which you may refer. These take you through the more functional aspects of media production. Many of the most well-known production handbooks are also part of the Focal Press imprint.

14.7 Completion

The completion stage of a production project has three subsections; delivery, distribution and wrap. This is not the post-production stage of the simple media production model. All media-related activities, such as editing and sound dubs, have been completed by now.

14.7.1 Delivery

One of the biggest challenges for anybody running a project, and more specifically a media project, is establishing when it actually closes. In engineering projects, such as the Channel Tunnel, the objective is to complete the Tunnel and have trains running along it. Its completion and project closure is clearly defined. In media projects, there is always going to be a high degree of ambiguity as to when the project is satisfactorily completed. There will always be a word, a phrase, a frame, an image or a graphic that someone will feel does not quite meet the needs of the production. It is the role of the project production manager, in partnership with the director and producer, to make that call. If the project manager is the individual monitoring and controlling the budgets, it is usually at this time that he or she will be reminding the rest of the team that funds are running extremely low. Budget and time remain key constraints.

It is also time to look back on the contract and confirm that all the elements of the project are prepared and ready for delivery. In modern multimedia projects, this can be quite complex. The main product, whether a website or a CD-ROM-based production, will be needed to be stored in some physical form and delivered as a master or gold disk. This will usually need to be supported by documentation that will set out the technical specifications and constraints alongside any agreed source code and third party warrantees. Any copyright clearance documents will also need to be delivered and signed off for music, voice-over artists, library footage and stills photography etc.

Distribution

Many texts have been devoted to the trials and tribulations of the film-maker, especially the independent film-maker who tries to get a programme distributed. Completing deals to secure exhibition of a speculative film project made outside of the seven Hollywood majors is a daunting prospect. Negotiations for distribution deals, whether through cinema release or by producing a project for television transmission, has to start at the beginning of the project. By the completion stage of the project, one should only be dealing with the mechanics of the distribution process. For those not dealing with the distribution of physical objects such as film or videotape, the Internet has had a profound effect upon the possible models of distribution. There is no longer a requirement for every finished product to be produced from one factory in one country when this can be replicated across the world by either remaining in electronic format or by being processed more locally at the point of final delivery. There is a certain irony in the fact that a CD-ROM with a face value of £0.30 (the pressing fee and packaging costs), although it embodies material of anything up to half a million pounds in production costs, will cost £5 or £10 to ship to its final destination across the world. We still wait for the paperless office and paperless communication.

14.7.2 Wrap (review and communicate)

At the end of the project, after sufficient time for team members to reflect on its successes and failures, a review should take place – ideally before the team move onto another production. It has been a common oversight in the audiovisual industry not to spend some time looking at the success and failure of a programme project from the perspective of the production processes involved. The prime and sometimes only criteria for measurement are whether the programme is a critical success, either because the customer enjoys it or because it's well received by audiences or reviewers, and whether it makes money.

The difficulty for the audiovisual industry is to establish what can be learned by the experiences of the production team. How can this learning be shared with others in the industry? When you are in an industry in which the saying 'You're only as good as your last job' is paramount, you have to maybe spend some time reflecting on what exactly was your last good job. However you view it, there is a lot to be gained by having a review and communicating it to all interested parties.

The review process should start by asking all of those involved in the project to think about and write down those things that they thought obviously went well and those things that they thought obviously went badly. They should then reflect on why these elements or processes went well or badly. More formally, you can begin to ask them to look at the production project cycle and go through each stage, identifying those elements that went well or did not go well.

Each person should therefore end up with a list as shown in the PPC review template (Table 14.4).

If this grid is handed out to everybody involved with the project, they can identify certain areas that concerned them and comment about them accordingly.

Table 14.4 PPC review template

Project element	What went well/ improved the project	What went wrong/ delayed or hindered the project
Initiation • assessment • evaluation		
Group production • definition • planning		
Production • media production • post-production		
Completion • delivery • wrap		
Staffing		
Methods		
Planning		
Monitoring		
Meeting objectives		
Unexpected results		
Stakeholder response (client, audience etc.)		
Project communication and feedback		

Many believe that just completing the production project is success and a good enough measure. However, there is value in making a clear assessment regarding:

- whether it fulfilled the project requirements
- the cost in terms of the true budget as opposed to the funded budget
- the time in terms of delays and areas of over-run
- the cost to individuals within the project team in coping with the stresses and strains put upon them because of either poor management or poor project planning.

The so-called 'softer' issues of team membership and team relationships are vital in understanding how a project can be successfully managed. A complex production project deserves, and possibly demands, at least a day set aside to evaluate the successes and failures of the project.

The outcome should be a report that:

- suggests new approaches and standards for future projects
- looks at ways of improving the current procedures
- considers buyer/supplier relationships in terms of core team partnerships, as well as subcontractors or freelance staff recruited by any of the key players in the production
- ideally, considers the training and courses that team members might need to go on in the future
- identifies any gaps in their knowledge for all or any of the team members.

In addition to the grid in the review template (Table 14.4), a project audit checklist that identifies all the questions in each area of the project will provide a useful tick list against which the discussion can take place.

A project review meeting could take the following form:

1 General introductions and scene setting
2 A quick summary of impressions and feelings from all of those present who represent the team production membership
3 A more formal approach of going through the stages of the project and examining people's comments on those stages as they are reached
4 Examining in some detail one or two elements that were particularly troublesome
5 Summarising in the meeting the general impressions of what has taken place over the project, and what has been achieved
6 Agreeing as to who will write up the notes and share them within the team before they are passed to other interested parties.

These meetings can be difficult, especially if there were aspects of the project in which individuals or teams of individuals came head to head and clashed over production or creative issues. If the project has ended in some disarray, then it may be useful to bring in an independent facilitator or some sort of skilled negotiator to manage the meeting. If the project has been tolerably successful but there have been some differences (hardly surprising in a creative industry), then these need to be explored. This has to be handled with a fair degree of sensitivity by either the project manager or someone deputed to take on the management of the review. In many cases, projects are made up of a supplier plus client or a production company and series producer. Whatever the case, there are usually two or three key parties involved. The final communication should be a document to which all feel they have made a contribution. In this manner a wealth of shared knowledge becomes available to colleagues, suppliers and new entrants to the industry.

14.8 References

1. Hoskins, C., McFadyen, S. and Finn, A. (1997). *Global Television and Film*, p. 51. Oxford University Press.
2. Anderson, E. S., Grud, K. V. and Hague, T. (1998). *Goal-Directed Project Management*, 2nd edn. Kogan Page.
3. *The Leadership Toolbox* (2000). Shell International Exploration Petroleum CD-ROM, distributed by TSSL Ltd, Hitchin, Hertfordshire, UK.

14.9 Further reading

Clevé, B. (1994). *Film Production Management*. Focal Press.
Millerson, G. (1992). *The Technique of Television Production*. Focal Press.
Croton, G. (1991). *Television Training: Approaches to Production and Direction*. BBC Books.
Watts, H. (1992). *On Camera*. BBC Books.

Glossary

Above the line costs – Refers to those costs that are directly attributable to a particular production

ACTT – Association of Cinema and Television Technicians

Audiovisual industry – This term is used to describe all aspects of the screen-based media industry within the European Union (EU). It is sometimes used in partnership with Cinematograph. It could therefore be used to describe all screen media with the exception of the cinema. In this book, it applies to all elements of the screen-based media

BBC – British Broadcasting Corporation

BBFC – The British Board of Film Classification – the body whose function is to classify films for both cinema and video according to their suitability for particular age groups. Such classification crudely depends upon the level of sex, violence, and bad language in a film, together with the context in which it is portrayed. Currently headed by Andreas Whittam-Smith

Below the line costs – Those not attributable to a particular production; could be considered as that proportion of fixed costs set against a particular production

BECTU – Broadcasting, Entertainment, Cinema and Theatre Union

Benchmark – Anything taken as a point of reference or standard by which to make a comparision

BETA – Broadcasting and Entertainments Trades Alliance (see BECTU)

BFI – British Film Institute – concerned with promoting film culture in the UK. Activities include research, production funding, publishing, education, and the National Film and Television Archive. The National Film Theatre provides exhibitions, along with the more recently opened BFI IMAX cinema. *The Museum of the Moving Image*, currently being relocated, is an illustration of the history of film and television

Broadcasting Standards Commission – Body with the combined brief of the old Broadcasting Standards Council (to draw up and enforce a broadcasting standards code relating to taste and decency) and that of the old Broadcasting Complaints Commission (to investigate and adjudicate upon complaints of unfair treatment and unwarranted infringement of privacy)

Churn – Stir or agitate violently – the numbers/quantity remain the same, but the associations change

Cinematograph – Term used in EU to decribe all film-based media

CBC – Canadian Broadcasting Corporation

Dolly – Part of the camera support equipment that allows studio cameras to be moved across the studio floor

EC – European Community

EEC – European Economic Community

EU – European Union (term used for EEC and EC post-1993)

GATT – General Agreement on Tariffs and Trade

IBA – Independent Broadcast Association – the regulatory body set up by the Government to monitor the work of the independent television companies dating from the initial transmissions of ITV (see ITC)

ILR – Independent local radio

INR – Independent national radio

IPPA – Independent Programme Producers' Alliance

IPS – Independent production sector – those companies that make programmes ranging from industrial and corporate to broadcast. They are not the franchise holders

ITC – Independent Television Commission – government body set up to replace the IBA to monitor and regulate the independent broadcast companies in accordance with the Broadcast Act 1990

ITN – Independent Television News

ITV – Independent Television

Key performance indicators (KPIs) – An inventory of measurable targets by which an entity may be assessed. These can be against external benchmarks or to agreed targets, and can include both hard (financial, output etc.) and soft (training, work environment etc.) measures

Media industry environment (MIE) – Refers to the cultural, political and econiomic framework within which any individual or firm must operate if part of the media industry

Mind map – Mind mapping is defined as a brainstorming tool which allows you to conceptualise ideas in a rapid and creative manner. It was developed in the mid-1970s by Tony Buzan, Peter Russell and Mark Brown

Mise-en-scene – Derived from French theatre criticism, this term literally means 'puttting in the scene'. As a film studies term, it refers to the visual aspects of the frame content controlled by the director. In Bordwell and Thompson's *Film Art*, these are defined as: 1) Setting; 2) Costume and make-up; 3) Lighting; 4) Figure expression and movement. Other writers have included additional aspects. However, *mise-en-scene* does not include technical codes such as framing, camera style or editing

Multimedia – Whilst there is some confusion over the use of this term generally, it can be defined as a computer-based audiovisual presentation – the convergence of the traditional media of graphics, sound, text and the moving image in a single delivery system

New media – An expression that refers to any of the more recent media channels of CD-ROM, Internet, Intranet, DVD and cable

PACT – Producers' Alliance in Cinema and Television

PSB – Public service broadcasting. A difficult concept to define accurately (see Chapter 2). In the UK, it usually refers to the terrestrial television channels (BBC1, BBC2, ITV, Channel 4 and Channel 5) together with most radio stations (BBC, INR, ILR)

Publisher–Broadcaster – The Publisher–Broadcaster maintains his/her remit through commissioning editors. They contract independent production companies to make the programmes by an invitation to a tender round process (see Channel 4 website for Independent Producers' guidelines). The transmission of the programme 'publishes' the commissioned programme

RAAs – Regional Arts Authorities, e.g. Eastern Arts, East Midlands Arts

RAI – Italy's PSB service

Screen-based media – Any image that is stored and reproduced by some mechanical means, whether chemical, electrical or electronic. Photography, film, television, audio recordings and computer-based media channels all fall within this definition

Semiotics – A method of studying the meaning of visual material. Originally derived form the work of Ferdinand de Saussure (*A Short Course in Linguistics*), it is essentially concerned with the process of signification – the way in which visual signs carry meaning and indeed are often polysemic

Skillset – Government-recognised and supported training organisation for broadcast, film and video

Spanish practices – This refers to obstructive work behaviours that, usually, remain within the letter of the law. They were especially prevalent in the newspaper industry

VSIPH – Very small independent production house – i.e. companies within the independent sector that have a turnover of less than £1 million and no parent company or third-party company share holding

ZDF – The second, PSB, television channel in Germany (Zweite Deutsche Fernsehen)

Bibliography

Although many texts are dated, latest editions apply.

Adorno, T. W. and Horkheimer, M. (1992). The culture industry: enlightenment as mass deception. In: *The Cultural Studies Reader* (S. During, ed.).

Alvorado, M. and Thompson, J. (1990). *The Media Reader*. British Film Institute.

Anderson, B. (1991). *Imagined Communities: Reflections on the Origin and Spread of Nationalism*. Verso Books.

Andersen, E. S., Grude, K. V. and Haug, T. (1995). *Goal-Directed Project Management*, 2nd edn. Kogan Page.

Ansoff, H. I. (1965). *Corporate Strategy*. McGraw-Hill.

Armstrong, A. (1990). *A Handbook of Personnel Management Practice*. Kogan Page.

Baker, M. (1992). *Marketing: An Introductory Text*. Macmillan.

Barendt, E. M. (1995). *Broadcasting Law – A Comparative Study*. Clarendon Press.

Barendt, E. M., Lustgarden, L., Norrie, K. and Stephenson, H. (1997). *Libel and the Media*. Clarendon.

Bazin, A. (1958). *William Tyler, or The Jansenist of Mise-en-Scene*. Translated from *Qu'est-ce que le Cinema?* Editions du Cerf.

Benjamin, W. (1985). Surrealism: the last snapshot of the European intelligentsia. In: *One Way Street*. Verso Books.

Benjamin, W. (1992). The work of art in the age of mechanical reproduction. In: *Film Theory and Criticism* (G. Mast *et al.*, eds). Oxford University Press.

Berelson, B. (1949). Communication and public opinion. In: *Mass Communication*. Columbia University Press.

Betts, C. W. (ed.) (1973). *The Film Business: A History of British Cinema 1896–1972*. Allen and Unwin.

BFI (1993). *BFI Film and Television Handbook 1993*. British Film Institute.

BFI Planning Unit (1993). *Guide to Funding for Low Budget Film and Video Production.* British Film Institute.

Block, P. L. (1996). *Strategies for Survival – The Small Television Production Company.* University of Hertfordshire.

Blumer, J. G. and Gurevitch, M. (1982). The political effects of mass communication in the media. In: *Culture, Society and the Media* (M. Gurevitch, T. Bennet, J. Curran and J. Woollacott, eds). Methuen.

Bolton, R. (1990). *Death on the Rock and Other Stories.* W. H. Allen.

Bordwell, D. (1990). German expressionism (1919–1924). In: *Film Art*, 3rd edn. McGraw-Hill.

Bordwell, D. and Thomson, K. (1990). *Film Art: an Introduction*, 5th edn. McGraw-Hill.

Brecht, B. (1971). Against Georg Lukacs. *New Left Review*, **84**.

Brewster, B. and Bordwell, D. (1974) Eisenstein's epistemological shift. *Screen*, **15(4)**.

Briggs, A. (1961). *The History of Broadcasting in the United Kingdom*, Vol. 1. Oxford University Press.

Briggs, A. (1965). *The History of Broadcasting in the United Kingdom*, Vol. 2. Oxford University Press.

Briggs, A. (1970). *The History of Broadcasting in the United Kingdom*, Vol. 3. Oxford University Press.

Briggs, A. (1979). *The History of Broadcasting in the United Kingdom*, Vol. 4. Oxford University Press.

Briggs, A. (1995). *The History of Broadcasting in the United Kingdom*, Vol. 5. Oxford University Press.

Budd, S. (1991). *The European Community, A Guide to the Maze.* Kogan Page.

Bull, J. A. (1988). *The Framework of Fiction.* Macmillan.

Burch, N. (1978). Porter, or ambivalence. *Screen*, **19(4)**.

Burns, T. (1979). *The BBC – Public Institution and Private World.* Macmillan.

Cantril, H. (1940). *The Invasion from Mars.* Harper and Row.

Channel 4 Television Company Ltd (1994). *An Introduction and Guide for Producers.* CH4.

Channel 4 Television Company Ltd (1984–94). *Report and Financial Statements.* CH4.

Charters, W. W. (1966). Motion pictures and youth. Reprinted in: *The Reader in Public Opinion and Communication* (2nd edn) (B. Berelsona and M. Janowitz, eds). Free Press.

Cheneviere, G. (1990). Chairman of the ECA Programme Committee. The European co-production association is five years old. *EBU Review*, **XLI(6)**.

Christie, I. (1979). French avant-garde film in the twenties; from specificity to surrealism. In: *Film as Film*. Arts Council of Great Britain.

Clegg, F. (1984). *Simple Statistics: A Course Book for the Social Sciences.* Cambridge University Press.

Collins, R. (1985). Canada: nation building threatened by the US dominated media? In: *Made for Television: Euston Films Limited* (T. Alvarado and N. Stewart, eds). British Film Institute.

Collins, R. (1989). *Broadcasting – The United Kingdom and Europe in the 1990s.* Rundfunk and Fernsehen.

Collins, R. (1990). *Television: Policy and Culture.* Unwin Hyman.

Collins, R. and Porter, V. (1981). *WDR and the Arbeiterfilm: Fassbinder, Ziewer and Others.* British Film Institute.

Cornford, J. and Robins, J. (1990). *Beyond the Last Bastion: Industrial Restructuring and the Labour Force in the British Television Industry.* Centre for Urban and Regional Development Studies, University of Newcastle upon Tyne.

Coase, L. (1937). The Nature of the Firm. In: *The Economic Nature of the Firm (A Reader).* Cambridge University Press

Coopman, J. (1999). *Who's Who in Television.* Profile Media.

Cottrell, L. E. (1993). *Performance – the Business and Law of Entertainment.* Sweet and Maxwell.

Cowling, A. and Mailer, C. (1990). *Managing Human Resources.* Edward Arnold.

Craig, D. (ed.) (1975). Letter to Minna Kautsky. *Marxists on Literature.* Penguin.

Crofts, S. (1976). Ideology and form: Chapeyev and Soviet realism. *Film Form,* **1**.

Crofts, S. and Rose, O. (1974). An essay towards man with a movie camera. *Screen,* **15(4)**.

Crone, T. (1989). *Law and the Media.* Focal Press.

Croton, G. (1991). *Television Training: Approaches to Production and Direction.* BBC Publications.

Curran, J. and Porter, V. (eds) (1985). *British Cinema History.* British Film Institute.

Curran, J. and Seaton, J. (1998). *Power Without Responsibility.* Routledge.

Curwin, J. and Slater, R. (1991). *Quantitative Methods for Business Decisions.* Chapman and Hall.

Davidson, A. (1992). *Under the Hammer: Greed and Glory Inside the Television Business.* Mandarin.

Davis, J. (1991). *TV, UK – A Special Report.* Knowledge Research.

De Cordova, R. (1985). The emergence of the star system in America. *Wide Angle,* **6(4)**.

Dembo, R. (1973). Gratification found by British boys. *Journalism Q.,* **50(3)**.

Demetz, P. (1967). Letter to Starkenberg, 1894. In: *Marx, Engels and the Poets.* University of Chicago Press.

Desaulniers, J.-P. (1987). What does Canada want? (L'histoire sans lecon). *Media Culture and Society,* **9(2)**.

Drummond, P. (1976). Notions of avant-garde cinema. In: *Film as Film.* Arts Council of Great Britain.

Dudley, A. J. (1976). *The Major Film Theory: An Introduction.* Oxford University Press.

During, S. (ed.) (1993). *The Cultural Reader.* Routledge.

Dworkin, G. and Taylor, R. (1992). *Blackstone's Guide to the Copyright Designs and Patents Act, 1988.* Blackstone Press.

Eberts, J. and Ilott, T. (1992). *My Indecision is Final: The Rise and Fall of Goldcrest Films.* Faber and Faber.

Economist (1990). Thatcherites of the small screen. *The Economist,* 3 February.

Eisenstein, S. (1986). Montage of attraction. In: *Film Sense.* Faber and Faber.

Eisenstein, S. (1988). The dramatology of film form. In: *Selected Works,* Vol. 1 (R. Taylor, ed.). British Film Institute.

Ellis, J. (1992). *Visible Fictions.* Routledge.

Engels, R. (edited by Craig, D.) (1975). *Marxists on Literature.* Penguin.

European Union (1992). *Audio Visual Policy Document.* HMSO.

BBC (1992). *Extending Choice.* BBC Policy Document.

Fazzani, L. and Hart, T. (1997). *Intellectual Property Law.* McMillan Law Masters.

Arts Council of Great Britain (1979). *Film as Film: Formal Experiment in Film, 1910–1975.* Arts Council of Great Britain.

Film Policy Review Group (1998). *A Bigger Picture, The Report of the Film Policy Review Group.* Department of Media, Culture and Sport.

Fisher, W. (1990). Let them eat Europudding. *Sight and Sound,* **59(4)**.

Gellner, E. (1983). *Nations and Nationalism.* Blackwell.

Gerbner, G. and Gross, L. (1976). Living with television: the violence profile. *J. Communication,* **26(2)**.

Giles, P. (1996). History with holes: Channel 4 films of the 1980s. In: *Television Times, A Reader* (J. Corner and S. Harvey, eds). Arnold.

Godwin, A. and Whannel, G. (eds) (1990). *Understanding Television.* Routledge.

Gorky, M. *et al.* (1977). *Soviet Writers' Congress 1934.* Lawence and Wishart.

Gray, A. and McGuigan, J. (ed.) (1993). *Studying Culture (An Introductory Reader)*. Edward Arnold.

Greiner, L. E. (1972). *Evolution and Revolution as Organisations Grow*. Harvard Business Review, July–August.

Grey, A. (ed.) (1996). *Turning It On, A Reader in Women and Media*. Arnold.

Gurevitch, M., Bennett, T., Curran, J. and Woollacott, J. (eds) (1982). *Culture, Society and the Media*. Methuen.

Handy, C. (1990). *Understanding Organisations*, 4th edn. Arrow Business Books.

Harcourt, A. (1986). *The Independent Producer: Film and Television*. Faber and Faber.

Harris, P. (1989). *An Introduction to Law*. Weidenfeld.

Hartley, R. E. (1993). *Business Ethics: Violations of the Public Trust*. Wiley.

Hartog, S. (1983). State protection of a beleaguered industry. In: *British Cinema History* (J. Curran and V. Porter, eds). Weidenfeld and Nicolson.

Harvey Jones, J. (1993). *The Trouble Shooter – On the Treadmill?* BBC television special on Independent Production for Edinburgh Television Festival (not broadcast).

Henderson, B. (1980). Two types of film theory. In: *Critique of Film Theory*. Dutton.

Hilbert, J., Sperling, H. and Rainnie, A. (1994). SMEs at the crossroads – scenarios on the future of SMEs in Europe. *Future of Industry Paper* Series, Vol. 9. Commission of European Communities.

Hinds, H. (1996). Fruitful investigations: the case of the successful lesbian text. The critical question. *Sight and Sound*, **29(4)**.

Hood, S. (ed.) (1994). *Behind The Screens, The Structure of British Television in the Nineties*. Lawrence and Wishart.

Horrie, C. and Clarke, S. (1994). *Fuzzy Monsters: Fear and loathing at the BBC*. Mandarin.

Hoskins, C., McFadyen, S. and Finn, A. (1997). *Global Television and Film – An Introduction to the Economics of the Business*. Oxford Press.

Huczynski, A. and Buchanan, D. (1991). *Organisational Behaviour*, 2nd edn. Prentice Hall.

Hutchinson, J. and Smith, A. (eds). (1994). *Nationalism*. Oxford University Press.

Jenks, C. (1992). *The Post-Modern Reader*. Academy Editions.

Johnson, G. and Scholes, K. (1993). *Exploring Corporate Strategy*, 3rd edn. Prentice Hall.

Juneau, P. (1984). Audience fragmentation and cultural erosion: a Canadian perspective on the challenge for the public broadcaster. *EBU Review*, **35(2).**

Keal, P. (1985). *The Citizen Kane Book – Raising Kane*. Methuen.

Kedourie, E. (1985). *Nationalism*. Hutchinson.

Keirsey, D. and Bates, M. (1993). *Please Understand Me*, 5th edn. Prometheus Nemesis Book Co.

Kennedy, C. (1993). *Guide to Management Gurus*. Century.

Key Note Publications Ltd (1991). Independent TV and Film Production. Key Note Publications Ltd.

Kitses, J. (1969). *Horizons West*. Thames and Hudson/British Film Institute.

Kracauer, S. (1990). *Theory of Film*. Oxford University Press.

Kracauer, S. (1992). From Caligari to Hitler. In: *Film Theory and Criticism*. Oxford University Press.

Kuhn, R. (ed.) (1985). *The Politics of Broadcasting*. Croom Helm.

Kumar, K. (1986). Public service broadcasting and the public interest. In: *The BBC and Public Service Broadcasting* (C. MacCabe and O. Stewart, eds). University of Manchester Press.

Leavis, F. R. (1930). *Mass Civilisation and Minority Culture*. Minority Press.

Le Bon, G. (date unknown). *The Crowd*. Ernet Benn.

Lyotard, J.-F. (1989). Defining the post-modern. In: *Post-Modern ICA Documents* (L. Appiganesi, ed.). Lodo, Free Association Books.

M&E Business Handbook Series (1991). Business/Finance/Law. Pitman.

Marinetti, F. T. (1973). The founding and manifesto of futurism, 1909; and The futurist cinema, 1916. In: *Futurist Manifestos* (U. Apollonio, ed.). Thames and Hudson.

Marquand, D. (1988). *The Unprincipled Society*. Fontana Press.

McIntyre, S. (1996). Art and industry: regional film and video policy in the UK. In: *Film Policy* (A. Moran, ed.). Routledge.

McLuhan, M. (1964). *Understanding Media*. Routledge and Kogan Page.

Mintzberg, H. (1980). *The Nature of Managerial Work*. Harper and Row.

Mintzberg, H. and Quinn, J. B. (1991). *The Strategy Process*. Prentice Hall.

Mitchell, G. (1979). The consolidation of the American film industry 1915–1920, parts one and two. *Cine-Tracts* nos. 6 and 7/8.

Monaco, J. (1981). *How to Read a Film*. Oxford University Press.

Moran, A. (Ed.). *Film Policy*. Routledge.

Morgan, G. (1986). *Images of Organisation*. Sage Publications.

Morley, D. and Robins, K. (1990). Non-tariff barriers: identity, diversity and difference. In: *The Single European Market and the Information and Communication Technologies* (Locksley, ed.). Belhaven.

Mulville, J. (1994). Independence days. *J. R. Television Soc.*, **July/August**.

Musser, C. (1983). Archaeology of the cinema. *Framework*, **22/23**.

Negrine, R. (1992). *Politics and the Mass Media in Britain*. Routledge.

Orakwue, S. (1994). Waiting to hear ... *J. R. Television Soc.*, **July/August**.

O'Sullivan, T. et al. (1994, 1995). *Key Concepts in Communication and Cultural Studies.* Routledge.

Pappas, J. L., Brigham, E. F. and Shipley, B. (1983). *Managerial Economics.* Penguin, Cassell.

Park, J. (1984). *Learning to Dream, The New British Cinema.* Faber and Faber.

Pascale, R. (1990). *Managing on the Edge.* Penguin.

Peacock, A. (1986). *Report of the Committee on the Financing of the BBC.* HMSO.

Peak, S. (1993). *The Media Guide.* Fourth Estate.

Peak, S. and Fisher, P. (1999). *The Media Guide 2000.* Fourth Estate.

Peters, T. and Waterman, R. H. Jr (1982). *In Search of Excellence.* Harper and Row.

Petrie, D. (1992). *New Questions of British Cinema.* British Film Institute.

Phillips, J. and Firth, A. (1995). *An Introduction to Intellectual Property Law.* Butterworths.

Porter, M. (1980). *Competitive Strategy.* The Free Press.

Porter, M. (1992). *The Competitive Advantage of Nations.* Macmillan Press.

Porter, V. (1985). European co-productions: aesthetic and cultural implications. *J. Area Studies,* **12**.

Pringle, P. (1991). *Electronic Media Management.* Focal Press.

BBC (1995). *Programmes and People.* BBC Policy Document. This account is taken from a lecture by Richard Dunn, Chief Executive Thames TV Ltd, *The 1990 Broadcasting Act: Benefit or Disaster?*, given at the RSA, London, 16 November 1994.

Pugh, D. S. and Hickson, D. J. (1989). *Writers on Organisations,* 4th edn. Penguin Business.

Rainnie, A. and Blair, H. (1998). *Flexible Films?* University of Hertfordshire Business School Working Paper Series No. 1.

Richter, H. (1986). *The Struggle for the Film: Towards a Socially Responsible Cinema.* Wildwood House.

Robertson QC, G. and Nicol, A. (1992). *Media Law.* Penguin Books.

Robins, K. and Cornford, J. (1992). What is flexible about independent producers? *Screen.*

Rotha, P. and Griffith, R. (1960). *The Film Till Now.* Twayne.

Roud, R. (1960). The French Line. *Sight and Sound,* **29(4)**.

Salt, B. (1976). The early development of film form. *Film Form,* **1**.

Salt, B. (1978). Film form 1900–06. *Sight and Sound,* **47(3)**.

Sarris, A. (1962–3). *Film Culture.* Winter.

Sarris, A. (1962). The world of Howard Hawks. In: *Focus on Howard Hawks* (J. McBride and P. Scannell).

Schumacher, E. F. (1973). *Small is Beautiful.* Harper and Row.

Schwartz, I. (1985). Broadcasting without frontiers in the European Community. *J. Media Law Pract.*, **6(1)**.

Seaton, J. (1991). *Power Without Responsibility.* Routledge.

Seaton, J. (1998). To be or not to be the BBC: broadcasting in the 1980s and 1990s. In: *Treaties Establishing the European Community.* European Commission.

Smith, A. D. (1991). *National Identity.* Penguin.

Smith, K. and Johnson, P. (1996). *Business Ethics and Business Behaviour.* Thomson Business Press.

Stacey, R. (ed.) (1993). *Strategic Thinking and the Management of Change.* Kogan Page.

Stacey, R. (1996). *Strategic Management and Organisational Dynamics*, 2nd edn. Pitman Publishing.

Staiger, J. (1980). Mass-produced photoplays, economic and signifying practices in the first years of Hollywood. *Wide Angle*, **4(3)**.

Stephane, R. (1988). Cinema and television in Europe: present situation and future prospects. *EBU Review*, **39(2)**.

Stokes, J. and Reading, A. (1999). *The Media in Britain – Current Debates and Developments.* Macmillan.

Storper, M. (1985). *The Changing Organisation and Location of the Motion Picture Industry – A Research Report.* UCLA Publishing.

The Broadcasting Act (1990). HMSO.

The Broadcasting Research Unit (1985). *The Public Service Idea.* BRU.

The Future of the BBC. Green Paper (1992). HMSO.

Broadcasting Research Unit. (1985). *The Public Service Idea.* Broadcasting Research Unit.

Thompson, K. and Bordwell (1983). Linearity, materialism and the study of early American cinema. *Wide Angle*, **5(3)**.

Tisdall, C. and Bozzollo, A. (1977). *Futurism.* Thames and Hudson.

Tonnies, F. (1887). *Community and Association RKP 1955*, p. 37. Routledge and Kegan Paul, 1955.

Towers, B. (1992). *Industrial Relations Practice.* Kogan Page.

Tracey, M. (1998). *The Decline and Fall of Public Service Broadcasting.* Oxford University Press.

Turvey, G. (1936). The culture of the popular front and Jean Renoir. Reprinted in *Media, Culture and Society*, Vol. 4, 1982. Academic Press Inc.

Ursell, G. (1995). *Organising Employment for Higher Performance in the UK Television Industry.* Paper presented at the 1995 Annual Conference of the Employment Research Unit, Cardiff Business School.

Vertov, D. (1972–3). Film directors: a revolution. *Screen,* **13(4)**.

Viljoen, D. (1991). *The Art of the Deal: An Independent Producer's Guide to Business Affairs.* IPPA Publications.

Walter, B. (1985). *One Way Street.* Verso Books.

Walter, B. (1992). The work of art in the age of mechanical reproduction. Reprinted in *Film Theory and Criticism* (G. Mast, M. Cohen and L. Braudy, eds). Oxford University Press.

Walsh, M. (1981). *The Brechtian Aspect of Radical Cinema.* British Film Institute.

Webb, I. (1984). *Survival and Growth: A Position Audit for the Small Expanding Business.* BIM.

Welsh, T. and Greenwood, W. (1999). *McNae's Essential Law for Journalists, 15th edn.* Butterworths.

Wiese, M. (1989). *Film and Video Marketing.* Focal Press.

Wiese, M. (1991). *Film and Video Financing.* Focal Press.

Williams, A. (1988). *The Impact of the New Technologies on the West German Media.* Contemporary German Studies, Occasional Papers No. 5. Strathclyde University.

Williams, R. (1990). *Technology and Cultural Form.* Routledge.

Wilson, R., Gilligan, C. and Pearson, D. (1992). *Strategic Marketing Management.* Butterworth Heinemann.

Winterbottom, M. (1985). In: *Production: Minder* (M. Alvorado and J. Stewart, eds). *Made for Television: Euston Films Limited.* BFI.

Wollen, P. (1975). The two avant-gardes. *Studio* Int., **180(978)**.

Wright, W. (1975). *Six Guns and Society.* University of California Press.

Further useful sources

Broadcast – weekly media newspaper

Websites

Arts Council of England – www.artscouncil.org.uk

BBC Code of Ethics – http://www.bbc.co.uk/info/news/news222.htm

British Film Commission – www.britfilm.co.uk

British Film Institute – www.bfi.org.uk

Department for Media, Culture and Sport (DCMS) – www.culture.gov.uk

European Union website – www.europa.eu.int (audiovisual index at EU website – www.europa.eu.int/comm/dg10/index_en.html)

Film Council – www.filmcouncil.org.uk

Managing in the Media

Financial Times on-line – www.ft.com

Financial Times – media news http://news.ft.com/industries/media

Greenpeace – http://www.greenpeace.org

Institute of Business Ethics – www.ibe.org.uk

Professor Tom Cannon, article on business ethics – http://www.bbc.co.uk/knowledge/business/tradesecrets/theme9a.shtml

UK media desk – www.mediadesk.co.uk (this provides links to many other relevant sites)

20th Century Media Time Line

Media Industry	1800s	1900–09	1910–19	1920–29	1930–39	1940–50
Film	Photography – Daguerreotype & Talbotype 1839	National Association of Cinematography Operators 1907	National Association of Theatre and Kine Employees (NATTKE) 1910	America dominates world film making 1920	Disney's *Silly Symphony*	Hitchcock moves to Hollywood 1940
	Muybridge's experiments with motion & picture photography 1873	Melies – *Voyage to the Moon* 1902	Griffith moves to Los Angeles, film production shifts from New York to West Coast 1910	Musicians Union 1921	Wellman's *Public Enemy* marks rise of gangster genre. *Dracula* & *Frankenstein*, the horror genre	Welles *Citizen Kane* 'the great American movie' 1941
	Edison's phonograph 1877	Development of narrative films, in US by Porter, in UK by Hepworth 1903–5	British Board of Film Censors formed 1912	Columbia founded. MGM consolidated. Leger's *Ballet Mecanique* 1923	Film Artistes Association 1932 (film extras)	British film industry revitalised with Coward's *In Which We Serve* 1942
	Eastman develops flexible rollfilm 1888		Griffith's feature film *Birth of a Nation* begins new period of film history 1915	Eisenstein's *Battleship Potemkin* 1925	Association of Cine Technicians (ACT) 1933	Rosselini's *Rome Open City* & De Sica's *Shoeshine* mark neorealism 1945
	The kinetoscope invented 1891–94		Wiene's *Cabinet of Dr Caligari*, German Expressionism in film begins. Chaplin, Pickford & Fairbanks form United Artists 1919	Vitaphone – sound on disc premier – *Don Juan* 1926	Astaire & Rogers in *Flying Down to Rio* – the urbane sophistication of 1930s films 1933. Flaraty completes *Man of Aran* 1934	American film industry's best box office year 1.7 billion dollars 1946
	Lumiere's first public film show in Paris 1895			The *Jazz Singer* first popular sound success 1927	Technicolour three strip process invented 1935	House Un-American Activities Committee begins hearings on 'Communist influence in Hollywood' 1947
				RKO formed. First all talking movie *Lights of New York* 1928	Capra's *Mr Deeds Goes to Town*, Renoir's *Le Crime de M Lange* 1936	The National Film Finance Corporation October 1948
					Michael Balcon takes over Ealing Studios 1938	Howard Hughes buys RKO 1948
					Hollywood's greatest year; Selnick's *Gone with the Wind* & MGM's *Wizard of Oz*, both directed by Victor Fleming. John Ford's *Stagecoach* 1939	Donen and Kelly *On the Town* new style musical 1949

(continues on pages 374, 376, 377 and 380)

20th Century Media Time Line

	1800s	1900–09	1910–19	1920–29	1930–39	1940–50
Media Industry						
Television & radio	Lumiere shows film to the public at Polytechnic			British Broadcasting Company 1922	BBC Television Service 1936–39	Transistor invented at Bell Telephone Laboratory 1947
				British Broadcasting Corporation 1926	Radio Luxembourg starts transmission 1933	BBC resumes television service 1949
					BBC World Service 1932	
New Media						
Government (continues on pages 378, 380 and 381)						
Policy		Sunday Trading Act 1909		Cinematograph Films Act 1927 established Quotas		Beveridge Report 1950
				Sykes Committee on Broadcasting 1923		
				Crawford Committee 1925		
Legal		1909 Cinematograph Act passed, placing controls on the public exhibition of films	1912 BBFC set up		Trade Marks Act 1938	
			1911 Official Secrets Act passed after paranoia over German spies			
	Berne Convention on copyright 1886		1914 Performing Rights Society set up			

20th Century Media Time Line

	1800s	1900–09	1910–19	1920–29	1930–39	1940–50
Technical		(continues on pages 379 and 381)				
Infrastructure	Still images transmitted over wires 1860				BBC transmit first '405 line high definition' TV 1936	
Recording						
Computing						First digital computer Eniac, a room-sized system of 18,000 vacuum tubes 1946
Film/photography	Photography 1830s					
Historical		(continues on page 379)				
		Death of Queen Victoria	First World War (1914–18)	General Strike 1926	Second World War (1939–45)	

Media Industry	1950–59	1960–69	1970–79	1980–89	1990–99
	(continued from pages 373 and 374, continues on pages 377 and 380)				
Film	Wilder's Sunset Boulevard 1950. The Eady Levy voluntarily in 1950. Compulsory by the Cinematograph Films Act 1957	Reisz's Saturday Night and Sunday Morning. Hitchcock's Psycho 1960	MGM actions its heritage – May 1970	Scorsese's Raging Bull 1980	Costner's Dances with Wolves. Scorsese's Goodfellas. Matsushita acquired Universal Studio 1990
	Kurosawa's Rashomon successful at Venice Film Festival. Cahiers du Cinema founded 1951	Dr No starts James Bond genre 1962	Bertolucci's Last Tango in Paris. Coppola's The Godfather. Goddard and Gorin Tout va Bien 1972	Spielberg's Raiders of the Lost Ark. Hugh Hudson's Chariots of Fire 1981	Demme's Silence of the Lambs. Scott's Thelma and Louise 1991
	Kelly & Donen's Singin' in the Rain. Zinneman's High Noon 1952	Kubrick's Dr Strangelove 1963	Warner Bros The Exorcist – renewed interest in shock effect of film. MGM opts out of film production 1973	Spielberg's E.T. Scott's Blade Runner 1982	Tax relief on films introduced by Norman Lamont 1992. Eastwood's The Unforgiven revives westerns. Cinema admissions up to 102 million 1992
	RKO liquidated. Cinerama and 3-D introduced 1953	McLuhan's Understanding Media published. Lester's A Hard Day's Night 1964	Bergman's Face to Face. Jaws sets box office record, disaster genre 1975	Marquand directs Return of the Jedi, the third of Lucas's Star Wars movies. Attenborough's Gandhi 1983	Spielberg's Jurassic Park takes 100 million dollars in 9 days at box office 1993
	Jan Truffaut's essay Une certaine tendance du cinema francais published in Cahiers de Cinema. Kazan's On the Water Front 1954	Bergman's Persona. Antonioni's Blow-Up. Ken Loach's Cathy Come Home for television 1966	Scorsese's Taxi Driver 1976	Rietman's Ghostbusters, biggest hit of the year. Cameron The Terminator. British cinema attendances lowest ever: 55 million 1984	Forrest Gump – retarded war hero becomes a box office success 1994
	Nicholas Ray's Rebel Without a Cause 1955	Forsyte Saga on BBC TV. Penn's Bonnie and Clyde 1967	Success of Woody Allen's Annie Hall marks a small shift of film from Hollywood back to New York 1977	Eady Levy abolished by Films Act. Zemeckis's Back to the Future. Frean's My Beautiful Launderette. Roger Moore's last Bond film 1985	Centenary of Cinema celebrated 1995
	Ford's The Searchers. Bergman's The Seventh Seal 1956	Kubrick's 2001. Christian Metz Essais sur la Signification au Cinema published 1968	Highly successful Saturday Night Fever earns more from soundtrack album than from box office 1978	Lynch's Blue Velvet. Ted Turner takes over MGM/UA 1986	Channel 5 1997
	Hitchcock's North by Northwest 1959	Peter Wollen's Signs and Meanings in the Cinema published. Hill's Butch Cassidy and the Sundance Kid. Peckinpah's The Wild Bunch. Hopper's Easy Rider 1969	Coppola's Apocalypse Now. Ridley Scott Alien 1979	Lyn's Fatal Attraction. Donner's Lethal Weapon 1987	

	1950–59	1960–69	1970–79	1980–89	1990–99
Media Industry					
Television & Radio				The Museum of the Moving Image opens in New York, 1988. When Harry Met Sally, Lee's Do the Right Thing, Greenaway's The Cook, The Thief, His Wife and Her Lover 1989	
	ITV regional franchises 1955	Pirate Radio (3 years)	Regional Commercial Radio 1973	Channel 4 1982, Initial levy set at 13.6% from franchised terrestrial channels	BSB & Sky merge to form BSkyB 1990
	1950–59 BBC radio provides three services named Light, Home, Third	BBC2 1964	Open University 1971	Direct broadcasting by satellite (DBS) 1989 Sky TV followed by British Satellite Broadcasting. Merged in 1992	Sky seizes Premier League rights in joint deal with BBC 1992
		Radio 1 1967	Upstairs Downstairs, Parkinson, Old Grey Whistle Test 1971	Boys from the Blackstuff 1982	C4 launches Big Breakfast 1992
		News at Ten & Forsyth Saga 1967	Capital Radio & LBC, first indie local radio 1973	BBC Breakfast Time 1983	New franchise holders Carlton, Meridian & Westcountry go on air 1993
		Dad's Army 1968	Fawlty Towers 1975	Blackadder 1983	Radio 5 Live 1994
		Monty Python 1969	South Bank Show 1978	Spitting Image 1984	Talk Radio 1995
		BBC Radio Light – Radio 2. Third – Radio 3. Home – Radio 4		Eastenders 1985	BBC radio has five networks with national and local radio stations, 230+ commercial stations 1999
New Media					BBC start global web casts 12.99

	1950–59	1960–69	1970–79	1980–89	1990–99
Government	(continued from page 374, continues on pages 380 and 381)				
Policy	Independent Television Authority (ITA) 1950	Pilkington Report 1960	Independent Broadcasting Authority (IBA) 1972	Range of anti Union legislation	Broadcasting Act 1990 responsible for the current ITC regime and the franchising system
	1954 IBA given power to interfere with the content of commercial radio and TV programmes		Annan Report 1977	BCC set up 1981	Publisher model embodied in law
	1959 Obscene Publications Act replaces the existing common law			The British Film Commission was established to market British Film abroad	1996 Broadcasting Act which sets up the machinery for the introduction of digital television
				The Peacock Report 1986	1996 BBC Charter renewed
				The Hunt Report 1982	MEDIA Programme launched by EU 1991
				Television Without Frontiers' EU Directive 1989	MEDIA Programme EU 1996
					Labour Government film policy review 'A Bigger Picture' March 1998
Legal	Universal Copyright Convention 1952	1961 *Lady Chatterley's Lover* obscenity trial	1973 House of Lords decides 'Thalidomide' case	Contempt of Court Act passed 1981	ECHR upholds UK blasphemy law as applied to films (*Visions of Ecstacy*) & UK ban on sale of satellite porn channel decoders (*Red Hot Dutch*)
	Defamation Act 1952	1966 UK accepts ECHR enforcement machinery	1978 Last prosecution for blasphemy – 'Gay News' case	Video Recording Act 1984	1990 & 1996 Broadcasting Acts introduce ITC duty & power to regulate domestic broadcasting
	Television Act 1954		1979 E court of HR rules that UK contempt law, as found in 'Thalidomide' case, infringes the ECHR	Copyright, Designs and Patents Act. Current form of law on copyright, moral rights and performing rights 1988	

	1950–59	1960–69	1970–79	1980–89	1990–99
Technical	(continued from page 375; continues on page 381)				
Infra-structure	BBC reach 97% of UK population with TV signal 1956	Colour TV PAL 625 lines in UK	Teletext 1974	First Systems for Satellite Broadcasts 1983	Sky Digital & On Digital launched 1998
		First commercial satellite 1965			World Wide Web 1990
				Cable TV starts (1979–80)	MPEG 1 encoding 1991
					Digital transmission by terrestrial, cable & satellite starts 1999
					Cable penetration passes 1 million barrier 1995
recording	Ampex 2® video recorder		Video Cassette Recorders (VCR) Betamax 1975 and VHS 1977	VHS and 8mm camcorders 1983	Domestic digital camcorders 1998
	Stereo records 1958		CD-Audio 1979	Video Disk 1982	Digital Versatile Disk 1998
computing	First synthesizer appears 1955, later to become synonymous with the name Robert Moog in the 1960s and 1970s		Intel Corporation introduces the microprocessor 1971. Apple II 1977. Floppy Drive 1978	IBM PC 1981 CD-ROM 1982 Apple Mac 1984	Windows 95 launched in 1995. Concept of Cyberspace is coined 1995
Film/Photography				Hand-held games devices 1989	
Historical	(continued from page 375)				
	Coronation Elizabeth II (1952)	Yury Gagarin orbits the earth 1961. First Beatle album 'Please Please Me' 1962	John Lennon shot 1970 Decimalisation 1971	Miners Strike. Grunwicks Canary Wharf Strikes	Hubble space telescope launched 1990
		Telstar – communications satellite 1962	Patrick Steptoe, Robert Edwards develop techniques for the 'test tube baby' 1976	Chernobyl explodes 1986	1992 Single European Market established
	Transatlantic telephone service 1956	First man on Moon 1969	First Thatcher Government 1979		Labour Government: Tony Blair 1997

	2000 – Fact	2000 – Fantasy?
Media Industry	(continued from pages 373, 374, 376 and 377)	
Film		
Television & Radio	Channel 4 licence renewal 2003	BBC is still considered too big and the licence fee is still being debated
New media	Web TV	
Government	(continued from pages 374 and 378)	
policy	Government subsidies set top box manufacturers to provide a cheap starter box to those who don't have digital so that the required 95% of the population can be reached, to turn off terrestrial analogue TV transmission. The new regulations under the Communications Commission decrees that no one corporation can own one-third of the carrier or provider.	Broadcasting/Communications Act 2002: The telecoms industry is redefined in two sectors – carriers and providers – there is no longer a distinction between telephone services and telephone or radio services – it's all data now.
	80% of population receive free to air digital TV 2006	ITV franchise and licence renewal 2004
		ICC – Independent Communications Commission set up with two subdivisions, one for the carriers and the other for the providers. A single unified body to supervise all channels to the consumer or industrial markets.
		A single ITV channel emerges to be broken up by 2010 by another Broadcasting Act invoked due to another Commission headed by Lord Branson, that suggests quality has dropped and that a single ITV company is anti-competition and against the interests of the viewing public.
		Health On Line now becomes the first stop for all people wishing to see a GP From home or from drop in centres at supermarkets or in the high street will be pre-screened, first by the electronic system then by a nurse, before you are given an appointment with a GP. For those who wish it they will be able to have their first booked appointment with the GP through web cam or digital TV links.
		2005 – 50 channels available to the home environment – and still nothing to watch. Television companies will form associations with the major supermarkets to sell the products as they are being advertised.

	2000 – Fact	2000 – Fantasy?
Government		
		BBC still debating how they will truly make good use of the digital age. Before Lord Dyke quits the BBC pundits will look back upon the period of John Birt as another golden age of television.
		2005 – pay and digital TV reaches 75% of all UK homes, outstripping all previous predictions. Digital radio goes through a surprising boom as people free to exchange telephone services listen to their favourite station whilst surfing the web.
Legal	2000 Expected date when Human Rights Act will come into force, incorporating ECHR into UK domestic law	
	New copyright directive to be in force – more restrictions on copying, levying on blank tapes	
Technical	(continued from pages 375 and 379)	
Infrastructure	Convergence of technologies will gather pace, web TV and TV web will become commonplace	It will become possible before 2010 to receive any channel, radio or TV, anywhere in the world. It will also become possible to timeshift any programme due to storage at the supplier's side, not at the user's side. Spare digital capacity will be multiplexed and used by international organisations to communicate with staff.
		Terrestrial analogue TV switched off 2006

Index

Index

Index

Index